THE OAKWOOD PRESS

BOGIE CAR

OF THE
SOUTH EASTERN & CHATHAM RAILWAY

by
David Gould

THE OAKWOOD PRESS

ISBN 0 85361 455 5

Typeset by Gem Publishing Company, Brightwell, Wallingford, Oxfordshire.

Printed by Alpha Print (Witney) Ltd, Crawley, Oxfordshire.

Published by
The OAKWOOD PRESS
P.O.Box 122, Headington, Oxford OX3 8LU

Contents

Introduction and Acknowledgements

'Seldom has a railway excited such blazes of sulphurous wrath by reason of its rolling stock as the South Eastern. Frenetic abuse and unstinted bad language have been hurled at everyone connected with the line on account of the third class carriages.'

These words were written by D.T. Timins in his article about South Eastern Railway (SER) third-class carriages, 'From Roofless Pen to Corridor Coach', which appeared in *The Railway Magazine* in 1899 (Vol. 4, p.495), a few months after that railway and its Kentish neighbour, the London, Chatham & Dover (LC&DR), had been joined together by a managing committee known as the South Eastern & Chatham Railway (SE&CR).

The SER had tried desperately to live down its former evil reputation but never really succeeded, despite the fact that from about 1888 all its new coaches were of excellent quality and pleasing to both the eye and the posterior. Richard Mansell, famous for his patent wheel with teak segments and iron tyre, was still carriage and wagon superintendent when the first bogie carriages were introduced in 1878. It was when he was succeeded by William Wainwright that carriage design was so radically improved; and the good work was carried on by his third son, Harry Smith Wainwright, who became carriage and wagon superintendent in 1896 (and also locomotive superintendent from 1899), continuing to turn out many beautiful coaches until his resignation due to ill-health in November 1913.

The elder Wainwright's coaches gained the approbation of Foxwell in 1888: 'The third class carriages on the Ramsgate and Hastings trains are more roomy than the average in England. The passenger communication with the guard is far superior to that mockery provided on our great lines to the North.'

Although Harry Wainwright introduced a great many types of carriage, there was a degree of standardisation. The typical coach of the 1900s would have had a low elliptical roof, Fox's patent bogies, Stone's electric lighting, a body width of only 8 ft, and a moulding style that embraced panels extending from the cantrail to the waist. Above all, coaches with a guard's compartment at one end would have featured a full-width, round-topped roof observatory; such coaches were usually dubbed 'birdcage' stock. Coaches also included a lower stepboard between the bogies, and adjustable round-section truss rods to support the underframe. Lower stepboards were discontinued about halfway through the production of 60 ft 3-coach sets, and the Southern Railway removed the lower stepboards from most of the other coaches in later years. Another feature, although not universal, was a single bar placed across the droplight of each door; most (but by no means all) carriages built between the 1890s and 1910 had them, but bars were not fitted retrospectively and by 1914 it seems that all the bars had been removed. All coaches with a body length of 50 ft or longer had compensating buffers of Spencer's patent design.

Many passengers would have been reassured to know that 'Mr Harry S. Wainwright, the genial and energetic locomotive and carriage Superintendent of the Joint Companies, is a firm believer in the excellence of British workmanship, and in its superiority over that of America or of any foreign country.' (*The Railway Magazine*, Vol. 4, p.504.)

One curiosity was the provision of notices in French in SE&C carriages. Apparently they were displayed not merely in stock used on Continental boat trains but in virtually all bogie carriages. Certainly in the 1920s almost all coaches running on the Dartford Loop Line (via Sidcup) had them and, according to R.W. Kidner's father, they were quite normal. The notices gave the usual warning about not leaning out of the window or misusing the alarm signal.

After Wainwright's time carriage design changed to something much plainer and austere; the low elliptical roof was retained for local stock, but for mainline trains the roof-height was increased and R.E.L. Maunsell, the new superintendent, introduced a new bogie which ultimately became standard on the Southern Railway. From 1st March, 1920, the rules about smoking in carriages were changed and red triangular 'no-smoking' labels were placed on selected compartments; the old arrangement had designated compartments for smoking with the implication that it was not allowed anywhere else. Henceforth one could smoke anywhere except where it was forbidden. The reason for this change was purely one of economy in labels; it was cheaper to provide 'no-smoking' labels because in those days very few compartments were set aside for those who did not indulge.

One of the earliest decisions made by the new Southern Railway Board was to cease the building of carriages at Ashford Works, for so many years the birthplace of SE and SE&C rolling stock. In October 1923 the Board decreed that Ashford would be retained for the construction of all wagons and for the repairs to all SE&C Section locomotives, carriages and wagons. When it came to repainting SE&C stock in SR colours, Ashford did most of the work, Lancing (the old London, Brighton & South Coast (LB&SC) carriage works) did a fair amount, and a small number was done at Eastleigh Works (ex-London & South Western).

During the 1920s, before there had been much electrification of ex-SE&C routes, the most notable feature of the stock running on what was now designated the Eastern Section of the SR was its variety. The carriages had to cater for a wide variety of differing publics: notabilities on their way to the Continent (by no means all the boat trains were formed of new corridor stock), the well-to-do people of the Kentish countryside, the rather mixed bag of season-ticket holders, and hordes of excursionists and hop-pickers, for which the least attractive stock was carefully set aside.

A great many trains were made up with one, two or even three 'trio' sets – those all-purpose 3-coach sets that so typified the SE&C. With their uniform profile and roof-height, they bestowed a neatness to the trains that was rarely found elsewhere. They also rode very well and were particularly comfortable.

Although many bogie coaches ran in 'set' trains, almost as many did not, at least until about 1931, when a great many were gathered together into 9-coach sets for excursion and relief services. During the 1930s, 1940s and 1950s these sets were berthed at all sorts of odd places, often several miles from their booked starting point: for example, Bellingham, Blackheath, Crystal Palace (High Level), Eardley (on the ex-LB&SC Central Section near Streatham), Grove Park, Herne Hill, Maze Hill, New Beckenham, Tattenham

Corner and Walmer all had a few sidings that housed from one to four sets used only at peak holiday times and for special traffic. Many were the empty carriage workings between these outstations and the booked starting point – usually Victoria or Charing Cross. There were a few carriage depots as well, such as Rotherhithe Road (Bermondsey) and Victoria, but these housed important main-line stock and there was never enough room to accommodate all the inferior stuff as well.

In the main, ex-SE&C coaches disappeared in 1958, this being the last summer for which extra trains were needed on the Victoria–Ramsgate line before its electrification. The once-numerous 'trio' sets bowed out in that year also. From then until 1962 the only SE&C survivors were those that had been converted for push-and-pull sets; these were the only ones with which I was personally acquainted when I used to see them at Oxted station during 1961/2 when they worked the Tunbridge Wells West hourly service. By then they looked quite antique.

As far as possible this book uses official sources, mainly carriage registers and carriage working notices. Inevitably it has made use of some published work, such as that of D.L. Bradley, H.C. Hughes, R.W. Kidner and J.T. Howard Turner and certain journals, such as *Engineering*, *The Railway Magazine*, *Model Railway News* and *Invicta*.

For assistance freely provided I am very grateful to Denis Cullum, who has amassed a vast collection of material relating to SR rolling stock; Tom Burnham, who looked up several references in *Engineering* and loaned his copies of *Invicta*; R.W. Kidner, whose knowledge of the SR in the 1928–32 period being second to none was so often able to state what *actually* occurred instead of what was *supposed* to happen; and Mike King, a noted SR carriage enthusiast who has himself collected a large amount of data and made it available.

In the present work I have occasionally quoted sources, but there is no room to do this for every statement made. I have tried very hard to ensure accuracy, particularly with numbers and dates, but doubtless there will be examples of misinterpretation on my part; for, when dealing with events that occurred so long ago, it is probably out of the question to be 100 per cent accurate.

East Grinstead, September 1993 *David Gould*

Chapter One

South Eastern & Chatham Railway Carriages – General Features

Bogies

Most SE&C 8-wheel carriages ran on Fox's patent pressed-steel bogies of 8 ft wheelbase, although some of the shorter carriages had 7 ft-wheelbase bogies instead. The frames, bolsters and swing beams were all of pressed steel plates made by the Leeds Forge Co. The top centre bearing block was of wrought iron and the bottom centre block and side radial blocks were of cast steel. There was a half-inch indiarubber pad between the blocks and the bolster. The cast-iron axleboxes were usually of J. Stone & Co.'s make. Bearing springs were built up of seven plates, 4 in. by ½ in., and two nests of elliptical springs were provided on each bogie to support the bolster. The wheels, usually 3 ft 6 in. diameter, were the Mansell pattern, with tyres and axles of mild steel, centres of wrought iron, between which were segments of hardwood. The combination of bogie springing and cushioned wheels provided superb riding qualities for SE&Cs carriages.

Brakes

The South Eastern Railway standardised on the automatic vacuum brake from September 1887; until then the simple vacuum brake had been used. From 1889, under the Regulation of Railways Act, all railways were required to fit automatic brakes to their carriage stock, and the SE completed this work in about 1893. The London, Chatham & Dover Railway began using the Westinghouse air brake from about 1888; until then it had used nothing but hand brakes. When the two companies came together in 1899 new stock came out dual-braked and the Chatham carriages had vacuum brakes added, but from about 1903 new stock was vacuum-fitted only and Chatham stock generally lost the air brake, despite its superiority. The Southern Railway also was a vacuum-braked line, except on the Isle of Wight; all the carriages sent there required conversion to Westinghouse air brakes.

Destination Boards

In 1901 *The Railway Magazine* stated that the SE&C was the most slipshod and inconsistent of all the companies in the matter of displaying destination boards on carriages. Whether true or not, the situation was soon to change. Instructions were sent out in 1901 that all main line and principal branch trains were to have a destination board placed on each alternate vehicle, normally on both sides. North Kent, Mid Kent and Bromley trains were to have boards only on the first and last coaches. By 1903, triangular or square boards had been provided for Mid Kent, Bromley and Oxted line trains, and guards were exhorted to turn the boards to their correct position before starting the train.

Destination boards were a strong point of the SE&C, and were perfectly practicable when, as was often the case, the same set of coaches was used on same 'out-and-home' working, day after day. On no account were roof boards of trains working in these 'fixed services' to be removed without authority, unless a coach was permanently transferred from the service from which it was boarded, and nor were boards to be taken off coaches sent to Ashford Works for repair.

Roof boards were vermilion with gold lettering shaded in black. Here are some examples of the wording displayed on them:

London, Ashford, Shorncliffe, Folkestone & Dover.
London, Tunbridge Wells, St. Leonards & Hastings.
Continental Boat Express, London & Folkestone Harbour.
Continental Mail Express, London & Dover Pier.
Continental Boat Express, London & Queenboro' Pier.

After Grouping, roof boards were seldom used on SE&C carriages; instead small boards bearing the ultimate destination (e.g. 'Victoria') were fitted to the bodyside at the luggage compartment. The LC&D had used similar single-name boards, but these were carried at or near the centre of each vehicle, in the top panel. These boards were about 2 ft 3 in. by 3½ in.

Fixed Trains

These were sets of carriages allocated to fixed workings, and from 1907 or possibly earlier they had train set numbers painted on the solebars. If a coach failed in service it could be removed and temporarily replaced by another of corresponding description but it was to be restored to its correct set as soon as possible. From 1910 'fixed trains' were sent to Ashford Works complete, and not separately as before, but vehicles could still be withdrawn in emergency. Right until 1922 the numbers were being carried on the solebars, but there is no record of their being displayed on the brake-ends. The Southern painted its own set numbers on the ends, and a distinction was made between sets allocated to individual services (non-interchangeable sets) and those not (interchangeable sets).

Formation of Trains

Every care was taken to see that best stock was kept in long-distance important services (leaving the worst stock for local services) made up of corresponding description as regards pattern, brake and passenger communication. There was little problem with bogie stock, most of which was uniform in width and height. In later years ex-LC&D stock was mixed in with some SE&C and the picture was not so satisfactory.

Four-wheeled stock was not to be formed in bogie stock trains, but in emergency could be marshalled at either end. Possibly fearing accidents, the SE&C instructed that if a passenger coach other than a brake was marshalled next to the locomotive the three compartments nearest to the engine were to be locked out of use; however, if the train was very crowded passengers were admitted at the discretion of the station staff and guard.

Normally a train on the SE&C had a brake coach at each end, a planned provision of first, second and third class accommodation (the proportions calculated by supposed demand) and a reasonable allocation of lavatory carriages. Some sets had only one brake coach, others had a 6-wheel full brake, and there was even one set without any brake compartment at all (Set

255 – Dorking to Cannon Street in 1919–22).

By 1922 all trains between London and stations beyond Tonbridge, Maidstone East and Gillingham were formed entirely of bogie stock.

Heating

For far too many years passengers in winter were expected to ride in cold, unheated trains. In the early 1900s the primitive footwarmer was still (apart from a hipflask) the passenger's only comfort. Between 1st November and 30th April these tins of hot water and sodium acetate cluttered the floors of passenger compartments of every train running 15 miles or more. Two footwarmers were placed in each first-class compartment, one in each second-class compartment and, on application, one in the third-class compartments. In local and suburban trains, presumably, passengers just froze.

The American Car Train of 1892 and the Folkestone Cars of 1897 were equipped with Baker heaters: boilers which circulated hot water in pipes around the saloons. It was not until 1905 that a complete steam-heated train was introduced, this having storage heaters devised by W.S. Laycock, a noted carriage-fittings company. On the storage system the radiator was filled with soda acetate solution which absorbed heat from the steam pipe (steam being supplied by the locomotive) and gave it off as it cooled. The steam supply was admitted again when the cooling had reached a predetermined point. Storage steam heating was in vogue for about two years, during which nine of the trains used in fast services were equipped.

They were heated from 1st November to 31st March, although boat trains would be heated, if required, until 30th April. Even this did no more than take the chill off, as the temperature was supposed not to exceed 60 degrees. From May 1907 steam heating on the non-storage system was standardised; with this there was a continuous supply of 'live' steam through the radiator. Policy was to equip all carriages intended for boat trains and certain other important services with heaters, but from March 1909 all main-line stock was so equipped, both in new construction and whenever an existing carriage was sent to Ashford for general repair. By February 1916 the SE&C had spent £30,000 on these improvements and needed a further £10,000 to complete the programme. By 1922 all bogie stock was steam-heated, except a few suburban examples with short life-expectancy. Presumably the carriages equipped with storage-system heaters were converted to non-storage.

Lavatory Carriages

Lavatories on trains were originally available only to first- and second-class passengers, and then only sparingly. Later, a popular type of coach was the lavatory tri-composite, with six compartments and six lavatories (two firsts, two seconds and two thirds). The SE&C did not favour corridor coaches because of the short distances involved so, until the arrival of the 1921 boat train, no service on the SE&C ever provided all passengers with lavatory access; those who required it had to choose their compartment very carefully.

In 1901 lavatory-fitted stock was kept exclusively in boat trains and other main-line expresses – which, regrettably, did not include Reading line trains. Later the SE&C relented and Reading line passengers gratefully received these facilities in 1908. After all, the journey time for the 68¾ miles from Charing Cross to Reading was only about three hours!

The starting station of each lavatory-fitted train was responsible for supplying water, soap, towels, water bottles, glasses and sanitary paper.

Lighting

Originally, oil-lighting of carriages was in use by both companies: on the South Eastern until 1887 and on the Chatham until the Managing Committee was formed. The SER used gas-lighting for new stock between September 1887 and December 1897, and much earlier stock was so-fitted during that time. From June 1898, new coaches were fitted with electric lighting, nearly all employing J. Stone & Co's system with accumulators charged by a dynamo driven by a belt from one of the bogie axles. Gas-lighting was, however, perpetuated on Post Office sorting vans, possibly because since much of the work in them was done while they were stationary there were fears that the batteries might not have lasted.

Although next to no gas-lit bogie coaches were converted, all the Chatham's oil-lit specimens were fitted with Stone's electric lighting between 1899 and 1903. Gas-lit coaches could not work on the Chatham section as a general rule, as there were no gassing facilities until some years later.

Each compartment usually was illuminated by two lamps in one fitting, known as a 'duplex'. The lighting was controlled by a rod at the end of each coach. By moving this to its fullest extent, all the lights were put on. By moving it gently until a spring was felt to drop in a notch half-way, only half the lights would be put on; and this would be done for the daytime services. Economically-minded, the SE&C instructed that lights must always be switched off when the train had arrived at its destination. Fifteen minutes before starting-time, half-lights would be switched on; and, at night, full lights immediately before departure. Boat trains, always given preferential treatment, had half-lighting switched on *thirty* minutes before departure.

With this system there was no through control of carriage lighting from the guard's compartment and it was not until 1920 that this facility was provided on new stock, when 3-coach sets Nos. 202 and 203 were introduced with through control. Except on the Isle of Wight, carriages were ultimately converted so that the guard could switch all the lights on and off from the brake compartment.

Gas-lit coaches co-existed with electrically-lit ones for many years, the chief gas-supplying depot being Rotherhithe Road. Many had been altered from the early Pintsch system to incandescent burners, which gave as good a light as, or better than, contemporary electric lamps. But the Southern was not very happy about gas lighting and withdrew the coaches steadily; by 1939 all were gone.

Livery

South Eastern carriages during the Wainwright era were crimson lake. LC&D carriages were varnished teak, with their oak underframes grained 'teak' and footboards, springs, axleboxes and couplings black.

In May 1899, shortly after the amalgamation, a minute of the Locomotive, Carriage & Wagon sub-committee recorded that a decision as to future carriage livery had been made:

> The top quarter panels to be varnished to imitate the London, Chatham & Dover Railway Carriages, and the bottom part to be of crimson lake, these two colors [*sic*] being a combination of the colors now in use on the Joint Lines.

Between 1899 and 1901 all repaints and new stock were in this style. The upper panels were painted and grained 'teak', while the lower panels and ends were crimson lake. The mouldings of the upper panels, as well as the underframes, were picked out in lake. Mouldings were lined with a broad gold line and fine-lined vermilion, and lettering was in gold with red blocking and black shading. The 3-compartment third brakes of 1900/1, for example, were painted in this style.

Apparently the 'khaki tops' did not weather well and by 1901 Chatham stock was being painted the 'standard colour' of that on the SE section. The 1901 livery was stated to be 'rich purple lake lined finely in gold'. Upholstery at this time was in Tashmere tapestry for first-class compartments, Tashmere velvet for the seconds, and a mysterious 'Railway Velvet' for the thirds (*The Railway Magazine*, Vol. 9, p.203).

The 'rich purple lake, fine-lined with gold' appears to have been the same colour as that used by the SER; the American Cars when rebuilt in 1896 were recorded as dark lake lined with gold and edged in vermilion. Carriages introduced in 1904 and 1906 were stated to be in this colour. Roofs were white before receiving a liberal coating of soot in normal service, underframes were black, and droplights were varnished wood. Lining on the moulding edges was gold for first and second class, but yellow on the thirds. Van stock was unlined.

Around 1910/12 carriages started to be painted in a light maroon or red-brown shade with gold lining. The 60 ft 3-coach sets of 1912 were lined in yellow, with gold lettering, blocked and shaded. Class numbers were 11 in. high, coach numbers 2½ in. high and 'S.E.&C.R.' 3 in. high. The painting of set numbers in large figures on the brake-ends of sets was first noticed in 1911.

In 1916 coaches began to be repainted in umber brown, said to be indistinguishable from that used by the London, Brighton & South Coast Railway. Lettering was gold, shaded red, and class numerals were reduced in size. By 1919 the only vehicles still in lake were Pullman cars and the Royal train stock. R.W. Kidner asserted in 1991 that the SE&C brown was not the same colour as LB&SC coach brown: 'My recall of the few coaches in SE&CR livery around 1926/7 was of a dark chocolate colour with a dash of purple. It was quite different from the colour of the former American Cars (by then Pullmans) which was I suppose the authentic lake, and faded to be lighter rather than darker.'

From October 1923 the Southern Railway began painting SE&C coaches and vans in sage green, with the mouldings picked out in yellow and black; roofs were white and underframes and ends were black. *The Railway Maga-*

zine observed that second-class coaches were being withdrawn for alteration to third-class and at the same time were being repainted standard green and lettered 'Southern Railway'. Lettering was in gold, shaded black; and the class designation was shown in words, not figures.

The brilliant malachite green was in use from about 1940; coaches in this colour were unlined, with the title 'Southern' on the waist, and the class shown in numerals instead of words. During the war several coaches were repainted grey. Malachite was continued during 1948 and 1949 by British Railways Southern Region, except that the 'Southern' title was omitted and coach numbers were given the prefix 'S'. For the next few years a colour that BR was pleased to call 'crimson lake' was applied to many SE&C coaches (carmine red might have been a more accurate description) with the coach number on the waist (originally at the left-hand end, later at the right). Some coaches even had the luxury of lining-out, with an orange-yellow and black line along the waist and above the windows. Corridor stock was crimson and cream, though very few examples of SE&C stock carried this hopelessly unsuitable colour scheme. Coach numbers were now given a suffix 'S' in addition to the prefix.

Here are a few examples of BR liveries carried by SE&C coaches and sets:

Second 1087 – still red, unlined, right-hand numerals, 7/58
Second 1070 – red, repainted green at Lancing, 11/60
Second 1093 – red, repainted green at Lancing, 12/59
Seconds 1104, 1111 – red, repainted green at Lancing, 1/61
Composite 5370 (Set 897) – painted red at Lancing, 1/56
First 7347 – still red, lined, left-hand numerals, 7/56
Set 587 – still malachite green, numerals in SR style but with 'S' prefix and suffix, 9/53
Set 596 – still red, unlined, right-hand numerals, 5/55
Set 611 – red, lined, left-hand numerals, n.d.
Set 634 – red, lined, left-hand numerals, n.d.

From July 1956 further repaints were in Southern Region green, unlined, with number shown on the waist at the right-hand end; the colour was slightly darker than malachite. The old red did not disappear until about early 1961. Here are some further examples, all being push-and-pull sets:

Set 656 – painted green at Lancing, 7/61
Set 660 – from red to green at Lancing, 6/59
Set 661 – from red to green at Lancing, 1/60
Set 662 – from red to green at Lancing, 12/59
Set 663 – red, lined, left-hand numerals, 1952/3

Pullman Cars

Pullman cars, the property of the Pullman Car Company, ran in certain main-line trains of the SE&CR from 1910 under contract. As they were not owned or staffed by the SE&C they are beyond the scope of a book on the subject of SE&C carriages, but some brief notes may be useful.

Ten Pullmans were introduced in 1910, followed by four in 1912 and five in 1914; all had buckeye couplers and Pullman gangways and were classed by the SE&C Type 'A'. Further examples, with six-wheeled bogies, had the same couplers and gangways and were designated Type 'B', of which four were introduced in 1914, two in 1920 and ten in 1921. Type 'C' were former South Eastern American Cars rebuilt by Pullman and Type 'D' were old SER vestibuled cars of 1897, rebuilt. Six cars (Type 'E'), which were brought into use in 1921, with screw couplings and British Standard gangways, had been London & North Western ambulance cars.

Originally, Pullmans ran only in boat trains, but in July 1919 *The Railway Magazine* noted that for the first time they were operating in Kent Coast fast trains also: the 7.55 am (SX), 8.15 am (SO) Folkestone to Cannon Street and 11.00 am Charing Cross to Folkestone; the 4.50 pm Folkestone to Charing Cross and 7.00 pm return; the 7.45 am Ramsgate to Cannon Street and 11.30 am Victoria to Ramsgate; and the 3.00 pm Ramsgate to Victoria and 7.00 pm return. They were first-class only and commanded a 2-shilling supplement. The 'Thanet Sunday Pullman' was introduced in July 1921 and was made up entirely of Pullman cars; and in 1922 a car was placed in the 8.05 am Margate to Cannon Street and 5.10 pm Holborn Viaduct to Margate business services.

Pullmans on the SE&C were always painted crimson lake, supposedly to match the Managing Committee's own carriages, and brown-and-cream cars did not start to appear on the Eastern Section of the SR until November 1924.

Route Restrictions

Chatham section bogie vans, brake vans with side lookouts, coaches 8 ft 6 in. wide, and the Folkestone Car Train were not permitted to run between Tunbridge Wells and Hastings or between Minster and Sandwich, owing to the Stour bridge. Chatham section bogie brake vans could not at first work over any part of the SE section. All ordinary carriages were barred from the Canterbury West and Whitstable Harbour branch. In 1902 the Folkestone Harbour branch could not accept American Cars, six-wheel or bogie vans, any bogie stock longer than 42 ft, gas trains or post office sorting vans. All bogie stock was prohibited from running into Moorgate Street station, and brake carriages with high roof observatories could not work over any part of the Metropolitan Railway. All coaches that were able to work to Hastings via Tunbridge Wells were marked 'H' on the solebars, but those that could travel to Hastings only via Ashford and Rye were marked 'A'.

Set Trains

In SE&C terminology there was a difference between 'set trains' and 'fixed trains' in that the former could not be dissembled in any circumstances; should there be a failure the whole set was to be withdrawn and a spare set substituted. The only bogie set trains were the few close-coupled suburban sets and the 3-coach sets known as 'Trios', introduced in 1909 and continuing in production until 1921. From 1911 set numbers were painted in large figures on the brake-ends of each set, in addition to the small numerals painted on the solebars. The SR continued this practice, and so did BR. As far as the Eastern Section was concerned, there were three categories of set trains; interchangeable (the Trios), non-interchangeable (sets allocated to specific regular workings), and 'general service and relief trains' (often referred to as 'long' sets and usually bearing a paper label number in addition to the painted set number).

Slip Coaches

These were special coaches marshalled at the rear of certain trains. Slip coaches were equipped for detaching from the main train at speed, and designed so that the brake pipe on the main train resealed itself to prevent a sudden brake application. The slip-coach guard, having operated the detaching mechanism, then applied the brake for a few seconds to ensure that the coach was well clear of the train as it sped on its way, and then allowed the coach to glide under momentum into the stopping station.

If there was one slip portion the coach carried red and white lights horizontally, and if there were two slip portions the rear (first) coach carried red and white lights vertically and the inner (second) coach carried them horizontally. By day, lamps were encircled by discs of the same colour as the lamps shown at night.

Coaches were not slipped during severe frost or ice or frozen snow on the rails or wheels. Instead, the train stopped to detach. 'Slipping' was revived after wartime suspension, but did not last long under Southern auspices.

Chapter Two

South Eastern Railway Bogie Carriages

The South Eastern Railway's first bogie carriage stock was introduced at the end of 1878, only five years after the appearance of Britain's very first bogie coaches (which were on the narrow-gauge Festiniog Railway). Thus, despite its relative poverty, the South Eastern was well to the fore with experimentation and improvements in its carriage stock, though only in a small way. Bogie coaches were heavier and more expensive to build than four- and six-wheeled coaches, which continued to appear in very large numbers not only for suburban services but main-line too. Bogie vehicles remained a rarity for the rest of the 19th century, but included several different types, many of them experimental. Of the more unusual varieties the close-coupled bogie stock built for suburban use probably came top, as it was later decided that such stock was too heavy and a reversion to non-bogie stock was made for suburban services; the remarkable 12-wheeled bogie composites of 1889, with their bewilderingly frequent conversion to lavatory/non-lavatory and close-coupled/long buffers, probably came a close second. And for luxury travel to rival the Pullman Car Co. the SER put into service some very fine American Cars – quite a contrast to its 4-wheeled 'dog-boxes'!

COMPOSITES

Nos. 1892–1937

There were three distinct batches of the SER's first bogie coaches. The first 20, Nos. 1892–1911, were ordered from Craven Brothers, of Darnall, Sheffield, in June 1878 at a cost of £650 each and were delivered to the SER in the following order:

1893–98:	10/78	1904/05:	12/78	1908/09:	3/79
1892/99–1903:	11/78	1906/07:	2/79	1910/11:	4/79

Body length: 40 ft 6 in. Body width: 8 ft 0¾ in.
Compartments: 4 1st, 2 2nd class. Seats: 24 1st, 16 2nd class.

A series of six, Nos. 1912–1917, was next constructed by the SER itself; bodies were slightly longer and there was a luggage compartment at each end of the coach.

1912/13:	12/78	1914:	5/79	1915–17:	6/79

Body length: 42 ft. Body width: 8 ft 0¾ in.
Compartments: 3 1st, 2 2nd class, 2 luggage.
Seats: 18 1st, 16 2nd class.

A second batch was ordered from Cravens at a cost of £675 each, similar to the first batch but with longer bodies. These 20 were numbered 1918–1937.

1918/19:	6/79	1924–27:	/79	1929–37:	/79
1920–23:	7/79	1928:	10/79		

Body length: 42 ft. Body width: 8 ft 0¾ in.
Compartments: 4 1st, 2 2nd class. Seats: 24 1st, 16 2nd class.

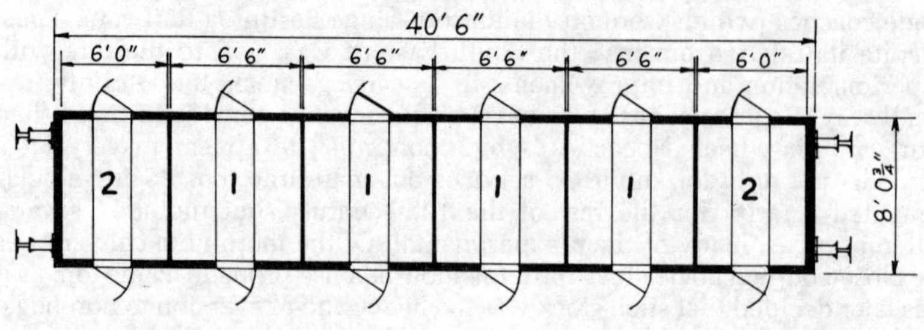
COMPOSITE
40' 6"
6' 0"
6' 6"
6' 6"
6' 6"
6' 6"
6' 0"
2
1
1
1
1
2
8' 0¾"
SE Nos. 1892 - 1911.
SEATING CAPACITY 24 F 16 S.

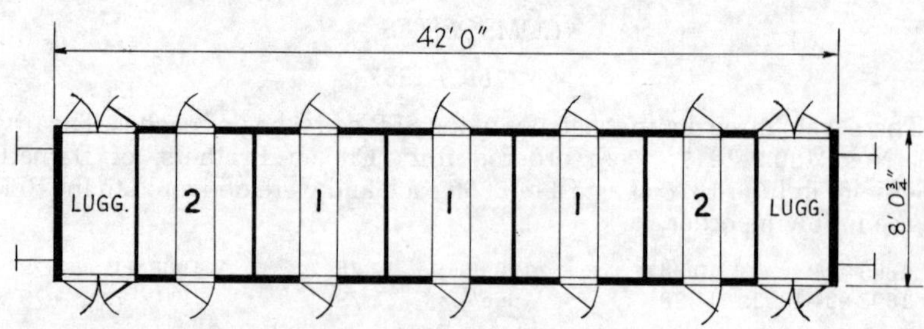
COMPOSITE
42' 0"
LUGG.
2
1
1
1
2
LUGG.
8' 0¾"
SE Nos. 1912 - 1917.
SEATING CAPACITY 18 F 16 S.

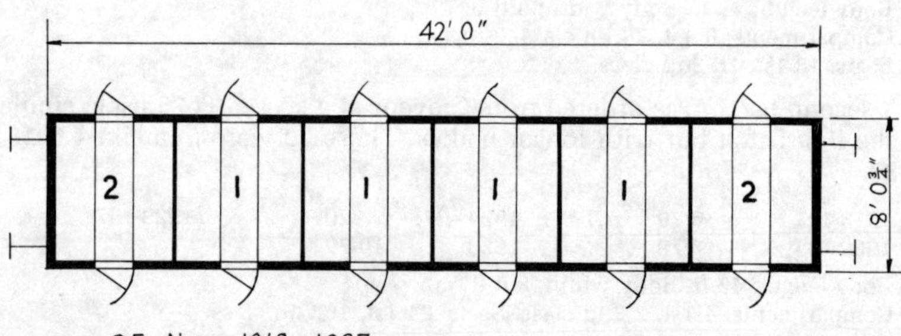
COMPOSITE
42' 0"
2
1
1
1
1
2
8' 0¾"
SE Nos. 1918 - 1937.
SEATING CAPACITY 24 F 16 S.

All three types were to the design of Richard Mansell, the South Eastern's carriage superintendent. The coaches were carried on 'American' bogies of 8 ft wheelbase; bogie centres were 25 ft 6 in. on the 40 ft 6 in. vehicles and 27 ft on the 42 ft ones. Underframes were of wood: soles and headstocks in Moulmein teak, the remainder in Quebec oak. The bodies were made of Moulmein teak with Honduras mahogany panels.

When new the coaches would have had Smith's simple (non-automatic) vacuum brake, which worked very well so long as the train did not become accidentally divided. Automatic vacuum brakes were fitted between 1887 and 1893. As for lighting, probably oil illumination was fitted when new, soon replaced by gas burners.

The 46 coaches ran in Continental boat trains and other main line services, and by 1900 were specially noted as being permitted to work over the Folkestone Harbour branch, which, because of a severe curve at the Harbour station, could not accept anything longer than 42 ft. Nos. 1899 and 1904 were lavatory-fitted at some stage and from October 1901 were not permitted to run in boat expresses, though they could work in other main-line services. No. 1906 became a Tri-Compo with two first, two second and two third class compartments; and Nos. 1913/15 were altered to brake composites with detaching (or 'slip') facilities. Apparently some of the first Craven series were rebuilt with elliptical roofs in place of their original arc roofs.

In 1906 No. 1897 was stationed at Queenborough Pier to stand as spare composite for the Vlissengen boat train. No. 1922, between about 1909 and 1913, was formed in 5-bogie set No. 17, which worked the 7.40 am Tonbridge to Cannon Street and 5.40 pm London Bridge to Penshurst. In 1915 and 1916 Nos. 1906 and 1913 (later 1915) were specially noted as being part of a train working the 8.33 am from Westerham to Cannon Street and 4.50 pm Charing Cross to Westerham.

All 46 coaches were withdrawn between 1914 and 1918 and the bodies broken up. Most of the underframes, however, did further service as aeroplane trucks between 1917 and 1924, when the last of these was broken up. None received a Southern Railway number.

Composites withdrawn complete

No.	*Laid aside*	*Broken up*	No.	*Laid aside*	*Broken up*
1898	6/15	7/15	1929	4/17	5/17
1911	6/16	10/16	1930	6/16	10/16
1916	c.14	c.14	1931	4/15	5/15
1924	4/17	5/17	1936	4/15	5/15
1925	4/17	5/17	1937	6/14	7/14
1926	6/16	10/16			
1927	6/15	7/15			

Underframes sent overseas as platform trolleys

Nos. 1932–35. Bodies broken up 9/17.

Underframes converted to aeroplane wagons for L&NWR, November 1917

No.	Body broken up	U'frame broken up	No.	Body broken up	U'frame broken up
1893	12/17	3/22	1910	12/17	/23
1895	12/17	4/22	1913	12/17	2/22
1900	11/17	/23	1914	2/18	
1902	11/17		1917	11/17	5/22
1909	12/17	1/24	1920	11/17	5/22

Underframes converted to supplementary aeroplane trucks, March 1918

No.	Body broken up	U'frame broken up	No.	Body broken up	U'frame broken up
1892	3/18	10/21	1907	3/18	8/23
1894	3/18		1908	3/18	9/23
1896	3/18	2/23	1912	3/18	2/22
1897	3/18	2/22	1915	3/18	2/22
1899	3/18	2/22	1918	3/18	9/23
1901	3/18		1919	4/18	1/24
1903	3/18	/23	1921	4/18	3/22
1904	9/17	1/24	1922	3/18	2/22
1905	3/18	3/24	1923	3/18	10/21
1906	3/18	10/21	1928	3/18	4/22

Ten vehicles surviving until 1923/4 were allocated SR numbers but were withdrawn without ever carrying them. The underframes of Nos. 1894, 1901, 1902 and 1914 were sent to Angerstein Wharf in 1921 as engineers' trucks; all were condemned in 1922.

CLOSE-COUPLED SUBURBAN STOCK

Nos. 1940–1957, 1984–1987

Because the carriage stock provided for suburban and local trains was so poor in the nineteenth century, the passengers who had to ride in it were not slow to complain to the railway company about its shortcomings. So Mansell introduced in 1880 eighteen bogie coaches, formed into two 9-coach trains, intended for suburban services; they were close-coupled and the compartments were made as narrow as possible in order to pack in the maximum number of passengers in the shortest possible train-length. Four additional carriages were built in 1881 and the sets altered to run as three 7-coach trains with one coach spare. Details of construction follow:

Second class. Nos. 1940–1943 (SR Thirds Nos. 883, 884)
Body length: 43 ft. Body width: 8 ft 4 in.
Compartments: 7. Seats: 70.

Third brake. Nos. 1944–1947 (SR No. 3234); Nos. 1986, 1987 (SR No. 3236)
Body length: 40 ft 6 in. Body width: 8 ft 4 in.
Compartments: 6. Seats: 60.

Third class. Nos. 1948–1953 (SR Nos. not carried)
Body length: 43 ft. Body width: 8 ft 4 in.
Compartments: 8. Seats: 80.

First class. Nos. 1954–1957 (SR Nos. 7239/40/42); Nos. 1984, 1985 (SR No. 7243)
Body length: 40 ft 6 in. Body width: 8 ft 4 in.
Compartments: 6. Seats: 48.

All were built by the SER at Ashford: Nos. 1940–57 in July 1880 and Nos. 1984–7 in May 1881. Roofs were a plain arc; height from rail level to top of roof was 11 ft 5½ in. on the Seconds and Thirds and 11 ft 6 in. on the Firsts and Third Brakes. The guard's compartment was equipped with a roof observatory, the top of which was 12 ft 10 in. above rail level.

Third class compartments were only 5 ft 3 in. wide, partition to partition, and each alternate partition was only as high as the seat-back. The extra body width allowed the second class passengers to be seated 5-a-side instead of the usual 4-a-side, whilst the first class compartments were designed to accommodate 4-a-side instead of the usual 3-a-side. Gas lighting, comprising one burner in each compartment, was fitted.

Body framing was teak and oak; roof and partitions pine; top quarter panels papier maché; and bottom quarter panels Honduras mahogany. The whole of the underframe was oak, soles and headstocks being steel plated. Only the outer ends of the Third Brakes had screw couplings and side buffers and there were no buffers at all intermediately. Instead, on each headstock was an oval cast-iron block through which the sprung drawbar passed. Thus, each bar, which had an indiarubber spring at each end and terminated near the centre of the coach, linked two carriages together. Bogie wheelbase was 8 ft.

Braking was by simple vacuum, but automatic vacuum brakes were fitted in 1890/1, by which time the three sets had the following formations:

Third Bke	1944	1947	1946	
Second	1943	1940	1941	
Third	1949	1952	1948	
Third	1951	1953	1950	
First	1955	1956	1954	Spare Second
First	1984	1957	1985	1942
Third Bke	1945	1987	1986	
AVB fitted:	11/90	12/90	4/91	3/91

It was found that suburban bogie coaches were rather heavy for the available locomotive power, but the three sets continued in use on the North Kent line for which they were built. Writing from memory in 1934, H. Dixon Hewitt recalled that in the 1899–1901 period the formation of the 'North Kent' trains was Third Brake, Third, Second, three Firsts, Third Brake. He also believed that the roof observatories were not added until after 1901, but this seems extremely unlikely.

In 1906 one of the sets was fitted with axle bearings of a type suitable for main line work, although the set itself still continued on North Kent services: Firsts Nos. 1954/85, Composite No. 2287 (see later section), Second No. 1941, Thirds Nos. 1948/50 and Third Brakes Nos. 1946/86. Apart from the addition of an elliptical-roof 2nd/3rd Composite the set was unaltered in formation after 15 years. From 1908 set numbers 92, 93 and 94 were applied to the three trains. No. 93, berthed at Orpington, worked London–Bromley North services.

By 1914 there had been some considerable reshuffling of the sets, some of which now had elliptical-roofed coaches mixed in. The new formations and set numbers from 1914 were as shown:

Set 398		**Set 399**		**Set 400**		**Set 401**	
3rd Bke	2293	3rd Bke	1947	3rd Bke	1946	3rd Bke	1986
Second	1943	Second	1940	First	1957	Second	1941
First	1955	First	1956	First	1985	First	1954
3rd Bke	2294	3rd Bke	1987	2nd/3rd	2286	2nd/3rd	2287

Steam heaters were fitted to No. 398 in October 1914, 399 in March 1915, 400 in November 1915 and 401 in December 1915. No. 399 had been old No. 94 and No. 401 had been old No. 92 until late 1915. All six of the Thirds were collected together in Set 402 with two ex-LC&D 6-wheeled Composite Brakes and never received steam heating, which was still something of a luxury for suburban trains.

Sets 398 and 399 were berthed at Ashford for leave trains to/from Westenhanger during 1917/18. Set 400 was at Addiscombe Road or Beckenham Junction and Sets 401 and 402 were spare at Walmer. Later in 1918 an elliptical-roof 2nd/3rd Composite, No. 2285, was added to Set 398. Meanwhile, Nos. 1942/44/45/84 were withdrawn in 1918, the bodies being broken up in April and the underframes used as flat platform trucks to carry aeroplane parts; all were condemned in 1922.

After World War I the remaining sets returned to the suburban area: No. 398 was at Nunhead, 399 at Maidstone West, 400 and 401 at Addiscombe and 402 at Orpington in 1920. Set 399 in 1922 was booked to work the 8.05 am Maidstone West to Charing Cross, returning from Cannon Street at 6.20 pm.

Nos. 400/1 were really 'half-sets' as the elliptical-roofed composites had long buffers at the outer ends; this made it easy to run the stock as either one long train for peak periods or two short trains for the off-peak. The new owners, the Southern Railway, sent the eight coaches into Ashford Works and in November 1924 they emerged in new livery with Southern numbers as 8-set No. 679. 5-set 398 was also sent to Ashford for relivery and became Southern set No. 678 in February 1924. Second class was redone as third class.

SE&C Set No. 399 never appeared in Southern livery and was condemned complete in April 1928. All six Thirds in Set 402 (Nos. 1948–53) were withdrawn in June 1927, also without having received their allocated SR numbers.

SR Set No. 679 ran until 1928, when it was disbanded and a six-coach train, with coaches from Set 678, was made up and sold to Gainsborough Films in August 1928. These coaches (SR Nos. 884, 3234/6 and 7239/40/3) were destroyed in a specially-staged wreck on the Basingstoke & Alton Light Railway near Herriard on 19th August, 1928, for a silent film entitled 'The Wrecker'; the smash was filmed from several angles so that in the final picture the impression was given that there were several wrecks.

A photograph taken of Third Brake No. 3236 about 1928 shows that the Southern had reduced the number of compartments from six to five with consequent enlargement of the luggage compartment.

SEC No.	*Class*	*SR No.*	*Re-No.*	*Set No.*	*Wdn*	*SEC No.*	*Class*	*SR No.*	*Re-No.*	*Set No.*	*Wdn*
1940	2nd	–		–	4/28	1945	3rd Bke			–	3/18
1941	"	883	11/24	679	10/28	1946	"	3234	11/24	679	8/28
1942	"	–		–	3/18	1947	"	–		–	4/28
1943	"	884	2/24	678	8/28	1986	"	3236	11/24	679	8/28
1948	3rd	–		–	6/27	1987	"	–		–	4/28
1949	"	–		–	6/27	1954	1st	7239	11/24	679	8/28
1950	"	–		–	6/27	1955	"	7240	2/24	678	8/28
1951	"	–		–	6/27	1956	"	–		–	4/28
1952	"	–		–	6/27	1957	"	7242	11/24	679	10/28
1953	"	–		–	6/27	1984	"	–		–	3/18
1944	3rd Bke			–	3/18	1985	"	7243	11/24	679	8/28

COMPOSITE LAVATORY

No. 1988 (SR No. 5178)

Body length: 38 ft. Body width: 8 ft.
Compartments: 2 1st, 3 2nd. Seats: 10 1st, 24 2nd.
1 Lavatory, with access to both 1st-class compartments. Gas lighting.

Sir Edward Watkin was Chairman of the South Eastern and of the Manchester, Sheffield & Lincolnshire Railway; this fact, and the fact that the two railways were not in competition with each other, meant that there was no surprise when the SER accepted two coaches built at Gorton Works, MS&L. One of them was a Royal saloon; the other was this very strange little composite coach, built to a style totally unlike that of the normal SER carriage.

This unique vehicle was received in late February 1881 and sent into traffic early in March. It was built as a Tri-Composite with the makeup '3 1 lav. 1 2 3', but the Thirds were up-graded to Seconds before the coach was sent into traffic. As built it was six-wheeled with Cleminson Radial Application, in which the two outer axles pivotted and were connected to the centre axle, which slid laterally. Wheelbase was 28 ft.

The body was made of teak and varnished. From rail level to the top of the plain arc roof measured 11 ft 5 in. The windows and door droplight frames had a sort of 'Gothic' shape with the bottom corners square and the top curved. But the most curious feature of the coach was the lavatory – or rather the access thereto, for it had two doors, giving access from both first class compartments. What must often have happened was that a person would attempt to enter the lavatory simultaneously from each compartment, resulting in embarrassed apologies from both sides. Then again, even if only one person entered, he or she would have to remember to lock both doors to ensure privacy – and probably forget to unlock one of them when he or she left, thus denying facilities to the 'rival' compartment! Amazingly, this arrangement was allowed to continue until 1925, when access from one of the compartments was permanently blocked off and an extra seat built in front of what had been the door, increasing the 1st-cass seating capacity to 11.

If the SER was satisfied with the lavatory arrangements it was not so pleased with the Cleminson truck and so in June 1888 normal 4-wheel bogies of 8 ft wheelbase were substituted, bogie centres being 23 ft. At the same time automatic vacuum brakes were fitted in place of the non-automatic kind.

No. 1988 was recorded in 1889 as being formed in a tidal boat train with a 6-wheel Saloon, two 6-wheel Lavatory Firsts and a 6-wheel Lavatory Second. As a bogie coach it was short enough at 38 ft to work into Folkestone Harbour station.

The Composite was equipped with steam heating in September 1915 and in 1923 it became Southern Railway property. Seating was altered to 11 first 30 third, and in January 1926 it received its Southern number 5178 at Ashford. Finally, after a surprisingly long life of nearly 50 years – it must have been solidly built – No. 5178 was withdrawn in December 1930.

ROYAL SALOON (CONTINENTAL)

No. 1.R

Body length: 54 ft 10 in. Body width: 8 ft 6 in.
Compartments: 1 1st, 1 saloon, two bedrooms, 3 lavatories.
Seats: 16.

Gorton Works, Manchester, Sheffield & Lincolnshire Railway, built this very fine 12-wheel Royal Saloon for the South Eastern, which received it in February 1883. Actually the vehicle was delivered at Antwerpen and spent almost all its life on the Continent, being stationed at Calais ready for use by the British sovereign whenever any Continental journeys were undertaken. It was built specifically for the Prince of Wales, later to become King Edward VII.

The Saloon had teak body framing, a clerestory roof (the height of which was 12 ft 6¼ in. above rail level) and a gangway or 'vestibule' at one end only. The 6-wheel bogies each had a wheelbase of 5 ft 6 in. plus 5 ft 6 in. Each of the two sleeping compartments included one bed and two seats; the saloon had two inward-facing couches seating four each; and the attendant's compartment, at the gangwayed end of the coach, had four seats.

Braking system was both automatic vacuum and Westinghouse air; electricity for lighting was supplied by cells; and heating was by stove and through pipes.

During World War I No. 1.R was stabled at Le Landy in St Denis, a suburb of Paris. In March 1919 it needed repairs and was sent by train ferry from Calais to Richborough, thence Ashford Works. Afterwards it returned to France.

No. 1.R came into Southern ownership in 1923 and the number 7931 was allocated to it, though not carried. In February 1927 an offer of 15,000 francs for the Saloon was made to the Southern Board and after due consideration the Board sold No. 1.R in October 1927 to M. Boutigny at Calais for 12,000 francs, the Saloon having been officially withdrawn from stock in September 1927.

COMPOSITES

Nos. 2275–2284 (SR Nos. 5302–10, 4185)

Body length: 50 ft 1 in. Body width: 8 ft 0¾ in.
Compartments: 4 (later 3) 1st, 3 2nd. Seats: 24 (later 17) 1st, 24 (later 22) 2nd. Automatic vacuum brakes, gas lighting.

Richard Mansell retired in 1882 and his replacement as carriage superintendent was William Wainwright, from the Midland Railway. He did not at first build any bogie stock but concentrated on putting into service large numbers of 6-wheelers; from 1887 elliptical roofs 11 ft 10 in. above rail level became standard and the appearance of the carriages was much improved.

Wainwright's first elliptical-roof bogie coaches were 10 Composites, Nos. 2275–84, ordered from Craven Bros. in August 1888. They were delivered in the following order:

2275/6	12/1888	2280	6/1889	2283	9/1889
2278	2/1889	2281/2	7/1889	2284	10/1889
2277/9	3/1889				

The most impressive feature of these carriages was their 6-wheeled bogies, each with a wheelbase of 11 ft 9 in. (5 ft 10½ in. plus 5 ft 10½ in.). The fixed windows measured 2 ft 2¾ in. high by 1 ft 4 in. wide; doors were 6 ft by 2 ft 1 in. Original cost of each coach was £805.

Hardly had they been in traffic when modifications began to be made. In November 1889 Nos. 2280/1 had the innermost first-class compartment stripped out and in its place two lavatory compartments were installed, side-by-side, one having access to a first-class compartment and the other to a second-class one. It is believed that all the other Composites were similarly rebuilt during the next two or three years. Nos. 2275–7 became all-first in April 1893 and No. 2280 was altered to all-second in December 1892, losing its lavatories in 1893.

During 1893 the whole series, with the exception of No. 2280, was taken off main-line services, their lavatories stripped out, and placed on suburban services as close-coupled carriages without side buffers. The lavatories of No. 2281 were removed in March 1893 and those of the others probably around the same time.

The six Composites and three Firsts were formed into three trains, two Composites and one First in each set, together with four newly-built 8-compartment Thirds, two of the 1880-built flat-roof Thirds and six newly-built 6-compartment Third Brakes. These are described in the next section. The three 7-coach close-coupled sets worked on the Mid Kent line in the same sorts of services as the earlier flat-roof bogie stock; meanwhile No. 2280, without lavatories, remained as a long-buffered vehicle on main-line services.

In 1899 there was a further change of mind; the Firsts and Composites were taken off the suburban services and reconverted back to long buffered coaches and had their lavatories restored. As it had been found that the six-wheeled bogies were somewhat heavy, they were replaced by normal 4-

wheel bogies of 8 ft wheelbase. Lavatories were fitted to Nos. 2275–7/81–4 in 1899 and Nos. 2278/9 in 1900. Four-wheeled bogies were fitted to Nos. 2275–7/81/3/4 in 1899, Nos. 2278/9/82 in 1900 and to second class No. 2280 as late as 1905. Nos. 2275–7, the three that had become all-firsts in 1893, reverted to Composites in about 1899.

An authority on the SE&CR, H.F. Andrews, wrote that a six-wheeled bogie was a difficult thing to make run truly straight without pivotting on the middle axle. The tyres of the centre wheels needed renewing about every 50,000 miles, and the SE&C could not afford this.

After conversion the Composites were placed in Charing Cross – Hastings fixed services and were not permitted to run on either the Tadworth or Folkestone Harbour branches. From May 1906, No. 2277 was booked to work in the 9.08 pm Cannon Street to Dover Pier mail train. No. 2278 was stabled at Loughborough Junction to run when necessary in the Vlissengen boat train between Victoria and Queenborough Pier. From October 1908 No. 2276 was formed in the 7.55 am Ramsgate to Charing Cross and the slow portion of the 5.10 pm Holborn Viaduct to Ramsgate (detached at Faversham). Meanwhile Second No. 2280 had been formed in Set Train No. 56 by 1913.

Between 1911 and 1916 Nos. 2275–84 were fitted with steam heaters. No. 2281 was berthed at Chilworth during 1915 and 1916, working with bogie First No. 192 in a return London service.

In 1923 the Composites had their second-class compartments altered to third, seating 27. No. 2276 was withdrawn in 1926 without receiving its new Southern number, but Nos. 2275/7–9/81–4 were renumbered 5302/04–10 between 1923 and 1926. Second class No. 2280 was retained as a Second for working in boat trains, renumbered 4185 in 1926 and given electric lighting. It was withdrawn in 1931.

The others retained gas-lighting to the end. In their final years no other SER coach was quite like them, for they were the only ones to have two lavatories side-by-side, with two frosted glass windows between two passenger compartments.

SEC	*SR*	*Re-No.*	*SR Set No.*	*Wdn*	*SEC*	*SR*	*Re-No.*	*SR Set No.*	*Wdn*
2275	5302	7/24		10/28	2280	4185	1/26		8/31
2276	–	–		6/26	2281	5307	10/26		6/34
2277	5304	10/23	698	8/29	2282	5308	12/24		6/34
2278	5305	10/23	688	10/31	2283	5309	1/24		3/34
2279	5306	10/23		8/29	2284	5310	1/24		3/34

THIRDS

Nos. 2285–2288 (SR Nos. 896–8, 891)

Body length: 44 ft. Body width: 8 ft 0¾ in.
Compartments: 8. Seats: 80.

THIRD BRAKES

Nos. 2289–2294 (SR Nos. 3240–3, 3238/9)

Body length: 44 ft. Body width: 8 ft 0¾ in.
Compartments: 6. Seats: 60.

These 10 vehicles appear to have been introduced specifically for suburban services, for they were mixed in with the arc-roof suburban stock of 1880/1. The four Thirds were built by the SER in December 1892 (2285/6) and March 1893 (2287/8) and fitted with close-coupling (drawbar and cast-iron block) about March 1893. Messrs Cravens Ltd built the six Third Brakes, delivering them in March (2289/90), April (2291/2) and May 1893 (2293/4). These were close-coupled at the inner end but had normal couplings and long buffers at the brake end.

All 10 coaches continued the body style begun in 1888, with rounded mouldings and elliptical roofs, the tops of which were 11 ft 9½ in. above rail level. Compartment width on the 3rd brakes was 5 ft 7¼ in., which was quite an improvement on the 1880 third-class compartments, but on the all-3rds width was only 5 ft 4½ in. Bogie wheelbase was 7 ft and bogie centres were 30 ft. Each of the brake coaches was equipped with a roof observatory for the guard and as it was 12 ft 10 in. above rail level it prevented the carriages from running over the Metropolitan Railway. Lighting was by gas on all 10 coaches.

Between 1893 and 1899 the coaches ran formed in three suburban 7-coach sets which included the 50 ft Composites of 1888/9 and some of the 1880-built arc-roof Thirds. The standard formation is believed to have been: Third Brake, two Thirds, two 12-wheel Composites, 12-wheel First, Third Brake. In the normal way these sets would never have run in multiple, as no station platforms on the SER were long enough to accommodate a 14-coach bogie train; but it is said that on one occasion an 'F' class 4–4–0 did draw out an empty train consisting of two 7-sets coupled.

Even a 7-coach train was reckoned to be too heavy for the motive power and so, around 1898/9, the coaches were withdrawn from the North Kent and Mid Kent line services and altered for main-line use; Nos. 2288–90 became long-buffered in 1898 and Nos. 2285–7/91–4 in 1899. Three of the Thirds (Nos. 2285–7) were altered in 1903 to Composites with five 2nd class and three 3rd class compartments seating 40 and 30 respectively.

At the time of the carriages' conversion from suburban to main-line use an example of each was photographed at Ashford Works and copies of the pictures appeared in *The Railway Magazine* in 1899, the captions describing them as 'new' and the 'latest type'. Somewhat misleading, but perhaps the buffers were new! In addition the droplights each had a metal bar across them, and the roofs were gleaming white.

Then in 1908 Third Brakes Nos. 2293/4 were again converted to close-coupling at the non-brake ends and formed into a 4-coach set with two of the 1880/1 coaches; by 1913 this was carrying the set number 81 and running on the Dartford lines.

Train 81	3rd Bke	2293	
	First	1955	Set Renumbered 398
	Second	1943	in 1914.
	3rd Bke	2294	

With the addition of 2nd/3rd Composite No. 2285, converted to close-coupling about 1918, the set became 5-set 398, as detailed in a previous section. Meanwhile 2nd/3rd Composites Nos. 2286/7 became the end coaches of close-coupled sets 400/1. Third Brake No. 2289 was in set 72 and No. 2290 in set 32. All 10 coaches had been given steam heating between 1912 and 1918. Gas lighting was retained.

The Southern Railway converted the 2nd/3rds back to all-thirds in 1923, renumbering them 896–8; No. 2288, which had always been all-third, was given the new number 891.

SEC	*SR*	*Re-No.*	*SR Set No.*	*Wdn*	*SEC*	*SR*	*Re-No.*	*SR Set No.*	*Wdn*
2285	896	2/24	678	/32	2290	3241	5/24	690	11/30
2286	897	11/24	679,678	/32	2291	3242	1/26		5/31
2287	898	11/24	679	6/32	2292	3243	10/26	689	9/30
2288	891	12/27		6/32	2293	3238	2/24	678	/32
2289	3240	9/24		12/33	2294	3239	2/24	678,679	7/32

No. 3240 became Mess and Tool van No. 730S at New Cross Gate in December 1933.

TRI-COMPOSITES

Nos. 84 and 85 (SR Nos. 5255 and 5256)

Body length: 44 ft. Body width: 8 ft 0¾ in.
Compartments: 2 1st, 2 2nd, 2 3rd, 1 luggage.
Seats: 12 1st, 16 2nd, 20 3rd class. Gas lighting.

Following William Wainwright's death in 1895 Harry Smith Wainwright became carriage superintendent of the SER. The style of his carriages was just the same as that of his father's. The first bogie coaches to emerge from Ashford Works during Harry's tenure were these two Tri-Composites built in June 1896; they had teak body framing and oak underframes with angle iron sole plates. Bogies, of 7 ft wheelbase, were pressed steel and bogie centres 30 ft. Height of the coaches from rail to roof was 11 ft 9½ in. A luggage compartment, with double doors on each bodyside, was stuck at one end of the coach.

Nos. 84 and 85 do not show up in any carriage working notice until 1910, when it was specified that they were to be kept to Ashford–New Romney through trains throughout that year.

In May 1913 both were steam heated, and in 1923, when the Southern became the owner, the second class seating was altered to third (five-a-side), the four compartments now seating 40 third class passengers. The coaches received their new numbers, 5255 in February 1927 and 5256 in October 1923. No. 5256 was one of the first two coaches to emerge from Ashford in Southern livery, the other being a Third Brake (No. 3254).

The coaches do not appear to have been formed in any set train, though both lasted until February 1936, when they were transferred to service stock. No. 5255 became 900S and 5256 became 901S, being Mess and Tool vans for the locomotive running department at Stewarts Lane.

THE 'AMERICAN CARS'

Nos. 32–36 and 47

Body length: 45 ft over corner pillars. Underframe: 51 ft 3½ in.
Body width: 8 ft 3¾ in. Open end platforms, with open fall-plates between cars.
Height from rail level to top of clerestory: 12 ft 9 in.

In 1891 the South Eastern ordered from the Gilbert Car Manufacturing Co. of Troy, New York State, USA, four Drawing Room Cars, one Buffet Car and one Baggage Car. These were supplied in sections, which were duly assembled at Ashford Works and completed (officially) in December 1891. Actually Nos. 32 and 36 were dated January 1892 and Nos. 33–35 February 1892.

All the cars ran on 'American' 8 ft bogies with standard SER Mansell wheels. Bogie centres were 32 ft 0¾ in. Buffing and draw gear also was added by Ashford, with automatic vacuum brakes and a handbrake at one end. Electric lighting, with dynamos and accumulators, was supplied. The accumulators had to be recharged at regular intervals.

Nos. 32–35 were first class Drawing Room Cars with 25 seats in each. The body was divided into two parts, with a drawing room and a smoking compartment. Seating in the drawing room comprised 14 revolving chairs, one couch and two single chairs. The smoking room had four fixed seats and three moveable chairs. A heater and ladies' lavatory was provided at one end of the car and a gentlemen's lavatory at the other. The hot-water heating stove was made by the Baker Heater Co. of Troy, N.Y., and the heating pipes were carried throughout the length of each car.

No. 36 was the Buffet Car; accommodation was in one saloon compartment with 28 fixed seats. A passageway through the centre of the car led to the 'buffet office', situated at one end, and at the other end were a heating stove, an attendant's store room and a lavatory.

No. 47, numbered in the separate van list, was the Baggage Car. It was completely open, an empty shell, without guard's accommodation and in fact fairly useless. J.T. Howard Turner believed that it never ran in service as a Baggage Car, and in June or July 1892 it was rebuilt as a first class Drawing Room Car, keeping the same number but now in the passenger carriage list. There were two saloon compartments with communicating door; each saloon contained two couches, four revolving chairs and two fixed chairs seating a total of 26 passengers. At one end of the car was a heater and lavatory, and at the other end was a seat for the conductor and another lavatory.

On 2nd March 1892 the Drawing Room Cars and two modified 4-wheel Brake vans made a demonstration run from Charing Cross to Hastings and back. The complete train was painted dark lake, lined in red and with green bogies. Later, the Buffet and Drawing Room Cars were placed singly or in pairs in various Dover and Hastings expresses and no additional charge or supplement was made for this luxurious form of travel. This uncharacteristically generous gesture on the part of the chairman, Sir Edward Watkin, was made probably not so much out of feeling of benevolence towards his passengers but to make a gesture of a rather different kind to the Pullman Car Co., whose luxurious vehicles always commanded a supplement. The Hastings run was competitive with that of the London, Brighton & South Coast Railway and doubtless Watkin hoped that his 'Cars' would steal a little traffic from that line; but in fact the American Cars were not very popular with passengers. No doubt some of them found the cars too hot, while others – accustomed as they were to closed-in compartments – disliked the open saloons with their lack of privacy.

However, the South Eastern persisted with the American Cars and in 1896 decided to make some of them available for second- and third-class passengers, at the same time rebuilding the bodies to a limited extent. The open end platforms were enclosed and bellows gangway connections were added at each end. Electric lighting was converted to J. Stone's system. Nos. 35 and 47 were retained as first class; No. 36 became second class, with 28 seats; while Nos. 32–4 were the third class conversions. Of these, Nos. 32 and 34 seated 38 and No. 33 seated 39 passengers.

No. 35, which retained its layout of main saloon and smoking saloon, with both revolving chairs and fixed seats, had oak panelled interiors, silk curtains to the windows, and lamps suspended from brackets. Floral upholstery in the main saloon was coloured green and gold. No. 47 kept its two main saloons, one of which was set aside for the use of ladies if required; interior panelling was in Hungarian ash. One saloon was trimmed with light gold velvet, the other trimmed with blue velvet.

No. 36, the second-class car, had three compartments: main, trimmed with claret and gold tapestry; smoking; and ladies', decorated in Louis XV style and seating four persons.

Each of the third-class cars had oak interiors with trimming in terra-cotta tapestry, and there was a smoking room trimmed with dark tapestry.

Five of the cars were placed into service on 1st December, 1896, on a train running between Charing Cross and Hastings. At first, 4-wheel brake vans ran with them to provide accommodation for luggage and guard but, later, 6-wheel brake vans were used. One of the first-class cars was formed in a Dover–Charing Cross service but by 1902 all six Gilbert cars were in use on what became known as 'The Hastings Car Train'. This service left Hastings at 8.40 am for Charing Cross, taking about 1¾ hours, and returned at 3.35 pm taking rather more than 1¾ hours. From about 1903 a bogie brake coach headed and tailed the train in replacement of the brake vans. In 1904 one of the new Lavatory Thirds was booked to run in the train additionally: on the 3.35 pm 'down' on Fridays, remaining in the train until the 8.40 am 'up' the following Monday.

By May 1907 the set had been numbered as Train No. 8, which incidentally was the same as its working number in the Carriage Working Notices. The brake coaches allocated to the train were usually 3-compart-

FIRST CLASS DRAWING ROOM CAR

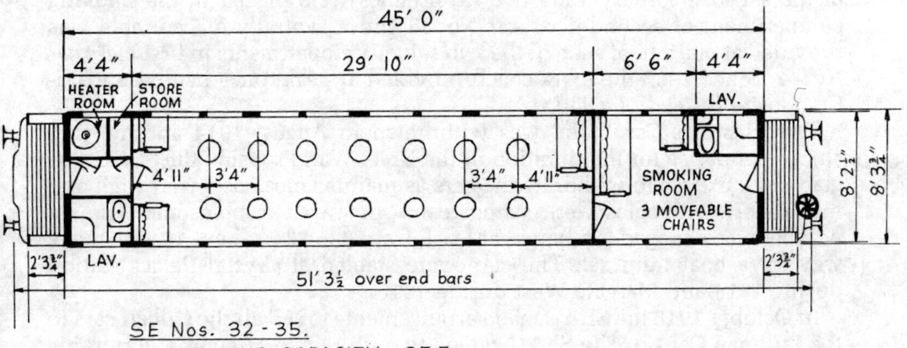

SE Nos. 32 - 35.
SEATING CAPACITY 25 F.

FIRST CLASS BUFFET CAR

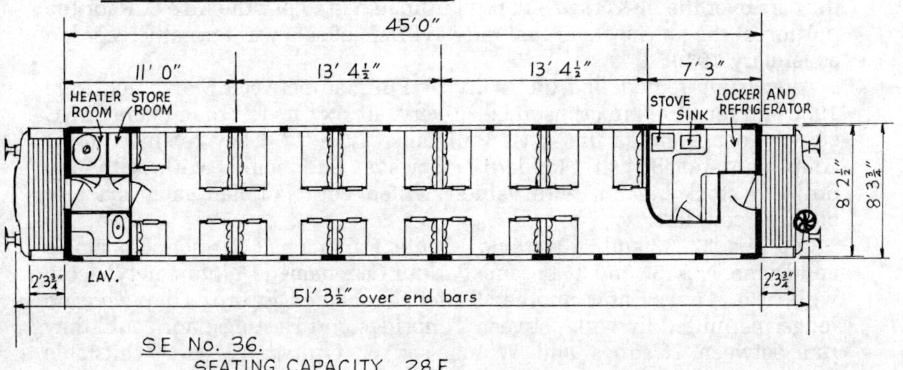

SE No. 36.
SEATING CAPACITY 28 F.

BAGGAGE CAR

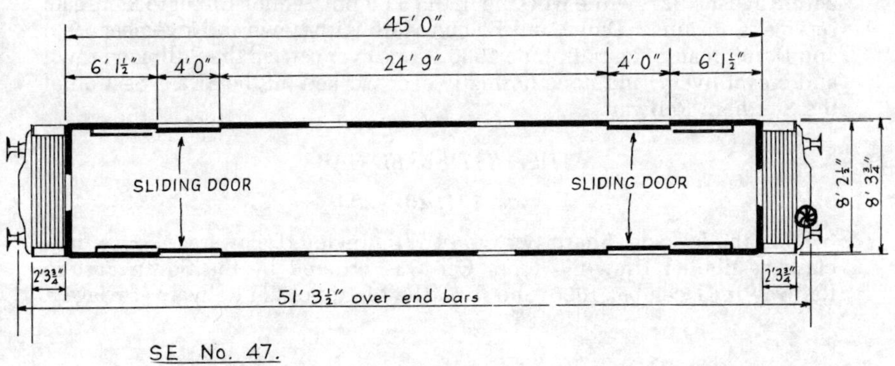

SE No. 47.

ment Third Brakes of 1900, but it is thought they were not numbered as part of the set. In February 1909 two drop tables were placed in the smoking compartment of second-class car No. 36 and a centrally-placed table was provided at one end of each of the two saloon compartments in first-class car No. 47. Since 1907 the extra coach provided at peak times had been a Tri-Composite instead of a Third.

The 'Hastings Car Train' was withdrawn in August 1914 and the cars stored out of use for the duration of the Great War. Probably the SE&C was glad of an excuse to withdraw the cars as maintenance costs were high and the 'American' bogies were stated to be somewhat troublesome. The set number was changed (on paper, at least) from 8 to 22 in about 1915 to make way for a boat train set. The cars were stabled at Crystal Palace station during 1915 and Margate West during 1916.

In October 1918 the SE&C made arrangements to sell all the Gilbert cars to the Pullman Car Co. The SE&C agreed to put the underframes and running gear in good order and to send the cars to Preston Park so that Pullman could make the necessary alterations to the bodies to bring them up to Pullman's standard; it is noteworthy that no charge was made to Pullman for transit of the cars over the SE&C system, but Pullman had to pay the LB&SCR for the portion of the journey over that railway! Date of sale was formally recorded as January 1919.

After being remodelled internally by Pullman between March and June 1920 and repainted in crimson lake livery, all six cars returned to the SE&C system to operate as first-class Pullmans, Type 'C'. They retained screw couplings and British Standard gangways, and could work with any ordinary stock but not with vehicles fitted with Pullman gangways and buckeye couplers.

Old Nos. 32, 33 and 34 were now Buffet Cars named *Carmen*, *Constance* and *Diana*. Nos. 35 and 36 became Parlour Cars named *Dolphin* and *Falcon*, while No. 47 was now another Buffet Car named *Figaro*. They were no longer permitted to work between Tonbridge and Hastings, nor could they run between Hastings and Winchelsea or Canterbury and Whitstable Harbour.

This remodelling gave the cars a further ten or so years of useful life, although unfortunately *Carmen* was wrecked in an accident at Sevenoaks on 24th August, 1927, while working in the 5.00 pm Cannon Street to Ramsgate service. *Constance*, *Diana* and *Falcon* were withdrawn in November 1928 and *Dolphin* and *Figaro* in June 1930. None ever carried the Pullman brown and cream livery, and none normally ever worked off the SE&C Section of the Southern Railway.

THE VESTIBULED CARS

Nos. 171, 201–208

From the Jackson, Sharp Car Co. of Wilmington, Delaware, USA, a first-class vestibuled Drawing Room Car was ordered by the South Eastern Railway in December 1896; and from the Metropolitan Railway Carriage &

Wagon Co. of Birmingham a complete Vestibuled Car Train of eight vehicles was ordered in January 1897.

The British cars were designed by H.S. Wainwright in conjunction with W.S. Laycock, of Sheffield, whose firm was a notable supplier of carriage fittings: in particular, buffers, couplers, window mechanisms and blinds, heaters and ventilators. According to *Engineering*, 10th September, 1897, Laycock had had considerable experience in the railways of the United States:

> We understand that the order for these cars was really placed through him, and the South-Eastern officials freely acknowledge that his knowledge of American practice in car equipment has been invaluable; and certainly Mr Wainwright, in conjunction with him, has embodied in these cars a combination of some of the best English and American features, together with an amount of artistic decoration of the highest order.

William Samuel Laycock was in business from at least 1866, at Ranmoor, Sheffield until the mid-1890s; then at Victoria Works, Millhouses, Sheffield until at least 1921. By 1925 the company had been amalgamated into one called Beckett, Laycock & Watkinson ('Beclawat').

The Metropolitan-built cars, Nos. 201–208, were delivered by September 1897 and the carriage register recorded that they were sent into traffic on 29th September, although a trial run of six of the cars had been made one week earlier.

All the cars were teak-built, of 'rigid' construction, lavatory-fitted, and ran on Fox's patent pressed-steel bogies of 8 ft wheelbase at 38 ft 3 in. centres. Length over body (exclusive of end doors, which were recessed) was 50 ft; length over vestibules was 56 ft 1 in.; width over cornices 8 ft 5 in.; and height from rail level to the top of the clerestory was 12 ft 9 in. The clerestories were of the American pattern downcurving towards each end of the cars. Automatic centre couplers of American design were provided within the train, but not at the outer ends of the brake cars, which had ordinary buffers and screw couplings. Retractable side buffers were provided on all the intermediate cars so they might run with ordinary coaches, including, on occasion, the Gilbert cars of 1892 (although the gangways could not be used if this happened). The new vestibuled cars had gangways similar to the Pullman type, but at the brake ends no gangway of any description was provided. Laycock supplied both the couplers and the gangways.

No. 201 was a first-class Drawing Room Car with 28 seats: 24 in the main saloon (16 transverse seats and eight inward-facing chairs) and four in the ladies' compartment. The interior was decorated in Louis XV style, with Italian walnut, slate-blue curtains, mirrors between the windows, and floral-patterned seat covers in 'neutral' colours.

No. 202 was a first-class Buffet Car with 28 seats: 12 in one saloon and 16 in the other saloon for smokers; at this end was a small buffet office. This car was decorated in Louis XVI style, with carved mahogany, golden-yellow curtains, and tapestry seat-coverings: slate-blue in the main saloon and tobacco-coloured in the smoking saloon.

No. 203 was a second-class car with 38 seats. This car comprised four small saloon compartments of which one was for ladies and two for smokers. Interior woodwork was in black walnut.

Nos. 204–6 were third-class cars with 42 seats each, 34 being in the main saloon and the remainder in a ladies' compartment. Fittings were of polished oak.

Nos. 207/8 were Third Brake cars with 22 seats each, a large luggage compartment and a guard's compartment with handbrake wheel. On these cars the clerestory was placed over the passenger half only, and did not extend the whole length of the car, stopping short at the inner end of the luggage compartment. The guard was provided with a roof observatory and the clerestory would have clashed with this.

The firm of Morison & Co., of Edinburgh, supplied all the decorative features of the interiors as well as the seats, lamps with electroliers, metalwork and upholstery. All these were designed by W.R. Reid, of Morison & Co.

Nos. 201–8, which although British-built were American in style, had inward-opening doors, one at each corner. Stone's electric lighting, with double accumulators and an axle-driven dynamo, was supplied on each car, which also was heated by a Baker stove with hot-water pipes.

Engineering recorded that the general manager of the Birmingham company, John Rawlins, 'naturally' took a leading part in the work of building the vestibuled train, making it an object of special attention.

The solitary Jackson, Sharp car, SER No. 171, was supplied in sections and erected at Ashford in October 1897. It comprised a non-smoking saloon with 12 seats, a ladies' compartment with five seats, a smoking compartment with 13 seats, and two lavatories. Body dimensions were 50 ft over pillars and 8 ft 4 in. wide. This car had the same type of gangways and couplers as the Metropolitan cars and could run with them. Heating was by means of a Baker stove.

Six of the Metropolitan cars entered regular service from October 1897 between London and Folkestone, the new train being dubbed 'The Folkestone Vestibuled Limited'. Two of the third class cars and the Jackson, Sharp first, being spare, were used on a service that left Tunbridge Wells for Charing Cross at 9.03 am and returned at 3.44 pm.

Writing in *The Railway Magazine* in 1899, D.T. Timins enthused over the third-class car running in the 'Folkestone Vestibuled Limited', 'unquestionably the most beautiful train in the British Isles. The design and decorations reflect no less credit upon the engineering skill of Mr Wainwright than upon his splendid artistic taste and judgment'. Both the main saloon compartment and the ladies' compartment were furnished in wainscot oak and finely upholstered, and the writer infinitely preferred these cars to any Pullmans; after all, Pullman was *American* and anything British was automatically superior!

Between 1902 and 1905 the formation of the Folkestone Car Train was booked as 3rd Bke 208, 2nd 203, 1st 202, 1st 201, 3rds 205/6 and 3rd Bke 207, with 3rd No. 204 as the spare car. The other spare car, No. 171, could be used on the Hastings line but the Folkestone cars, being wider, were barred from that line south of Tunbridge Wells, and also between Minster and Sandwich.

In 1906, workings of the Folkestone Car Train, which since 1903 had run non-stop between Cannon Street and Folkestone and was the fastest train on the SE&C, were: 8.30 am Folkestone Central to Charing Cross, 4.28 pm Charing Cross to Dover Harbour, thence empty to Folkestone Central. On Mondays a bogie Lavatory Composite and bogie Third were added on the 8.30 am 'up' and returned on Fridays by the 4.28 pm 'down'.

From about 1907 the Folkestone cars were numbered as Train No. 7 and the extra coaches on Mondays and Fridays were a Tri-Composite and brake van. About 1908 the spare car No. 204 was upgraded to second class, seating capacity remaining at 38. In September 1911 several structural alterations were made to No. 171. The smoking compartment was enlarged and a longitudinal partition removed in order to make one open compartment, and in addition a cross-partition was moved. The cross-partition dividing the lavatory from the compartment was made up complete.

All the cars were withdrawn after the outbreak of World War I in August 1914 and placed in store at Battersea; in 1915 the set was renumbered 21 – as the number 7 was required for a boat train set – and stabled at Crystal Palace, then at Margate West. In October 1918 the SE&C agreed to sell to the Pullman Car Co. all eight Metropolitan cars, the Jackson, Sharp car and the six Gilbert cars for £15,000. At the time the original cost of all 15 cars was stated to have been about £28,000. Pullman's contract dated 31st May, 1912, to run Pullman cars on the SE&C was extended for 12 years from 1919 and now included the 15 ex-SE&C cars, which became Pullman property in January 1919.

At Preston Park between March and November 1919 the Third Brakes were rebuilt to match the other cars; the luggage and guard's compartments, as well as the roof observatory, being done away with. The clerestory was extended over the whole car length. Internally, all cars were brought up to Pullman standards but exteriors were largely unaltered. As the cars would continue to run on the SE&C, they were repainted in crimson lake livery instead of the brown and cream used elsewhere. All were classed Type 'D'. No. 201 became a Buffet Car named *Hilda*, and Nos. 202–6 became Parlour Cars (first class) named *Dora, Mabel, Stella, Dorothy* and *Venus*. Nos. 207/8, the former Third Brakes, were remodelled as Buffet Cars and named *Thistle* and *Albatross*: a curious pairing of names. Finally, No. 171 became a Parlour Car named *Tulip*.

The original couplers and gangways were retained, and similar couplers and gangways were fitted at what had been the brake ends of *Thistle* and *Albatross*. J.T. Howard Turner recorded that in about 1925 standard Pullman gangways were fitted in replacement.

Withdrawal of the reconditioned cars began with *Stella* in April 1928. *Venus* followed in November 1929 and all the rest in June 1930. But it was not the end for *Albatross* and *Thistle*, for they were converted at Preston Park into 'supply' (or kitchen) cars without passenger accommodation and repainted all-over brown. They returned to service in May 1931, still named but without the title 'Pullman' on the fascia. Even on final withdrawal in

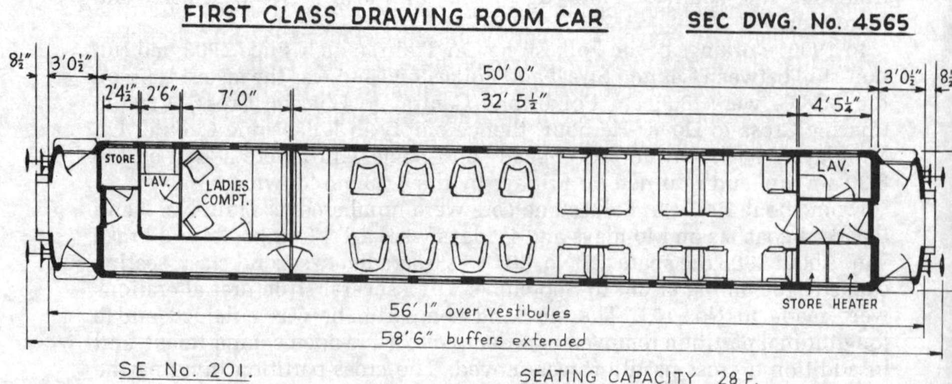
FIRST CLASS DRAWING ROOM CAR
SEC DWG. No. 4565
8½″
3′0½″
50′0″
3′0½″
8½″
2′4½″
2′6″
7′0″
32′ 5½″
4′5¼″
STORE
LAV.
LADIES COMPT.
LAV.
STORE
HEATER
56′ 1″ over vestibules
58′ 6″ buffers extended
SE No. 201.
SEATING CAPACITY 28 F.

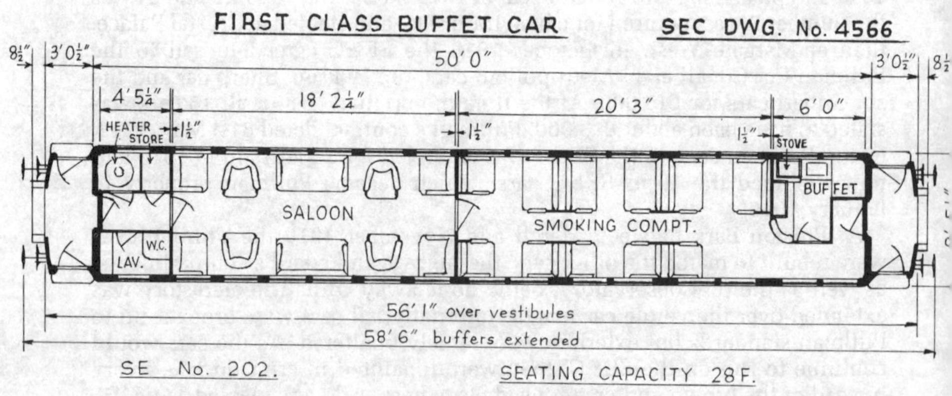
FIRST CLASS BUFFET CAR
SEC DWG. No. 4566
8½″
3′0½″
50′0″
3′0½″
8½
4′5¼″
18′ 2¼″
20′3″
6′0″
HEATER
STORE
1½″
1½″
1½″
STOVE
BUFFET
SALOON
SMOKING COMPT.
W.C.
LAV.
56′ 1″ over vestibules
58′ 6″ buffers extended
SE No. 202.
SEATING CAPACITY 28 F.

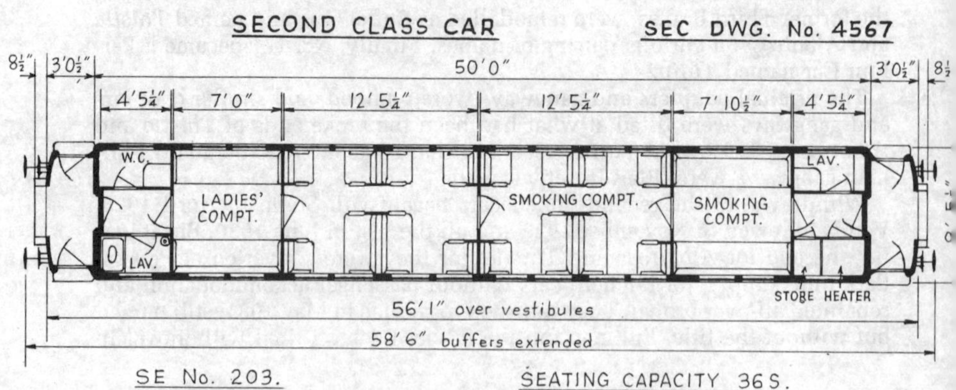
SECOND CLASS CAR
SEC DWG. No. 4567
8½″
3′0½″
50′0″
3′0½″
8½
4′5¼″
7′0″
12′ 5¼″
12′ 5¼″
7′ 10½″
4′5¼″
W.C.
LADIES' COMPT.
SMOKING COMPT.
SMOKING COMPT.
LAV.
LAV.
STORE
HEATER
56′1″ over vestibules
58′ 6″ buffers extended
SE No. 203.
SEATING CAPACITY 36 S.

1938 they were not scrapped but became mobile offices at Lancing Carriage Works. There they stayed for many years. In October 1952 L.E. Brailsford wrote that at Lancing there were 'two of these cars still on their wheels and now used as offices. Everyone there shews them to you as "Pullmans" which in a sense is incorrect. Correct in that their last owner was the Pullman Co. and they were run as Pullmans; but not as regards their origin and first use.'

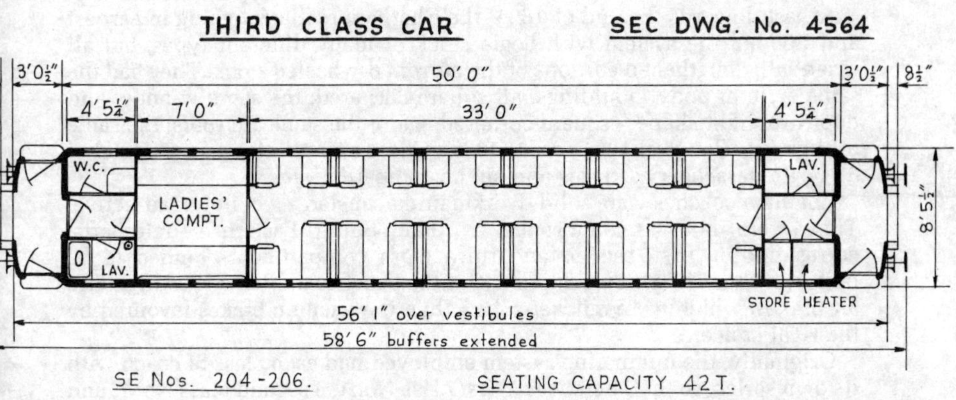

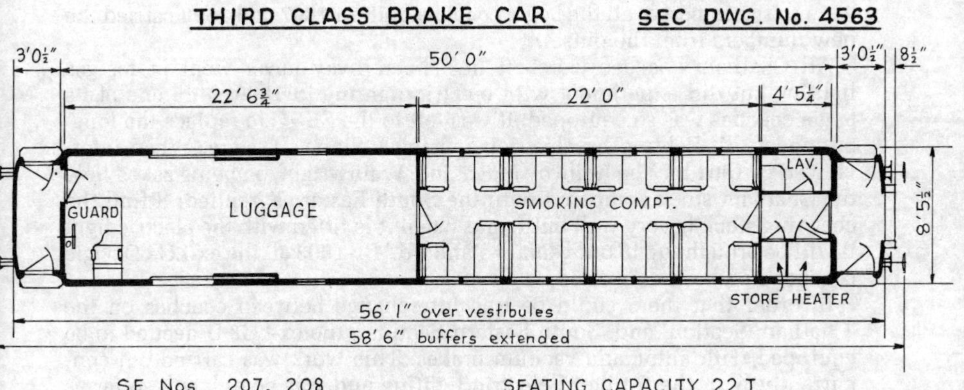

Chapter Three

London, Chatham & Dover Railway Bogie Carriages

For most of its life the London, Chatham & Dover Railway went on building 4- and 6-wheeled carriages, the later ones of which showed very little advance on the earlier. Then in 1885 it made a bold and daring experiment. It built a bogie coach! Seven months later, it built yet another. Then, either through lack of funds or lack of conviction that bogies really were the up-and-coming thing, the Chatham had a breathing-space until 1887, when it put into service no fewer than four new bogie coaches.

At last, towards the end of 1894, the Chatham really got going in earnest and flooded the system with bogie stock of many different types, but all essentially lengthened editions of the current 6-wheeled stock. They had the same style of body mouldings, all square-cornered; the same window and door droplight shape – square-cornered again; the same arc roofs; the same oil lighting. Between 1885 and 1898 the Chatham put into service a total of 83 bogie passenger carriages and six bogie guard's vans.

Chatham coaches were solid, workmanlike, austere – yet not unattractive. They were not as comfortable as their South Eastern counterparts; corresponding first, second and third class compartments tended to be narrower than the South Eastern's. But the coaches did have Westinghouse air brakes, which were quicker-acting than the vacuum brakes favoured by the rival concern.

Originally, the numbering system employed had each class of coach with its own series, so that there was a first class No. 1, a second class No. 1, and so on. In 1897 the Chatham introduced a renumbering scheme whereby all its coaches and passenger vans would be in one series, and several coaches were so renumbered; all the bogie coaches built in 1897 and 1898 carried the new numbers from the outset.

All Chatham coaches were oil lit. The railway never went in for gas lighting but did experiment with electric lighting in 1896; only one of its bogie coaches was so equipped. It was left to the SE&C to replace the long-outmoded oil lighting by electricity, using J. Stone's system. When interviewed in 1901 by *The Railway Magazine*, Wainwright, on being asked how the Chatham stock compared with the South Eastern's, replied: 'I find the coaching stock is very well built, and when it is fitted with the electric light it will be brought up to our general standard.' By 1903 all the ex-LC&D bogie coaches had been converted.

In order that there could be free interchange between coaches on the 'Chatham Section' and 'South Eastern Section', the ex-LC&D needed to be equipped with automatic vacuum brakes. This work was carried out concurrently with the fitting of electric lighting and was completed, so far as bogie stock was concerned, by 1903. Certain coaches thus became dual-braked, but the majority had the Westinghouse gear stripped out.

Features common to all Chatham bogie coaches were a body width of 8 ft, height from rail to roof 11 ft 7½ in. (1897 onwards) or 11 ft 6½ in. (1885–96), a bogie wheelbase of 8 ft and wheels of 3 ft 7 in. diameter.

COMPOSITES

Nos. 52–57 (SEC Nos. 2699–2704, SR Nos. 5179–84)

Body length: 40 ft. Bogie centres: 25 ft.
Compartments: 4 1st, 2 2nd. Seats: 24 1st, 16 2nd.

These six Composites were the Chatham's first bogie coaches, and all were built at Longhedge Works. No. 52 had wheels of 3 ft 6 in. diameter, but all the others were 3 ft 7 in. Electric lighting was fitted to No. 56 in December 1896 but only four years later the standard SE&C lighting replaced it.

When new, the Composites were classed as boat train stock. Automatic vacuum brakes and electric light were fitted to the series during 1901/2, and the SE&C passed them for working into Folkestone Harbour station. Steam heating was available to Nos. 2699, 2700/03 in 1912 and 2701/02/04 in 1914. No. 2704 in 1914 had one of the first-class compartments downgraded to second so that the seating capacity was now 18 first and 24 second-class.

All six vehicles came to the Southern Railway in 1923 and the second-class compartments were altered to thirds seating 10 passengers each. All the Composites received their Southern numbers of 5179–84, but were withdrawn in the early 1930s. However, two were sent to the Isle of Wight in 1933 for further service, Nos. 5182/4 being renumbered 6358/9 and re-equipped with Westinghouse air brakes, which were standard on the Island. No. 5182 had one of its first-class compartments altered to third so as to match No. 5184.

After a working life of over 60 years these two, as Nos. 6358/9, were withdrawn in 1948 and 1949 respectively.

No.	*Built*	*SEC*	*Reno'd*	*SR*	*Reno'd*	*To IOW*	*IOW No.*	*Wdn*
52	5/85	2699	4/03	5179	4/26	–	–	3/31
53	12/85	2700	7/01	5180	4/26	–	–	12/30
54	6/87	2701	3/02	5181	2/28	–	–	8/30
55	"	2702	4/06	5182	6/28	5/33	6358	5/48
56	10/87	2703	12/00	5183	4/26	–	–	6/31
57	"	2704	5/02	5184	6/24	5/33	6359	4/49

THIRDS

Nos. 347–351 (SEC Nos. 3301–05, SR Nos. 849–53)

Body length: 40 ft. Bogie centres: 25 ft.
Compartments: 7. Seats: 70.

Possibly the Chatham would have liked to own more bogie coaches but they were expensive to build and after the first six Composites were completed in 1887 no more 8-wheeled stock came out for another seven years. At last, between 1894 and 1896, five coaches were put into service: 7-compartment Thirds each seating 70 passengers in somewhat cramped conditions.

Vacuum brakes and electric lighting were fitted in 1900 to No. 347 and in 1902 to the remaining four vehicles. In SEC days the coaches were permitted to work over the Folkestone Harbour branch.

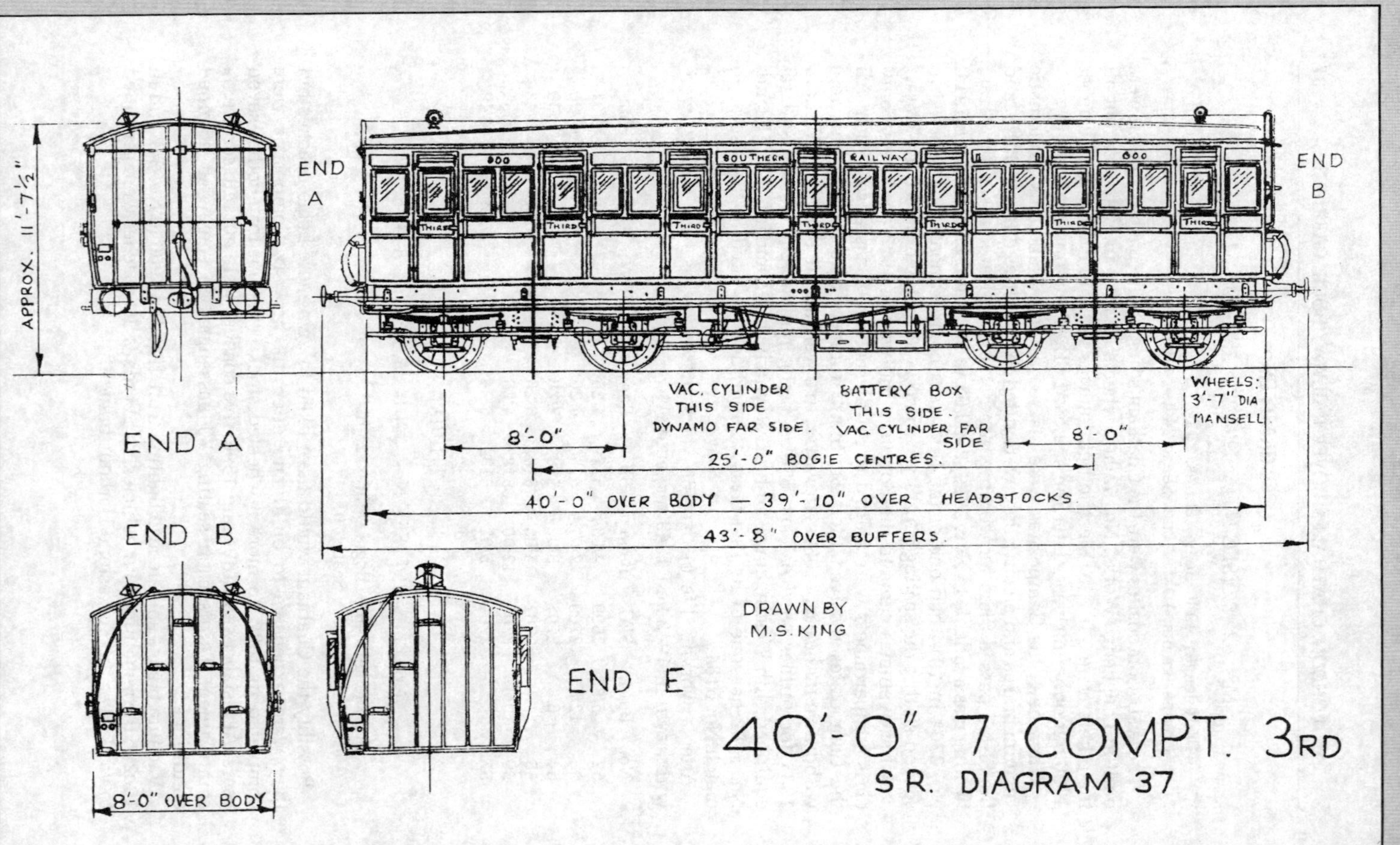

APPROX. 11'-7½"
END A
END B
SOUTHERN
RAILWAY
THIRD
VAC. CYLINDER THIS SIDE DYNAMO FAR SIDE.
BATTERY BOX THIS SIDE. VAC. CYLINDER FAR SIDE
WHEELS: 3'-7" DIA MANSELL
8'-0"
8'-0"
25'-0" BOGIE CENTRES.
40'-0" OVER BODY — 39'-10" OVER HEADSTOCKS.
43'-8" OVER BUFFERS.
END A
END B
8'-0" OVER BODY
DRAWN BY M.S. KING
END E
40'-0" 7 COMPT. 3RD
S R. DIAGRAM 37

It is not known whether any were formed into numbered sets, either by the SE&C or the Southern. All were taken into Southern stock in 1923, having been fitted with steam heating, and all received their new numbers. Probably most were used as strengthening vehicles on branch lines: No. 851, for example, was working between Appledore and Dungeness on 17th October, 1929, boarded 'New Romney Branch'.

In May 1933 three were sent to the Isle of Wight, having been re-equipped with Westinghouse brakes, and performed yeoman service there as part of Set 497 until withdrawal in 1948/9.

No.	*Built*	*SEC*	*Reno'd*	*SR*	*Reno'd*	*To IOW*	*IOW No.*	*Wdn*
347	11/94	3301	12/01	849	2/24	–	–	12/30
348	9/95	3302	3/00	850	2/24	5/33	2418	5/48
349	12/95	3303	10/05	851	3/26	–	–	12/31
350	3/96	3304	9/02	852	2/27	5/33	2419	4/49
351	5/96	3305	9/02	853	12/28	5/33	2420	4/49

THIRDS

Nos. 1069–1090 (SEC Nos. 3388–3409, SR Nos. 899–918, 3270/71)

Body length: 46 ft. Bogie centres: 30 ft.
Compartments: 8. Seats: 80.

The majority of LC&D bogie stock was built in the last two years of its separate existence, and all were numbered in the new 'one-sequence' number series.

In 1897/8 the Gloucester Railway Carriage & Wagon Co. built 22 8-compartment Thirds for the LC&D. The SE&C replaced the Westinghouse brakes by vacuum and the oil lighting by electricity in 1899 (Nos. 3388/9 and 3405) and 1902 (the remainder). From about 1912, steam heaters were installed.

In May 1912, Nos. 3396 and 3402 were converted to push-and-pull Third Brakes, reducing the seating capacity to 70. One of the end compartments was altered to a driver's compartment (also luggage and guard). With similarly converted Brake Composites they ran first of all on the Greenwich Park branch with the locomotive (a class 'P' 0–6–0 tank) between the two coaches. By 1915 the two 2-coach trains had been numbered 271 and 272 and continued working between Nunhead and Greenwich Park until the branch was closed on 1st January, 1917. Set 272 then worked between Margate Sands and Minster, and later Set 271 worked in the same area, both sets during 1918 being berthed at Ramsgate Town. About October 1919 they were again transferred, this time to Aldershot Town for working the Ash shuttle service on which they remained until withdrawal in early 1936.

The remaining 20 Thirds came to the Southern and all received their new numbers. In 1930/1 13 were sent to the Isle of Wight; of these, two were rebuilt into 7-compartment Third Brakes. Westinghouse brakes were fitted in all cases. One of the converted Third Brakes was involved in an accident at Watchingwell in 1939 and condemned, but all the other Isle of Wight coaches lasted until 1948/9. Those remaining on the Mainland had been withdrawn in 1929/30.

No.	*Built*	*SEC*	*Reno'd*	*SR*	*Reno'd*	*To IOW*	*IOW No.*	*Wdn*
1069	8/97	3388	12/99	899	1/28	–	–	3/30
1070	"	3389	12/99	900	1/28	6/31	2423	4/49
1071	"	3390	2/08	901	10/28	6/31	2424	5/48
1072	"	3391	10/05	902	10/24	–	–	11/29
1073	9/97	3392	10/05	903	12/25	–	–	11/29
1074	"	3393	11/08	904	6/24	6/31	2425	4/49
1075	"	3394	1/07	905	8/24	6/31	2426	5/48
1076	"	3395	1/05	906	10/26	–	–	11/29
1077	10/97	3396	10/06	3270	6/28	–	–	1/36
1078	"	3397	4/05	907	12/27	5/31	2427	5/48
1079	"	3398	1/07	908	5/29	5/31	2428	4/49
1080	2/98	3399	4/05	909	10/26	5/31	4110	2/39
1081	"	3400	4/07	910	6/25	7/30	2421	5/48
1082	"	3401	10/03	911	10/24	–	–	11/29
1083	"	3402	11/03	3271	6/27	–	–	2/36
1084	3/98	3403	10/06	912	11/24	5/31	2429	5/48
1085	"	3404	4/05	913	6/24	–	–	11/29
1086	4/98	3405	12/99	914	1/28	5/31	2430	5/48
1087	"	3406	1/07	915	6/24	–	–	11/29
1088	"	3407	5/06	916	10/28	5/33	4117	5/48
1089	"	3408	5/06	917	?	7/30	2422	5/48
1090	"	3409	7/06	918	?	5/31	2431	5/48

COMPOSITES

Nos. 1091–1100 (SEC Nos. 2707–16, SR Nos. 5263–70, 6605/06)

Body length: 45 ft. Bogie centres: 30 ft.
Compartments: 3 1st, 4 2nd. Seats: 18 1st, 32 2nd class.

A series of ten 45 ft Composites was built by the Birmingham Railway Carriage & Wagon Co. for the LC&DR late in 1897.

The SE&C fitted vacuum brakes and electric lighting to Nos. 2707 and 2716 in 1899 and the remainder in 1901. Air brakes were removed from all but No. 2712. They were given steam heaters between 1912 and 1916.

In May 1912 two of the Composites, Nos. 2711/13, were rebuilt with a driving and brake compartment at the expense of a second-class compartment at one end. Each was fitted with what the carriage register described as a 'through driving rod' for pull-and-push working. Brake Composite No. 2713 was paired with Third Brake No. 3396 and eventually given the set number 271, while No. 2711 was paired with No. 3402, becoming Set 272. These Third Brakes had similarly been rebuilt from Thirds, as described in the previous section. When the Southern took over these push-and-pull sets – the only 8-wheeled ones bequeathed by the SE&C – it renumbered them 732 and 733. They were repainted in SR colours in June 1928 and June 1927 respectively. Until their withdrawal in early 1936 these sets operated the Ash–Aldershot shuttle.

No alterations were made to the remainder. In 1923 seating capacity was altered to 24 first, 40 third class. Two vehicles were withdrawn in 1930, leaving six to be transferred to the Isle of Wight for further useful service. The second class compartments had been altered to thirds, seating 5-a-side, in 1923.

The Island vehicles received Westinghouse brakes and were formed into sets until their withdrawal in 1948 and 1949.

No.	Built	SEC	Reno'd	SR	Reno'd	To IOW	IOW No.	Wdn
1091	11/97	2707	1/01	5263	12/25	6/31	6395	4/49
1092	"	2708	5/03	5264	7/27	6/31	6396	5/48
1093	"	2709	11/04	5265	1/28	5/31	6397	4/49
1094	12/97	2710	1/05	5266	7/27	–	–	3/30
1095	"	2711	10/06	6605	6/27	–	–	1/36
1096	"	2712	2/08	5267	6/24	–	–	7/30
1097	"	2713	11/03	6606	6/28	–	–	2/36
1098	"	2714	9/04	5268	2/24	5/33	6360	
1099	"	2715	5/03	5269	3/29	5/34	6361	
1100	"	2716	2/99	5270	2/27	5/31	6398	2/39

COMPOSITE LAVATORY

Nos. 1150–1161 (SEC Nos. 2717–28, SR Nos. 854–65)

Body length: 42 ft. Bogie centres: 27 ft.
Compartments: 3 1st, 3 2nd, 2 lavs. Seats: 13 1st, 19 2nd.

Of all the Chatham's bogie coaches the pick of the bunch was this series of lavatory-fitted Composites, which were the only such equipped bogie coaches in the collection. Moreover, there were internal corridors, so that all first-class passengers had access to their lavatory, and all second-class passengers had access to theirs, but there was no communication between the two classes. By LC&D standards these 12 Composites were of a very advanced design, for even by 1898 the provision of sanitary facilities on the Chatham main line was virtually nil. Two 6-wheel Composites and a handful of 6-wheel Saloons: that was it.

The carriages were built by the LC&D itself, at Longhedge Works, and put into service during 1898. Electric lighting and vacuum brakes (in addition to the Westinghouse brakes) were installed to Nos. 1150/1 in 1899 and to the other ten during 1901. SE&C Nos. 2717–28 – as they became – were permitted to work over the Folkestone Harbour branch. Steam heaters were put in between 1911 and 1922.

In 1911 a start was made to convert the coaches into all-thirds, seating 40 but still keeping the lavatories. Nos. 2718/20/27/28 were downgraded in 1911, 2722 in 1912, 2724/6 in 1913, 2721 in 1920 and 2717/23/25 in 1921. Uniquely, No. 2719 ran as a first/third Composite from 1914 to 1922, when it became the last of the 12 to be made all-third. No. 2719 regularly worked on to the LB&SCR, which was a 'Westinghouse' line, so its dual brakes were very necessary. During 1915 it was formed into an un-numbered 'set' that was booked to work the 9.33 am through train from Ashford to Brighton and 1.55 pm return, locomotives being changed at Hastings. By 1916 the same 'set' that included No. 2719 was scheduled to work the 1.30 pm (Saturdays)

Folkestone Junction to Charing Cross. Certain other Lavatory Composites had worked several Charing Cross–Reading services since 1909. During 1917 seven Lavatory Thirds were stabled for special working only: Nos. 2724/28 at Ashford, 2718/22 at Faversham, 2720 at Rotherhithe Road and 2726/27 at Victoria.

All 12 coaches came to the Southern in 1923 as dual-braked Thirds and were renumbered 854–865. Westinghouse fittings were removed from Nos. 854/57/59/60 in November 1930. The SR did not seem to regard Chatham coaches with much favour and, as they were unsuitable for service in the Isle of Wight because of their lavatories (not permitted on Island trains), this particular series was rendered extinct in 1933.

Three, however, did become Mess and Tool Vans in November 1933 and were attached to the Locomotive Running Department for the Bricklayers Arms breakdown train. These three, Nos. 725S, 726S and 727S, were observed by R.W. Kidner on 29th June, 1935 attached to the Nine Elms breakdown train, although at New Cross. No. 726S was condemned in August 1941 and No. 725S was transferred to Hither Green in October 1941.

No.	*Built*	*SEC*	*Reno'd*	*SR*	*Reno'd*	*Wdn*	
1150	12/97	2717	12/99	854	9/26		To 725S, 11/33
1151	"	2718	12/99	855	11/26	11/30	
1152	2/98	2719	7/05	856	12/26	3/33	
1153	"	2720	6/04	857	7/26	2/33	Sold
1154	3/98	2721	7/03	858	7/26	9/30	
1155	4/98	2722	7/06	859	6/28		To 726S, 11/33
1156	5/98	2723	1/05	860	2/26	2/33	Sold
1157	"	2724	11/08	861	5/29	3/33	
1158	6/98	2725	3/04	862	10/26	3/33	To 727S, 11/33
1159	"	2726	2/05	863	1/27	3/31	
1160	7/98	2727	1/05	864	3/27	10/31	
1161	"	2728	7/05	865	2/26	10/30	

TRI-COMPOSITES

(Nos. 1162–1167 (SEC Nos. 2729–34, SR Nos. 5257–62)

Body length: 45 ft. Bogie centres: 30 ft.
Compartments: 3 1st, 2 2nd, 2 3rd. Seats: 18 1st, 16 2nd, 20 3rd.

One might imagine that the Chatham was going in for a competition to build the largest variety of coaching stock types, for the next batch to enter service was a small number of Tri-Composites. These were built by the Birmingham Railway Carriage & Wagon Co. and delivered at the same time as the bi-composites already described – that is to say, November and December 1897. Although similar to these, the Tri-Composites were not merely the same vehicles with reclassified compartments; the compartments did in fact differ dimensionally. In the Tri-Composites both first- and second-class compartments were an inch wider, and the third-class were narrower by 3½ in. than the seconds. Actual makeup was '3 2 1 1 1 2 3'.

The SE&C fitted vacuum brakes to Nos. 1165/6 in 1899, 1162–4 in 1901 and 1167 in 1902. Westinghouse brakes were, in turn, removed from all save

No. 1165/7 (SEC 2732/4). Electric lighting was installed in 1901 (Nos. 1162–5) and 1902 (1166/7).

At first, ex-Chatham stock did not appear on very many trains operating within the South Eastern section. However, by 1909 certain train services on the Charing Cross–Redhill–Reading line were particularly specified to be formed of 'Chatham Section' stock, so clearly this stock was already being considered suitable chiefly for secondary services – and train services did not come much more than 'secondary' than the Reading line one, with its three-hour through journeys. Four un-numbered 'sets' operated on this line in 1909, each being formed of a LC&D Lavatory Composite, a Tri-Composite, a Third and a brake van – all bogie stock. A typical 'Not Saturdays' carriage working began with the 9.55 am Reading to Charing Cross, returning at 2.05 pm. The 'set' then worked the 6.40 pm 'up' train to Charing Cross, empty to Cannon Street, and 10.42 pm thence to Dorking. On Saturdays the workings were 7.48 am Reading to Charing Cross, 2.12 pm return then as Monday to Friday.

All six Tri-Composites were steam-heated between 1913 and 1922. During 1916, No. 2732 was booked to work with a bogie Brake Composite between Holborn and Gravesend West, being berthed at Swanley. In 1919 No. 2733 was formed in Set 34 with two 50-seat 6-wheel Thirds and a 6-wheel brake van, being berthed at Caterham. Later, with the addition of a Lavatory Third, the set was transferred to Dover, working to and from Margate Sands and Ramsgate Town. Meanwhile No. 2729 was kept as spare coach on the Sheppey Light Railway.

The Southern Railway inherited the six Tri-Composites and, with the abolition of second class in September 1923, increased the seating capacity of the former 2nd-class compartments to 10 each; total capacity was now 18 1st and 40 3rd.

Four vehicles were transferred to the Isle of Wight in the early 1930s (the other two having been withdrawn) and had their Westinghouse brakes reinstated. All four were placed in set trains with other Chatham stock and served the Island passengers well until shortly after World War II.

Much of the Chatham stock remained in regular service until March 1949, having been painted in malachite green a short time previously. After withdrawal many coaches were transferred back to the Mainland and stood in sidings at South Croydon for some months to await breaking up. No. 6388 (ex-5259) became a mess and tool van No. DS 1858, but its final withdrawal date is not known.

No.	*Built*	*SEC*	*Reno'd*	*SR*	*Reno'd*	*To IOW*	*IOW No.*	*Wdn*
1162	11/97	2729	11/08	5257	11/26	–	–	2/31
1163	"	2730	7/05	5258	12/28	6/31	6394	5/48
1164	"	2731	3/04	5259	10/24	4/34	6388	4/49
1165	"	2732	10/06	5260	1/28	6/32	6399	4/49
1166	"	2733	10/06	5261	7/26	–	–	11/30
1167	12/97	2734	5/06	5262	2/27	4/34	6400	4/49

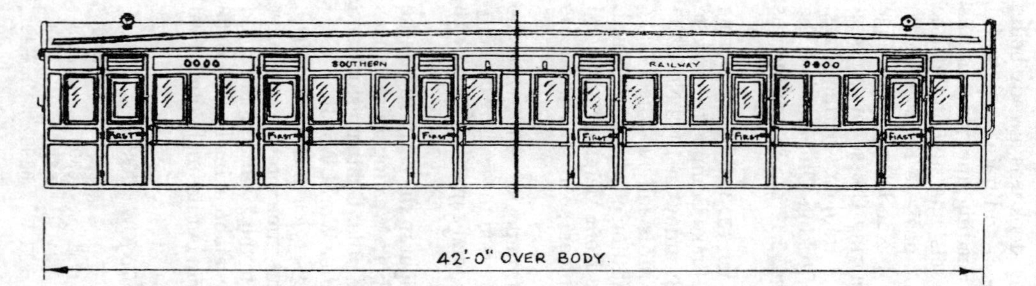
END A
END B
SOUTHERN
RAILWAY
FIRST
42'-0" OVER BODY
42'-0" 6 COMPT. 1ST
S.R. DIAGRAM 484
ONE VEHICLE LATER DOWNGRADED TO 3RD CLASS - DIAGRAM 54.

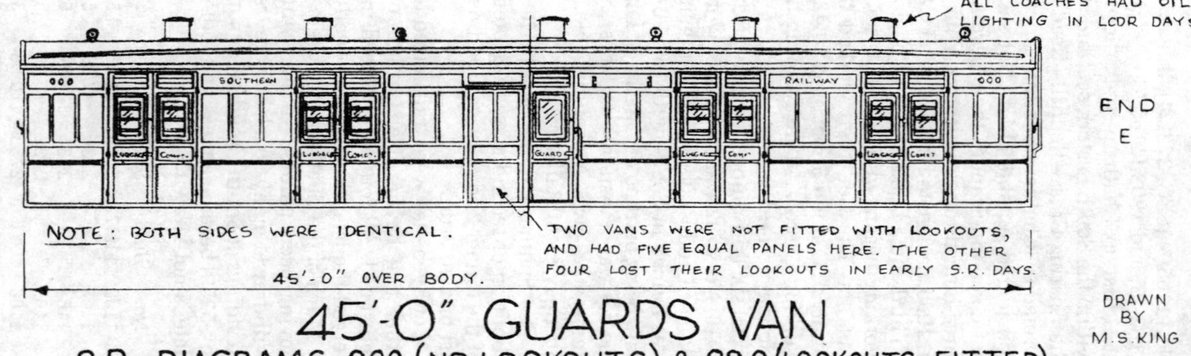
ALL COACHES HAD OIL LIGHTING IN LCDR DAYS
END E
END E
SOUTHERN
RAILWAY
GUARD
NOTE: BOTH SIDES WERE IDENTICAL.
TWO VANS WERE NOT FITTED WITH LOOKOUTS, AND HAD FIVE EQUAL PANELS HERE. THE OTHER FOUR LOST THEIR LOOKOUTS IN EARLY S.R. DAYS.
45'-0" OVER BODY.
45'-0" GUARDS VAN
S.R. DIAGRAMS 889 (NO LOOKOUTS) & 890 (LOOKOUTS FITTED)
DRAWN BY M.S.KING

FIRSTS

Nos. 1168–1177 (SEC Nos. 2631–40, SR Nos. 7244–53)

Body length: 42 ft. Bogie centres: 27 ft.
Compartments: 6. Seats: 36.

The Lancaster Railway Carriage & Wagon Co. built ten 42 ft 6-compartment Firsts for the LC&DR and delivered them between September and November 1897. Automatic vacuum brakes and electric lighting were fitted during 1901, Westinghouse brakes being retained on No. 1176 only. No. 1177 had to wait until 1905 before it received AVB and at the same time was repainted in SE&C dark lake.

This group of carriages, in early SE&C days, was permitted to run on the Folkestone Harbour branch.

From 1912, as the coaches entered Ashford Works for overhaul, they were given steam heaters; No. 2631 in 1922 was the last of the series to receive this addition to passenger comforts.

All 10 came to the Southern Railway, who altered the seating to accommodate 4-a-side instead of the normal 3-a-side for first class compartments. New SR numbers were applied as the coaches passed through Ashford Works. Most were run as loose vehicles, but No. 7245 almost certainly was formed in 5-set 688 until 1932, when the coach was downgraded to third class and renumbered 871. This new number was carried for only a year, when the coach was withdrawn and altered to mess and tool van No. 760S (December 1933). No. 7250 also became a mess and tool van on withdrawal at the same time: No. 759S. Both were based at Ramsgate locomotive depot.

No.	*Built*	*SEC*	*Reno'd*	*SR*	*Reno'd*	*Wdn*	
1168	9/97	2631	6/04	7244	2/26	3/33	
1169	"	2632	7/05	7245	10/23		Re-No. 871, 10/32 To 760S, 12/33
1170	"	2633	3/04	7246	2/27	3/33	
1171	"	2634	10/06	7247	6/27	5/32	
1172	10/97	2635	10/06	7248	6/26	12/30	
1173	"	2636	7/08	7249	8/26	2/32	
1174	"	2637	3/04	7250	3/29		To 759S, 12/33
1175	11/97	2638	3/04	7251	5/29	1/32	
1176	"	2639	1/05	7252	8/24	2/32	
1177	"	2640	7/05	7253	2/29	3/33	

SECONDS

Nos. 1178–1183 (SEC Nos. 2906–11, SR Nos. 866–871)

Body length: 42 ft. Bogie centres: 27 ft.
Compartments: 7. Seats: 56.

Another group of carriages, comprising only six vehicles, was ordered from a contractor: this time it was the Metropolitan Railway Carriage & Wagon Co., who delivered these 7-compartment Seconds to the LC&D in

December 1897 and January 1898. As usual with second-class coaches, each compartment seated 4-a-side in moderate comfort.

Vacuum brakes were fitted to the group in 1901 (Nos. 1178/80) and 1902 (remainder) and Westinghouse gear stripped from all save No. 1181 (SE&C 2909). Electric lighting replaced the primitive oil-pots in 1899 (1180), 1901 (1178) and 1902 (remainder). From about 1912, steam heaters were fitted to all six vehicles.

Chatham coaches do not show up in many booked carriage workings, and it seems likely that most were taken off main-line work quite early, being used for strengthening the normal formations or for secondary services. Relatively few were formed into sets, but No. 2911 (formerly 1183) did go into Set 17 between 1909 and 1913, as did a Chatham first, No. 2637.

The Southern Railway reclassified the group as Thirds, seating 5-a-side (70 in total), and gave them numbers 866–71 in the third-class list. Information on their use in Southern days also is lacking, but thanks to R.W. Kidner's observations in 1928/9 we do know that Nos. 868/70 were formed in 5-bogie sets 687 and 688 respectively. They were specially noted because they were the only arc-roofed coaches in a set composed otherwise of elliptical-roofed stock. In addition, No. 869 was in 3-set 648 in the early 1930s.

All six were sent to the Isle of Wight between 1932 and 1934 and kept the services going there for 15 years or so. They needed refitting with Westinghouse brakes before transfer. All were formed into numbered sets for use in the Island. No. 870 (as IOW No. 2437) was officially photographed on 13th June, 1934, as it waited at Southampton to be hoisted on to a floating crane for transfer to Cowes. That year was the first that the whole of the service between Ryde and Ventnor was formed of bogie stock, except on summer Saturdays.

Chatham coaches withdrawn in 1948 tended to stay on the Island, their bodies being sold as huts, sheds, etc. for farmers and others. Coaches withdrawn in 1949, however, were returned to the Mainland and stood at South Croydon sidings for some time. No. 2437 was one such, and after withdrawal from passenger service it was converted into a service vehicle No. DS 1827. Its final withdrawal date is unknown.

No.	*Built*	*SEC*	*Reno'd*	*SR*	*Reno'd*	*To IOW*	*IOW No.*	*Wdn*
1178	12/97	2906	10/06	866	5/29	3/33	2433	4/49
1179	"	2907	7/05	867	7/27	6/34	2434	4/49
1180	"	2908	1/01	868	10/28	6/34	2435	5/48
1181	1/98	2909	5/06	869	8/24	6/34	2436	5/48
1182	"	2910	4/04	870	10/23	6/34	2437	4/49
1183	"	2911	2/06	871	9/27	6/32	2432	4/49

THIRD BRAKES

Nos. 1184–1189 (SEC Nos. 3410–15, SR Nos. 3246–51)

Body length: 45 ft. Width over side observatories: 9 ft 0¾ in.
Compartments: 5 3rd-class, plus guard and luggage compartments.
Seats: 50. Bogie centres: 30 ft.

To build six bogie Third Brakes, yet another contractor was used by the LC&D: Brown, Marshalls & Co. All were delivered in February 1898 and unusually all were dual-braked from the outset – vacuum and Westinghouse. However, the SE&C removed the air brake equipment from all six in due course. Electric lighting was installed in No. 1189 in 1901 and in the remainder during 1902.

Chatham practice with regard to brake coaches differed from the South Eastern's in that the guard's compartment was placed between the passenger compartments and the luggage compartment, which was located at one end. The general angularity of LC&D carriages was carried even to the side lookouts, which projected 6 in. on each bodyside: they were flat-topped with a 90-degree angle, although, wonder of wonders, there was a gentle curve towards the bodyside on the lower part of each lookout. The guard's compartment had a door communicating with the luggage compartment, which could hold three tons; external double doors also gave access to it.

5-set No. 17, formed in about 1909, included four LC&D coaches which, in January 1913, were recorded as 3rd Brake 3410, First 2637, Second 2911 and 3rd Brake 3415; there was also an early SE Composite, No. 1922. Surviving SE&C papers indicate that this set was running on the Dartford lines in 1913. In 1910 its booked workings took in the 7.40 am Tonbridge to Cannon Street, 9.04 am Cannon Street to Caterham and 10.41 am return to Charing Cross, 11.45 am Charing Cross to Reigate and 1.00 pm return to London Bridge, then 5.40 pm (not Saturdays) or 2.13 pm (Saturdays) to Penshurst and empty to Tonbridge. About 1914 the set was disbanded.

During the latter days of World War I there was such a shortage of goods brake vans for the vastly inflated goods traffic that several passenger brakes had to be used. Some were fitted with stoves for the comfort of the guard; many others were not. LC&D Third Brakes Nos. 3411/14/15 were allotted to goods train services during 1918 and 1919 and were among those not stove-fitted. The coaches were by now steam heated, but this was of no use in goods trains as there were no connections between locomotive and coach if goods wagons came between them.

All six Third Brakes came to the Southern and gained their new numbers 3246–51. At some stage in their careers they lost the side lookouts, a piece of flat sheet steel being put across the resulting gap in the bodyside. In the 1920s No. 3247 ran in 5-set 691 (recorded by L. Pegrum as being 4 LC&D, 1 SE), which also included ex-SEC Third Brake No. 3305. Until 1932 No. 3249 was in 3-set 648 with Third No. 869 and First No. 7252.

No. 3248 was withdrawn in 1930, but from 1931 the other five all went to the Isle of Wight. Before being transferred, No. 3247 (with a 7-compartment ex-LC&D Second) spent some time at Grove Park sidings apparently withdrawn; it was noted there in March 1932. Whatever its intended fate, it did go across to the Island eventually but not until May 1933. For Isle of Wight service the coaches were again Westinghouse-fitted and all five ran in set trains until withdrawal in 1948.

No. 4115 (formerly 3247) was sold as a body, which became a henhouse on a farm at Atherfield on the south-west coast of the Island. In 1975 its owner donated it to the Wight Locomotive Society and it was delivered to the Isle of Wight Steam Centre at Haven Street on 30th June, 1975. As far as is known, it is the only *complete* LC&D bogie coach body to have been preserved. Other such bodies on the Island have generally been cut into halves.

No.	*Built*	*SEC*	*Reno'd*	*SR*	*Reno'd*	*To IOW*	*IOW No.*	*Wdn*
1184	2/98	3410	7/02	3246	9/24	6/32	4113	5/48
1185	"	3411	10/02	3247	4/24	5/33	4115	5/48
1186	"	3412	10/03	3248	3/27	–	–	3/30
1187	"	3413	11/08	3249	8/24	6/32	4114	5/48
1188	"	3414	1/05	3250	2/27	5/31	4109	5/48
1189	"	3415	10/06	3251	11/24	5/33	4116	5/48

GUARD'S VANS

Nos. 1190–1195 (SEC Nos. 568–73, SR Nos. 648–53)

Body length: 45 ft. Width over side observatories: 9 ft.
Compartments: 1 guard, 2 luggage. Bogie centres: 30 ft.

The final type of bogie vehicle ordered during the last years of the Chatham's separate existence was a passenger Guard's Van. There were six, all built by the Midland Railway-Carriage & Wagon Co., and they were delivered early in 1898. Original numbers were 1190–95, but the SE&C renumbered them in its separate van list as 568–73. In 1902 the SE&C added vacuum brakes to Nos. 568/70–73 and to No. 569 in 1903, so that the vans were now dual braked; but No. 568 lost its Westinghouse fittings before Grouping.

For brake vans these really were quite impressive vehicles, and even the lordly SE&C did not have any bogie brake vans until 1905 – and then only two! The guard's compartment was located in the centre of the vehicle, with side lookouts to standard Chatham design, and it was flanked by two large luggage compartments with sets of double doors on the bodyside.

These vans were not allowed to work over any part of the Metropolitan Railway and, until 1908, they were also barred from the South Eastern system. From 1908 they began working between London, Redhill and Reading and were formed in un-numbered 'sets' for several of those round-about and slow services.

By 1917 the side lookouts on Nos. 568/9 had been removed and the vans could then work over any part of the system; those of No. 573 came off in about 1921 and the Southern was left to remove the lookouts on the remaining three vans. Later in 1917, Nos. 570–3 were specially passed to work between London and Dover, Folkestone and Margate Sands by either route.

In the early 1920s the six vans were allocated to Reading–Charing Cross services for conveying Huntley & Palmer's traffic. About 800 tons of biscuits from the Reading factory were carried each week over this route, according to H.F. Andrews, an SE&C authority.

All six vans came to the Southern; at various unknown dates they had been equipped with electric lighting and steam heating for the guard. Like

The South Eastern's first bogie coach: Composite No. 1892, built by Cravens in 1878. Arc roof, 'American' bogies, safety chains at each end and gas lighting. Body length 40 ft 6 in. *Author's Collection*

SER Third No. 2287, built in 1893 with short buffers, but here shown as altered with long buffers in 1899 at Ashford Works. Elliptical roof, safety chains, bar across each droplight and gas lighting. Body length 44 ft. The coach became SR third No. 898 in 1924. *Author's Collection*

SER Third brake No. 2294, built by Cravens in 1893 (short-buffered at non-brake end, but altered to long buffers in 1899). Elliptical roof, safety chains, bar across each droplight, round-topped roof observatory and gas lighting. Body length 44 ft. Became SR No. 3239 in 1924. *Author's Collection*

SER vestibuled car No. 203, built by Metropolitan RCW Co in 1897 for the Folkestone Car Train. Fox's pressed steel bogies, clerestory roof, electric lighting. Sold to the Pullman Car Co. in 1919, becoming parlour car *Mabel*.

Lambert Weston & Son, Folkestone

SE&C English Royal Saloon No. 1.R, built by Metropolitan Amalgamated RCW Co. in 1903. Fox's bogies, clerestory roof, safety chains at each end, corridor vestibule at one end only. Became SR No. 7930 in 19125. *Author's Collection*

A view taken on 27th April, 1914, to show Dover Marine station under construction also shows one of the firsts with saloon from the 1907/8 batch Nos. 939–46, 958–60 with 50 ft body, *or* Nos. 821 or 822 built in 1909 with 51 ft body. *Author's Collection*

SE&C Lavatory Composite Brake No. 1045, built by Metro in 1909 with 50 ft body. The photo was taken at Tonbridge on 21st July, 1928; although the coach is still in SE&C livery it carries a Southern set number, 534. No. 1045 became SR Third Brake No. 3350 in 1929. *P. Hornblower*

Details of SE&C lettering style. Although this example is actually a 4-wheel 3-compartment Third Brake, the style is applicable to bogie coaches. *Author's Collection*

LC& DR 45 ft composite No. 1098, built by Birmingham RCW Co. in 1897. Arc roof, safety chains, Westinghouse air brakes, oil lighting. Became SE&C No. 2714, SR No. 5268 and finally to Isle of Wight as SR No. 6360 in 1933. *Birmingham RC&W Co.*

LC&DR 42 ft Lavatory Composite No. 1152 of 1898, running as SE&C No. 2719 with three 2nd class compartments, two lavatories, three 1st class compartments, electric lighting and vacuum brakes. Altered to 1st/3rd Composite in 1914 and to all-Third in 1922, becoming SR No. 856 in 1926. *Lens of Sutton*

LC&DR 46 ft Third No. 1077 built by Gloucester RCW Co. in 1897, renumbered 3396 by the SE&C and converted to push-and-pull Third Brake about 1914. Here shown with class 'P' tank locomotive and similarly-converted Composite at Greenwich Park station. The Third Brake became SR No. 3270 in 1928. *Author's Collection*

44 ft Third No. 882 as altered by the Southern in 1936. It was built in 1900 as SE&C Composite No. 2372, becoming SR No. 5210; withdrawn in 1942. Photographed at Templecombe, 6th July, 1938. *H.C. Casserley*

46 ft Lavatory Third No. 913 in Set 913 at Maze Hill, 2nd July, 1947. This coach was originally SE&C First No. 3509, built in 1904, and became SR First No. 7344, being downgraded in 1940. *D. Cullum*

Third No. 915 push-and-pull set No. 482 at Dunton Green, 19th April, 1952. The coach was built originally as steamcar No. 7 by Metro in 1906 and was altered to Trailer Composite No. 6367 in 1924 (later No. 5581). Inward-opening doors, bars across droplights, and L-section truss rods bolted to *outside* of solebar. *J.H. Aston*

46 ft Third No. 921 in Set 912 at Maze Hill, 2nd July, 1947. Built as SE&C No. 707 in 1906, it received its SR number in 1923 and was withdrawn in 1951. *D. Cullum*

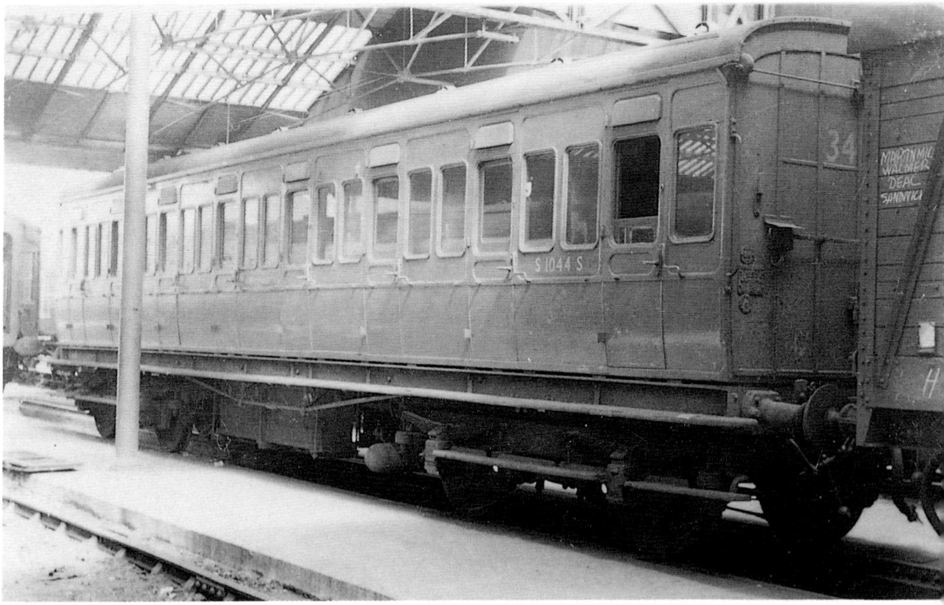

46 ft Third No. 1044, originally SE&C No. 3478, built by Oldbury RCW Co. in 1901. The coach ended its days in Margate Miners' set No. 346, being withdrawn in 1957.
Lens of Sutton

46 ft Third (7-compartment) No. 930 in Set 912 at Maze Hill, 2nd July, 1947. This was built in 1900 as a Second, SE&C No. 2320, and withdrawn in 1951. Note triangular 'No Smoking' labels on one compartment only. *D. Cullum*

48 ft Lavatory Third No. 944 in Set 913 at Tonbridge, 29th May, 1950, still in Southern Railway livery. Built by Gloucester RCW Co. in 1906 as SE&C No. 868, it was withdrawn late in 1951. *D. Cullum*

50 ft Lavatory Third No. 959 in Set 898 at Tonbridge, 10th September, 1949. Built in 1909 as SE&C No. 1088, it had the same layout of compartments and lavatories as No. 868, but was less cramped. It was withdrawn in 1951. *D. Cullum*

Corridor Third No. 964 (corridor side) at Tonbridge, 29th May, 1950. This was built as No. 1353 by the SE&C in 1920. High elliptical roof, British standard gangways and Spencer's patent buffers. All six of these Thirds were later formed in Set 389, as shown here. *D. Cullum*

Corridor Third No. 963 (compartment side) at Tonbridge, 29th May, 1950. Originally SE&C No. 1352 when built in 1920. This coach had SR bogies, and there was only one lavatory for the eight compartments. *D. Cullum*

60 ft Third No. 1087, with matchboarded lower panels, in Set 918 at Allhallows, 24th August, 1955. It was built at Ashford as No. 1405 in 1922 with Spencer's buffers, L-section truss rod, low elliptical roof. The coach was withdrawn at the end of 1959. *R.M. Casserley*

Third No. 2451 at Bembridge (I.O.W.) on 26th June, 1950. This was converted from Third Brake No. 3382 (SE&C 1141) of 1911 in 1949. The two additional compartments, without bodywork mouldings, may be seen at the right-hand end. *D. Cullum*

Second (formerly Third) No. 2439 at Ryde St Johns, 29th September, 1965. This was another conversion from a 54 ft Third Brake in 1948, being originally No. 3372 (SEC 1117) of 1911; the new compartments are at the right-hand end, but much of the original bodywork has been covered with galvanised steel sheets. *J.H. Aston*

SER Third Brake No. 1946, built in 1880 and here shown in SR livery as No. 3234 with 'American' bogies, gas lighting, close-coupled at inner end. Alternate compartment partitions are half-height only. Four 'Smoking' labels are etched on the glass; body length 40 ft 6 in. *Author's Collection*

SR Third Brake No. 3236, built by the South Eastern as No. 1986 in 1881. One of the six compartments was later altered to an enlarged luggage compartment. Body length 40 ft 6 in., 'American' bogies, gas lighting, close-coupling, 'smoking' labels. *Author's Collection*

Lavatory Third Brake, No. 3244 or 3245, built by Metropolitan RCW Co. in 1900 as a 3-compartment 3rd brake and given a lavatory and short corridor in 1904. Shown here running as the front coach behind class 'U' No. 1634 on a Victoria to Ramsgate train leaving Bromley South. *H.C. Casserley*

LC&DR Third Brake No. 1185, built by Brown, Marshalls in 1898 and renumbered SE&C 3411. Side lookouts were removed in 1923, and the SR gave the coach the new number 3247. Photographed here at Grove Park on 12th March, 1932, No. 3247 was later sent to the Isle of Wight as No. 4115. *R.W. Kidner*

45 ft Third Brake No. 3263 in Set 913. This was built by Metro in 1901 as SE&C No. 3494. Note the louvres on the luggage compartment doors. The coach was withdrawn in 1951. *Lens of Sutton*

45 ft Third Brake No. 3266 in Set 696, formed (as sometimes happened) with brake-end inwards. The coach was built as SE&C No. 3497 by Metropolitan RCW Co. in 1901 and withdrawn in 1956. Photographed at Addiscombe, 22nd June, 1947. *D. Cullum*

50 ft Third Brake No. 3299 in Set 669 at Bellingham, 28th April, 1948, recently repainted (malachite green, 'S' prefix to numbers, no ownership title). Built by Metropolitan Amalgamated RCW Co. in 1906 as SE&C No. 850, it was withdrawn in 1952. *D. Cullum*

Lavatory Third Brake No. 3316, one of only two to this design, at Margate, 22nd August, 1950. It was built by Metropolitan Amalgamated in 1907 for a boat train, was 50 ft over body and originally numbered 947. It has been detached from Set 686 with one buffer-head missing. *D. Cullum*

An end view of Third Brake No. 3311 (built at Ashford as SE&C No. 969 in 1908), showing the later style of roof observatory with flattened top, droplight in the body end originally for use of the slip-coach guard, and vertical rodding connected by means of bevel gears with handbrake. Seen at Maze Hill, 6th April, 1949. *D. Cullum*

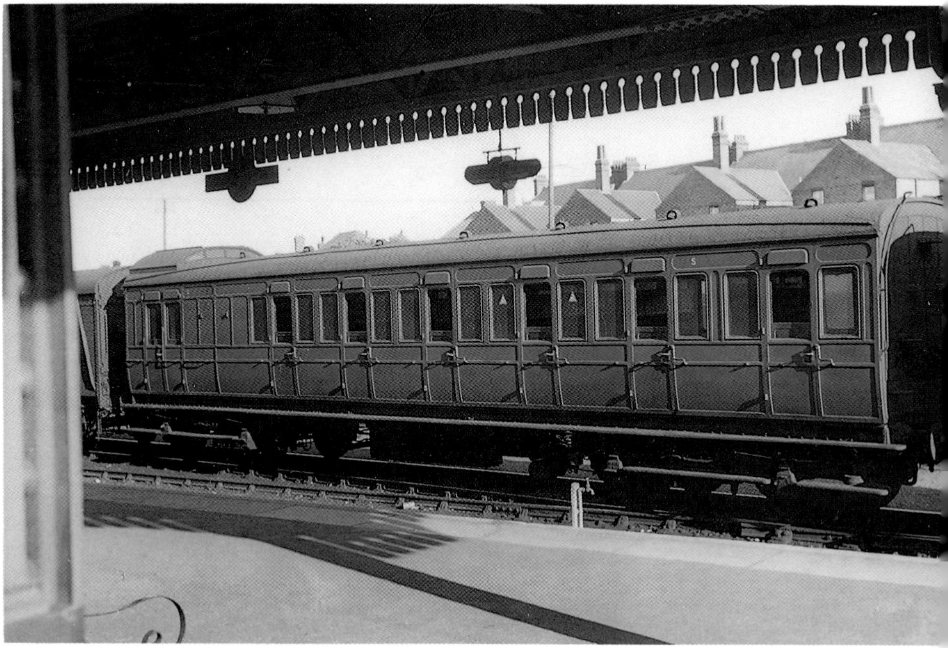

SE&C No. 1052, built in 1909 by Metropolitan Amalgamated and renumbered by the SR as 3325 (Trio set 531). The vehicle has 'Ashford Gothic' moulding style, Spencer's buffers, and flattened roof observatory. Seen at Margate, 20th August, 1950.
D. Cullum

At the other end of Set 531 was Lavatory Third Brake No. 3346, renumbered from SE&C 1041 in 1928; Margate, 20th August, 1950. *D. Cullum*

all Chatham bogie stock, they did not last very long in Southern ownership, with the exception of two transferred to the Isle of Wight. Remarkably, these two were not withdrawn until 1957 – the last survivors of the 89 LC&D bogie carriages built between 1885 and 1898.

No.	*Built*	*SEC*	*Reno'd*	*SR*	*Reno'd*	*To IOW*	*IOW No.*	*Wdn*
1190	2/98	568	12/01	648	2/24	–	–	3/32
1191	"	569	12/02	659	11/23	4/32	1011	3/57
1192	3/98	570	3/02	650	11/23	–	–	10/31
1193	"	571	3/02	651	7/26	5/33	1012	5/57
1194	"	572	3/02	652	4/24	–	–	2/32
1195	"	573	12/01	653	2/24	–	–	2/32

SR No. 650: Westinghouse gear removed August 1930.

The total number of ex-LC&D bogie vehicles sent to the Isle of Wight was 41: 39 passenger carriages and 2 vans. Many of them were repanelled with steel sheeting, in an effort to modernise their appearance.

PULL-AND-PUSH WORKING

As mentioned previously, four LC&D bogie coaches were modified by the SE&C for pull-and-push working, using mechanical control. The regulator control on the locomotive was connected to the regulator handle in the end carriage driving compartment by shafting running under the coaches, with couplings having universal joints between the coaches, and connected to the driving gear by means of bell cranks and rods.

A report in October 1927 found that this system was not entirely satisfactory because of backlash and springing that took place in the gear between the regulator handle in the driving compartment and the regulator handle on the locomotive. Sometimes the system worked; sometimes it didn't.

The LB&SC push-and-pull sets had a much better system, using compressed-air control, and one such set (No. 754) was tried out on several Eastern and Western Section services between November 1928 and February 1929, including the Ash–Aldershot service from 11th to 14th December, 1928. On 25th March, 1929, the Rolling Stock Committee recommended that air-control be fitted to all pull-and-push units and the rod system be abolished. Sets 732/3 were duly converted to compressed-air control in 1930; the only other SE&C pull-and-push sets were some 6-wheeled 3-coach ones, but these were all withdrawn at the end of 1929, probably without having been converted.

Chapter Four

South Eastern & Chatham Railway Bogie Carriages

From 1st January, 1899, the two rival railways of Kent came together with a sigh of relief. Although retaining their separate legal identities they were now worked as one by a Managing Committee, and the ruinous competition between the two was ended at once. More money was now available for improving the main lines, and renewing the locomotive and carriage stock. Harry Wainwright was now in charge of both and, as far as carriage design was concerned, there was no break in continuity from South Eastern practice.

All new carriages put into service had automatic vacuum brakes (some of the first having Westinghouse in addition, for working on what became known as the Chatham Section); and all were electrically lit using the system devised by J. Stone & Co. of Deptford, in which an axle-driven dynamo charged double batteries fixed beneath the underframe. The compartment lights were wired in two circuits and were controlled by a rod at the end of each coach. Full lighting was used at night-time and half-lighting during the day.

Almost every year saw some fresh improvement in SE&C carriage design. At first, body length was short, only 44 ft, but gradually this increased to 60 ft. Compartment dimensions, particularly those of the third class, also became more generous: rising from 5 ft 7 in. to 6 ft. Most coaches were lavatory-fitted, too, although as usual not all passengers had access to this necessary compartment. The Managing Committee, it would appear, convinced itself that such facilities were not really required by every passenger on journeys of short duration. As coaches generally were only 8 ft wide, putting in a corridor resulted in too much loss of seating accommodation.

COMPOSITES

Nos. 682–696 (SR Nos. 5185–5199)
Nos. 2347–2396 (SR Nos. 5200–5219 and 7255–7284)

Body length: 44 ft. Bogie centres: 29 ft.
Compartments: 4 1st, 2 2nd. Seats: 24 1st, 16 2nd.

The first 15 of these Composites were ordered by the South Eastern from the Gloucester Railway Carriage & Wagon Co. in May 1898. They were completed and delivered in 1899: Nos. 682–5 in March, 686–9/91/4–6 in April and 690/2/3 in May.

The teak body framing had panels of mahogany. Height of the vehicles from rail to top of roof was 11 ft 9½ in. Stone's electric lighting was fitted, and the coaches ran on Fox's patent pressed-steel bogies of 8 ft wheelbase.

Contracts were placed in September 1899 with Brown, Marshalls & Co. for 25 Composites to the same design, and in January 1900 with the Metropolitan Railway Carriage & Wagon Co. for another 25. They were delivered to the SE&C in the following order:

Brown, Marshalls batch		*Metro batch*	
Nos.	*Received*	*Nos.*	*Received*
2372–77	2/1900	2347–56	9/1900
2378–81	3/1900	2357–63/65	10/1900
2382–85/89	4/1900	2364/66/67	11/1900
2388/90/91	5/1900	2368/69/71	12/1900
2386/87/92–94	6/1900	2370	1/1901
2395/96	7/1900		

Built to Drawing No. 1104, these 50 coaches cost £1,470 each and had teak body framing and steel and wood underframes.

In 1902/3 thirty of the Brown, Marshalls and Metropolitan Composites were converted to all-firsts by upgrading the second class compartment at each end of the coach; this small modification was recorded as costing £23 per coach! Those involved were Nos. 2347–9/51/3/5/6/8/60/2/3/5/8/70/1/3/6/8–81/3–6/8/9/91/4/6. Most were done in 1902, leaving only two, Nos. 2351 and 2386, to be upgraded in 1903.

Six coaches were Westinghouse-piped in addition to having vacuum brakes, these being Nos. 2353/55/62/78/84/93. The pipes were later removed by the Southern Railway.

The other 35 coaches were retained as Composites. From May 1909 No. 2375 was formed in Train No. 16, a 4-coach set which was booked to work the 7.55 am Ramsgate Harbour to Charing Cross and the rear portion of the 5.10 pm Holborn Viaduct to Ramsgate Harbour, being slipped at Faversham.

From 1909 all 65 coaches were fitted with steam heaters at a cost of £38 10s. each, the first two to be equipped being Nos. 2352 and 2375. It took several years before the last was equipped and No. 2373 rolled out of Ashford in 1922.

No. 2375 was still in Set 16 in 1914; in that year four Composites were allotted as 'extra coaches' on certain Maidstone East trains: Nos. 2350, 2357, 2367 and 2382. About 1915 or 1916 4-set 16 was renumbered 31, and No. 2375 was removed from it; but sister coach No. 2374 was then placed in 4-set 24 (formerly 10), which was based at Ramsgate Harbour for working the Granville Express. Meanwhile by about 1916 Nos. 682, 689, 692 and 696 had been formed into Caterham and Tadworth lines 4-sets, each of which consisted of three 6-wheelers and one bogie composite. No. 694 was now in 4-set 31 (old No. 16). By 1917 both Sets 24 and 31 were spare, without regular workings, because so many train services had been withdrawn. No. 24 was disbanded in early 1919 and No. 31 about 1920/1. Composite No. 2374 then went to Caterham 4-set 47 by 1920. Composites Nos. 686 and 688 were in 5-sets 256 and 261 by 1919; these were berthed at Dorking or Tonbridge, being exchanged every Saturday.

In the final year of the Managing Committee's reign the workings of these 5-coach sets included the 8.25 am Tonbridge to Frant, 9.05 am Frant to Cannon Street and 6.27 pm (not Saturdays) or 1.34 pm (Saturdays) London Bridge to Tonbridge via Oxted and Edenbridge. The other set took in the 7.23 am Dorking to Cannon Street and 6.36 pm (not Saturdays) Cannon Street to Reigate or 1.24 pm (Saturdays) Cannon Street to Dorking.

All 65 coaches came to the Southern Railway on 1st January, 1923, the Composites receiving new numbers 5185–5219 and the Firsts 7255–84. After the abolition of second class in September 1923 the seating of the Composites became 24 first and 20 third. A few ran in set trains but the great majority were used as loose coaches. Many of the Firsts found use in first-class-only sets used only on days when there were race meetings: Sets 341, 344, 345, 346 and 347 (allocated to the Western Section in the middle-to-late 1930s) each included ex-SE&C Firsts.

In 1936 all the Composites – except No. 5194, which had been withdrawn in 1933 – were downgraded to Thirds, seating 60 passengers each in considerable luxury (compartments of the ex-Firsts were 7 ft 5 in. wide). In 1939/40 some of the all-Firsts were similarly downgraded, although still remaining in the same sets. Only three unconverted Firsts survived World War II, all the others being withdrawn or converted to service stock. The last of the converted Composites was withdrawn in July 1955.

Summary of Composites and Firsts

SEC	*SR*	*Re-No.*	*Third*	*Set*	*Wdn*	*SEC*	*SR*	*Re-No.*	*Third*	*Set*	*Wdn*
682	5185	11/28	858		2/38	2393	5218	10/26	890		12/43
683	5186	1/26	859		6/42	2395	5219	11/23	891		6/42
684	5187	8/26	860	301	9/43	2347	7255	4/24		691,347	7/39
685	5188	1/28	861		2/43	2348	7256	7/27		345	12/41
686	5189	8/29	862	686,39	12/49	2349	7257	9/24		341,515	4/48
687	5190	10/26	863		8/43	2351	7258	12/25		341,345	12/41
688	5191	11/26	864	301	11/42	2353	7259	11/23	846	347	3/43
689	5192	7/26	865	662	11/40	2355	7260	9/26	847	899	10/49
690	5193	7/24	866		12/41	2356	7261	3/24		341,347	7/39
691	5194	11/26			7/33	2358	7262	6/26	911	344,686	12/51
692	5195	6/26	867	517	7/43	2360	7263	11/24		657	9/36
693	5196	2/25	868	687,515	4/48	2362	7264	11/27		913	10/48
694	5197	12/25	869		7/39	2363	7265	11/23		910	/44
695	5198	3/27	870	688,517	9/43	2365	7266	7/26	900	346	4/50
696	5199	2/27	871	516,921	7/55	2368	7267	11/27	851		1/42
2350	5200	6/28	872		3/42	2370	7268	11/24		341,345	8/42
2352	5201	12/24	873	921,899	10/49	2371	7269	10/23		696	6/32
2354	5202	8/26	874		3/42	2373	7270	1/26		345	1/42
2357	5203	5/28	875		4/44	2376	7271	4/24		691	7/39
2359	5204	9/27	876		10/43	2378	7272	1/27		909	8/44
2361	5205	6/25	877		12/42	2379	7273	9/26	901	346	4/50
2364	5206	11/26	878	775,905	1/48	2380	7274	11/27	898		3/42
2366	5207	2/25	879	301	10/42	2381	7275	1/27	857		8/42
2367	5208	3/27	880		2/43	2383	7276	9/24		341	/42
2369	5209	10/23	881	520	12/46	2384	7277	6/27	852		12/41
2372	5210	8/29	882		5/42	2385	7278	12/24		600	/42
2374	5211	9/27	883		6/43	2386	7279	2/24		696,517	/43
2375	5212	2/27	884	301?	3/43	2388	7280	8/26	902	346	7/55
2377	5213	8/28	885	695	2/51	2389	7281	2/26		696	6/51
2382	5214	9/29	886	516,913	12/51	2391	7282	7/26			2/42
2387	5215	3/26	887		12/41	2394	7283	1/24			/42
2390	5216	11/25	888	516,913	12/51	2396	7284	9/26	903	346	7/55
2392	5217	5/24	889		2/42						

Note: 2-set 39, the Salisbury–Idmiston workmen's train, included Third No. 862 during 1948 and 1949.

For Composites Nos. 5185–5219, the set numbers shown in the list refer to the coaches when running as Thirds. Latterly, Third No. 868 ran in Set 515 and No. 871 was in Set 921. Three of the Thirds were noted as being loose push-and-pull fitted trailers in 1941: Nos. 863, 877 and 883, stationed at Yeovil, Swanage and Lymington respectively.

First No. 7255 ran in Set 347 latterly, and No. 7257 was in Set 515 between 1941 and 1948. Nos. 7259/60/67/74/75/77 became Thirds in mid-1939, and Nos. 7262/66/73/80/84 in mid-1940. No. 7272 was withdrawn following damage by enemy action during World War II in August 1944.

The following coaches were converted to service stock:

860 To Mess & Tool Van 1847 S, 9/43.
863 To Mess & Tool Van 1844 S, 8/43. Wdn 12/60.
864 To Stores Van 1772 S, Eastleigh, 11/42.
867 To Mess & Tool Van 1838 S, 7/43. Wdn 10/62.
870 To Mess & Tool Van 1841 S, 9/43.
875 To Stores Van 1954 S, 4/44. Wdn 7/44.
883 To Mess & Tool Van 1835 S, 6/43.
7256 To Stores Van 1695 S, 12/41. 'For use between Victoria and Banstead only.' Wdn 12/42.
7258 To Stores Van 1696 S, 12/41. As above. Wdn 12/42.
7268 Underframe to match truck 1722 SM, 8/42. Working with Taylor & Hubbard travelling crane 1722 S.
7282 To Stores Van 1708 S, 2/42. Eastleigh. Wdn 5/45.

BOGIE SALOONS

Nos. 176, 177 (SR Nos. 7912, 7913)

Body length: 38 ft. Bogie centres: 24 ft.
Height, rail to roof: 11 ft 10½ in. Bogie wheelbase: 7 ft.

Two first class Family Saloons were built by the SE&CR and completed in February 1900. They had teak body framing with mahogany panels and mouldings; the cross bars, diagonals and longitudinals, and bolster bars of the underframes were oak. The channel iron soles and headstock plates were fitted in with teak.

At one end of the carriage was a luggage compartment with double doors on each bodyside for access. Next came the saloon compartment, with two large windows flanked by droplights. A single door and transverse vestibule allowed access to the vehicle. A short centre corridor, on each side of which was a small compartment (one containing a water closet and the other a wash basin), led to a smoking compartment at the other end of the carriage. Seating in the saloon compartment consisted of two armchairs, and three couches around a central table.

The saloons could be used by wealthy people who wished to travel in privacy, the vehicle being attached to any scheduled train as required. However, with the increase in the number of ordinary coaches fitted with lavatories, use of Family Saloons declined and in 1907/8 these two were converted into Invalid Saloons.

In December 1907 No. 177 was fitted with double doors in place of the single door each side (to facilitate movement of stretchers) and a cross-partition was removed so that the entrance vestibule was now part of the saloon. The saloon compartment was equipped with a long couch, a hammock, two chairs and a table. No. 176 was similarly altered in February 1908. Seating capacity, formerly 18, was now 12 (seven in the saloon and five in the end compartment).

The pair received steam heaters in 1911 and on becoming Southern Railway property received new numbers 7912 (January 1927) and 7913 (September 1927). The Westinghouse brake pipes with which they had been fitted since new were removed in 1925. At some stage the luggage compartment doors were fitted with droplights.

No. 7912 was disposed of in October 1935, but No. 7913 had a much longer life; in fact the coach still exists. In March 1936 it was sold to the Longmoor Military Railway, where it was used as an officers' saloon, numbered 118 and finally ARMY 3006. It was in occasional use right up to the closure of the railway in 1969. The saloon was then acquired for preservation by the Transport Trust, being moved to the Severn Valley Railway on 20th September, 1971. It had been hoped to keep it at Liss for a proposed Southern Steam Centre, but this scheme was thwarted by local opposition.

On the Severn Valley the saloon was painted maroon with Southern number 7913 displayed, but its only use was on occasional filming work. The Transport Trust decided to dispose of No. 7913 and the Kent & East Sussex Railway Locomotive Trust purchased it; arrival on the K&ES was in July 1985. As yet it has not been used as much restoration needs to be undertaken first.

FIRST CLASS

Nos. 222–224, 247–249 (SR Nos. 7233–7238)

Body length: 38 ft. Bogie centres: 24 ft.
Compartments: 4 plus coupé. Seats: 25.
Lavatories: 2 (access from two compartments).
Height, rail to roof: 11 ft 10½ in. Bogie wheelbase: 7 ft.

These six very short coaches were built by the SE&C in 1900, Nos. 222/3 being completed in April, 247/8 in May, and 224 and 249 in June of that year. The teak body framing was finished off with mahogany panels and mouldings, whilst the underframes were the same as those used for Saloons Nos. 176/7.

Their short length permitted them to work on the Folkestone Harbour branch, and presumably they were designed for that purpose, being formed with 6-wheeled stock in Folkestone boat trains. Little else is known about their movements as they do not appear to have been attached to sets at any time.

Steam heating equipment was fitted to No. 248 in 1912, 249 in 1914, and to the remaining four in 1916.

On passing to the Southern they were renumbered 7233–8 and retained until the early 1930s, being employed probably on relief boat trains.

SEC	*SR*	*Re-No.*	*Wdn*	*SEC*	*SR*	*Re-No.*	*Wdn*
222	7233	5/26	6/31	247	7236	7/26	5/33
223	7234	6/26	7/33	248	7237	7/27	2/32
224	7235	1/27	3/31	249	7238	5/24	5/34

SECOND CLASS

Nos. 259–262 (SR Nos. 4182–4184, 846)

Body length: 38 ft. Bogie centres: 24 ft.
Compartments: 5. Seats: 36.
Lavatories: 2 (access from 2 compartments).
Height, rail to roof: 11 ft 9½ in. Bogie wheelbase: 7 ft.

These four Seconds were the last examples of 38 ft bogie stock, being built at Ashford in December 1900. Body framing was teak, with mahogany panels and mouldings, and underframes were the same as those on saloons Nos. 176/7. They were also the last with bogies of only 7 ft wheelbase; all other stock had 8 ft bogies as standard.

As with the 38 ft Firsts, these Seconds were used on Folkestone boat trains. No. 259 received steam heaters in 1910, Nos. 261/2 in 1911, and No. 260 in 1912. The only one to be attached to a set was No. 262, which replaced a 6-wheel second in 5-set 32 in about 1920. During 1922, Set 32 (which also included First No. 2347) was booked to work the 9.05 am Bexhill to Cannon Street and 6.16 pm return trains, Mondays to Fridays.

The Southern apparently could not decide what to do with the Lavatory Seconds when it took them over. Originally all four were to have been reclassified as Thirds (Nos. 845–8), but only No. 260 was renumbered. The other three were retained as Seconds and continued to run in relief boat trains, for which second class accommodation was still required. These became Nos. 4182–4. Later still, one of these was downgraded to Third and became No. 847 (the number it was originally intended to carry). Seating capacity as Thirds was increased from 36 to 44 by removal of the centre armrests.

No.	*To be re-no.*	*Date*	*Transfd*	*Re-No. (2nd)*		*To 3rd*		*Wdn*
259	845	–	11/25	4182	7/27	–	–	9/31
260	846	5/24	–	–	–	–	–	12/31
261	847	–	11/25	4183	4/26	847	10/30	3/34
262	848	–	11/25	4184	4/26	–	–	6/31

SECOND CLASS

Nos. 2315–2326 (SR Nos. 925–936, 4186–4189)

Body length: 46 ft. Bogie centres: 31 ft.
Compartments: 7. Seats: 56.

The Metropolitan Railway Carriage & Wagon Co. constructed 12 second class coaches at its Saltley Works, Birmingham, in 1900 for the SE&C, and delivered them between January and April. Each coach cost the SE&C £1,420. Nos. 2315/6/8 were sent into traffic in February 1900; 2317/9/20/2 in March; 2323/4 in April; and 2321/5/6 in May.

They were built to Drawing No. 1254. Body framing was teak and underframes steel and wood. The bogies, of 8 ft wheelbase, were fitted with Timmis's bolster springs. Height from rail level to centre of roof was 11 ft 9½ in. The Westinghouse pipes with which all were fitted in addition to vacuum brakes were soon removed.

From May 1908 No. 2323 was booked to be included in the formation of the 11.00 am Charing Cross to Dover Harbour and 2.25 pm return. This was a six-coach train made up entirely of bogie stock.

All 12 Seconds received steam heaters (which increased the theoretical value of each coach by £39) from 1911, beginning with Nos. 2315/8/9; Nos. 2316/20/2/6 were done in 1912, 2317/23 in 1913, 2321 in 1914, 2324 in 1915 and 2325 in 1916.

By about 1920 some of the Seconds were formed in sets: No. 2319 in 4-set 39, No. 2317 in 4-set 55, No. 2322 in 6-set 80, No. 2318 in 5-set 85, No. 2315 in 6-set 87 and No. 2316 in 8-set 259. Many of these sets included 6-wheeled coaches as well as bogies. The 1922 workings show that 6-set 80 was booked for the 8.01 am Caterham to Cannon Street; at Purley the 7.49 am from Tadworth, worked by 5-set 85, was attached to it. These two sets returned on the 5.06 pm from Charing Cross, being divided at Purley; Set 80 at the front for Caterham and Set 85 at the rear for Tadworth. 6-set 87 worked the 9.25 am Guildford to London Bridge via Redhill, returning to Guildford from Cannon Street at 6.00 pm. 4-sets 39 and 55 worked between Tonbridge and London, the former via Sevenoaks and the latter via Redhill. Finally, Set 259 was berthed at Bickley for suburban workings.

When the Seconds came to the Southern there seemed to be uncertainty as to how they should be classified, just as with the 38 ft Seconds of 1900. Some became Thirds while others remained as Seconds, although three of these were later downgraded. The Seconds were formed in relief boat trains until their 'demotion', some being berthed at Blackheath carriage sidings. SR numbers given to Seconds were 4186–4189 and to Thirds, 925–34/6. As Thirds they seated 70 passengers.

The following table summarises the history of these 12 coaches under the Southern regime:

No.	*To be re-no.*	*Date*	*Transfd*	*Re-No. (2nd)*		*To 3rd*		*Set No.*	*Wdn*
2315	925	–	11/25	4186	1/26	925	10/31		6/42
2316	926	5/24	–	–	–	–	–		6/39
2317	927	9/26	–	–	–	–	–	907	6/42
2318	928	5/24	–	–	–	–	–	907	12/43
2319	929	–	11/25	4187	1/26	929	10/31	907?	6/42
2320	930	–	11/25	4188	3/26	930	10/30	912	3/51
2321	931	1/24	–	–	–	–	–	913,686?	12/51
2322	932	10/24	–	–	–	–	–	907	12/43
2323	933	1/24	–	–	–	–	–	907	12/43
2324	934	8/24	–	–	–	–	–	910	5/44
2325	935	–	11/25	4189	1/26	–	–		10/31
2326	936	8/24	–	–	–	–	–	680?,912	3/51

Set numbers shown are those applicable to the later years; No. 936 was formed in 6-set 693 between 1931 and 1944 and No. 927 was recorded in 4-set 672 at an unknown date. The sets numbered in the 900s were formed in 1931 and were used mainly on summer Saturday services between Victoria and Ramsgate, at other times being berthed in sidings in many scattered locations.

Seven of the former Seconds on being withdrawn from service were re-used as service vehicles. Details follow:

925 to stores van 1734 S, 6/42. 'Stores Department, Eastleigh'.
926 to mess & tool van 1437 S, 6/39. Exmouth Jn, then Purley. Wdn. 4/43.
927 to stores van 1735 S, 6/42. 'Stores Department, Eastleigh'.
928 to mess & tool van 1930 S, 12/43. ARP repair train.
929 to stores van 1732 S, 6/42. 'Stores Department, Eastleigh'.
932 to mess & tool van 1931 S, 12/43. ARP repair train.
933 to mess & tool van 1932 S, 12/43. As above. Wdn 7/46.

THIRD CLASS

Nos. 2305–2314, 3453–3487, 697–716
(SR Nos. 919–924, 995–1053)

Body length: 46 ft. Bogie centres: 31 ft.
Compartments: 8. Seats: 80.

This type was built in three batches: 10 in 1900 by the Metropolitan RC&W Co., 35 by the Oldbury RC&W Co. in 1901 and, in 1906, 20 by the SE&C itself. These are the delivery dates:

Metro batch:		*Oldbury batch:*		*SE&C batch:*	
Nos.		Nos.		Nos.	
2305–08	3/1900	3453	12/1900	697–701	8/1906
2309/10	4/1900	3454–59	1/1901	702–706	10/1906
2311	5/1900	3461/62	2/1901	707–711	12/1906
2312–14	7/1900	3466–68/70	3/1901	712–716	2/1907
		3471/73	4/1901		
		3460/63–65/69/72/74	5/1901		
		3475/76	6/1901		
		3477/78	7/1901		
		3479	9/1901		
		3480–82	10/1901		
		3483/84	11/1901		
		3485–87	12/1901		

The coaches, built to Drawing No. 1255, had teak body framing and steel and wood underframes. Bogies were fitted with Timmis's bolster springs. The Oldbury batch was recorded as having Stone & Co.'s patent axleboxes. Wheels, of 3 ft 6 in. diameter, were the usual type of wood disc with steel tyres. The Ashford batch had the quarter lights bedded on felt, with 1½ in. teak mouldings. Underframes of Nos. 697–716 consisted of angle soles, channel iron headstocks and bolsters, the crossbars and all other parts being of oak.

In addition to vacuum brakes, Westinghouse pipes were fitted to Nos. 2305–14 and 3453–75 but by 1920 had been removed from all except Nos. 2307, 2308, 2310, 2313, 3466 and 3472.

From May 1908 No. 3464 worked regularly in the Charing Cross–Dover train described in the previous section; makeup of this train was booked to be Third Brake Lavatory, First, Second No. 2323, Third No. 3464, Tri-Composite Lavatory and 5-compartment Third Brake.

Between 1911 and 1916 all 65 Thirds received steam heaters (No. 2310 was steam-piped only, between 1916 and 1921, when it received steam heating complete).

No. 3475 was recorded in January 1913 as being formed in Train No. 56, which worked over the Dartford lines. Several sets at that time were recorded in detail, with formations, seating capacities and theoretical book cost, when consideration was given to converting the coaches to electric stock, but nothing came of the plan then.

In the early 1920s, however, when the South Eastern & Chatham Power and Construction Company was formed to begin serious work on electrification of lines, the 46 ft Thirds were considered ideal for alteration to electric carriages. Presumably they would have been formed in 4-car multiple units: Motor Third, Trailer Composite, Trailer Third, Motor Third. On the formation of the Southern Railway the rolling stock clerks allocated all but six of the Thirds to the electric stock list and the numbers 8999–9057 were kept blank for them. The remaining six were given 'steam' numbers from the outset, and Nos. 701/3/7/16, 2309 and 3473 duly became SR Nos. 919–924 late in 1923. Three Thirds actually received their 'electric trailer third' numbers: Nos. 713 to 9012 in January 1924, 2314 to 9023 in March 1924 and 3458 to 9029 in November 1923.

But it did not take the Southern long to decide to electrify its lines on the London & South Western system, using 3-car units (not 4-car), with separate 2-car trailer sets (third-class only); and so there was for the moment no use for the SE&C 8-compartment Thirds as electric stock, for London, Brighton & South Coast stock was used for the earliest SR trailer sets. In 1924, then, the 46 ft Thirds were re-allocated 'steam' numbers between 995 and 1053, many actually receiving these numbers. No. 9029 was renumbered 1025 in July 1924.

With the advancement of electrification, further coaches were required, all being converted from steam stock, and in 1928 it was at last decided that the SE&C 46 ft Thirds would, after all, be just the thing for trailer sets. From March 1928 a start was made on altering them to work with 11-compartment Thirds with LSW bodywork, one of each type being formed in each trailer set. These sets were numbered 1121–1167 and 1188. The SE&C Thirds became Nos. 8975–8998, 9133–9155 and 9296, being renumbered randomly. Six more were done in 1931, Nos. 9156/58/60/62/64/66 for Sets 1189–94. Virtually all that was done was to convert the vacuum brakes to Westinghouse air, replace the steam heaters by very feeble electric heaters, and fit the necessary control cables. No trailer set ever had a driving position, and so shunting had to be carried out using motor units. Trailer sets ran during peak periods, one being formed between two motor units.

Sets 1121–67 had Nos. 8975–98 and 9133–55 in numerical order, Set 1188 had No. 9296, and Sets 1189–94 included Nos. 9156/8/60/2/4/6 in numerical order. Original underframes and bogies were retained.

No. 8981 (formerly SE&C 2308), in Set 1127, had matchboarded sides, noted by R.W. Kidner in 1928. The 46 ft Thirds were not built new with this feature, but it is believed that it was a method devised in the 1919–23 period for re-panelling any defective stock, as well as being applied to much *new* stock at that time.

From the total of 65 8-compartment Thirds 54 were converted to electric stock, leaving 11 running as 'steam' Thirds. Of these, No. 924 was quite early transferred to the Western Section (the former L&SW) and on 4th November, 1926, was formed in the 5.40 am Waterloo to Weymouth. That morning the train overran signals between Farnborough and Fleet and crashed into the rear of the 4.15 am milk-churn train from Victoria to Yeovil. No serious harm was done to the ex-SE&C coach, which was back on its home territory by about 1930, and later formed in Set 698.

Longest-lived of the 46 ft Thirds was No. 1044 (SE&C 3478). In the 1930s it was formed in 7-set 662, during the 1940s it was in Set 920, and finally from 1955 until its withdrawal in 1957 it was part of the Margate-based miners' train, No. 346.

The following table shows the renumbering details of all the 46 ft Thirds.

SEC	*SR Steam*		*SR Electric*		*Wdn*
697	995	12/24	–	–	3/51
698	996	1/27	8983	4/28	9/40
699	–	–	9136	1/29	/46
700	–	–	8994	5/28	/46
701	919	?	–	–	5/44
702	999	?	9150	2/29	2/48
703	920	?	–	–	6/39
704	–	–	9137	10/28	/47
705	1001	9/26	9147	2/29	11/40
706	–	–	8998	4/28	3/43
707	921	11/23	–	–	3/51
708	1003	12/24	8977	3/28	3/43
709	–	–	8995	5/28	2/44
710	1005	3/26	9153	2/29	/47
711	1006	6/26	9151	2/29	9/43
712	1007	3/26	8984	5/28	/47
713	9012	1/24	8978	3/28	/47
714	1009	7/24	9144	2/29	4/48
715	1010	12/25	9160	2/31	12/43
716	922	10/23	–	–	5/50
2305	1011	12/24	9296	7/30	/47
2306	1012	12/25	9162	2/31	4/41
2307	1013	12/25	8976	3/28	/46
2308	1014	3/25	8981	4/28	9/43
2309	923	12/23	–	–	5/50
2310	1015	3/27	8992	4/28	12/44
2311	–	–	9141	12/28	/46
2312	1017	3/26	8993	4/28	2/44
2313	1018	1/26	8997	5/28	9/43
2314	9023	3/24	8986	5/28	9/43
3453	1020	12/25	9156	2/31	1/42
3454	1021	3/26	8979	3/28	9/42
3455	1022	8/26	9158	2/31	/46
3456	1023	1/27	8989	5/28	/48
3457	1024	4/26	8985	5/28	9/43
3458	9029 1025	11/23 7/24	9164	3/31	/43
3459	1026	11/24	8988	5/28	9/43
3460	1027	1/25	9148	2/29	/46
3461	1028	1/26	8980	4/28	4/42
3462	–	–	8975	3/28	/47
3463	–	–	8991	4/28	/47
3464	–	–	8996	5/28	/47
3465	–	–	8987	5/28	/47
3466	–	–	9138	1/29	4/44
3467	1034	6/26	9139	1/29	/46
3468	1035	12/24	9140	1/29	8/37
3469	–	–	9152	2/29	/47
3470	1037	?	9149	1/29	12/43
3471	1038	?	9135	11/28	11/42
3472	1039	?	8990	5/28	/47
3473	924	12/23	–	–	5/50
3474	1040	?	9166	3/31	7/48
3475	1041	12/26	9146	2/29	/47
3476	1042	2/25	9133	4/28	/47
3477	1043	2/27	–	–	8/42
3478	1044	7/26	–	–	9/57
3479	1045	3/26	9145	2/29	9/43
3480	–	–	9142	12/28	9/43
3481	–	–	9143	12/28	7/48
3482	–	–	9134	11/28	/47
3483	1049	1/25	–	–	8/56
3484	1050	1/26	9154	2/29	6/43
3485	1051	11/25	8982	4/28	/47
3486	1052	9/26	–	–	12/31
3487	1053	9/26	9155	2/29	/47

Trailer Third No. 9140 (SE&C 3468) was withdrawn after accident damage at Epsom Downs on 13th August, 1937. Other accident damage withdrawals were Nos. 9156 (SE&C 3453) at Cannon Street, 28th January, 1942, and 9135 (SE&C 3471) at Waddon, 4th November, 1942. No. 8983 (Set 1129) was badly damaged by bombing at Victoria on the night of 7th/8th September, 1940, and was withdrawn.

Only two Thirds – one steam, one electric – were re-used as service vehicles. No. 920 became a Mess and Tool van No. 1436 S in June 1939, originally being sent to Exmouth Junction; from April 1945 it was attached to the Paint Section at Purley, and withdrawn in 1960. No. 9162 became 1631 S, a yard wagon at Lancing Works, in April 1941 but was withdrawn in August 1945.

THIRD BRAKES

Nos. 2295–2304, 3488–3499 (SR Nos. 3244/5, 3252–69, 7914/5

Body length: 45 ft. Bogie centres: 30 ft.
Compartments: 3, plus guard and luggage. Seats: 30.

This group of coaches was built by the Metropolitan RC&W Co. at Saltley in two batches and they were received by the SE&CR on the following dates:

Nos.		*Nos.*	
2295	5/1900	3488–90	1/1901
2296	6/1900	3491/3/4	2/1901
2297–2301	7/1900	3495–99	3/1901
2302–04	8/1900	3492	5/1901

Built to Drawing No. 1256, the coaches had teak body framing and steel and wood underframes. The large luggage compartment had two sets of double doors each side; unusually these doors were fitted not with the usual droplights but with louvres. The guard's compartment, at the outer end of the coach, was equipped with a raised observatory in normal SE&C style, height above rail level being 12 ft 9½ in. or 1 ft higher than the roof.

Bogies had Timmis's bolster springs and the wood disc wheels, with steel tyres, were 3 ft 6 in. diameter. The 1901-built series was specially noted as having J. Stone & Co.'s patent axleboxes. All the coaches when new were equipped with Westinghouse brake pipes in addition to vacuum brakes. By 1901, as *The Railway Magazine* noted, several modern SE&C coaches were working on the LCD line hauled by vacuum-braked SE&C locomotives; presumably the Westinghouse fittings were for emergency use only, as the coaches were air-piped but not air-braked.

Very drastic alterations were made to Nos. 2301 and 3493 during 1902/3: conversion to Saloon First Brakes for use in a new Royal Train, no less. All the compartments were stripped out and in each coach a saloon compartment 17 ft long was built in their place. Between the saloon and the reduced luggage compartment were individual WC and lavatory compartments, separated by a central corridor. No. 2301 now seated 12 persons in four inward-facing settees, while No. 3493 seated 9 people, 4 of whom were in individual armchairs. Further details of the SE&C Royal Train may be found in a later section.

Two more of the Third Brakes received structural alterations, these being Nos. 2297 and 2298 in March 1904. A lavatory compartment was somewhat awkwardly put in a corner of what had been part of the luggage compartment and a side corridor was incorporated, reducing the capacity of two of the three compartments from 20 to 12. This corridor opened out into the end-most compartment, whose capacity was thus reduced from 10 to 8. On the whole these alterations seem to have been more trouble than they were worth, but presumably were done for some specific purpose, for no more coaches were altered. A reduction of seating capacity from 30 to 20, just for the sake of one lavatory, was not a very appealing notion to the SE&C. From July 1909 No. 2297 was specially provided to work in the 8.15 am Deal to Hastings train as a through portion, with two corridor composites, working to Brighton.

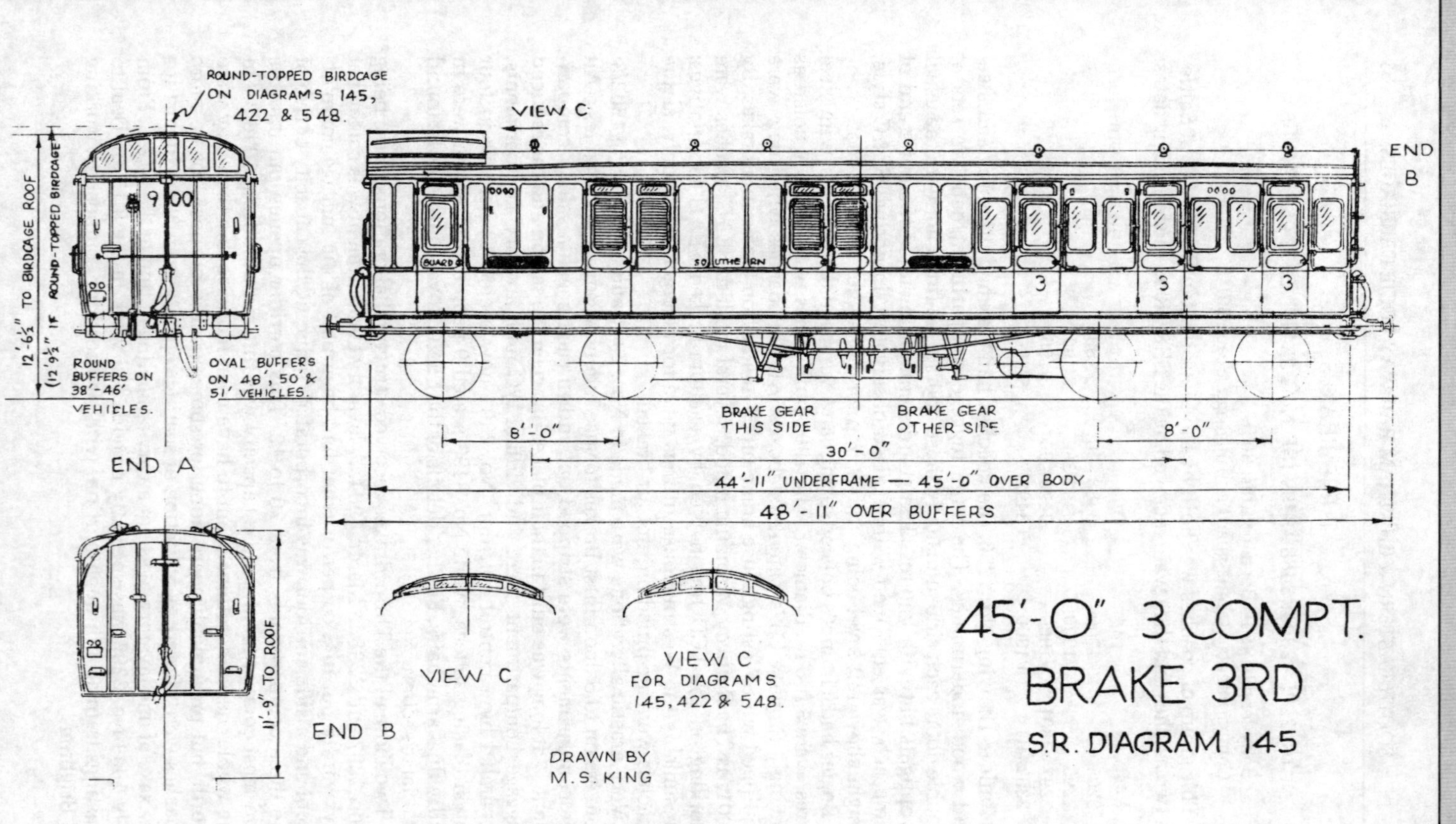
ROUND-TOPPED BIRDCAGE ON DIAGRAMS 145, 422 & 548.
VIEW C
END B
12'-6½" TO BIRDCAGE ROOF
(12'-9½" IF ROUND-TOPPED BIRDCAGE)
9100
GUARD
SOUTHERN
3
3
3
ROUND BUFFERS ON 38'-46' VEHICLES.
OVAL BUFFERS ON 48', 50' & 51' VEHICLES.
BRAKE GEAR THIS SIDE
BRAKE GEAR OTHER SIDE
8'-0"
8'-0"
30'-0"
44'-11" UNDERFRAME — 45'-0" OVER BODY
48'-11" OVER BUFFERS
END A
11'-9" TO ROOF
VIEW C
VIEW C FOR DIAGRAMS 145, 422 & 548.
END B
DRAWN BY M.S. KING
45'-0" 3 COMPT. BRAKE 3RD
S.R. DIAGRAM 145

No. 2304 was upgraded to Second Brake, seating 24 passengers four-a-side, during 1905 and remained so until 1923. It was booked to work in the Hastings Car Train as front coach in one direction and rear coach in the other. Another 3-compartment Third Brake was employed at the opposite end.

Four of the Third Brakes were fitted with 'storage' steam heating apparatus. These were Nos. 2295 in February 1904, 2297/8 in March 1904, and 3496 at around the same time. From May 1906, steam-heated Third Brakes were reserved for the 10.25 am Deal to Victoria and 3.02 pm Herne Hill to Deal. Formation of the 10.25 am leaving Deal was 3rd Brake (2295 or 3496) and Tri-Compo Brake (148 or 152) for Victoria, followed by London & North Western, Great Western and Midland through carriages, detached at Herne Hill. The Midland carriages worked through to Bradford, Manchester and Leicester. The SE&C coaches worked empty from Victoria to Herne Hill, where they were attached to the through North to Deal service, leaving at 3.02 pm if on time.

By mid 1908 No. 2295 was working as part of a 3-coach 'fixed train' on certain Hastings line train services, as follows: 5.35 am Cannon Street to Hastings and 9.40 am thence to Victoria, 2.42 pm Victoria to Ashford and 6.00 pm thence to Hastings, 9.00 pm Hastings to Charing Cross. These workings continued unchanged into 1910, by which time the set had been definitely numbered 59. Also on the Hastings line in 1909 was No. 3496, working as part of a 3-vehicle 'fixed' train on the 2.45 pm Hastings to Victoria and 6.00 pm return. In 1910 this working was altered to take in the 12.30 pm Hastings to Ashford, thence 2.18 pm to Victoria, returning to Hastings as before on the 6.00 pm from Victoria. This was short-lived, for in October 1910 No. 3496 was formed in a new 3-set No. 57 for Victoria–Ashford services.

Steam heaters of the 'non-storage' type were fitted to all the remaining Third Brakes between 1912 and 1915. No. 2295 ran as a 2nd/3rd Composite Brake between 1912 and 1920, one compartment being upgraded and seating 8 passengers. In 1914/5 No. 3497 worked with Composite No. 995, the two coaches being berthed at Reigate.

From about April 1916, owing to a shortage of goods brake vans, several passenger coaches with guard's accommodation began to be used in goods trains. Nos. 2296–98 and 2300 were the first to be so allotted. They were fitted with side lamp irons and labelled: 'Goods Pilot Service for working between Hither Green Sidings and Plumstead only.' In 1917 this became 'Goods Pilot Service for local working in the London District.' By 1918 the temporary goods brakes now comprised Nos. 2296, 2300, 2302, 3491, 3492 and 3496–98. As they were not fitted with stoves they were supposed to be confined to short journeys in the London area only. By the end of the year *all* the 3-compartment Third Brakes still in original condition had been allotted to goods train service. Only the 2nd/3rd Brake and the lavatory-fitted pair were excluded. All were returned to passenger service, probably in 1919. No. 2299 was placed in 5-set 53, which worked the 7.47 am Reading to Charing Cross and 6.27 pm return, and Lavatory 3rd Brake No. 2297 was in 5-set 256.

The Southern's renumbering scheme sorted the coaches into three different groups. The lavatory-fitted pair, Nos. 2297/8, became SR 3244/5; those remaining in their original condition became SR 3252–69; and the two Royal Train Saloon Brakes became Nos. 7914/5. Only Nos. 3244/5, 3264/6 still had their Westinghouse pipes in 1923.

The 3-compartment Brakes show up in many photographs taken of Southern Railway trains on the Eastern Section. As they were extremely useful for the amount of luggage they could carry, they found themselves formed in holiday trains to the Kent Coast. Some had set numbers, others did not; but almost all carried paper labels to identify the working. These paper numbers (in 1926) ran from 330 to 506 and bore no relation to any painted set numbers. A label was carried inside the windows of the brake coaches and on the solebar of each coach. Virtually all the 3-compartment coaches were formed into numbered sets during the 1930s, staying intact more-or-less until withdrawal from service from the 1940s onwards.

The following table shows renumbering details and SR set numbers of all the 45 ft Third Brakes.

SEC	*SR*	*Re-No.*	*Set No.*	*Wdn*	*SEC*	*SR*	*Re-No.*	*Set No.*	*Wdn*
2295	3252	7/26	905	1/48	3489	3259	3/24	667	4/42
2296	3253	5/28	917	12/52	3490	3260	8/26	689	12/38
2297	3244	11/28	907	4/44	3491	3261	8/26	908	5/50
2298	3245	12/27	910	6/44	3492	3262	8/26	912?	c11/40
2299	3254	10/23	903	8/45	3493	7915	10/25		5/41
2300	3255	7/26	909	c9/44	3494	3263	8/26	913	3/51
2301	7914	10/25		5/41	3495	3264	1/24	897	9/51
2302	3256	10/26	909	4/42	3496	3265	11/26	896	12/49
2303	3257	1/27	897	4/44	3497	3266	3/24	696	12/56
2304	3269	11/24	898	4/51	3498	3267	11/26	905	/46
3488	3258	1/24	908	5/50	3499	3268	2/26	914	/47

Nos. 7914/5 were not used as Royal Train vehicles after 1939, but were formed in the Necropolis funeral train that ran between the private Waterloo Necropolis station and Brookwood Necropolis. Unfortunately both Saloons were destroyed by enemy action at Waterloo on 15th April, 1941.

No. 3254, along with Composite No. 5256, was the first SE&C coach to receive SR green livery, being done at Ashford on 2nd October, 1923. Upon withdrawal, six of the Third Brakes became service vehicles:

3244 to Mess & Tool van 1966 S, loco running dept. 4/44.
3245 to Mess & Tool breakdown van 1969 S, 6/44. Wdn 1/64.
3254 to Mess & Tool van 244 S, 8/45. Wdn 1956.
3256 to Mess & Tool van 1719 S, 4/42. Signal & telegraph dept. Wdn post-1968.
3257 to Mess & Tool van 1967 S, loco running dept. 4/44.
3259 to Mess & Tool van 1720 S, 4/42. S&T dept. Wdn 4/58.

Those vehicles lasting into British Railways ownership received a 'DS' prefix in place of the 'S' suffix to their numbers. DS 1719 seems to have spent a considerable time on the Western Region of BR, even before the boundary changes of 1st January, 1963. Mr M.E.M. Lloyd noted the vehicle at Barmouth in June 1961 (*Model Railway News* December 1963); it is thought to have been still on that Region when withdrawn – the oldest survivor of the SE&C 1900-built Third Brakes.

COMPOSITES

Nos. 2327–2346, 3428–3452
(SR Nos. 7285–7304, 5220–5244)

Body length: 44 ft. Bogie centres: 29 ft.
Compartments: 3 1st, 3 2nd. Seats: 18 1st, 24 2nd.
Height, rail to top of roof: 11 ft 9½ in.

These 45 Composites were ordered to be built by two contractors, the Metropolitan Railway Carriage & Wagon Co. (20) and Messrs Cravens Ltd (25). They were delivered at Ashford as follows:

Metro batch

Nos.		*Nos.*		*Nos.*	
2327–30	12/1899	2337–39	3/1900	2344	6/1900
2331	1/1900	2340/41	4/1900	2345/46	7/1900
2332–36	2/1900	2342/43	5/1900		

Cravens batch

Nos.		*Nos.*		*Nos.*	
3428–31	12/1900	3438/39	6/1901	3448/49	10/1901
3432/33	2/1901	3440/41	7/1901	3450/51	11/1901
3434/35	4/1901	3442–45	8/1901	3452	12/1901
3436/37	5/1901	3446/47	9/1901		

The Metropolitan batch was sent into traffic between June and August 1900, and the Cravens group between March 1901 and April 1902 – approximately four months between their receipt and their commissioning.

The coaches were built to Drawing No. 1253, and had an asymmetrical layout: two second-class compartments at one end and a further second-class compartment at the other, the three first-class compartments (at 7 ft 6½ in. across, the widest-ever on the SE&C) between them. Body framing was as usual teak, with underframes of steel and wood; the bogies had standard Mansell wood wheels, 3 ft 6 in. diameter, with steel tyres. Nos. 3428–52 were noted as having J. Stone & Co.'s patent axleboxes, and all had Timmis's bolster springs. Nos. 2327–46 cost the SE&C £1,429 each, but the Cravens batch was dearer at £1,600 apiece.

Nos. 2327–46 and 3428–39 were Westinghouse-piped when new, but by October 1905 the pipes had been removed from the latter group; by 1919 only No. 2344 still retained them.

In 1909 No. 3450 was specially noted as formed in Train No. 29, the Victoria portion of the 8.37 am Ashford to Holborn Viaduct and Victoria service. This portion was slipped at Herne Hill. A complication was that, although No. 3450 was officially part of Set 29 (which included a 6-wheel slip coach, a Composite, Third and Brake Van), it was actually part of the Holborn Viaduct portion – which ran leading in the up direction. No. 3450 was however reunited with its set in the down direction, leaving Holborn at

4.12 pm and returning to Ashford as part of the 4.12 pm from Victoria. From October 1909 No. 3450 was altered to work as part of the Victoria portion – so that Train No. 29 could remain intact – and the return working to Ashford now left Victoria at 6.27 pm.

Many of the Composites were formed into sets (known as 'fixed trains') between 1908 and 1910, but vehicle numbers are unknown. One that was specified was No. 2346, formed in 3-set 71 about mid-1909. It was booked to work the 6.58 am Faversham to Victoria and 5.36 pm Victoria to Ramsgate Harbour, returning to Faversham on the 9.20 pm from Ramsgate. In October 1910 it was allocated a new working: 8.11 am Maidstone East to Victoria and 4.14 pm return. In the 1914 carriage working notice Composites Nos. 2335, 2340 and 3429 were specially noted as 'extra coaches' on the Maidstone East line. By then Set 71 had been disbanded.

Steam heating equipment was fitted to all 45 coaches from 1910 onwards as they went through Works, and the last was not done until 1922.

Set 29, which may still have included Composite No. 3450, continued to be based at Ashford for the Victoria service until 1920, when it was moved to Maidstone East; since 1918 it had been formed entirely of bogie stock. In 1922 it formed the 9.32 am Maidstone East to Holborn and 6.37 pm Victoria to Maidstone East.

Known set allocations during 1922 include Nos. 2329/31 in 6-set 53, 2339 in 4-set 88, 2341 and 2337 in 3-sets 245 and 246. Set 53 was stationed at Reading for a daily Charing Cross working, Set 88 at Caterham for the 8.24 am to Cannon Street, and Sets 245/6 were at Swanley or Maidstone East, being exchanged every week. Most of the other Composites were 'loose' stock.

On inheriting these 45 Composites the Southern Railway decided for some unknown reason to reclassify Nos. 2327–46 as all-first, and with four-a-side seating moreover. These 20 duly became Nos. 7285–7304 in the first-class series: each with a total seating capacity of 48. The former second-class compartments, at 6 ft 8½ in., were rather narrower than what the first-class passenger was accustomed to. The other 25 vehicles were retained as Composites, although with the second-class compartments altered to third with 5-a-side seating; the new numbers were 5220–5244. The first-class compartments were unchanged at 3-a-side seating: total capacity 18 first, 30 third.

By 1931 Nos. 5230 and 5241 had been formed in SR Set 696 on the Eastern Section, and by 1935 No. 5228 was in Set 685 and No. 5224 in Set 693. Of the Firsts, in 1935 Nos. 7296/7 were both in Set 687. Some of the coaches were transferred to the Western Section, and those formed in Race Sets 346 and 347 were among them. At least two were used as strengthening coaches on the Somerset & Dorset line in the 1930s, and H.C. Casserley's camera caught Nos. 5239 and 7298 together at Templecombe in July 1937. Both were very clean.

Three of the Firsts were downgraded to third-class in 1939: No. 7299 to 897 and Nos. 7301/2 to 904/5. These latter two remained in the same set (346) however.

The following list shows renumbering dates and set numbers applicable to the late 1940s period.

SEC	*SR*	*Re-No.*	*Set No.*	*Wdn*	*SEC*	*SR*	*Re-No.*	*Set No.*	*Wdn*
2327	7285	1/28		c/39	3431	5223	8/26	692	3/40
2328	7286	10/23	698	/44	3432	5224	9/24	693	2/43
2329	7287	10/29	310	11/41	3433	5225	7/24	705,520	12/46
2330	7288	3/24		/42	3434	5226	4/28		3/42
2331	7289	4/24		/42	3435	5227	12/24	899	10/49
2332	7290	2/24		/43	3436	5228	1/24	685,899	10/49
2333	7291	7/26	902,898	4/51	3437	5229	12/23	520	/47
2334	7292	8/26		/36	3438	5230	11/24	696,526	10/42
2335	7293	10/23	679,345	8/42	3439	5231	2/27	918	10/42
2336	7294	10/26		11/40	3440	5232	12/25	669	4/51
2337	7295	12/24	347	7/39	3441	5233	1/24	515	4/48
2338	7296	11/28	687,662	2/42	3442	5234	2/27		8/45
2339	7297	10/28	687,685	5/42	3443	5235	5/27	908	5/50
2340	7298	12/23	345	1/42	3444	5236	7/24	516,666	9/51
2341	7299	3/27		11/40	3445	5237	7/26	687	9/44
2342	7300	11/26	526	/42	3446	5238	4/25	519,900	1/58
2343	7301	7/26	346	7/55	3447	5239	7/24	775,905	1/48
2344	7302	9/26	346	7/55	3448	5240	5/28		11/41
2345	7303	8/26	902?	10/41	3449	5241	5/24	696	6/51
2346	7304	7/27	902	c4/47	3450	5242	1/27	680,908	2/41
3428	5220	2/26	797	3/40	3451	5243	1/27		/36
3429	5221	2/27	515	4/48	3452	5244	12/25	669	4/51
3430	5222	2/24	688?	8/44					

Nos. 5243 and 7292 on withdrawal had their underframes transferred to ex-LSW Post Office Vans Nos. 4907 and 4910 in 1936. No. 7294 was withdrawn after being damaged by enemy action in November 1940. Nos. 7299, 7301/2 were withdrawn as Thirds 897 and 904/5. Several bodies were grounded at various places, being used as temporary accommodation, mostly being broken up after the War. No. 5237, for example, became a mess room for women carriage cleaners at New Cross Gate in 1945 (noted by H.C. Casserley). No. 5240, the longest-surviving body, was grounded at Ashford Works and in January 1964 was purchased by Kent & East Sussex Railway volunteers and transported to Tenterden Town station for use as a mess-room. By 1991 it was in poor condition, and is believed to be regarded with disfavour by certain members.

Seven vehicles upon withdrawal were converted to service vehicles.

5234 to match truck 1997SM, 8/45. Underframe only. Working with travelling crane 1997 S (Taylor & Hubbard, 1945).

5242 to yard wagon 1600 S, 2/41. Lancing Works only.

7287 to Stores Van 1697 S, 11/41. Eastleigh.

7293 to match truck 1723SM, 8/42. Underframe only. Working with travelling crane 1723 S (Taylor & Hubbard, 1943).

7296 to Stores Van 1698 S, 2/42. Eastleigh.

7298 to Mess & Tool Van 1537 S, 1/42. Underframe only, replacing defective frame on vehicle. Withdrawn 5/1961.

7303 to Stores Van 1689 S, 10/41. 'For use between Victoria and Banstead only.' Withdrawn 12/42.

NON-GANGWAYED CORRIDOR COMPOSITES

Nos. 225–239
(SR Nos. 892–5 or 4180/1, 5245–54, 7254)

Body length: 44 ft. Bogie centres: 29 ft.
Compartments: 3½ 1st, 2 2nd. Seats: 15 1st class, 13 2nd class.
Height, rail to top of roof: 11 ft 10½ in. Lavatories: 2.

In June 1898 the South Eastern contracted the Ashbury Railway Carriage & Iron Co. of Openshaw, Manchester, to build 15 bogie Composites for £1,700 each. They were expected to be delivered at London Bridge early in 1899, but in fact were completed much later than this, not arriving until 1900/1. By this time the price had increased to £1,771 per vehicle. Completion and delivery dates were:

Nos.		*Nos.*	
225/26	5/1900	234	3/1901
227/28	7/1900	235/36	4/1901
229/30	8/1900	237–39	5/1901
231–33	11/1900		

The specification included some dimensions: doors 6 ft high by 2 ft 1 in. wide; floor to underside of roof 7 ft 6 in.; diameter of wheels 3 ft 6 in.; bogie wheelbase 8 ft; torpedo ventilators 8 in. diameter.

Each coach had two lavatory compartments, one being available to all first-class passengers and the other available to all second-class by means of internal side corridors. Lavatory fittings were Beresford's, with a square-top washbasin 2 ft by 1 ft 4 in. There were two water tanks, each holding 16 gallons.

Electric lighting was by J. Stone & Co., two lamps to one fitting (the 'Duplex' arrangement) being found in each compartment. Hinged doors gave access from the corridors to the compartments.

Underframes were of Quebec oak with steel solebars and stepboards of pitch pine. Bogies were assembled using Fox's patent pressed steel plates. Ashford gave the Ashbury company detailed painting instructions, which included 'one coat of lake brown, two coats of crimson lake, one coat of body varnish. Mouldings to be picked out with gold size, gilded, and fine lined with gold.' Three more coats of body varnish completed the painting.

In 1902 No. 225 was altered to all-first for use in the Royal Train. A corridor connection was fitted at what had originally been the first-class end of the coach, reducing the seating in the end compartment by one. The former second-class compartments were upgraded to seat nine persons instead of 13; total capacity of the coach was now 23. Further details of the SE&C Royal Train may be found in a later section.

In 1909 No. 231 was formed in Train No. 29, which worked regularly between Ashford and Victoria as described in the previous section. Apart from Composite No. 3450, this set comprised 6-wheeled vehicles: slip-fitted Brake Composite No. 2063, 6-compartment Third No. 567, and Brake Van No. 8. This formation was maintained until about 1915. No. 231 then became a loose coach and No. 234 was formed into the altered Set 29, whose workings in 1922 took in the 9.32 am Maidstone East to Holborn Viaduct and 6.37 pm return.

Four of the Corridor Composites were altered to all-second, seating 35 passengers each, in 1910 (Nos. 232/6/8) and 1911 (No. 229). They were used in boat trains as Lavatory Seconds.

All 15 vehicles received steam heating equipment, beginning with Nos. 232/6/8 in 1910 and finishing with No. 228 in 1916. Only three were formed in sets in the SE&C's last years: Nos. 234 in Set 29, 239 in Set 53 and 227 in Set 258. The last-mentioned two sets worked on the Reading line.

On coming to the Southern in 1923 the coaches were divided into three groups for the purposes of renumbering. Those remaining as Composites were given the numbers 5245–54; the four Seconds were allocated numbers in the third-class series (892–5) but in 1925 two of these were renumbered as Seconds (4180/1); and the First, No. 225, received the SR number 7254. Later, the two Seconds became Thirds, carrying the numbers they had originally been allotted; seating capacity was 37 each. Full details of the renumbering of the Seconds follow:

No.	*To be re-no.*	*Date*	*Transfd*	*Re-No. (2nd)*		*To 3rd*		*Set No.*	*Wdn*
229	892	–	11/25	4180	6/26	892	11/31	921	10/52
232	893	10/23	–	–	–	–	–	698,921	10/52
236	894	–	11/25	4181	10/27	894	4/30	921,686?	12/51
238	895	11/23	–	–	–	–	–	680,919	12/41

Of the Composites, No. 5254 was recorded in Set 691 between 1931 and 1935, and No. 5246 in Set 688 between 1931 and 1935. Other set numbers shown were applicable to the late 1940s.

SEC	*SR*	*Re-No.*	*Set No.*	*Wdn*	*SEC*	*SR*	*Re-No.*	*Set No.*	*Wdn*
226	5245	12/27	899	12/49	234	5251	9/26	914	6/42
227	5246	10/23	688,?	2/51	235	5252	12/27	695	2/51
228	5247	8/24		9/30	237	5253	3/24	695	c10/47
230	5248	3/29	674	5/42	239	5254	4/24	691	1/42
231	5249	4/28	687,?	/51	225	7254	10/25		5/41
233	5250	1/28		/44					

From September 1923 the Composites were classed as first/third, seating 15 1st and 14 3rd. As for the solitary First, that remained in the Royal Train until 1939, when with three other ex-Royal vehicles it ran as part of the Necropolis funeral train (Set 100). Its life in this special private service was short for, on 15th April, 1941, it was wrecked at Waterloo Necropolis station when high-explosive bombs and incendiaries fell there.

Of the other coaches, some after withdrawal became grounded bodies for a few years, but none was used in departmental service.

FIRST CLASS

Nos. 187–196, 3765–79 (SR Nos. 7310–7334)

Body length: 45 ft. Bogie centres: 29 ft 11 in.
Compartments: 6. Seats: 36.
Height from rail to top of roof: 11 ft 9½ in.

COMPOSITES

Nos. 3780–3784 (SR Nos. 7305–7309)

Body length: 45 ft. Bogie centres: 29 ft 11 in.
Compartments: 3 1st, 3 2nd. Seats: 18 1st, 24 2nd.
Height from rail to top of roof: 11 ft 9½ in.

These 30 coaches were built by the SE&CR in two batches: Nos. 187–196 in 1903 and Nos. 3765–84 in 1904; of this second batch, 15 were built as Firsts identical to the 1903 series, whilst the final five emerged as Composites designated Chatham Section stock, although structurally they were identical to the Firsts, all compartments being 7 ft 3½ in. across.

Building dates are as shown:

Nos.		*Nos.*	
187/88	10/1903	3765–69	4/1904
189–96	11/1903	3770–74	5/1904
		3775–79	6/1904
		3780–84	9/1904

Each coach had teak body framing with mahogany panels and mouldings. Quarter-lights were bedded on felt, and the partitions were double-boarded with a layer of felt between them. The underside of the roofs was covered with uralite and lincrusta. Underframes had angle soles strengthened by flitch plates, with channel iron headstocks and bolster crossbars, all other parts being of oak. Each coach was fitted with six Duplex electric lamps controlled by a main switch at the end. The five Composite coaches had three first-class compartments at one end and three seconds at the other.

Few of the coaches seem to have been allocated to any specific working. No. 193 was recorded as being in Train No. 56 in January 1913; this was a set used in the suburban area and included four other bogie coaches: First No. 2373, Second No. 2280, Composite No. 688 and Third No. 3475. Nos. 189–92 and 194–6 were 'loose'. In 1914 Composite No. 3782 was part of a pool of coaches used as strengtheners on Maidstone East trains. No. 194 was based at Dorking and worked with Composite No. 687 during 1914; by late 1915 it had been replaced by No. 192 working with Composite No. 2281 and based at Chilworth instead of Dorking. One of the Firsts, No. 191, was running in 8-set 259 by 1919 (a set formed of a mixture of 6-wheeled and bogie coaches) and berthed at Bickley.

The coaches began to be equipped with steam heating apparatus in 1912 and the process was complete by early 1922. All 30 came to the Southern and the five Composites were reclassified as Firsts, seating 36 each as did the other 25 coaches. Nos. 3780–4 were renumbered 7305–9, Nos. 187–96 became 7310–9 and Nos. 3765–79 were now Nos. 7320–34. Many were later formed into first-class-only race sets, but around 1939 14 of the Firsts were downgraded to third-class, even though continuing to run in the same sets, which bore the numbers 341, 344, 346 and 347.

The table shows the dates of renumbering, set numbers carried in later life, and 'third-class' numbers where carried.

SEC	*SR*	*Re-No.*	*Third*	*Set*	*Wdn*	*SEC*	*SR*	*Re-No.*	*Third*	*Set*	*Wdn*
3780	7305	10/26	907	344	1/47	3765	7320	12/24	855		1/42
3781	7306	6/24		686	12/48	3766	7321	10/25		346	2/42
3782	7307	1/28	853		9/44	3767	7322	2/26		341,515	4/48
3783	7308	11/25	908	344	1/47	3768	7323	9/27	910	344	1/47
3784	7309	3/24	848		9/42	3769	7324	10/26	896		6/43
187	7310	10/23			c7/39	3770	7325	7/26		347	c7/39
188	7311	10/23		519,898	1/56	3771	7326	8/29		695	2/51
189	7312	8/26	906	346,688	2/54	3772	7327	2/26			/41
190	7313	9/26			/42	3773	7328	8/26	856		3/42
191	7314	5/24		347	c12/39	3774	7329	5/24		695	2/51
192	7315	10/23	849	341	9/44	3775	7330	8/26		662,688	7/46
193	7316	7/26	854		/43	3776	7331	1/26	850		2/42
194	7317	2/27			10/41	3777	7332	2/26		912	3/51
195	7318	1/26			3/40	3778	7333	12/25	899		3/42
196	7319	6/24	909	344	1/47	3779	7334	12/27		344	11/41

Nos. 7314/22 were originally in Set 341, and between 1931 and 1935 No. 7325 was in Set 689 before going to Set 347 in the late 1930s. Several of the coach bodies were used as huts during and for a few years after World War II. No. 854 was at Guildford Locomotive Depot in April 1943, but in 1945 H.C. Casserley noted that part of it was in use as a lineman's hut at New Cross Gate. Nos. 7313/17/21/27 were noted as grounded bodies at Eastleigh, Southampton Docks, Alresford and Sheerness respectively.

Six of the coaches on withdrawal became service vehicles, as shown below:

850 to Stores Van 1707 S, 2/42. 'Stores Dept. Eastleigh.'
853 underframe to match truck 1770SM, 8/45. Working with Grafton travelling crane 1770 S at Ashford Works.
896 to Mess & Tool Van 1832 S, 6/43. Calor gas lighting fitted.
7317 to Stores Van 1690 S, 10/41. 'For use between Victoria and Banstead only.' Wdn 12/42.
7330 underframe to 1579SM, 7/46. Match truck working with Taylor & Hubbard crane No. 1579 S.
7334 to Stores Van 1699 S, 11/41. Eastleigh. Wdn 5/45.

The last example in capital stock was No. 7311, withdrawn from 8-set 898 in January 1956. It was noted by H.C. Casserley as having been cut up at Newhaven during the following March. During the 1950s and early 1960s Newhaven was responsible for burning a very large number of withdrawn, wooden-bodied coaches and was probably the chief carriage 'graveyard' of the Southern Region.

LAVATORY FIRST CLASS

Nos. 3500–3511 (SR Nos. 7335–7346)

Body length: 46 ft. Bogie centres: 31 ft.
Compartments: 5. Seats: 26.
Height, rail to top of roof: 11 ft 9½ in. Lavatories: 4.

The Midland Railway-Carriage & Wagon Co. of Shrewsbury built 12 Lavatory Firsts for the SE&C, and they were delivered in 1904: Nos. 3500/01/04/05 in February, 3502/03/06–09 in March and 3510/11 in April. The register records that each coach cost £1,606 10s., and was paid for out of revenue. Stone's lighting equipment, with duplex lamps in each compartment, was installed. Bogies were Fox's patent pressed-steel type, with Mansell wood-centred wheels.

In 1909 No. 3500 was booked to be formed in Boat Train No. 6A, which worked the 9.05 am Cannon Street to Dover Pier and 3.25 pm return.

All 12 Firsts were later steam-heated, and all came to the Southern Railway, who renumbered them 7335–7346. Some were later placed in first-class-only race sets, though a couple of others found themselves in special-traffic sets, which were mainly used on Kent Coast holiday trains. Two were downgraded to third-class and renumbered 912 and 913 in about 1939. The Southern thought it would be a big joke to form coach 913 into *Set* 913, just to confuse observers and historians; and this coach did in fact remain in Set 913 until withdrawal in December 1951. Nos. 7338/40 were in 4-sets 855 and 854 in 1931; the other three vehicles in each of these were ex-LB&SC.

The following table shows renumbering and withdrawal dates of the 12 Lavatory Firsts.

SEC	*SR*	*Re-No.*	*Third*	*Set*	*Wdn*	*SEC*	*SR*	*Re-No.*	*Third*	*Set*	*Wdn*
3500	7335	8/29	912	913	12/51	3506	7341	7/26			11/40
3501	7336	1/27		334,335	/43	3507	7342	1/28		303	c/44
3502	7337	7/24		897	10/43	3508	7343	7/26		695,334	7/46
3503	7338	11/24		855,345	/41	3509	7344	11/24	913	913	12/51
3504	7339	10/24		903	/45	3510	7345	1/26		302	2/51
3505	7340	11/25		854,345	/41	3511	7346	5/26		688	7/46

As Firsts, Nos. 7335/44 had been in Set 344, and No. 7342 was in Set 347 before being transferred to Set 303 about 1940. After withdrawal, some of the coach bodies were grounded as huts at various locations: for example Baynards, which in 1948 was home to Nos. 7339/46. Only one coach was transferred to the service vehicles list, this being No. 7337 which became Mess and Tool Van 1850 S in October 1943, receiving calor gas lighting. No. 1850 S was withdrawn in July 1960.

The body of No. 7336 was recorded by H.C. Casserley as sold to Keyes timber merchants of Berkhamsted in June 1950.

LAVATORY THIRD CLASS

Nos. 3515–3524 (SR Nos. 872–881)

Body length: 42 ft 6 in. Bogie centres: 28 ft 6 in.
Height, rail to roof: 11 ft 9½ in. Bogie wheelbase: 7 ft.
Compartments: 6. Seats: 52.
Lavatories: 4 (access from 4 compartments).

These were the first SE&C coaches ever built that gave third-class passengers access to lavatories; until now, only first- and second-class passengers had been so-favoured.

The SE&C itself constructed these 10 vehicles at Ashford Works: Nos.

3515–19 in December 1903 and 3520–24 in March 1904. For accountancy purposes the last two were regarded as Chatham Section stock as they theoretically replaced four withdrawn ex-LC&D 4-wheeled coaches. The teak body framing was finished off with mahogany panels and mouldings. Quarter-lights were bedded on felt. Each passenger compartment was fitted with two torpedo ventilators and each lavatory had just one. Stone's electric lighting was fitted, each compartment having a duplex light rated as 8 candle power each, while the lavatories were fitted with a single light of 8 candle power, all lights being controlled by a main switch at the coach end.

Lavatories were fitted with metal washbasins and Beresford's earthenware water closet pans. The seat was teak and the seat lid mahogany – nothing but the best, even for third-class! Not forgotten were a sanitary paper holder, a towel roller and even a coathook. Typically for the SE&C, there was a droplight in addition to a top ventilator.

Underframes consisted of angle soles with channel iron headstocks and bolster crossbars, all other parts being oak.

When new these Lavatory Thirds were put into trains working the following 'fixed services':

10.16 am Hastings to Charing Cross, 1.40 pm Charing Cross to Hastings and 5.58 pm return.
8.15 am Charing Cross to Hastings.
11.18 am Hastings to Charing Cross, 3.44 pm Charing Cross to Hastings and 7.15 pm return.
11.00 am Charing Cross to Hastings, 2.17 pm Hastings to Charing Cross and 5.58 pm return.
8.40 am Hastings to Charing Cross and 3.35 pm return.
10.30 am Victoria to Hastings and 5.00 pm return.
8.56 am Hastings to Charing Cross and 4.50 pm return (fast portion).
8.35 am Deal to Victoria and 5.00 pm return.
5.46 am Cannon Street to Hastings and 10.34 am Hastings to Charing Cross.
4.50 pm Charing Cross to Hastings (slow portion) and 8.52 pm return.

By May 1907 Nos. 3521 and 3523 were allocated to the through service between Deal and the Great Western and Great Central Railways that had started in 1903. Leaving Deal, the front four coaches (GC Composite, GW slip Composite, SEC Third 3521 or 3523, GW Composite Brake) were for Birkenhead etc.; then came an SEC Tri-Composite Brake (No. 161 or 162) for Reading. At the rear were a bogie Composite (3 1st 3 2nd), a 60-seat 6-wheel Third and a Brake Van for Charing Cross. At Folkestone Junction a bogie Composite, bogie Third and 6-wheel Brake Van were added and, finally, at Ashford a van from Margate to London.

By summer 1910 the 10.38 am Deal to Reading was booked to include No. 3515 or 2523 in the formation.

All 10 Lavatory Thirds received steam heating apparatus after 1909, and all became Southern Railway property in 1923; they were renumbered 872 to 881. It is not known if any were allocated to set trains; probably not, as Thirds tended to be more commonly used as loose strengthening vehicles. In 1935 the last was withdrawn. It seems likely that they disappeared earlier than many of their contemporaries because the accommodation standards were rather poor, compartments being only 5 ft 7½ in. across at a time when 6 ft was the norm for third-class compartments. Renumbering and withdrawal dates are given below:

SEC	*SR*	*Re-No.*	*Wdn*	*SEC*	*SR*	*Re-No.*	*Wdn*
3515	872	11/24	5/34	3520	877	5/28	3/34
3516	873	2/26	3/34	3521	878	10/29	12/33
3517	874	6/26	3/34	3522	879	?	3/34
3518	875	11/26	8/34	3523	880	?	7/34
3519	876	1/24	7/35	3524	881	1/26	6/34

The third class numbers 872–881 were re-used in 1936 for downgraded Composites Nos. 5200–09, as described in a previous section.

No. 3521 was one of the last SE&C coaches to receive its SR green livery, very few remaining in SE&C brown by October 1929. Strangely enough, it was the very first SE&C-built bogie carriage to be converted to a service vehicle. In December 1933 it became Mess and Tool Van No. 731 S, allocated to the locomotive running department at New Cross Gate.

FIRST SALOON LAVATORY

Nos. 3512–3514 (SR Nos. 7916–7918)

Body length: 50 ft 1 in. Bogie centres: 33 ft 6 in.
Compartments: 2. Seats: 32 (20 in No. 3514 only).
Height, rail to top of roof: 11 ft 9 in. Lavatories: 2.

Contracts were placed with the Midland Railway-Carriage & Wagon Co. in November 1903 for three first class Saloons, and the vehicles were delivered to the SE&CR in June 1904. They were of similar body construction but No. 3514 had different seating arrangements from the other two.

Each vehicle was composed of two large saloon compartments divided by a sliding door, so that two parties could use the whole coach at one time without getting in each other's way. A lavatory compartment, full-width across the coach, was located at each outer end. Nos. 3512/13, built to Drawing No. 1925, were fitted with eight inward-facing couches, each designed to seat four passengers. No. 3514, to Drawing No. 1926, was fitted with chairs (originally seating 28, later reduced to 20) and the external doors were positioned differently from those of Nos. 3512/3. These doors were 2 ft 3 in. wide.

All three vehicles had teak body framing with Honduras mahogany panels, whilst the underframes (to Drawing No. 1928) had steel soles, bolsters and longitudinals, all other parts being oak. Interior cabinet work was of walnut in No. 3512, mahogany in No. 3513 and satinwood in No. 3514. The cost of these luxurious saloons was £1,718 10*s*. each, charged to revenue account.

No. 3514, which had green moquette velvet upholstery, was placed in the Royal Train, along with Saloon Brakes Nos. 2301 and 3493 and First No. 225, already described in previous sections. It is possible that the other two were, in later years, regularly attached to certain Kent Coast business trains for the exclusive use of members of the Association of Regular Kent

Coasters, but evidence is lacking; all that is known is that unspecified saloons were reserved for these season-ticket holders from 1912.

All three first class Saloons were later steam-heated and came to the Southern, being renumbered 7916–18; No. 7918 (formerly 3514) was retained as a Royal Train vehicle until 1939 when, with three other ex-Royal carriages it became part of Set 100, the Necropolis funeral train. Unfortunately this was burnt out by incendiaries that fell on Waterloo Necropolis Station on 15th April, 1941.

During the summer of 1938 Nos. 7916 and 7917 both had booked workings on Western Section main-line trains: on Thursdays one was attached to the 8.30 am Waterloo–Bournemouth as far as Winchester, thence locally to Southampton, returning on Fridays in a van train from Southampton Terminus to Clapham Junction; and the other saloon was attached on Thursdays to the 9.00 am Waterloo–Exeter Central, returning on Fridays in the 8.43 am Exeter–Salisbury and 7.50 pm thence to Waterloo.

On withdrawal, the body of No. 7917 was sent to Plumstead; it had been badly damaged by a high-explosive bomb that fell on Clapham Junction carriage shed on 8th September, 1940.

SEC	*SR*	*Re-No.*	*Wdn*
3512	7916	7/24	9/42
3513	7917	12/25	11/40
3514	7918	10/25	5/41

THE KING'S SALOON

No. 1 R (SR No. 7930)

As earlier recorded, three coaches – Nos. 225, 2301 and 3493 – had been converted in the latter part of 1902 to run as part of a new Royal Train, for which the new King's Saloon was at that time under construction. In February 1902 the Lancaster Railway Carriage & Wagon Co.'s tender to build a Royal Saloon for £3,670 had been accepted by the Managing Committee; but in June a further £500 was authorised for improved interior decorative work to the Saloon. By this time the Lancaster company had lost its separate identity as in April 1902 it became part of the giant Metropolitan Amalgamated Railway Carriage & Wagon Co.; and so it was that company that finally delivered the completed Royal Saloon to the SE&C in March 1903. Quoted cost of the saloon was £4,170 – well over twice as much as a normal coach at that time.

The coach measured 50 ft 1¾ in. by 8 ft 0¾ in. over body. The roof was graced by a clerestory with downcurving ends; height from rail level to the top of this clerestory was 12 ft 11⅞ in. Fox's pressed-steel 8 ft bogies were at 33 ft 6 in. centres. Internal layout was arranged thus: at one end was a large, full-width lavatory compartment and adjacent to this was the King's Saloon compartment. Next came a large saloon for his equerries, after which one came to the Queen's saloon compartment. These three saloons all contained a good mix of armchairs, settees and tables, total seating capacity being 18.

At the opposite end of the carriage was a small coupé compartment with two seats for the Queen's ladies-in-waiting, as well as a lavatory for the use of the Queen; at this end was an external gangway to connect the saloon with first class coach No. 225.

It is odd that the coach should have borne the same number as the saloon kept at Calais, but to avoid confusion it was known officially as the English Royal, whilst the other was referred to as the Continental Royal. On the English saloon there were no sleeping facilities, so it was suitable only for short-distance day travel; on the SE&C its main function was to convey King Edward VII and Queen Alexandra to and from Dover for their Continental journeys, and to convey foreign royalties visiting Britain.

In 1905 the 4-coach Royal Train was augmented by three additional new Saloons: Nos. 3514, 3785 and 3786. These usually tended to be kept as spare vehicles, capacity of the train being increased or decreased as required for each occasion it was employed.

The train saw intensive use in 1910, when King Edward died, by foreign rulers arriving to attend his funeral. On 19th May, 1910, the train conveyed the German Emperor from Port Victoria to Victoria in the morning; then the same afternoon conveyed the King of Bulgaria and Prince Danilo Alexander of Montenegro from Dover to Victoria. Formation of the train on this date was: Brake Saloon 3493, Corridor First 225, Royal Saloon 1 R, Saloon 3514 and Brake Saloon 2301. Some of the 'back-up' Saloons were used in another train from Dover to Victoria: Nos. 821, 3787, 3785 and 3512 (with 6-wheel Brake Vans). This special train conveyed Archduke Ferdinand of Austria and Duke Albrecht of Wurtemberg.

Between 1910 and 1921 No. 1 R was used by King George V and again by visiting Kings. On 3rd July, 1917, the train ran as a 'private special' from Victoria to Dover, formed with the same vehicles as in 1910; stock was returned empty to Ashford, where it was berthed when not in use.

No. 1 R received steam heating apparatus in March 1914; if the carriage register is to be believed this improvement increased the theoretical book value of the saloon from £4,170 to £4,259 10s.

The saloon passed to the Southern, who renumbered it 7930 in October 1925 at Eastleigh Carriage Works along with the other Royal Train vehicles (2301, 3493, 3514, 3786 and 225). Perhaps Eastleigh thought it would do a better repainting job than Ashford, which at that time was still responsible for maintenance of all Eastern Section stock.

After Grouping No. 7930 tended to be less used, appearing only on Derby Day and annually between London and Portsmouth for Cowes yachting week. On 19th May, 1937, the Royal Train, conveying King George VI, Queen Elizabeth and Princess Elizabeth, ran from Victoria to Cosham for the Spithead Review (which was on the 20th) and returned from Portsmouth (South Jetty) on 21st May. In both directions it was hauled by ex-LSW class 'T9' No. 716 and had the usual formation of Saloon Brake, Royal Saloon, Saloon, Corridor First and Saloon Brake. The last day in Royal service of No. 7930 was 24th July, 1939, when King George VI travelled in it from Portsmouth to London. Stored during World War II, it was officially withdrawn in September 1947.

Too good to scrap, the saloon was acquired by a Southern officer and used by him as a holiday home at Newhaven, where it remained for many years. Denis Cullum, who worked in the Waterloo station offices, believes that the official who owned the saloon was Sidney Smart, superintendent of operation on the Southern since 1945 (his slogan was 'Punctuality is *really* necessary.').

In November 1958 the ex-Royal Saloon was noted at Newhaven Harbour painted white with black ends and underframe; the paint dates 31.8.28 and 1.4.37 were still visible in white figures on the solebar. In 1960 C.W. Underhill noted that the coach underframe still retained gold lining, and much of the interior was still in original condition. Stephen Musgrave recorded that in 1960 the saloon was still maintained in a tolerable state at Newhaven Harbour and was repainted while with black ends and underframe only that year. The solebars were once maroon [*sic*] with gold-leaf decorations. (*Model Railway News*, Vol. 36, pp. 375 and 440.)

How or why it came to be moved from Newhaven to Glenfinnan, on the West Highland line, is a mystery, but certainly it was there in both 1967 and 1968, in use as a camping coach, of which BR once had a great number berthed at various holiday locations. Nothing seems to have been reported about it since. The original armchair from the King's compartment was privately preserved; it was upholstered in soft green leather to match the green satin upholstery of the coach. (*Railway Magazine*, Vol. 114, p.296.) As No. 7930 does not appear in any recent stock lists, one can only assume it was broken up after camping coaches were done away with by BR.

At about the time the SE&C ordered the King's Saloon, it also ordered from Wagon-Lits a new Continental Royal saloon, this being numbered 2 R; it was always the property of the Royalty, however, and never owned by the SE&C. It is not mentioned in any SE&C or SR carriage register, but the Southern issued a diagram of the Saloon. It was 56 ft 8 in. over body, 9 ft 2¼ in. wide and had a clerestory roof, the top of which was 13 ft 1¾ in. above rail-level. Bogies, of 8 ft 2½ in. wheelbase, were at 31 ft 2 in. centres.

TRI-COMPOSITE BRAKES

Nos. 148–162 (SR Nos. 6607–6621)

Body length: 46 ft. Bogie centres: 31 ft.
Height, rail to roof: 11 ft 9½ in. Height to top of observatory: 12 ft 9½ in.
Compartments: 2 1st, 2 2nd, 2 3rd.
Seats: 12 1st, 16 2nd, 20 3rd class.

These 15 vehicles were built by the SE&C at Ashford in 1905 and were completed in the following order:

148–152	3/1905	158–160	5/1905
153–157	4/1905	161/162	6/1905

Body framing was teak with mahogany panels and mouldings, and the quarterlights were bedded on felt. The rather cramped guard's compartment included a dogbox, coupling box, locker and a seat for the guard. Underframes were of angle soles with channel iron headstocks and bolster cross bars, all other parts being oak. Six Duplex lamps and one single lamp (for the guard) were controlled by a main switch at the coach end.

Nos. 161 and 162 were built new with steam heating apparatus on the 'storage' system, each compartment being fitted with a 4 ft 6 in. storage heater. The guard's compartment had two steam gauges: one for engine pressure and the other for train pressure, with a regulating stopcock between. Three other coaches received storage heaters subsequently: Nos. 148/52 in December 1905 and No. 150 in October 1906.

When new, the first 10 of the Tri-Composite Brakes were allocated to the following train services (from May 1905):

1. 9.08 am Charing Cross to Bexhill, 2.46 pm return, 5.56 pm Charing Cross to Tonbridge.
2. 10.30 am Victoria to Bexhill and 5.22 pm return.
3. 9.23 am Tonbridge to Charing Cross, 11.15 am Charing Cross to Bexhill and 3.48 pm return.
4. 12.40 pm Charing Cross to Bexhill and 7.12 pm return.
5. Spare at Bexhill.
6. 7.40 am Tonbridge to London Bridge (not Mondays). 4.32 pm Charing Cross to Tonbridge (not Saturdays).

7 & 8. Deal and Reading Express (local portion).

9. 8.31 am Deal to Charing Cross and 4.32 pm return.
10. 9.28 am Holborn to Dover and 3.55 pm return.

The Bexhill trains shown above were actually through portions, attached at Crowhurst to up Hastings trains and detached from down Hastings trains at the same place. The Bexhill branch had been opened in 1902 to compete with the Brighton traffic to that resort, and the SE&C thought that probably the best way to stimulate traffic on its line was to run through carriages. The Tri-Composite Brakes did not remain on these services for very long, however, being replaced by new corridor Tri-Composite Brakes about 1908.

In 1906 Nos. 148 and 152, the pair that had been recently fitted with steam heaters, were allocated to the Victoria portion of the 10.25 am Deal to Manchester service (one in use, the other spare). Return working left Herne Hill for Deal at 3.02 pm. From February 1907 an extra steam-heated Tri-Composite Brake – presumably No. 150 – was included. Also in 1907 No. 161 or 162 was scheduled to run as the Reading portion of the 10.40 am Deal to GWR through service.

In 1908 No. 160 was formed into a 3-coach 'fixed train' with Third Brake No. 2295 and Tri-Composite No. 888, working between Hastings and London. In October 1910 it was replaced by No. 162, the other two coaches remaining in the set, which was given the number 59. The set was booked to work the 5.35 am Cannon Street to Hastings, 11.00 am Hastings to Victoria, 2.42 pm Victoria to Ashford and 6.00 pm thence to Hastings, and finally the 9.00 pm Hastings to Charing Cross.

Other numbered 3-sets formed around 1909/10 that included a Tri-Composite Brake were Nos. 23, 24, 61, 66, 82 and 83. By 1915 there were 14 of these 3-sets, with scattered numbers, and so a renumbering scheme was drawn up whereby the sets were grouped together and given the numbers 58 to 71, designated Type 'B'. Old Set 24 became 69, and 83 became 65, for example.

In February 1916, because of a shortage of goods brake vans, Set 60 was temporarily disbanded and its brake coaches (150 and 841) were used as goods brakes in the London area, being fitted with side lamp irons for the purpose. Early in 1917 Nos. 150 and 841 were withdrawn from goods working and reinstated as passenger stock.

Five of the coaches had been fitted with storage heaters, but this system was not perpetuated and the remaining 10 received non-storage heaters: Nos. 156/9 in 1910, 155/7/60 in 1911, 149/51/3/8 in 1912 and 154 in 1913. As stated, 14 of the Tri-Composites were in 3-sets; the remaining coach, No. 152, was in 6-set 87 during 1920–22, and was allocated to a Dorking–Cannon Street service.

On coming to the SR in 1923 Nos. 148–162 were renumbered 6607–21 and in September of that year, when second class was abolished, the seating was altered to 12 first, 40 third. Sets 58–71 were renumbered 515 to 528 in the same order, although Set 528 seems to have been disbanded early; its Composite Brake, No. 6619 (formerly 160), was later recorded in 4-set 668 but was withdrawn following accident damage at Margate on 24th August, 1933. The other 'odd' one, No. 152, became SR 6611 and was formed in Set 695 – the former SE&C Set 87.

The 3-sets worked all over the Southern's Eastern Section in the same 'link' as the later 60 ft 3-sets, even though the seating capacity fell somewhat short of that found in the longer coaches. Nos. 515–20 and 526 were augmented to 8-sets for Kent Coast holiday traffic, probably about 1939.

The second Composite Brake to be withdrawn was No. 6612 (in Set 526) in September 1942. Withdrawals continued slowly and the last to go was No. 6617 in December 1954. It had only recently been transferred from Set 896 to Set 696. Three coaches saw further life after withdrawal as service vehicles, and these are listed below.

Summary of Composite Brakes

SEC	*SR*	*Re-No.*	*Set*	*Wdn*	*SEC*	*SR*	*Re-No.*	*Set*	*Wdn*
148	6607	6/27	520	12/46	156	6615	4/26	522,669	12/53
149	6608	12/26	518	4/44	157	6616	3/27	519,900	9/53
150	6609	9/26	517	6/43	158	6617	12/27	525,896	12/54
151	6610	3/28	523	2/43	159	6618	11/27	521	/47
152	6611	7/26	695	2/51	160	6619	7/27	528,668	8/33
153	6612	6/27	526	9/42	161	6620	7/27	524	5/43
154	6613	5/27	527	9/46	162	6621	12/26	516	8/47
155	6614	3/29	515	4/48					

6608 to Mess & Tool Van 1919 S, 4/44. Traffic Dept. Wdn 2/46.
6609 to Mess & Tool Van 1960 S, 5/44. Engineers Dept., Redbridge.
6618 to Mess & Tool Van 379 S, 1947. Motive Power Dept., Reading.

SECR DIAG. No. S. 2811/2. SR DIAG. No. 36 or 236.

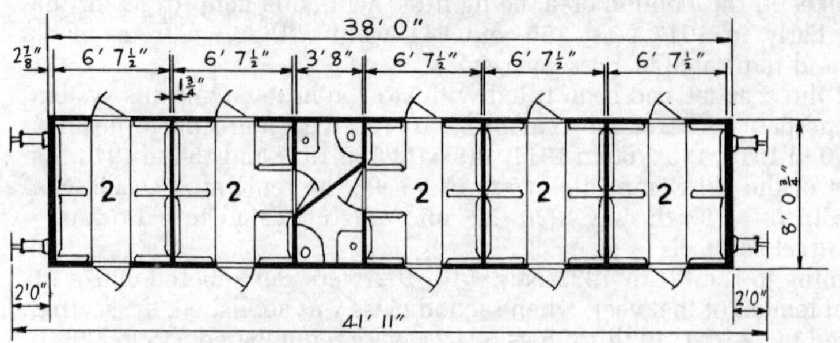

SEC Nos. 259-262. SR Nos. 4182, 846, 4183 (847), 4184.

SEATING CAPACITY 36S, LATER 44T.

SECR DIAG. No. SR DIAG. No. 37.

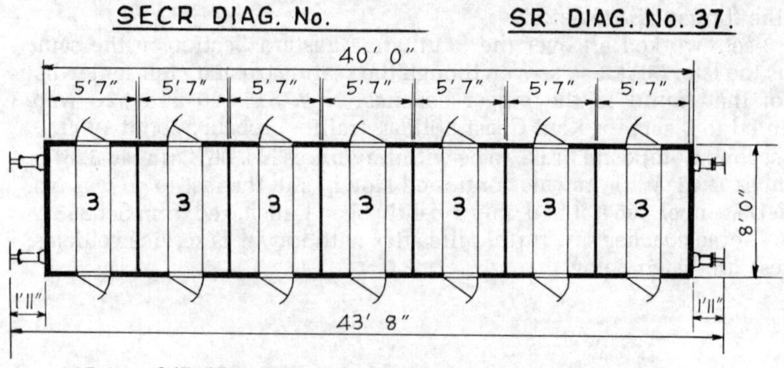

LCD Nos. 347-351. SEC Nos. 3301-5. SR Nos. 849-853.

SEATING CAPACITY 70T.

SECR DIAG. No. C5/2831. SR DIAG. No. 38.

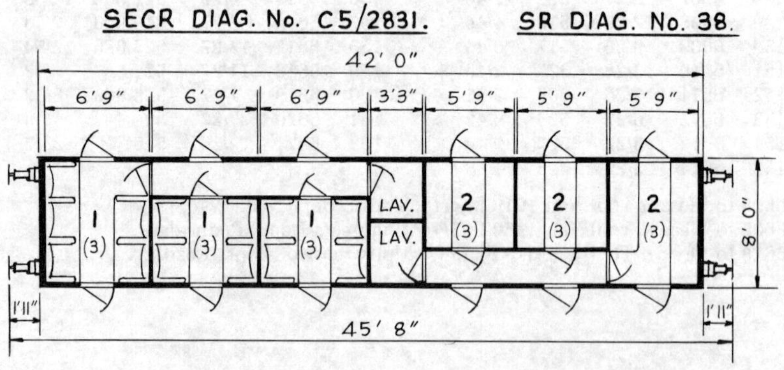

LCD Nos. 1150-1161. SEC Nos. 2717-28. SR Nos. 854-865.

SEATING CAPACITY 13F 19S, LATER 40T.

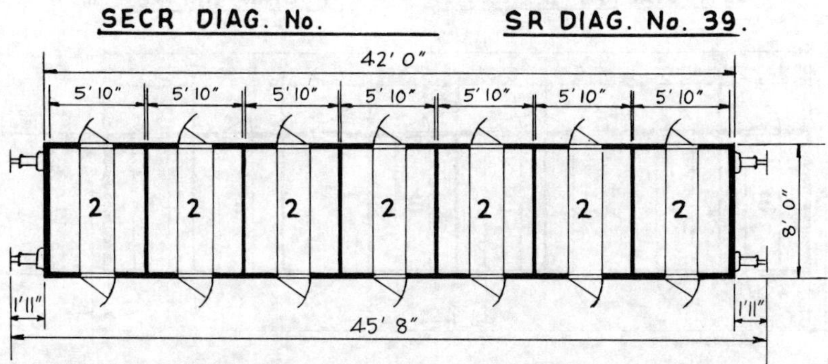

LCD Nos. 1178-1183. SEC Nos. 2906-2911. SR Nos. 866-871.

SEATING CAPACITY 56S, LATER 70T.

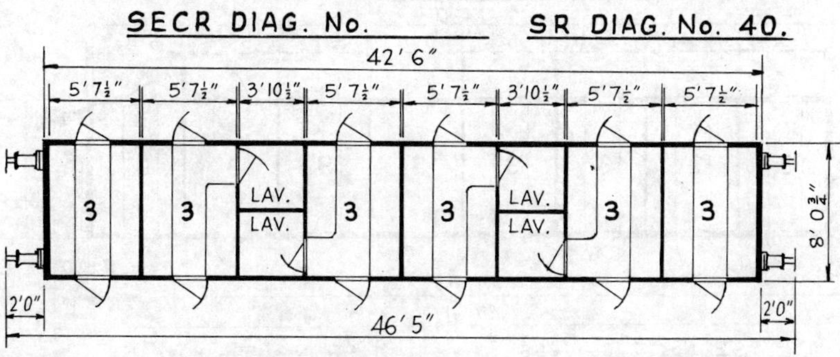

SEC Nos. 3515-3524. SR Nos. 872-881.

SEATING CAPACITY 52T.

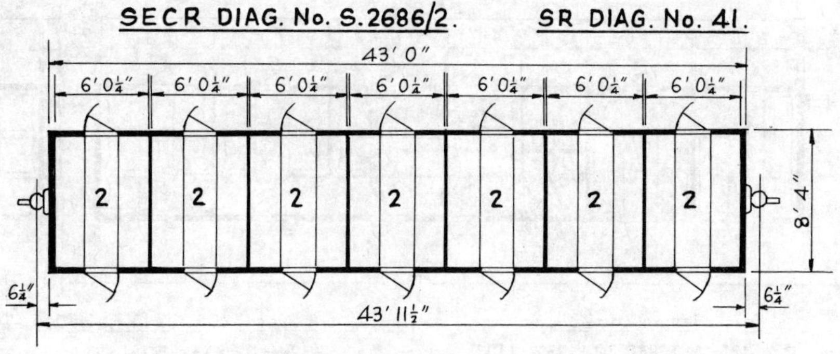

SE Nos. 1940-1943. SR Nos. 883, 884.

SEATING CAPACITY 70S, LATER 70T.

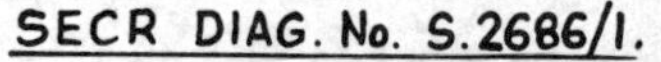

SR DIAG. No. 42.

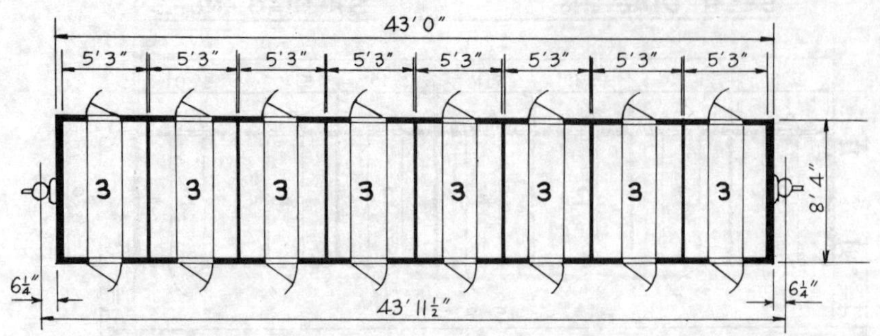

SE Nos. 1948-1953. SR Nos. NOT CARRIED.

SEATING CAPACITY 80T.

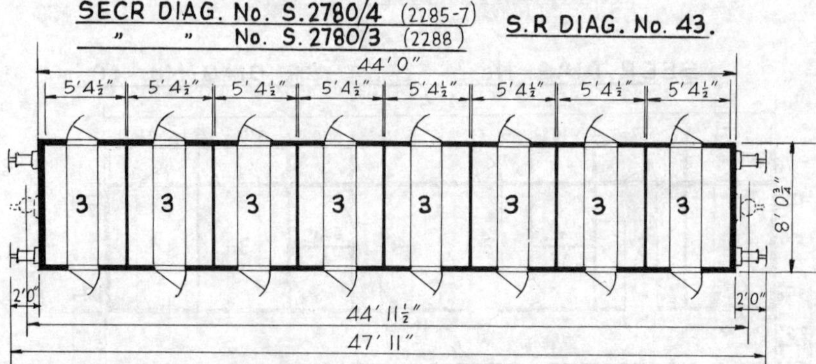

S.R DIAG. No. 43.

SE Nos. 2285-2288.

(2285-7 ALTERED TO 2nd/3rd COMPO., 1903)

SR Nos. 896-8, 891.

(896 close-coupled)

SEATING CAPACITY 80T. 2285-7: 40S 30T.

SECR DIAG. No. S.2805/1 (225)
" " No. S.2805/2 (226-8/30/1/3-5/7/9)
" " No. S.2805/3 (229/32/6/8)

SR DIAG. No. 485
" " No. 294
" " No. 44 or 237

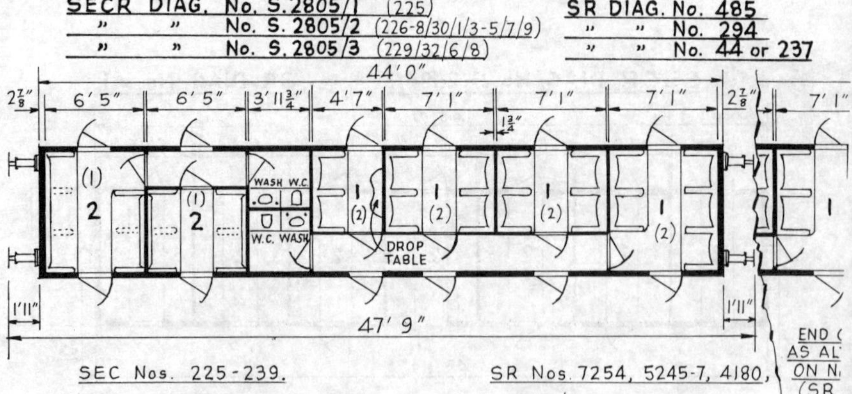

SEC Nos. 225-239.

No. 225 ALTERED TO FIRST, 1902.

Nos. 229/32/6/8 ALTERED TO SECONDS, 1910/11.

SR Nos. 7254, 5245-7, 4180, 5248/9, 893, 5250-2, 4181, 5253, 895, 5254.

SEATING CAPACITY 15F 13S, LATER 15F 14T.

225: 23F. 229/32/6/8: 35S, LATER 37T.

SECR DIAG. No. **SR DIAG. No. 45. No. 146.**

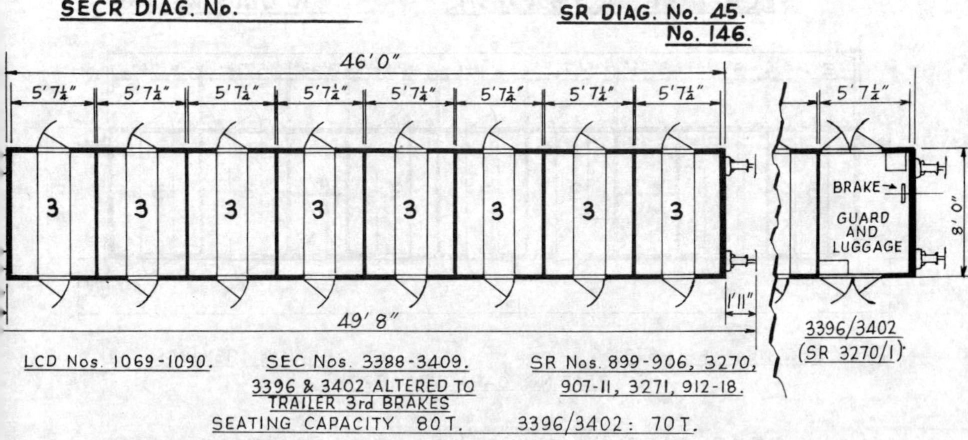

LCD Nos. 1069-1090. SEC Nos. 3388-3409. SR Nos. 899-906, 3270, 907-11, 3271, 912-18.

3396 & 3402 ALTERED TO TRAILER 3rd BRAKES

SEATING CAPACITY 80T. 3396/3402: 70T.

SECR DIAG. No. S.2783/2. **SR DIAG. No. 46.**

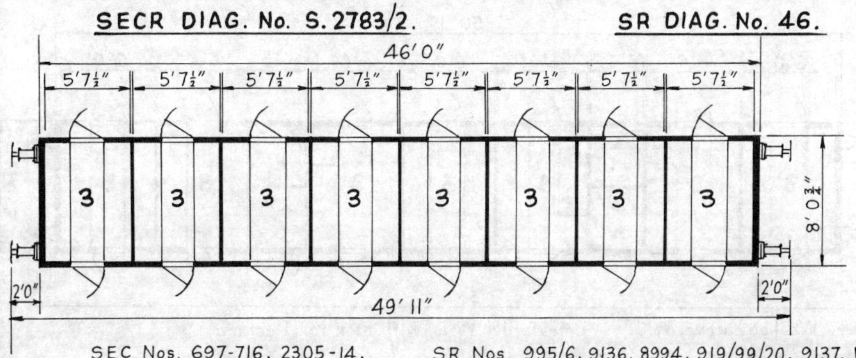

SEC Nos. 697-716, 2305-14, 3453-87.

SR Nos. 995/6, 9136, 8994, 919/99/20, 9137, 1001, 8998, 921, 1003, 8995, 1005-7, 8978, 1009/10, 922, 1011-14, 923, 1015, 9141, 1017/18, 8986, 1020-28, 8975/91/96/87, 9138, 1034/5, 9152, 1037-9, 924, 1040-5, 9142/43/34, 1049-53.

SEATING CAPACITY 80T.

SECR DIAG. No. S.2793/1. **SR DIAG. No. 47 or 238.**

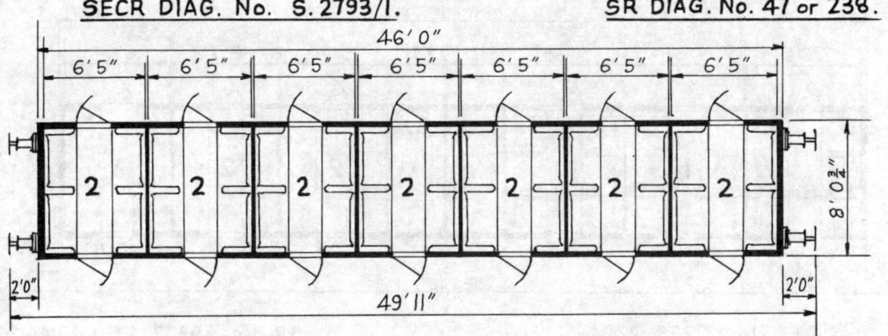

SEC Nos. 2315-2326. SR Nos. 4186, 926-8, 4187/8, 931-4, 4189, 936.

SEATING CAPACITY 56S, LATER 70T.

SECR DIAG. No. S.2783/1. SR DIAG. No. 48.

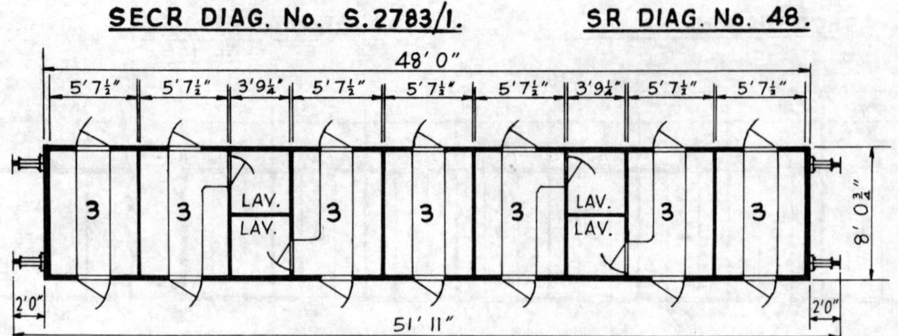

SEC Nos. 861-879. SR Nos. 937-955.

SEATING CAPACITY 62T.

SECR DIAG. No. S.2320/1. SR DIAG. No. 49.

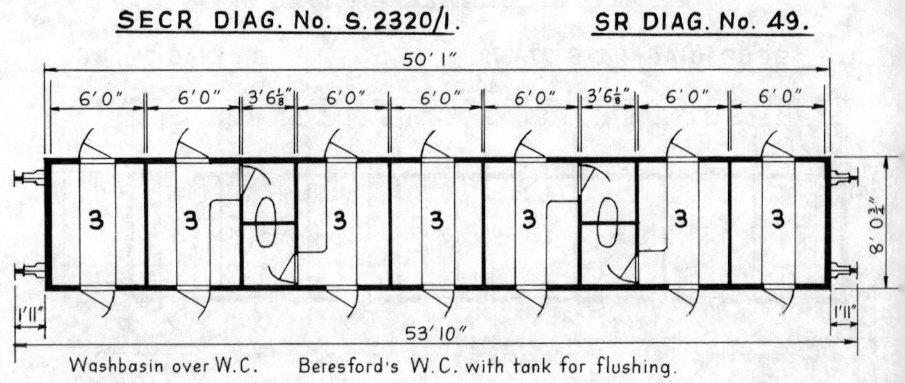

Washbasin over W.C. Beresford's W.C. with tank for flushing.

SEC Nos. 1085-89. SR Nos. 956-960.

SEATING CAPACITY 62 T.

SECR DIAG. No. S.2326/2 (2275-9/81-4). SR DIAG. No. 302. S.2811/3 (2280). No. 239.

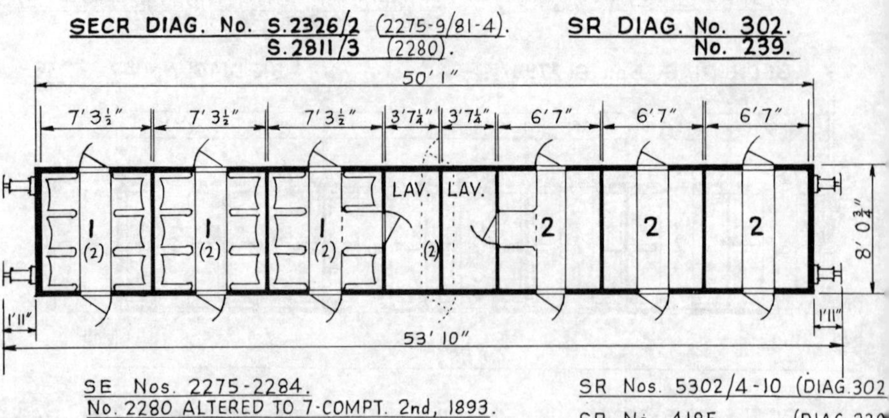

SE Nos. 2275-2284.
No. 2280 ALTERED TO 7-COMPT. 2nd, 1893.
LAVS. STRIPPED AND 8-SEAT COMPT.
7' 3½" WIDE PUT IN ITS SPACE.

SR Nos. 5302/4-10 (DIAG.302
SR No. 4185. (DIAG. 239

SEATING CAPACITY 17F 22S, LATER 17F 27T. 2280: 56S, LATER 70T.

SECR DIAG. No. S.2305/3. SR DIAG. No. 141.

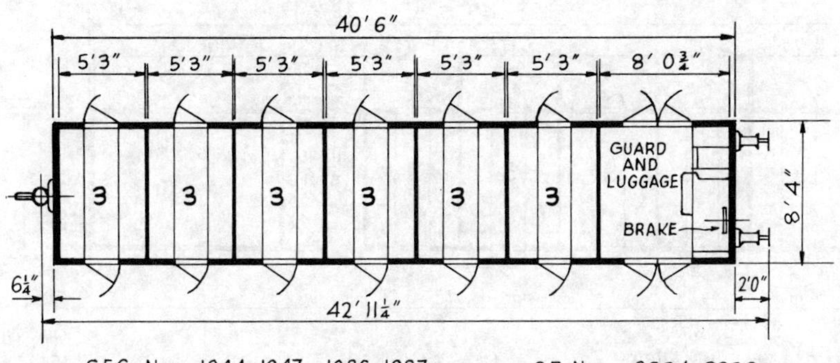

SEC Nos. 1944-1947, 1986, 1987. SR Nos. 3234, 3236.

SEATING CAPACITY 60 T.

SECR DIAG. No. S.2303/4. SR DIAG. No. 142.

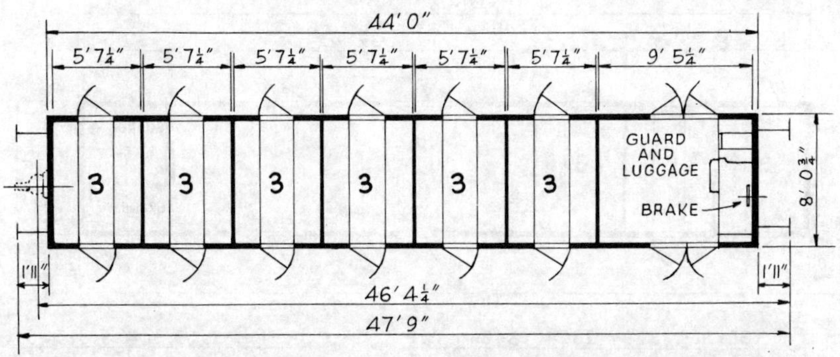

SE Nos. 2289-2294. SR Nos. 3240-43 (long-buffered), 3238/9 (close-coupled).

SEATING CAPACITY 60 T.

SECR DIAG. No. S.2303/5. SR DIAG. No. 143.

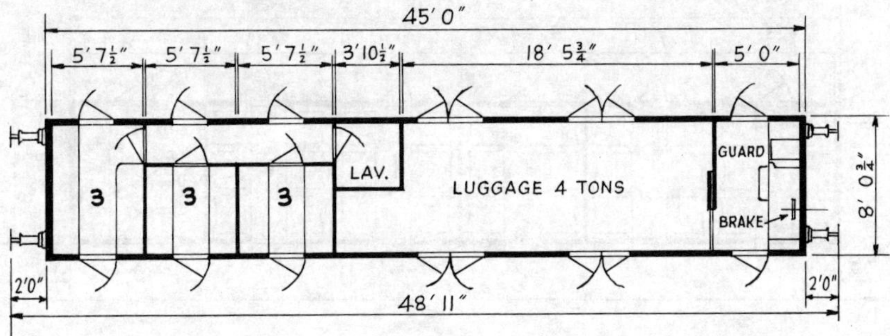

SEC Nos. 2297, 2298. SR Nos. 3244/5.

SEATING CAPACITY 20 T.

SECR DIAG. No. SR DIAG. No. 144.

LCD Nos. 1184-1189. SEC Nos. 3410-3415. SR Nos. 3246-3251.

SEATING CAPACITY 50 T.

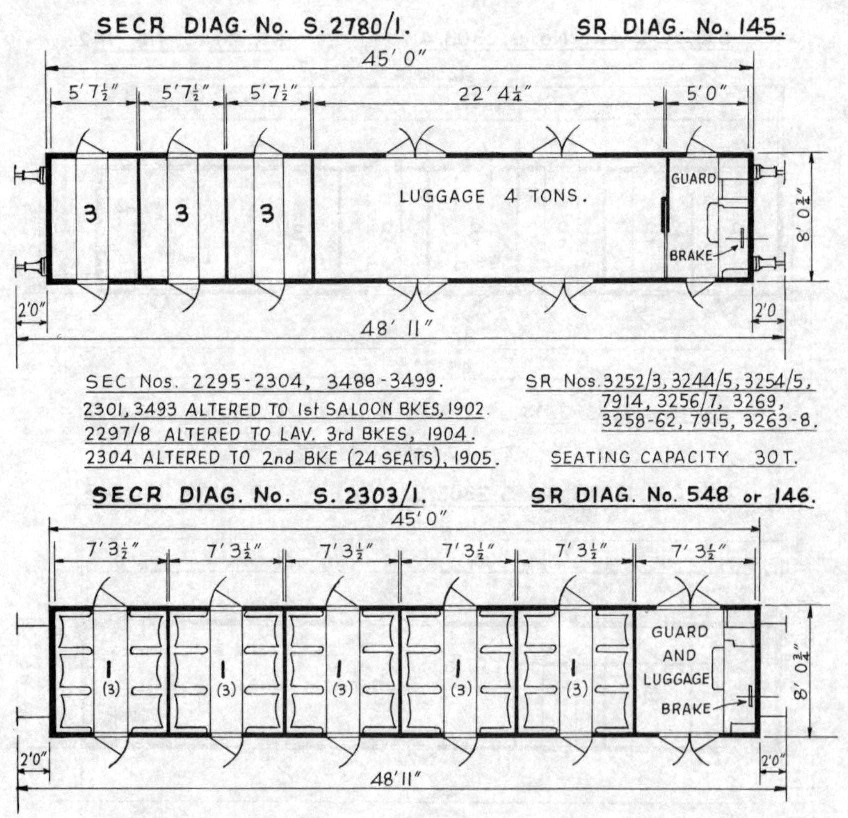

SEC Nos. 2295-2304, 3488-3499.
2301, 3493 ALTERED TO 1st SALOON BKES, 1902.
2297/8 ALTERED TO LAV. 3rd BKES, 1904.
2304 ALTERED TO 2nd BKE (24 SEATS), 1905.

SR Nos. 3252/3, 3244/5, 3254/5, 7914, 3256/7, 3269, 3258-62, 7915, 3263-8.

SEATING CAPACITY 30 T.

SEC Nos. 250-254.

SR Nos. 7735-7739. (DIAG. 548)

SEATING CAPACITY 30 F.

7739/37 ALTERED TO 3rd BKES 3590/1 (DIAG. 146), 5/40.

SECR DIAG. No. S.2332/2. SR DIAG. No. 147.

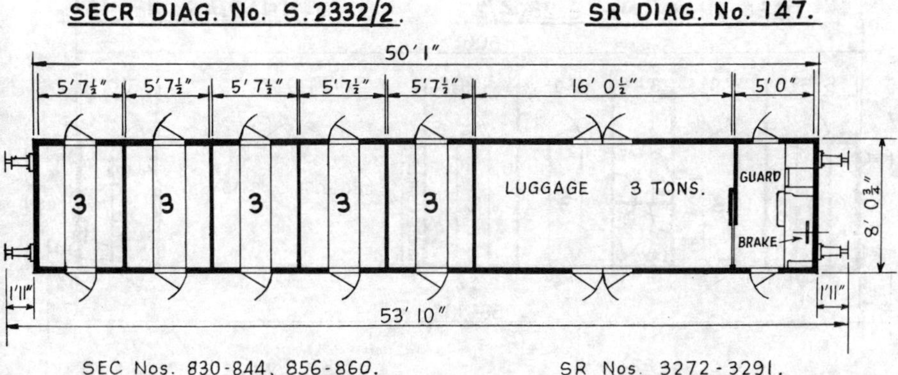

SEC Nos. 830-844, 856-860. SR Nos. 3272-3291.

SEATING CAPACITY 50 T.

SECR PLAN FF. SR DIAG. No. 148.

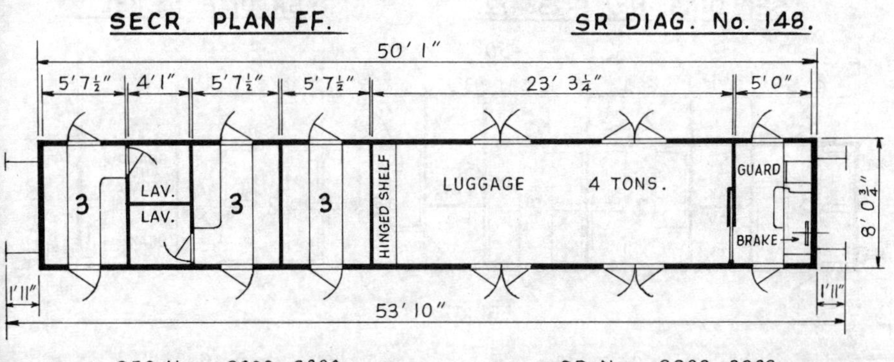

SEC Nos. 3808, 3809. SR Nos. 3292, 3293.

SEATING CAPACITY 26 T.

SECR DIAG. No. S.2307/2. SR DIAG. Nos. 149 and 150.

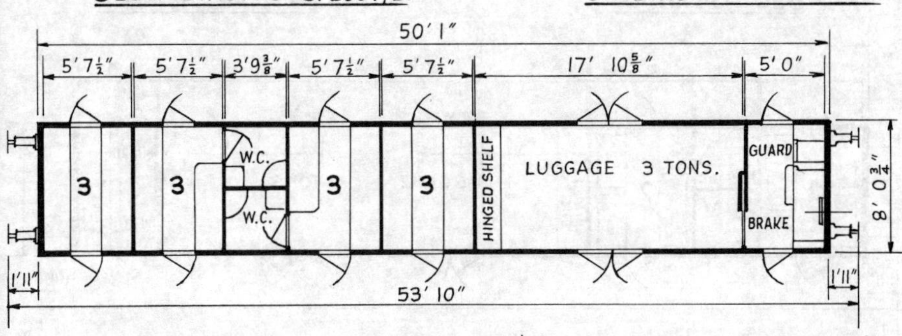

SEC Nos. 845-855 (EXTREME HEIGHT 12′9″). SR Nos. 3294-3304 (DIAG. 150).

" " 963-972 (EXTREME HEIGHT 12′ 6½″). " " 3305-3314 (DIAG. 149).

SEATING CAPACITY 36 T.

SEC DIAG. No. S.2304/2. **SR DIAG. No. 151.**

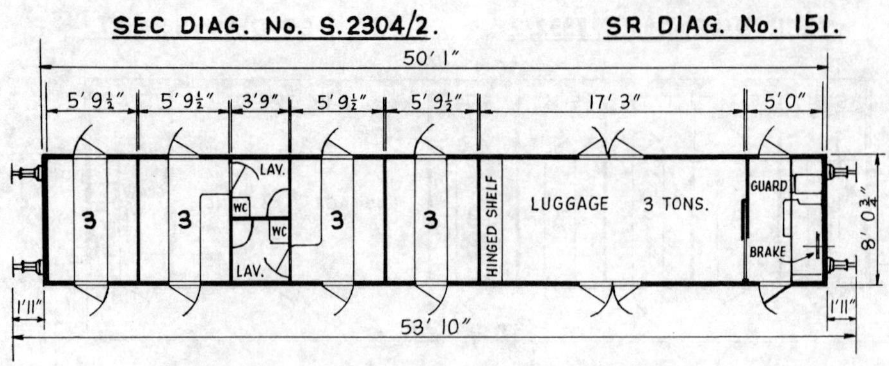

SEC No. 824. SR No. 3315.

SEATING CAPACITY 36 T.

SEC DIAG. No. S.2334/2. **SR DIAG. No. 152.**

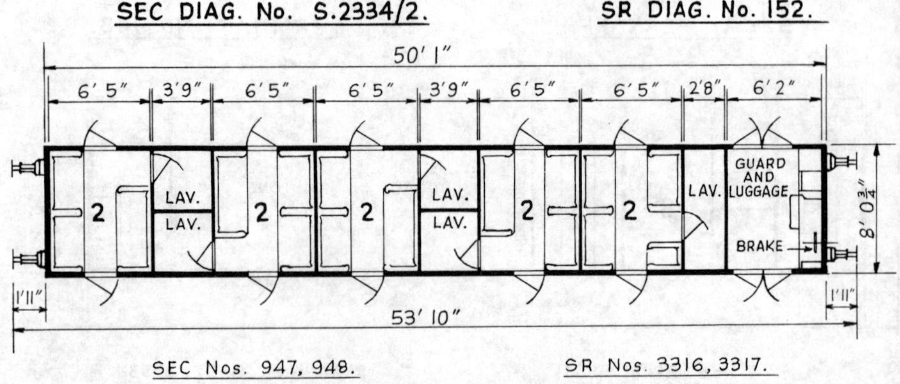

SEC Nos. 947, 948. SR Nos. 3316, 3317.

SEATING CAPACITY 35 S, LATER 40 T.

SECR PLAN D. **SR DIAG. No. 153.**

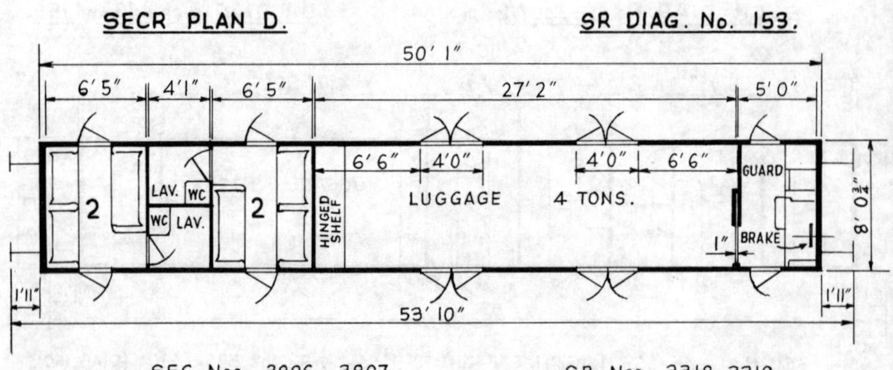

SEC Nos. 3806, 3807. SR Nos. 3318, 3319.

SEATING CAPACITY 14 S, LATER 16 T.

SECR DIAG. No. S.2316/1. SR DIAG. No. 154.

50′ 1″
6′5″ 3′9″ 6′5″ 27′ 5¾″ 5′0″
2 LAV. LAV. 2 HINGED SHELF LUGGAGE 4 TONS. GUARD BRAKE
8′ 0¾″
1′11″ 53′ 10″ 1′11″

SEC Nos. 951, 952. SR Nos. 3320, 3321.

SEATING CAPACITY 14S, LATER 16T.

SECR DIAG. No. S.2318/2. SR DIAG. No. 155.

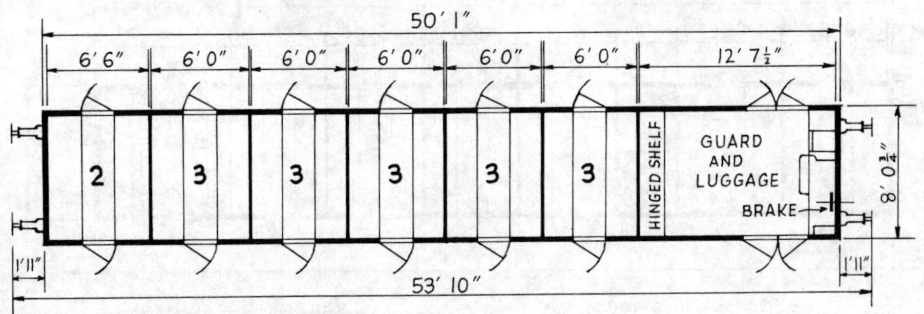

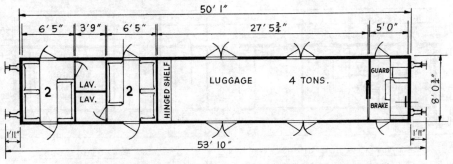

SEC Nos. 1049-1062, 1075-1078. SR Nos. 3322-3339.

SEATING CAPACITY 8S 50T, LATER 60T.

SECR DIAG. No. S.2318/1. SR DIAG. No. 156.

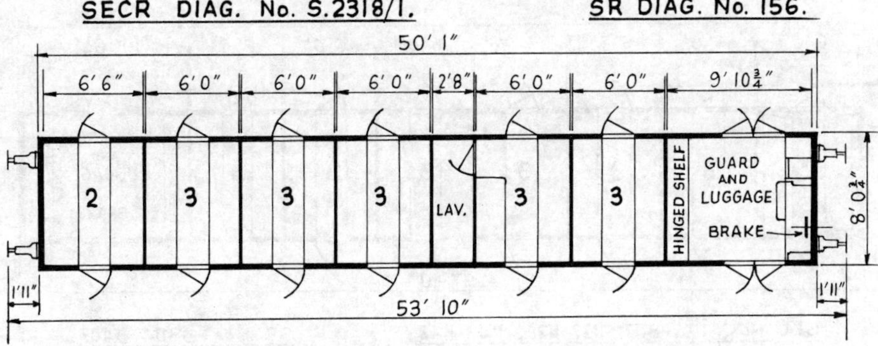

SEC Nos. 1035-1048, 1071-1074. SR Nos. 3340-3357.

SEATING CAPACITY 8S 48T, LATER 58T.

SECR DIAG. No. S.2322/1. SR DIAG. No. 158.

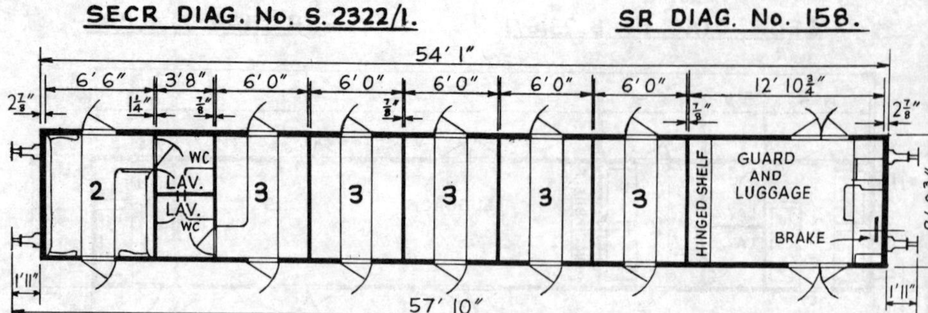

SEC Nos. 1096-1101, 1115-1121, 1136-1142. SR Nos. 3364-3383.

SEATING CAPACITY 7S 48T, LATER 56T.

SECR DIAG. No. S.2321/2. SR DIAG. No. 157.

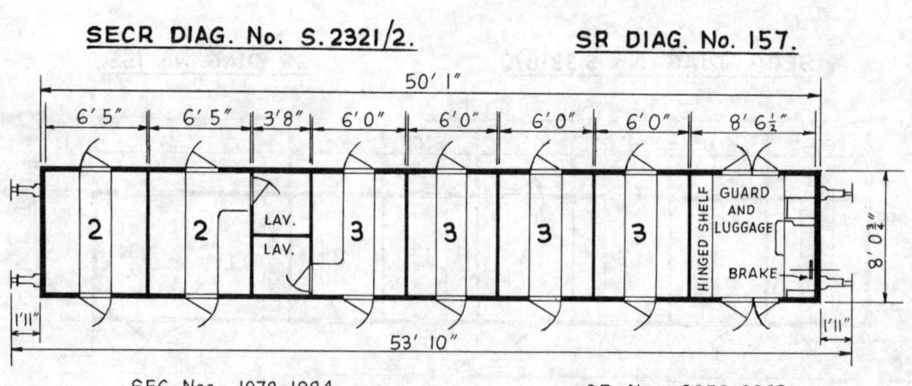

SEC Nos. 1079-1084. SR Nos. 3358-3363.

SEATING CAPACITY 15S 38T, LATER 56T.

SECR DIAG. No. S.2322/2. SR DIAG. No. 159.

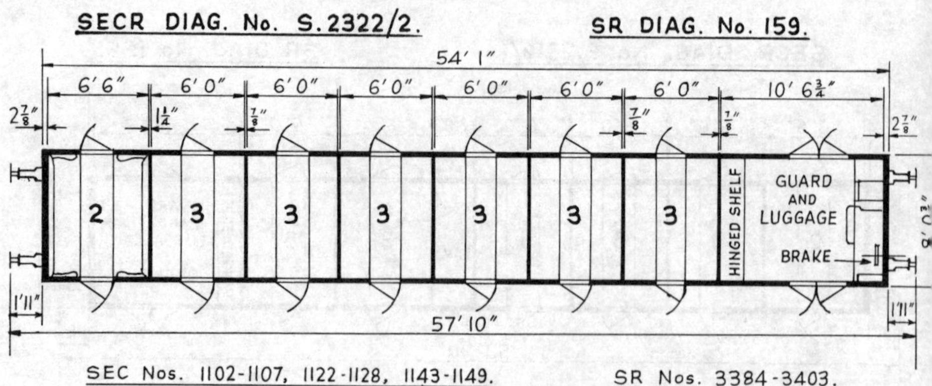

SEC Nos. 1102-1107, 1122-1128, 1143-1149. SR Nos. 3384-3403.

SEATING CAPACITY 8S 60T, LATER 70T.

SECR DIAG. No. S.2431. **SR DIAG. No. 160.**

60' 1"
6'0" 6'0" 6'0" 6'0" 6'0" 6'0" 6'0" 6'0" 11' 0¼"
3 3 3 3 3 3 3 3
HINGED SHELF
GUARD AND LUGGAGE
BRAKE
1'11¼"
63' 10½"

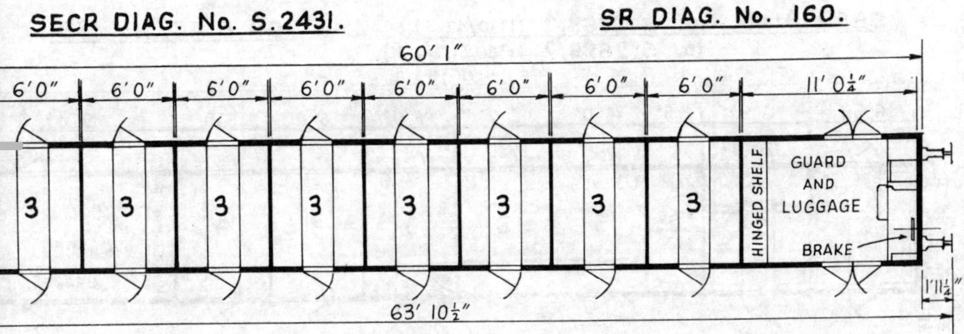

SEC Nos. 1164-70, 1179-1202, 1263-79, 1308-18, 1335-37.

SR Nos. 3404-3465.

3433 PULL & PUSH FITTED, 1942. (DIAG. 160A)

SEATING CAPACITY 80 T.

SECR DIAG. No. S.2773/1. **SR DIAG. No. 161.**

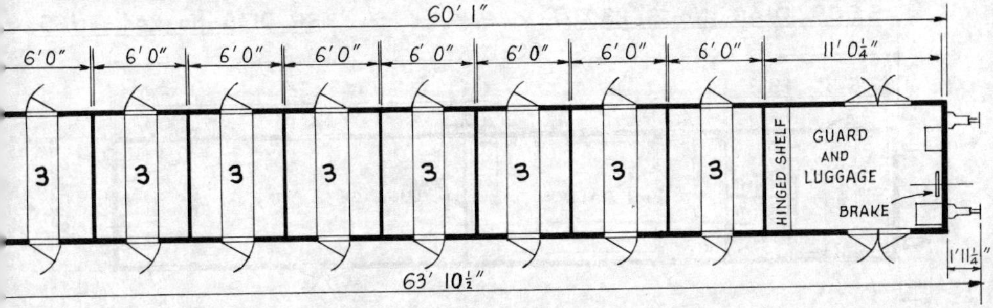

60' 1"
6'0" 6'0" 6'0" 6'0" 6'0" 6'0" 6'0" 6'0" 11' 0¼"
3 3 3 3 3 3 3 3
HINGED SHELF
GUARD AND LUGGAGE
BRAKE
1'11¼"
63' 10½"

SEC Nos. 1338-41, 1348, 1359, 1360, 1366-68.

SR Nos. 3466-3475.

3467 PULL & PUSH FITTED, 1947. (DIAG. 166)

SEATING CAPACITY 80 T.

SECR DIAG. No. S.2432. **SR DIAG. No. 162.**

60' 1"
6' 5½" 6' 5½" 3'8" 6'0" 6'0" 6'0" 6'0" 6'0" 12' 4½"
2 2
LAV.
LAV.
3 3 3 3 3
HINGED SHELF
GUARD AND LUGGAGE
BRAKE
1'11¼"
63' 10½"

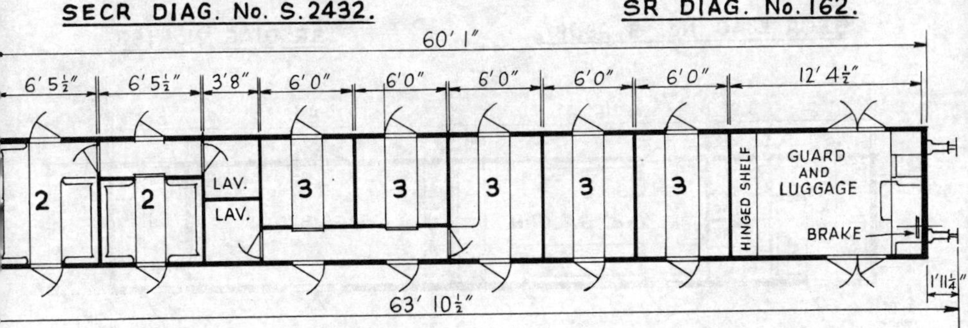

SEC Nos. 1157-63, 1171-74, 1223-52, 1287-1300, 1323-29.

SR Nos. 3476-3537.

3505 PULL & PUSH FITTED, 1942. (DIAG. 162A) LAVS. STRIPPED.

SEATING CAPACITY 13 S 40 T, LATER 54 T.

SECR DIAG. No. S.2763/2 (1330/42-4).
No. S.2689/2 (1350/61/2/9-71).

SR DIAG. No. 163.

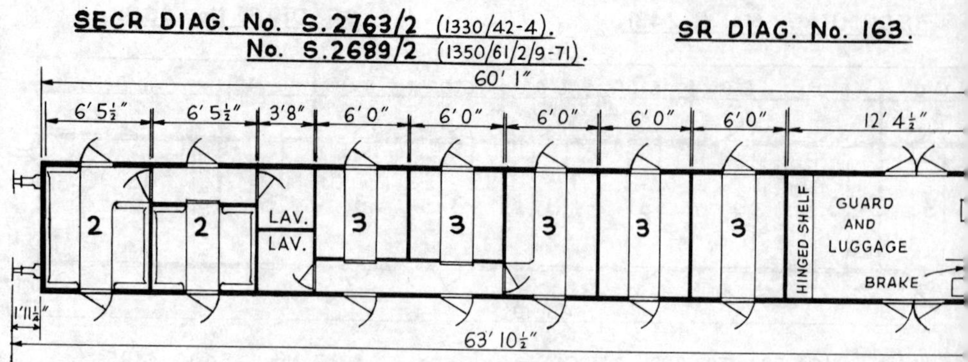

SEC Nos. 1330, 1342-44, 1350, 1361, 1362, 1369-71.

SR Nos. 3538-3547.

SEATING CAPACITY 13 S 40T, LATER 54T.

3539 ALTERED TO PULL & PUSH COMPO BKE 6410, 6/41. (DIAC
SEATING 13F 40T. LAVS. STR

SECR DIAG. No. S. 2307/1.

SR DIAG. No. 244 or 168.

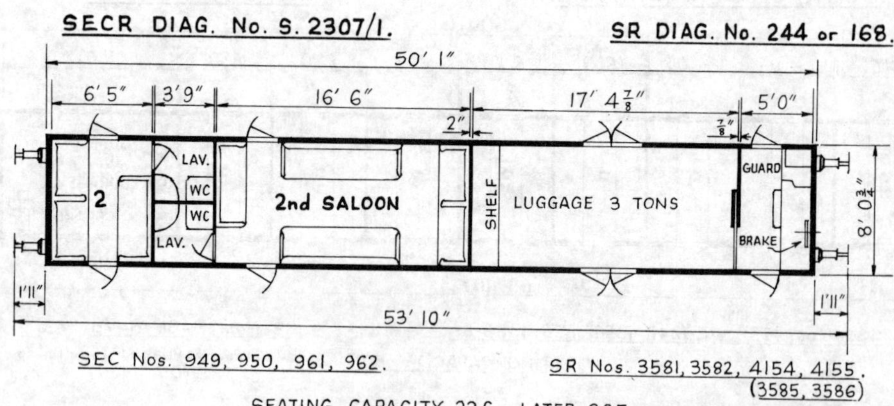

SEC Nos. 949, 950, 961, 962.

SR Nos. 3581, 3582, 4154, 4155.
(3585, 3586)

SEATING CAPACITY 22S, LATER 26T.

SECR DIAG. No. S. 2308/2.

SR DIAG. No. 168.

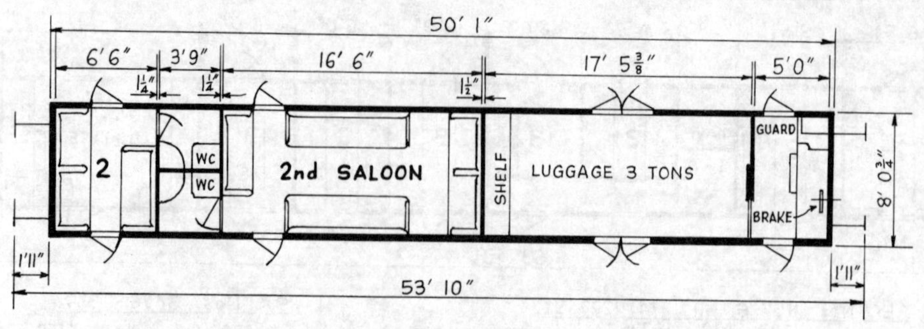

SECR No. 823.

SR No. 3580.

SEATING CAPACITY 22S, LATER 26T.

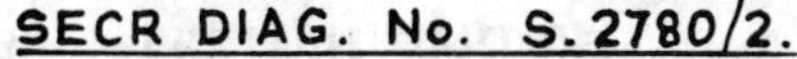

SECR DIAG. No. S. 2780/2. SR DIAG. No. 289.

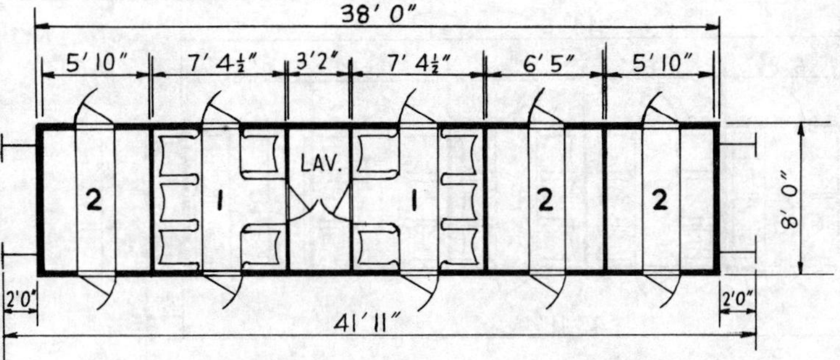

SE No. 1988. SR No. 5178.

SEATING CAPACITY 10F 24S, LATER 11F 30T.

SECR DIAG. No. S. 2790/1. SR DIAG. Nos. 290 and 291.

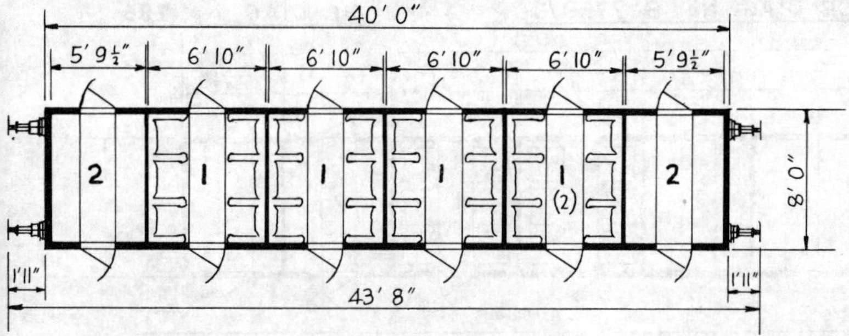

LCD Nos. 52 - 57. SEC Nos. 2699 - 2704. SR Nos. 5179 - 5183 (DIAG. 290)

SEATING CAPACITY 24F 16S, LATER 24F 20T (DIAG. 290)
2704 ALTERED TO 18F 24S, 1914; LATER 18F 30T (DIAG. 291 - 5184)

SECR DIAG. Nos. S. 2794/2 (COMPO.), S. 2794/3 (FIRST). SR DIAG. Nos. 292 or 486.

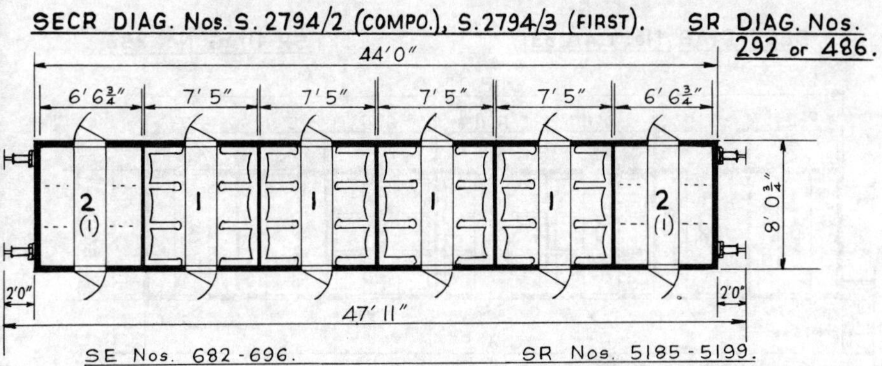

SE Nos. 682 - 696. SR Nos. 5185 - 5199.

SEC Nos. 2347 - 2396.

SEATING CAPACITY 24F 16S, LATER 24F 20T.

THIRTY ALTERED TO ALL-FIRST, SEATING 36 F. 1902/3.

SR Nos. 7255-7, 5200, 7258, 5201, 7259, 5202, 7260/1, 5203, 7262, 5204, 7263, 5205, 7264/5, 5206, 7266, 5207/8, 7267, 5209, 7268/9, 5210, 7270, 5211/2, 7271, 5213, 7272-5, 5214, 7276-9, 5215, 7280/1, 5216, 7282, 5217/8, 7283, 5219, 7284.

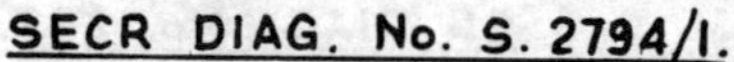

SR DIAG. Nos. 293 or 487.

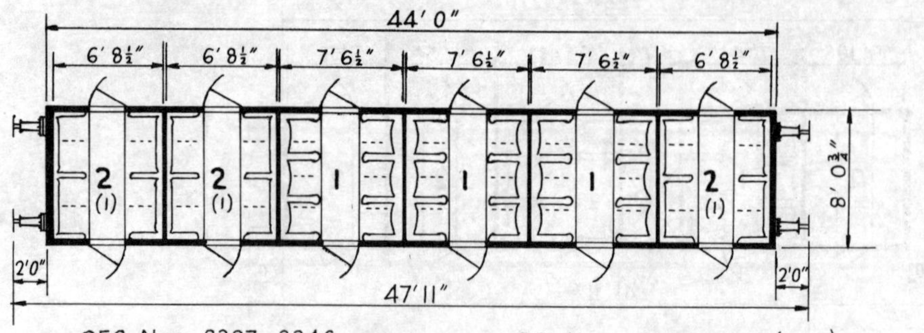

SEC Nos. 2327-2346.
SEC Nos. 3428-3452.
SR Nos. 7285-7304 (D.487). ------ SEATING ON DIAG. 487.
SR Nos. 5220-5244 (D.293).
SEATING CAPACITY 18F 24S, LATER 18F 30T OR 48F.

SECR DIAG. No. S. 2793/3.

SR DIAG. No. 295.

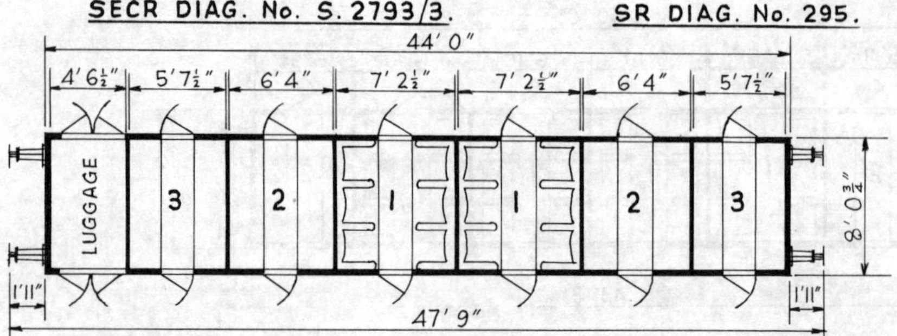

SE Nos. 84, 85.
SR Nos. 5255, 5256.
SEATING CAPACITY 12F 16S 20T, LATER 12F 40T.

SECR DIAG. No. C4/2831.

SR DIAG. No. 296.

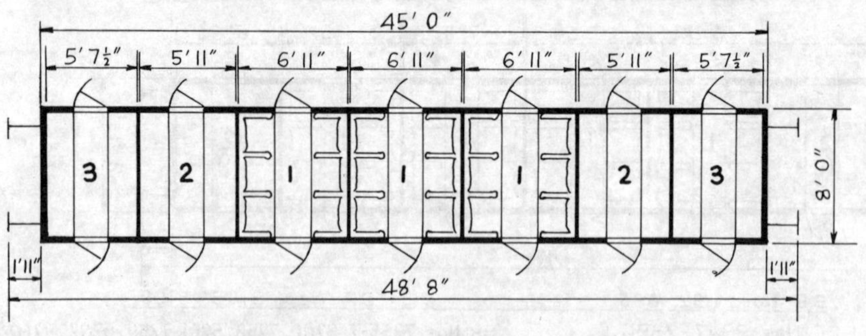

LCD Nos. 1162-1167. SEC Nos. 2729-2734. SR Nos. 5257-5262.
SEATING CAPACITY 18F 16S 20T, LATER 18F 40T.

SECR DIAG. No. C3/2831. **SR DIAG. No. 297.**

No. S.2790/2 (2711/13). **No. 421.**

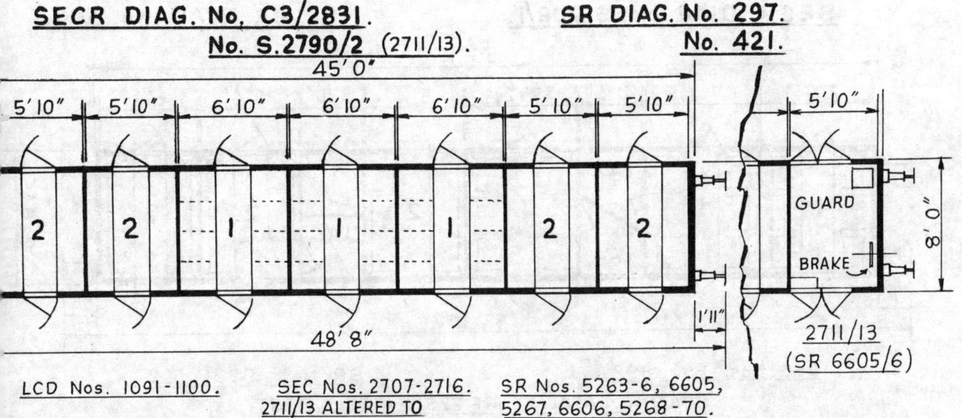

LCD Nos. 1091-1100. SEC Nos. 2707-2716. SR Nos. 5263-6, 6605, 5267, 6606, 5268-70.

2711/13 ALTERED TO TRAILER COMPO BKES.

SEATING CAPACITY 18F 32S, LATER 24F 40T. 2711/13: 18F 24S, LATER 18F 30T (DIAG. 421).

SECR DIAG. No. S. 2335/2. **SR DIAG. No. 298.**

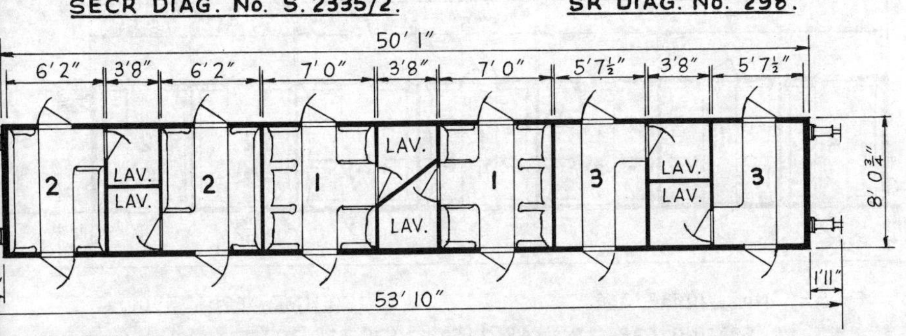

SEC Nos. 667-681. SR Nos. 5271-5285.

SEATING CAPACITY 10F 14S 16T, LATER 10F 32T.

SECR PLAN CC. **SR DIAG. No. 299.**

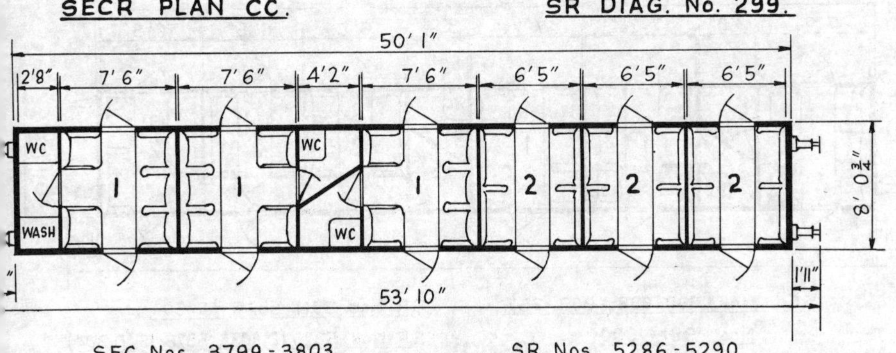

SEC Nos. 3799-3803. SR Nos. 5286-5290.

SEATING CAPACITY 15F 24S, LATER 15F 30T.

SECR DIAG. No. S.206/1. SR DIAG. No. 300.

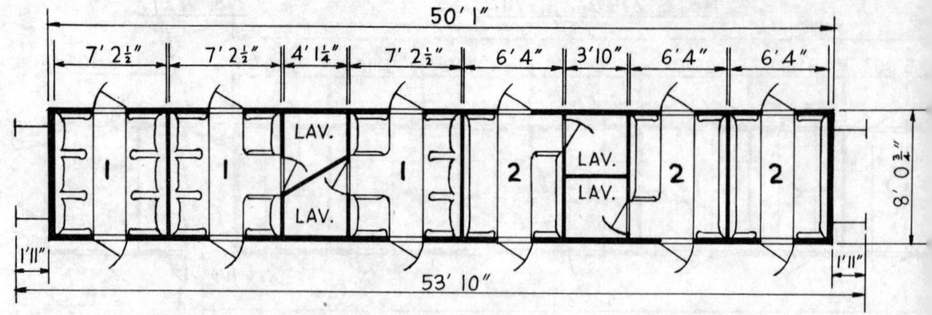

SEC Nos. 892-898. SR Nos. 5291-5297.

SEATING CAPACITY 16F 22S, LATER 16F 26T.

SECR DIAG. No. S.2321/1. SR DIAG. No. 301.

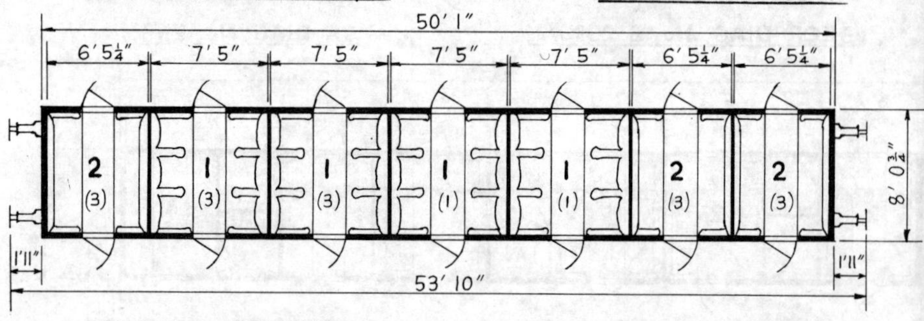

SEC Nos. 1063-1066. SR Nos. 5298-5301.

SEATING CAPACITY 24F 24S, LATER 24F 30T. 5301 SEATING ALTERED 1942. 16F 50T.

SECR DIAG. S.2309. SR DIAG. Nos. 303 and 304.

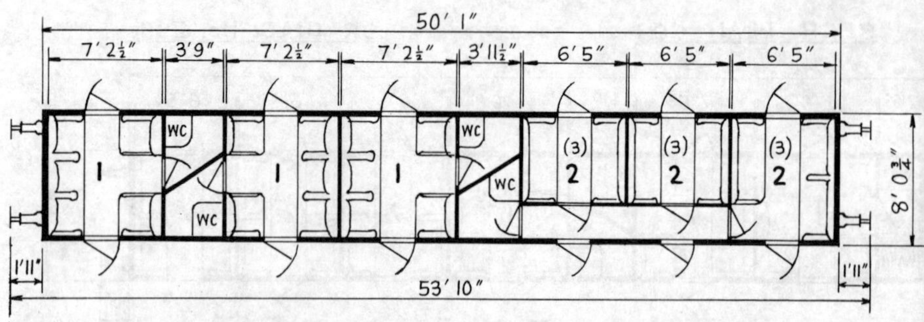

SEC Nos. 930-938, 953-957.
Nos. 981-1000.

SEATING CAPACITY 15F 19S (DIAG. 303).
LATER 15F 20T (DIAG. 304).

SR Nos. 5311-5324 (D. 303).
SR Nos. 5325 (D.303), 5326-28 (D.304), 5329-34 (D.303), 5335-39 (D.304), 5340/1 (D.303), 5342 (D.304), 5343 (D.303), 5344 (D.304).

Built as SE&C No. 1082 by Metropolitan Amalgamated in 1910, this Lavatory Third Brake became SR No. 3361 and is here shown at Margate on 22nd August, 1950, formed in Set 666. It displays the 'Ashford Gothic' style of mouldings. *D. Cullum*

54 ft Lavatory Third Brake No. 3366, built in 1910, formed in Set 913 and rebuilt as Third No. 2446 for the Isle of Wight in 1948. Seen at Maze Hill, 2nd July, 1947. *D. Cullum*

Trio set No. 626 at New Cross Gate. Nearest is 60 ft Third Brake No. 3463 (SE&C No. 1335 of 1914), which was withdrawn in 1957. *Lens of Sutton*

Plain-panelled 60 ft Third Brake No. 3474, as converted to a push-and-pull driving trailer to replace the original Third Brake in Set 31. The coach was built in 1921 as SE&C No. 1367. Here shown at Wareham on the Swanage branch train, 14th July, 1960. *H.C. Casserley*

SEC 60 ft Lavatory Compo Brake No. 1247, built by Cravens in 1913, became SR Third Brake No. 3511 in trio Set 606. The picture was taken after withdrawal from service of the set in April 1956. *Lens of Sutton*

Plain-panelled 60 ft Lavatory Third Brake No. 3543 after withdrawal in August 1958. It was built as Compo Brake No. 1361 in 1920 and was in trio Set No. 634 in Southern days. It had L-section truss rods supporting the underframe. *Lens of Sutton*

In 1950 a 'new' push-and-pull set, No. 662, was made from two coaches of trio Set No. 637. The lavatories were stripped and a driver's compartment was built at the end of Third Brake No. 3546. The set was painted in lined-out red livery. Here shown, ex-Works, at Eastleigh, 29th July, 1950. *A.E. West*

Third Brake No. 3560 in articulated Set No. 513 at Kensington Olympia on the peak-only Clapham Junction service, 17th March, 1956. The coach was built originally as steamcar No. 3 in 1906, and in 1924 was articulated to Third No. 975 (formerly steamcar No. 8) for working on the Sheppey Light Railway.

R.M. Casserley

Third Brake No. 3583 in push-and-pull Set No. 482 at Dunton Green, 19th April, 1952. Built as steamcar No. 6 by Metro in 1906, it was altered to Trailer Third Brake No. 4109 in 1924, but became No. 3583 in 1930. The vehicle had inward-opening doors, bars across droplights, and L-section truss rods bolted to the outside of the solebar.

J.H. Aston

SE&C Second Brake with saloon No. 962, built for a boat train by Metropolitan Amalgamated in 1908. Here shown as Southern No. 3586 in Set 906 at Tonbridge, 29th May, 1950. The luggage van doors have droplights instead of louvres, and the lavatory window is also a droplight. *D. Cullum*

45 ft Third Brake No. 3590 in Set 346 at Tattenham Corner on 13th April, 1948. It was downgraded from First Brake No. 7739, which had been built at Ashford in 1904 as SE&C No. 254. It has a round-topped observatory. *D. Cullum*

54 ft Third Brake No. 4138, as rebuilt for Isle of Wight service from 7-compartment Third Brake No. 3394 in 1948. The SE&C number was 1126, and the coach was built at Ashford in 1911. Seen at Newport (IOW), 28th June, 1949, the destination board reads: 'Ryde Pier–Havenstreet–Newport–Cowes'. *A.E. West*

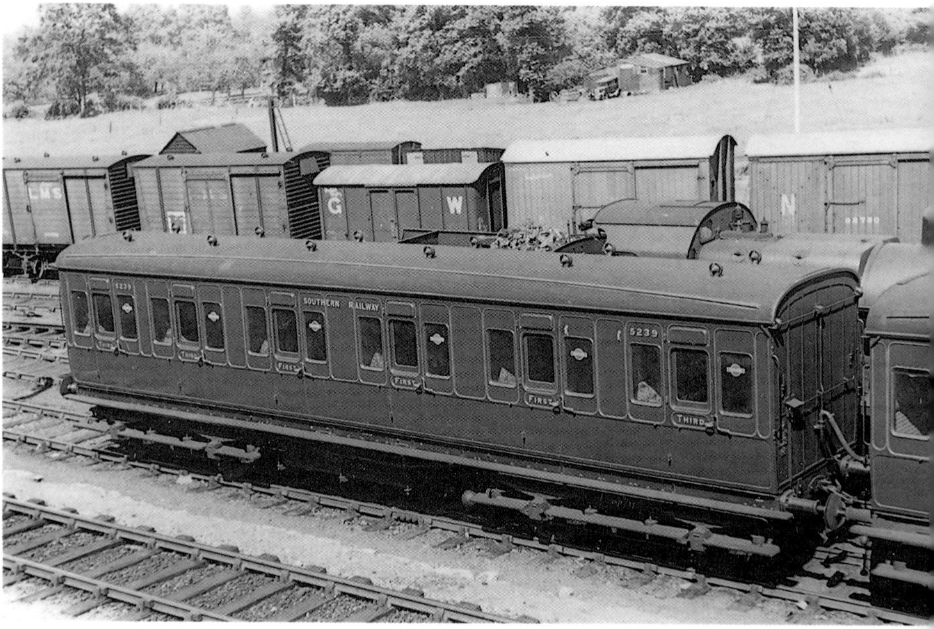

44 ft Composite No. 5239 at Templecombe, 23rd July, 1937. It was built by Cravens in 1901 as SE&C No. 3447, and is here shown painted in sage green with full lining-out in yellow and black. *H.C. Casserley*

44 ft non-gangwayed corridor Composite No. 5252, in Set 695, at Tattenham Corner on 13th April, 1948. It was built as SE&C No. 235 by the Ashbury Railway Carriage & Iron Co. in 1901. Half-compartment (coupé) to the left of the lavatory. *D. Cullum*

50 ft Composite No. 5279, with six lavatories, in Set 912 at Maze Hill, 1st December, 1946. It was built at Ashford in 1906 as Tri-Composite No. 675. The two former 2nd-class compartments are at the left-hand end. The coach was withdrawn in 1951.
D. Cullum

50 ft Composite No. 5286 in Set 666 at Margate, 22nd August, 1950. Five of this type were built for boat trains by Metro in 1905; this example was originally No. 3799. All three first-class compartments had lavatory access, but none of the second-class did.
D. Cullum

SE&C No. 1063 was a 50 ft Composite built at Ashford in 1910. It became SR No. 5298 in 1928. Here shown formed in push-and-pull Set 715 at Tunbridge Wells West, 7th July, 1948.
D. Cullum

50 ft Composite No. 5314 at Maze Hill. Built by Metro in 1907 for a boat train, it was originally SE&C No. 933. All compartments had lavatory access, the second-class by means of a short corridor. Withdrawn in May 1956. *Lens of Sutton*

51 ft Composite with first-class saloon, No. 5354, in Set 913 at Tonbridge, 29th May, 1950. As SE&C No. 3797, it was built for a boat train in 1905 by Metropolitan Amalgamated; there were only two examples of this design. This one was withdrawn in 1952. *D. Cullum*

51 ft Composite No. 5379, built as Tri-Composite No. 814 at Ashford in 1909. No. 5379 is shown here at Lenham formed in Set 334, which included vehicles of LSW origin. The former second-class compartments are at the left-hand end of the carriage. Picture taken on 7th May, 1949. *D. Cullum*

54 ft Lavatory Composite No. 5420, the centre coach of Set 531, at Margate on 20th August, 1950. Metropolitan Amalgamated built this coach for the SE&C in 1909 and its original number was 1026. Rounded upper mouldings and square lower mouldings were a feature. *D. Cullum*

60 ft Lavatory Composite No. 5449 (SE&C No. 1208, built by Metro in 1913) at Guildford, 14th September, 1953. This type had two large windows each side of the first-class saloon. Coach is in malachite green, numbers are displayed in SR position with prefix and suffix letters, and third-class compartments are not identified by figure '3' on the doors. *H.C. Casserley*

This was the prototype plain-panelled Composite, SE&C No. 1319 of 1914, here shown at London Bridge running as SR No. 5494 in Set 625. The first-class saloon had only one large window each side. No. 5494, which had a body length of 60 ft, was withdrawn in 1958. *Lens of Sutton*

Ex-LC&D 40 ft composite of 1887 as running in the Isle of Wight and modified with steel panels. Its original number was 57; it became SE&C No. 2704, then SR No. 5184, being renumbered 6359 for IOW service. Photographed at Ryde Pier Head, 29th March, 1948. *J.L. Smith*

A 'Chatham' coach in the Isle of Wight still with its full complement of mouldings: No. 6397 at Ryde St Johns Road on 18th April, 1949. Built by Birmingham RCW Co. in 1897 for the LC&D, it was originally numbered 1093, then SE&C No. 2709 and SR No. 5265. Body length was 45 ft. The air-brake pipe, which can be seen at the end of the coach, may be distinguished from a vacuum-brake pipe by virtue of its being much slimmer. *J.L. Smith*

Another Birmingham-built LC&D 45 ft Composite, but this one has had its appearance altered by sheet steel covering the bodywork. No. 1099 was built in 1897, became SE&C No. 2715 and SR No. 5269, and was sent to the Isle of Wight in 1934 as No. 6361. Ryde St Johns, 29th March, 1948. *J.H. Aston*

54 ft Composite No. 6365, modified for Isle of Wight service from Lavatory Composite No. 5404 (SE&C No. 1111 of 1911) in 1947. The lavatory and adjacent compartments have been knocked into one saloon, and all the body moulding has been covered with steel sheets. Seen at Ryde St Johns Road, 26th June, 1950. *D. Cullum*

'etail of brake-end and round-topped bservatory of Brake Composite No. 6615 ;E&C No. 156 of 1905). Note that the set umber had to be applied off-centre because f the presence of a vertical moulding on ie centre-line. Also visible are the vertical rake rodding connected to the guard's hand-rake wheel by bevel gears, and the orizontal rodding that operated the light-witches. Tunbridge Wells West, 1st inuary, 1949. *D. Cullum*

6 ft Brake Composite No. 6617 (Set 525) in down train hauled by class 'E1' 4–4–0 No. 507 near Bromley South on 6th August, 938. The coach was built at Ashford in 1905 s No. 158, a Tri-Composite Brake, the make-p being: Guard, 2, 2, 1, 1, 3, 3. *H.C. Casserley*

Corridor Brake Composite No. 6624 (compartment side) at Lenham in Set 334, 7th May, 1949. It was built as Tri-Composite Brake No. 915 in 1907 (Guard, 3,3,2,1,1).
D. Cullum

Corridor Brake Composite No. 6625 (corridor side) at Herne Hill in Set 334, 26th December, 1947. Built by the SE&C in 1907 as No. 916, it had the same makeup as No. 915.
D. Cullum

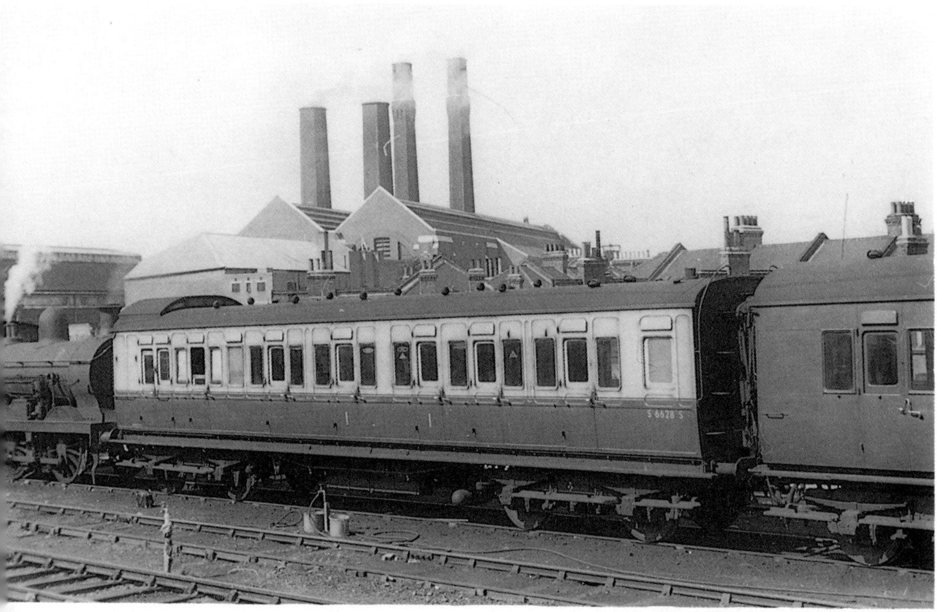

Corridor Brake Composite No. 6628 (compartment side) at Maze Hill in Set 389, 8th September, 1956. It is painted in BR crimson and cream livery and the dividing line pays no heed to the position of the mouldings. SE&C No. 911 was built at Ashford in 1907 and its original makeup was Guard, 3,3,1,1,2,2. Set 389 is here shown about to leave Maze Hill on empty stock to Charing Cross for the 2.25 pm to Hastings.

H.C. Casserley

Corridor Brake Composite No. 6634 (corridor side) at Ashford, 30th June, 1951, formed with a Corridor Third in 2-set 331. No. 6634 was built in 1907 as No. 905, with the makeup Guard, 3,3,3,3,1,1. The corridor connection is of the British Standard type, and has been fitted with adaptors so that it may be coupled to Pullman-gangwayed stock. No. 6634 was withdrawn in 1953. *A.E. West*

Corridor Brake Composite No. 6636 (corridor side) in 2-set No. 333. As No. 908 the coach was built at Ashford in 1907, and was of the same type as No. 905. Withdrawn in 1951. *Lens of Sutton*

Former Slip Brake Composite No. 976, built at Ashford in 1909. It was renumbered 6637 by the SR in 1928 and is here shown formed in Set 920 at Maze Hill on 19th September, 1956. *H.C. Casserley*

SECR DIAG. No. S.2308/1. SR DIAG. No. 305.

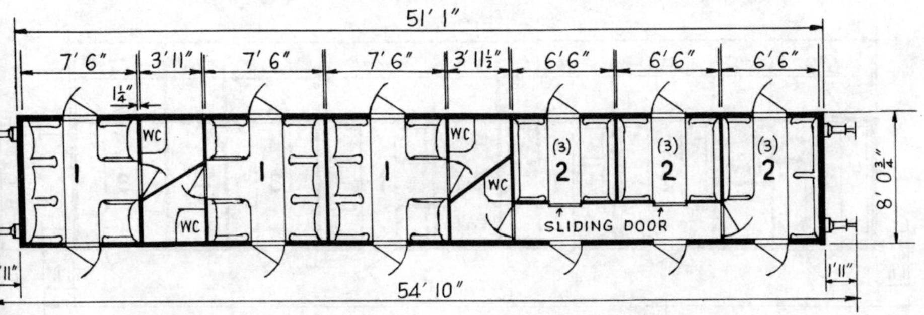

SEC Nos. 815-820. SR Nos. 5345-5350.

SEATING CAPACITY 15F 19S, LATER 15F 20T.

SECR DIAG. No. S.205. SR DIAG. No. 306.

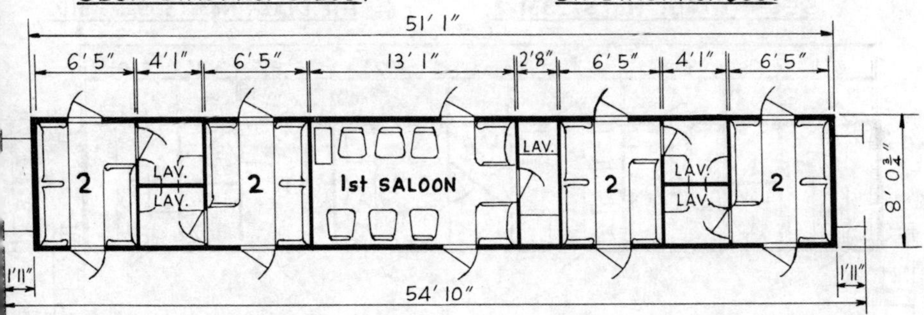

SEC Nos. 889-891. SR Nos. 5351-5353.

SEATING CAPACITY 10F 28S (SALOON ORIGINALLY WITH TWO SETTEES SEATING 4 EACH), LATER 8F 28S, LATER 8F 32T.)

SECR PLAN B. SR DIAG. No. 307.

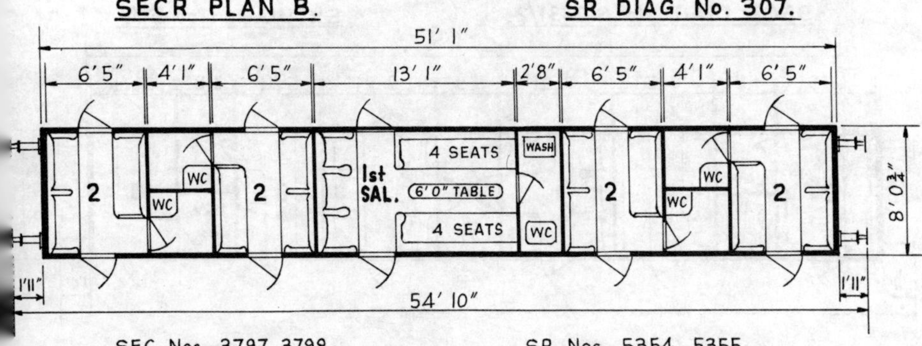

SEC Nos. 3797, 3798. SR Nos. 5354, 5355.

SEATING CAPACITY 11F 28S, LATER 9F 28S (SETTEES REPLACED BY SIX INDIVIDUAL ARMCHAIRS), LATER 9F 32T.

SECR DIAG. No. S.2335/1. **SR DIAG. No. 308.**

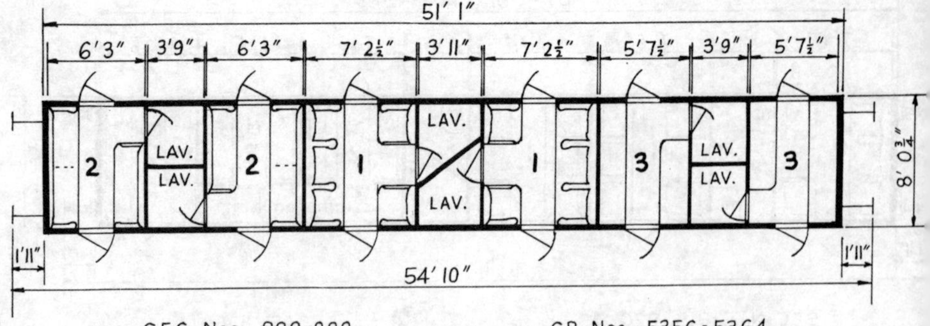

SEC Nos. 880-888. SR Nos. 5356-5364.

SEATING CAPACITY 10F 14S 16T, LATER 10F 32T.

SECR DIAG. No. S.2331/2. **SR DIAG. Nos. 309 and 310.**

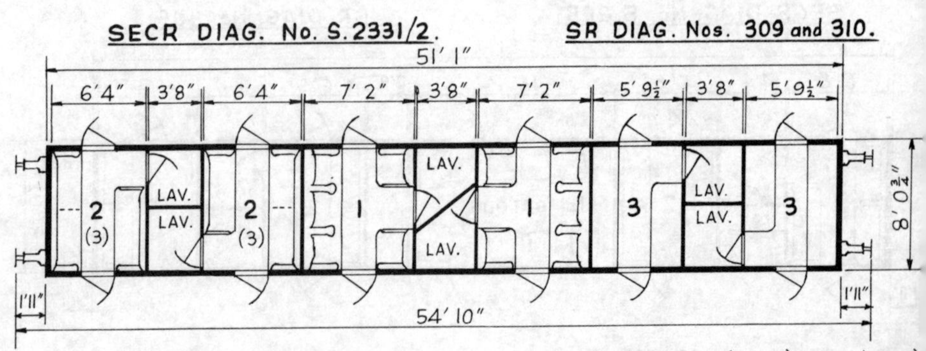

SEC Nos. 800-814. SR Nos. 5365-72 (D.310), 5373 (D.309)
5374 (D.310), 5375 (D.309),
5376 (D.310), 5377-79 (D.309).

SEATING CAPACITY 10F 14S 16T (DIAG. 309).
LATER 10F 32T (DIAG. 310).

SECR DIAG. No. S.2331/2. **SR DIAG. No. 311.**

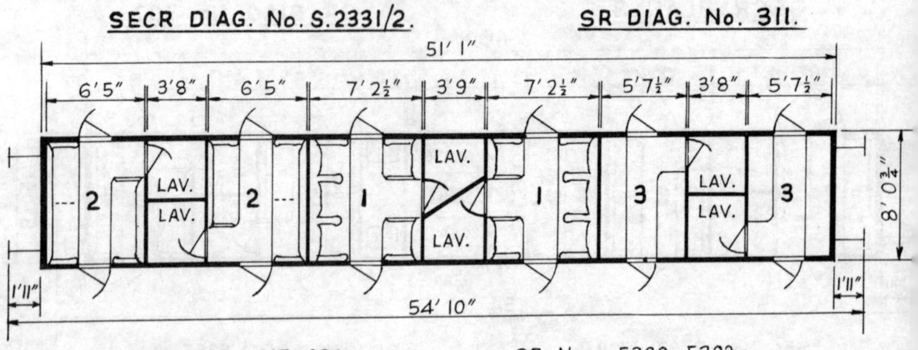

SEC Nos. 917-929. SR Nos. 5380-5392.

SEATING CAPACITY 10F 14S 16T, LATER 10F 32T.

SECR PLAN EE. **SR DIAG. No. 312.**

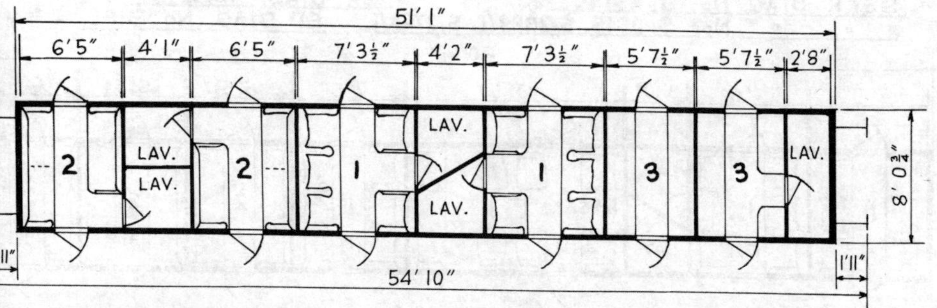

SEC Nos. 3804, 3805. SR Nos. 5393, 5394.

SEATING CAPACITY 10F 14S 18T, LATER 10F 34T.

SECR DIAG. No. S. 2311/2. **SR DIAG. No. 313.**

SEC Nos. 1090-1095, 1108-1114, 1129-1135. SR Nos. 5395-5414.

SEATING CAPACITY 22F 24S, LATER 22F 30T.

SECR DIAG. No. S. 2311/1. **SR DIAG. No. 314.**

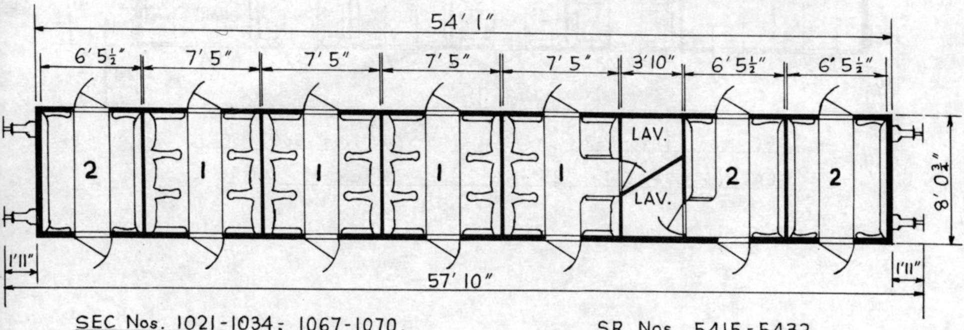

SEC Nos. 1021-1034; 1067-1070. SR Nos. 5415-5432.

SEATING CAPACITY 23F 23S, LATER 23F 28T.

SECR DIAG. No. S. 2314. SR DIAG. No. 315.
" " Nos. S. 2315, S. 2689/1, S. 2763/1. SR DIAG. No. 316.

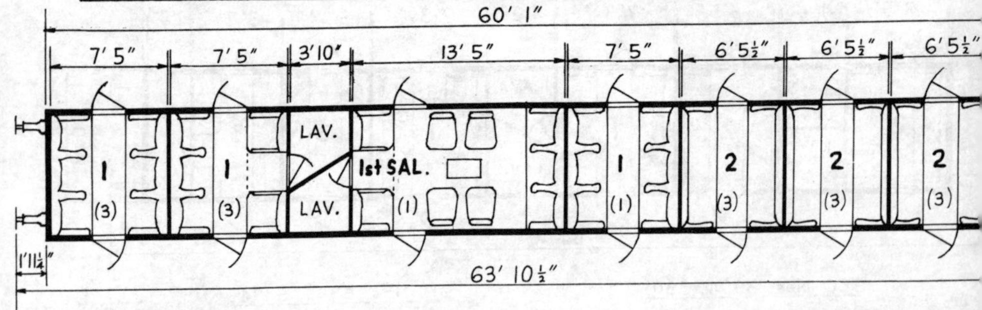

SEC Nos. 1150-56, 1175-78, 1203-10, 1253-56, 1280-86. (S.2314).
SEC Nos. 1211-22, 1257-62, 1301-07, 1320-22, 1331-33. (S.2315).
SEC Nos. 1319, 1334, 1345-47. (S.2689/1).
SEC Nos. 1349, 1357/58, 1363-65. (S. 2763/1).

SEATING CAPACITY 26 F 24 S, LATER 26 F 30 T.

SR Nos. 5433-51, 5459-62, 5452-58 (D.3
SR Nos. 5463-5493 (D. 316).
SR Nos. 5494-5498 (D. 316).
SR Nos. 5499-5504 (D. 316).

5473 PULL & PUSH FITTED, 1942. LAVS
STRIPPED, SEATS ALTERED 20 F 50 T (D.316

SECR DIAG. No. S. 2303/2. SR DIAG. No. 422.

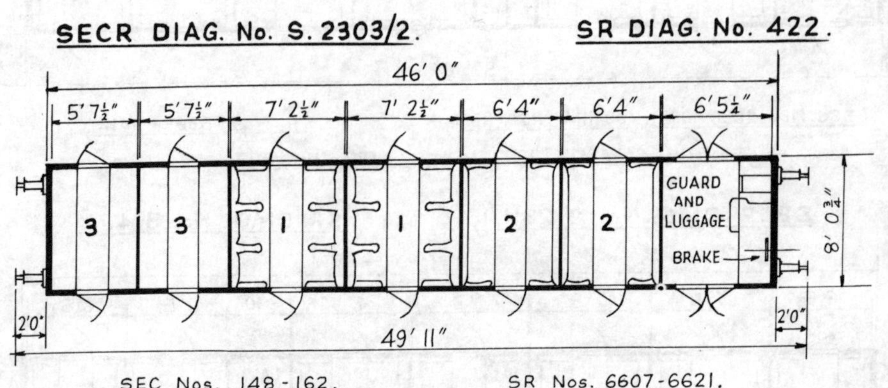

SEC Nos. 148-162. SR Nos. 6607-6621.

SEATING CAPACITY 12 F 16 S 20 T, LATER 12 F 40 T.

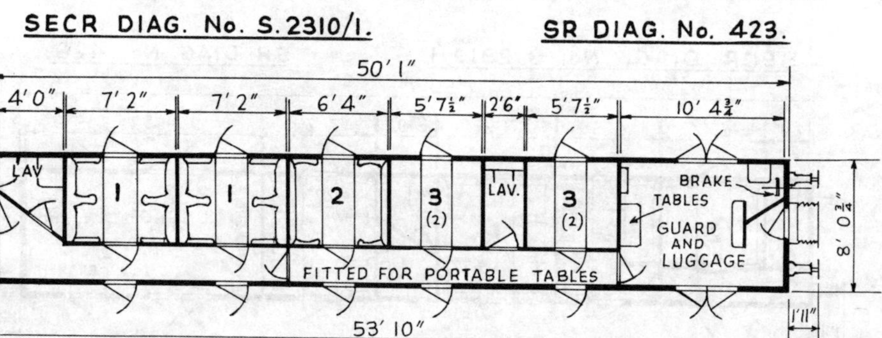

SEC Nos. 913-916. SR Nos. 6622-6625.

SEATING CAPACITY 8F 6S 12T, 8F 18S (1921-4), 8F 18T.

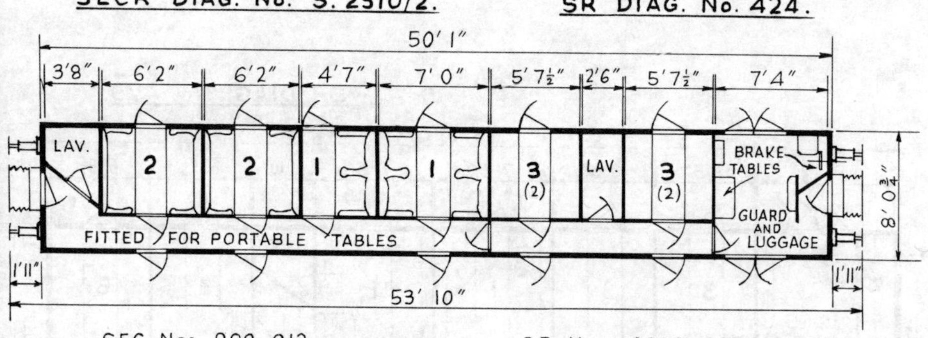

SEC Nos. 909-912 SR Nos. 6626-6629.

SEATING CAPACITY 6F 12S 12T, 6F 24S (1921-4), 6F 24T.

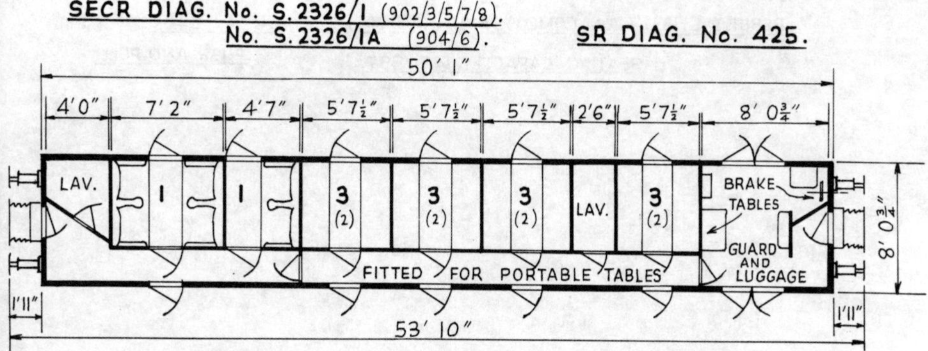

SEC Nos. 902-908. SR Nos. 6632/33, 6630, 6634, 6631, 6635/36.

SEATING CAPACITY 6F 24T. 904/6 TO 6F 24S (1911),
902/3/5/7/8 TO 6F 24S (1921). ALL TO 6F 24T (1924).

SECR DIAG. No. S.2319/1. SR DIAG. No. 426.

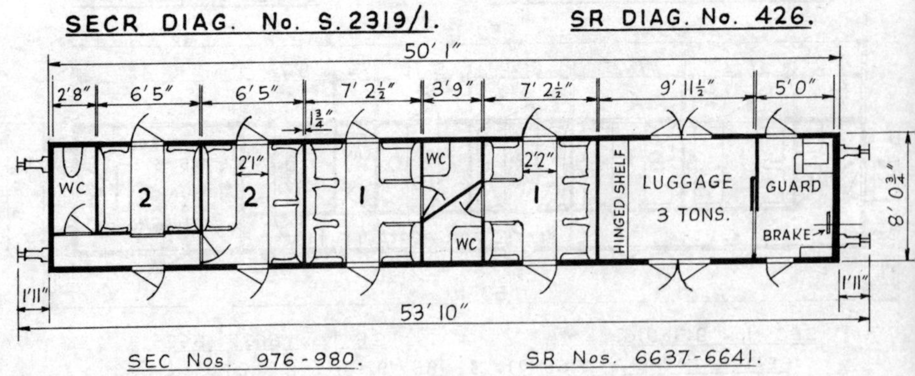

SEC Nos. 976-980. SR Nos. 6637-6641.

SEATING CAPACITY 10F 13S, LATER 10F 14T.

SR DIAG. No. 429.

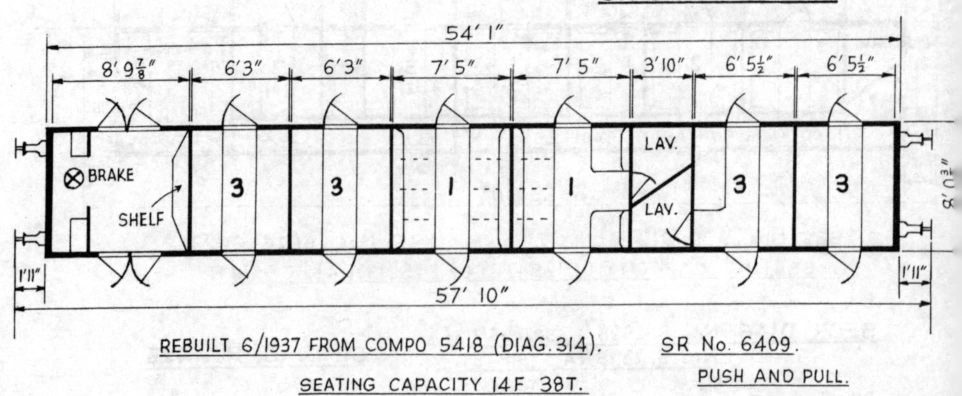

REBUILT 6/1937 FROM COMPO 5418 (DIAG. 314). SR No. 6409.

SEATING CAPACITY 14F 38T. PUSH AND PULL.

SECR DIAG. No. 1236. SR DIAG. No. 482.

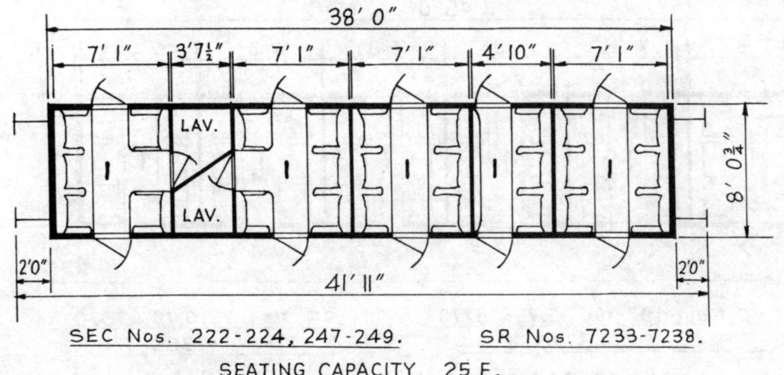

SEC Nos. 222-224, 247-249. SR Nos. 7233-7238.

SEATING CAPACITY 25 F.

SECR DIAG. No. S.2686/3. SR DIAG. No. 483.

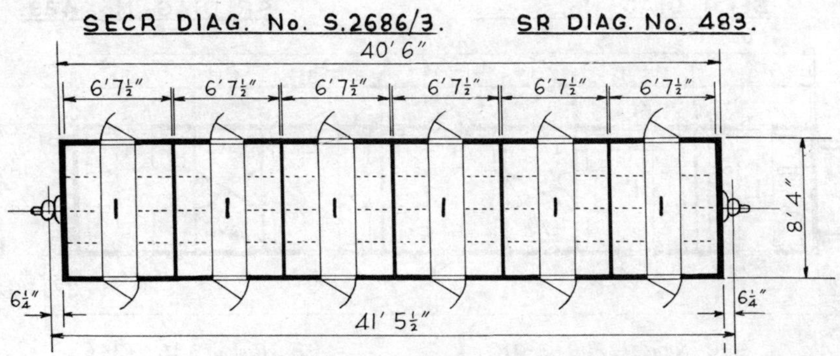

SE Nos. 1954-1957, 1984, 1985. SR Nos. 7239, 7240, 7242, 7243.

SEATING CAPACITY 48 F.

SECR DIAG. No. C1/2831. SR DIAG. No. 484.

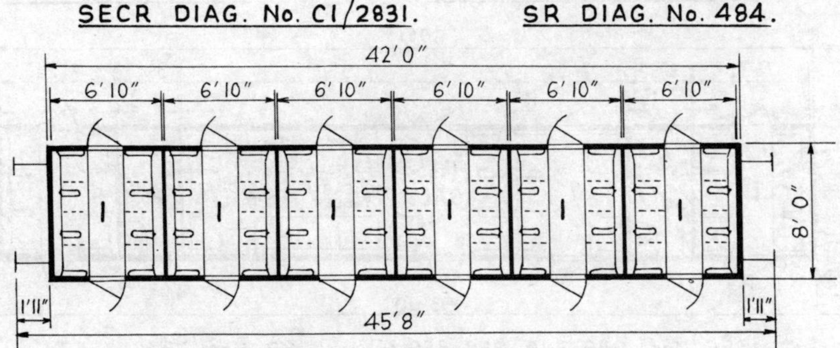

LCD Nos. 1168-1177. SEC Nos. 2631-2640. SR Nos. 7244-7253.

SEATING CAPACITY 36F, LATER 48F.

SECR DIAG. No. S.2794/4. SR DIAG. No. 488.

45' 0"
7' 3½"
7' 3½"
7' 3½"
7' 3½"
7' 3½"
7' 3½"
1
1
1
1
1
1
8' 0¾"
2'0"
2'0"
48' 11"

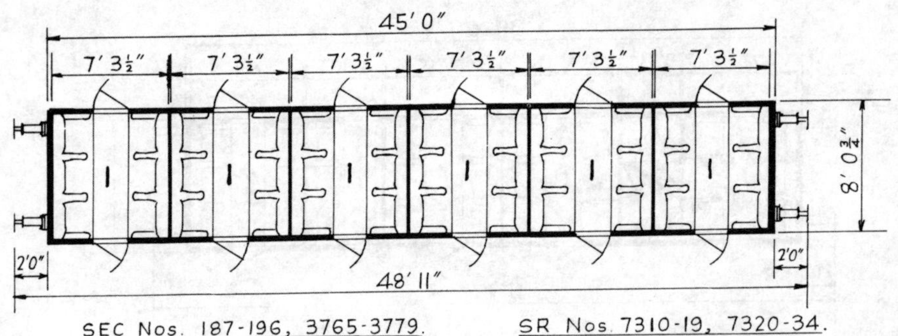

SEC Nos. 187-196, 3765-3779. SR Nos. 7310-19, 7320-34.
" " 3780-3784. " 7305-7309.

SEATING CAPACITY 36F (3780-84: 18F 24S).

SECR DIAG. No. SR DIAG. No. 489.

46' 0"
7' 3½"
7' 3½"
4' 1"
7' 3½"
7' 3½"
4' 1"
7' 3½"
1
1
LAV.
LAV.
1
1
LAV.
LAV.
1
8' 0¾"
2'0"
2'0"
49' 11"

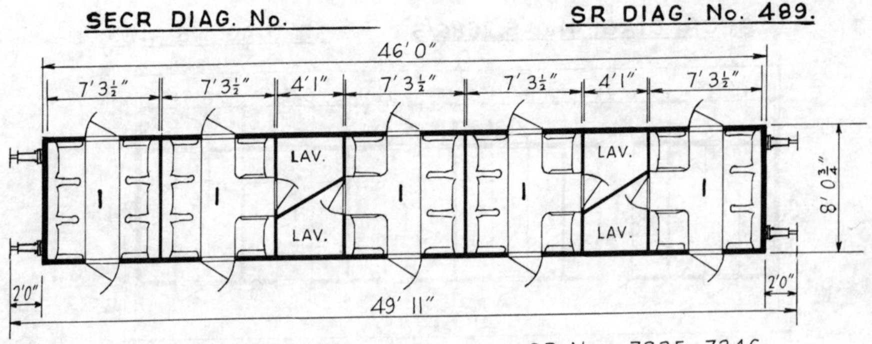

SEC Nos. 3500-3511. SR Nos. 7335-7346.

SEATING CAPACITY 26F.

SECR DIAG. No. S.2336. SR DIAG. No. 490.

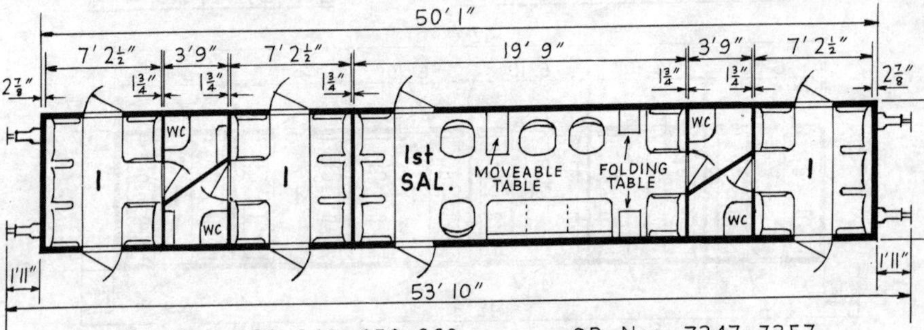

50' 1"
7' 2½"
3' 9"
7' 2½"
19' 9"
3' 9"
7' 2½"
2⅞"
1¾"
1¾"
1¾"
1¾"
1¾"
2⅞"
WC
1
WC
1
1st
SAL.
MOVEABLE
TABLE
FOLDING
TABLE
WC
WC
1
8' 0¾"
1'11"
1'11"
53' 10"

SEC Nos. 939-946, 958-960. SR Nos. 7347-7357.

SEATING CAPACITY 27 F.

SECR DIAG. No. S.206/2. SR DIAG. No. 491.

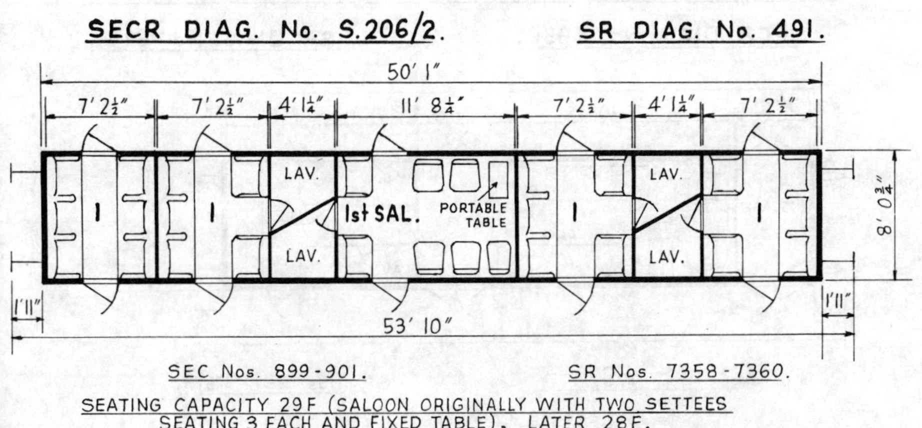

SEC Nos. 899-901. SR Nos. 7358-7360.

SEATING CAPACITY 29F (SALOON ORIGINALLY WITH TWO SETTEES SEATING 3 EACH AND FIXED TABLE), LATER 28F.

SECR PLAN AA. SR DIAG. No. 492. No. 549.

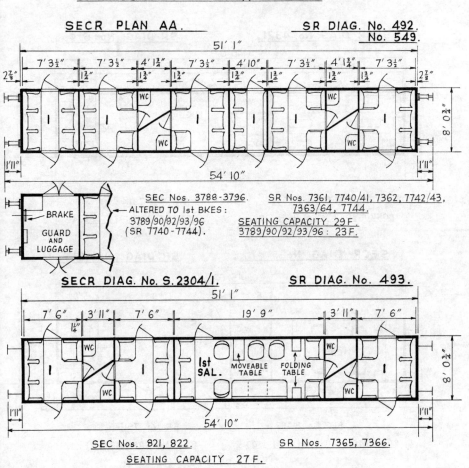

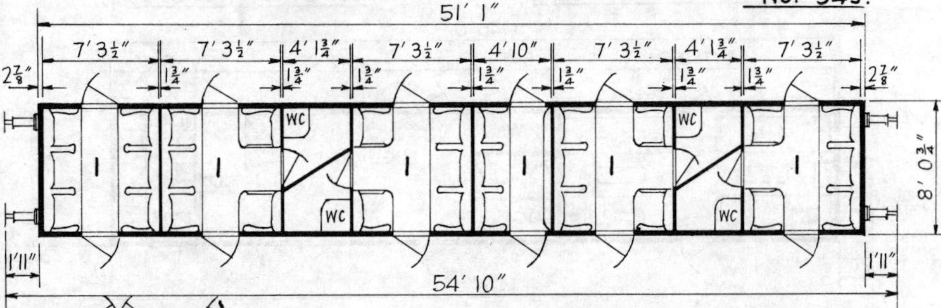

51′ 1″
7′ 3½″ 7′ 3½″ 4′ 1¾″ 7′ 3½″ 4′ 10″ 7′ 3½″ 4′ 1¾″ 7′ 3½″
2⅞″ 1¾″ 1¾″ 1¾″ 1¾″ 1¾″ 1¾″ 1¾″ 2⅞″
WC WC WC WC
8′ 0¾″
1′ 11″ 54′ 10″ 1′ 11″

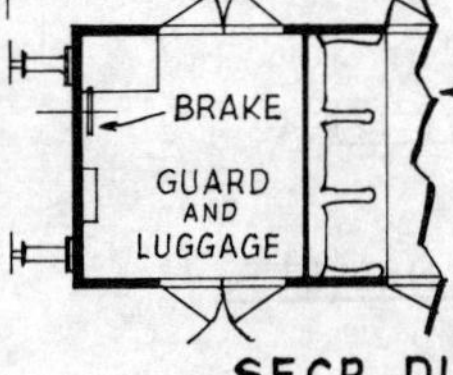

BRAKE
GUARD AND LUGGAGE

ALTERED TO 1st BKES: 3789/90/92/93/96 (SR 7740-7744).

SEC Nos. 3788-3796. SR Nos. 7361, 7740/41, 7362, 7742/43, 7363/64, 7744.

SEATING CAPACITY 29F.
3789/90/92/93/96: 23F.

SECR DIAG. No. S.2304/1. SR DIAG. No. 493.

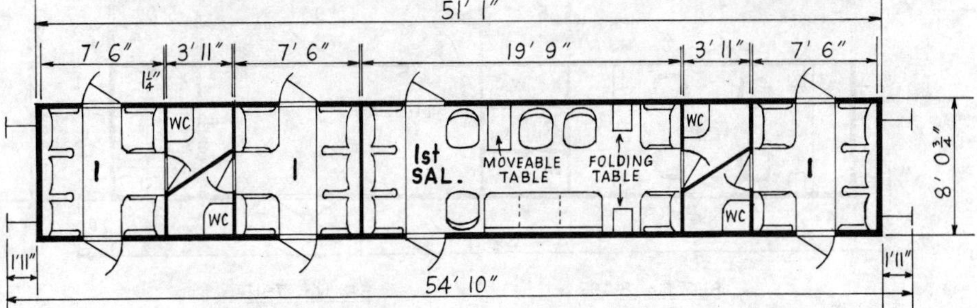

51′ 1″
7′ 6″ 3′ 11″ 7′ 6″ 19′ 9″ 3′ 11″ 7′ 6″
1¼″
WC WC 1st SAL. MOVEABLE TABLE FOLDING TABLE WC WC
8′ 0¾″
1′ 11″ 54′ 10″ 1′ 11″

SEC Nos. 821, 822. SR Nos. 7365, 7366.

SEATING CAPACITY 27F.

SECR DIAG. No. 4330. SR DIAG. No. 613.

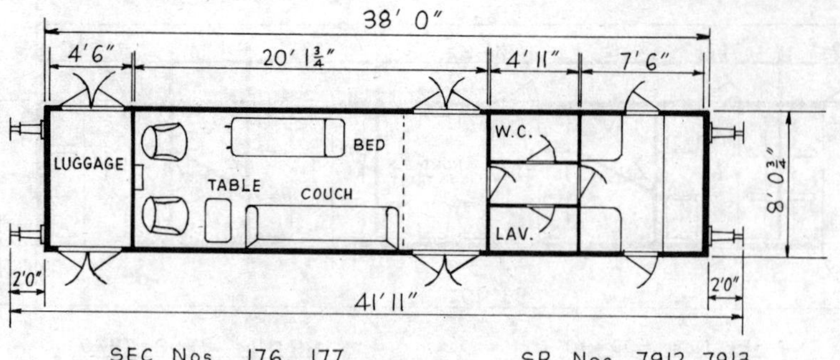

SEC Nos. 176, 177. SR Nos. 7912, 7913.

SEATING CAPACITY 12F.

SECR DIAG. No. 4321. SR DIAG. No. 614.

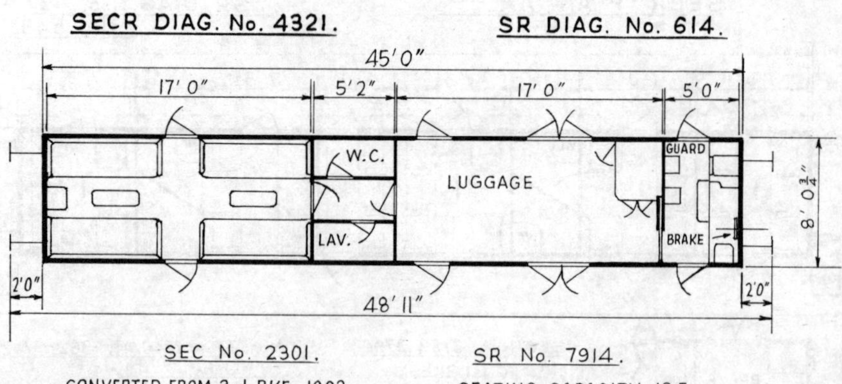

SEC No. 2301. SR No. 7914.

CONVERTED FROM 3rd BKE, 1902. SEATING CAPACITY 12F.

SECR DIAG. No. SR DIAG. No. 615.

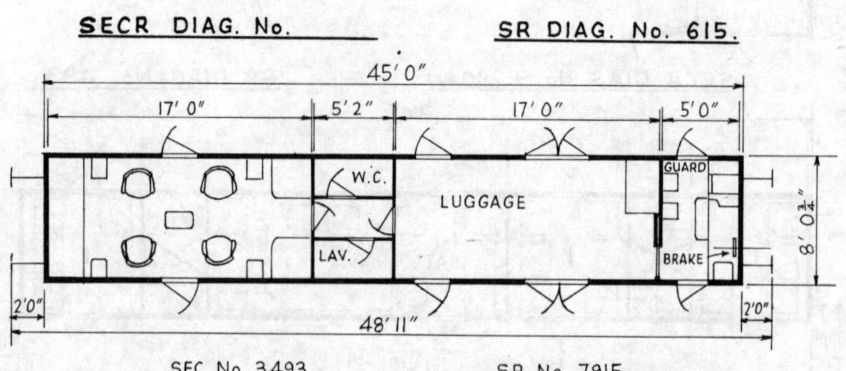

SEC No. 3493. SR No. 7915.

CONVERTED FROM 3rd BKE, 1902. SEATING CAPACITY 9F.

SECR DIAG. No. SR DIAG. No. 616.

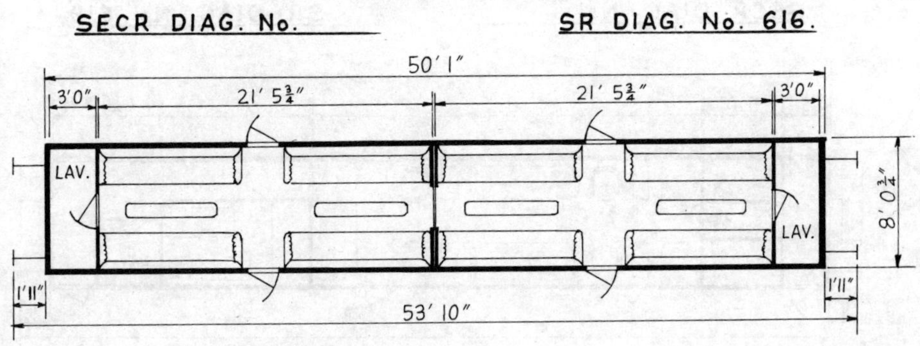

SEC Nos. 3512, 3513. SR Nos. 7916, 7917.

SEATING CAPACITY 32F.

SECR DIAG. No. SR DIAG. No. 617.

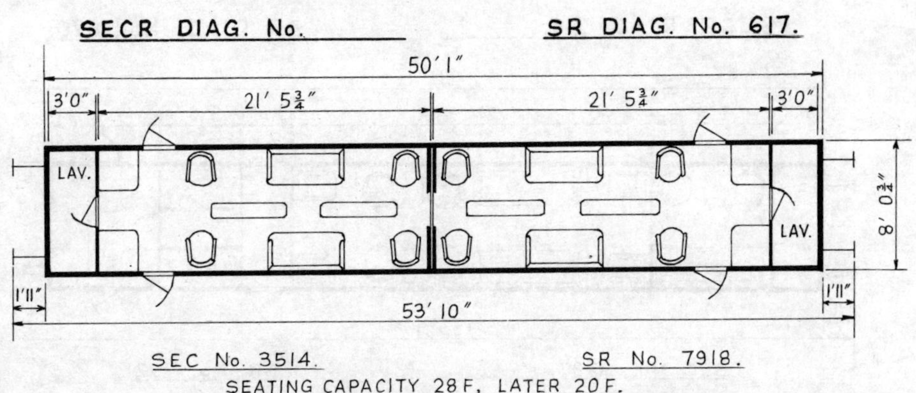

SEC No. 3514. SR No. 7918.

SEATING CAPACITY 28F, LATER 20F.

SECR DIAG. No. SR DIAG. No. 618.

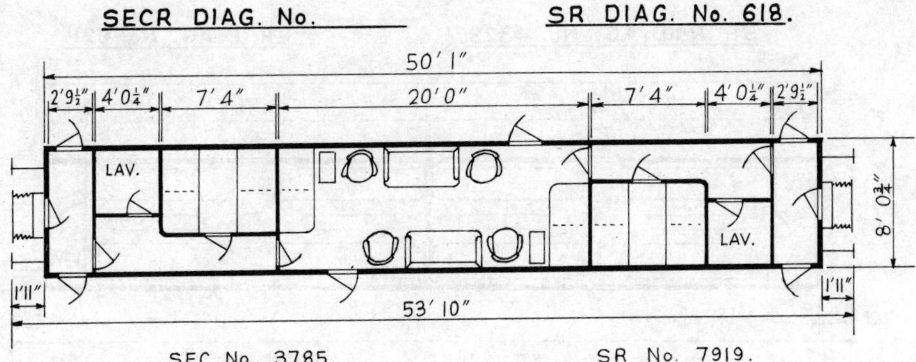

SEC No. 3785. SR No. 7919.

SEATING CAPACITY 22F, LATER 20F.

SECR DIAG. No. SR DIAG. No. 619.

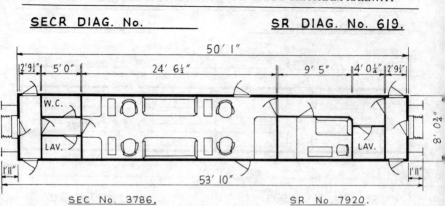

SEC No. 3786. SR No. 7920.

SEATING CAPACITY 21F, LATER 19F.

SECR DIAG. No. SR DIAG. No. 620.

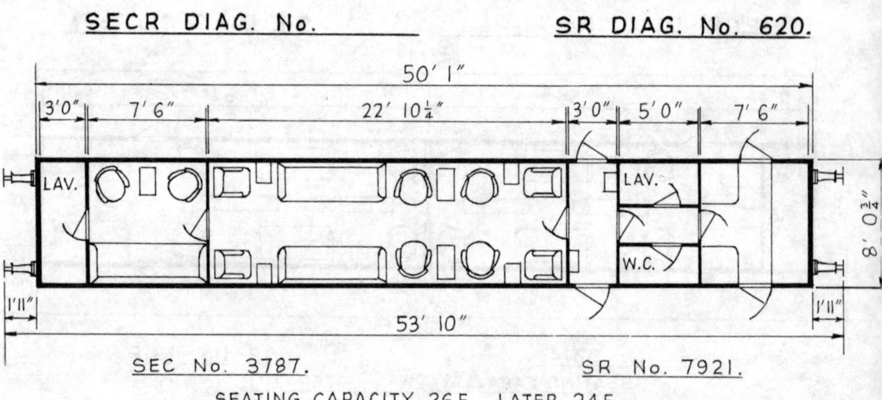

SEC No. 3787. SR No. 7921.

SEATING CAPACITY 26F, LATER 24F

SECR DIAG. No. 4329. SR DIAG. No. 621.

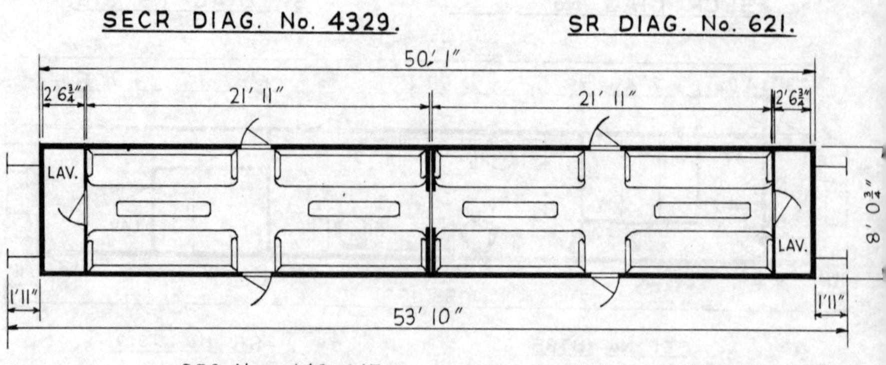

SEC Nos. 140-147. SR Nos. 7922-7929.

SEATING CAPACITY 48S, LATER 48T.

SECR DIAG. No. 4318. SR DIAG. No. 622.

50′ 1¾″
4′ 6¼″ 8′ 0″ 17′ 11¼″ 8′ 0″ 5′ 0″ 4′ 10½″
LAV. LAV.
8′ 0¾″
11″ 53′ 10″ 1′ 11″

SEC No. 1 ROYAL SALOON. SR No. 7930.

SEATING CAPACITY 20.

SECR DIAG. No. 4319. SR DIAG. No. 623.

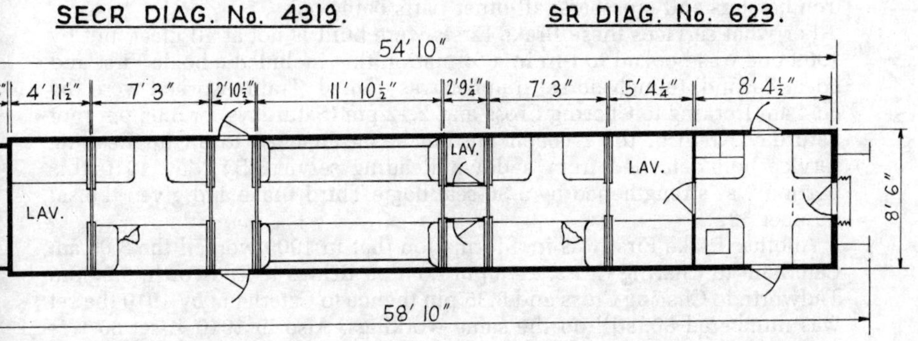

SEC No. 1 ROYAL SALOON (CONTINENTAL). SR No. NOT CARRIED.

SEATING CAPACITY 12, PLUS 2 IN SLEEPING COMPT.

SECR DIAG. No. SR DIAG. No. 625.

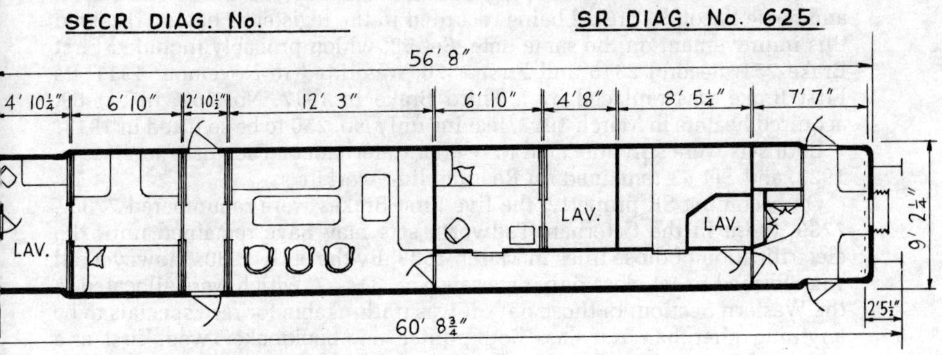

SEC No. 2 ROYAL SALOON (CONTINENTAL).

PROPERTY OF THE ROYALTY.

FIRST BRAKES

Nos. 250–254 (SR Nos. 7735–7739)

Body length: 45 ft. Bogie centres: 29 ft 11 in.
Height, rail to roof: 11 ft 9½ in.
Height, rail to top of observatory: 12 ft 9½ in.
Compartments: 5. Seats: 30.

A new departure for the SE&CR was this type of brake coach with first class accommodation only. Only five were built, all completed at Ashford in December 1904; they had teak body framing with mahogany panels and mouldings, and quarter lights bedded on felt. Each of the five compartments was lit by a Duplex electric lamp, with a single lamp in the guard's compartment, all controlled by a main switch at the coach end and an additional switch in the guard's compartment for the single lamp there. The raised roof observatory, with the then standard round top (5 ft 6 in. radius), prevented the carriages from working over the Metropolitan Railway via Snow Hill and the Widened Lines. The underframe consisted of angle soles with channel iron bolsters and crossbars, all other parts being oak.

For what services these Brake Firsts were built is not at all clear, but by 1909 one was booked to run in a formation that included a bogie First and bogie Second, though no set number was quoted. Trains worked were the 8.54 am Dorking to Charing Cross and 2.12 pm (Saturdays) or 5.06 pm (not Saturdays) return, the 3-coach portion being attached to an up Reading service and detached from a down Reading service. By May 1910 this portion was strengthened by a 36-seat bogie Third Brake and given the set number 53.

Another Brake First was in a formation that in 1909 worked the 8.06 am Caterham to Charing Cross, 2.48 pm London Bridge to Tadworth, 5.27 pm Tadworth to Charing Cross and 6.35 pm thence to Caterham; by 1910 the set was numbered 80, still on the same workings. Also in 1910, 4-set 85 was formed and included two Brake Firsts, working in the 9.15 am Tattenham Corner to Charing Cross and 5.55 pm London Bridge to Tadworth (not Saturdays) or 3.47 pm Charing Cross to Tadworth (Saturdays).

Set 85 was steam-heated in August 1911, Nos. 253/4, 6-wheel Third 2206 and bogie Second 2318 all being recorded in the register as having received this improvement on the same date. Set 53, which probably included First Brake 251, Second 2315 and First 2376, was fitted in November 1911. Its First Brake was replaced by a Third Brake in 1917. No. 252, in Set 80, acquired heaters in March 1912, leaving only No. 250 to be so fitted in 1913.

Both sets were still allocated to regular Caterham or Tadworth services in 1922, and Set 53 remained on Reading line workings.

On becoming SR property, the five First Brakes were renumbered 7735–7739; those in the Caterham/Tadworth sets may have remained until the electrification of those lines in March 1928. By the early 1930s, however, all were formed in 1st-class-only race sets Nos. 344–7, which were allocated to the Western Section. In those days it was unthinkable for race specials to be anything other than first class; both punters and bookmakers went 'first' as a matter of course. The fact that the sets could not be used for any purpose other than race traffic did not worry the Southern unduly.

No. 7739 was downgraded to third class in May 1940 and renumbered 3590, and a month later No. 7737 received the same treatment and took the number 3591. Both remained in their respective sets. The various renumberings, set numbers and withdrawal dates are summarised below.

SEC	*SR*	*Re-No.*	*3rd Bke*	*Set Nos.*	*Wdn*
250	7735	5/28		346,760	10/43
251	7736	1/24		347	7/39
252	7737	1/27	3591	344	/47
253	7738	11/26		345	9/41
254	7739	1/28	3590	346	9/55

Set 760, to which No. 7735 was transferred about 1940, was a special Paddock Wood–Maidstone West 3-set which, although it had many changes of formation in its long life, always retained the same set number.

Set 344 was berthed at Brentford in 1938, at Teddington in 1941, was third-class only by 1945 and allocated to Salisbury–Bulford workmen's services. Set 346 was berthed at Brentford during the late 1930s, was transferred to Christchurch–Wareham workmen's services about 1940, was at Eatleigh in 1945 and Hamworthy Junction the following year. From 1950 it was the regular booked set on the Margate–Canterbury miners' train, which worked three return trips every 24 hours at shift times. It was formed of six coaches from 1951 and five from 1954 until its withdrawal from service.

From first-class season ticket holders between Tadworth and London to coalminers between Chislet and Ramsgate – No. 3590 certainly conveyed a variety of passengers in its time.

FIRST SALOON LAVATORY

Nos. 3785–3787 (SR Nos. 7919–7921)

Body length: 50 ft 1 in. Bogie centres: 33 ft 6 in.
Height, rail to top of roof: 11 ft 9 in.

These three saloon carriages were ordered from the Metropolitan Amalgamated Railway Carriage & Wagon Co. in August 1904. They were constructed at the works of the former Lancaster RC&W Co. and delivered to the SE&CR in February 1905. Although all three were different they had some features in common, such as overall dimensions and method of construction. Body framing was teak with mahogany panels; underframes were oak with steel soles, bolsters and end longitudinals. The 8 ft bogies were fitted with Kitson's patent cushioned wheels with wrought-iron centres.

No. 3785, dual-braked, had a beautifully symmetrical layout, one half exactly balancing the other half. There was a centrally placed saloon compartment 20 ft long flanked by two 'cabin' compartments with a lavatory at each end and a transverse entry vestibule. Gangway connections were fitted at both ends. Seating capacity was 22 (later reduced to 20) and the coach was placed in the Royal Train.

No. 3786, vacuum-braked and air-piped, featured a large saloon compartment 24 ft 6 in. long, a 'cabin' compartment 9 ft 5 in. long (really a saloon, if a rather cramped one) and a lavatory at this end. At the other end were separate WC and lavatory compartments, separated by a short corridor. At the extreme ends were entry vestibules and gangway connections. Seating capacity was 21 (later 19) and this coach also went into the Royal Train.

No. 3787, dual-braked, was composed thus: full-width lavatory at one end, small saloon, large saloon 22 ft 10 in. long, transverse entry vestibule, separate lavatory and WC compartments with short corridor between, and ordinary compartment at the other end. Seating capacity was 26, later 24, and the coach was not gangwayed at the ends.

With the completion of Nos. 3785/6, the Royal Train could now be made up to its maximum length of seven vehicles, although it did not always run as a full-length train.

Saloon Brake	2301,	converted 1903	(SR 7914)
Saloon	3514,	built 1904	(SR 7918)
Royal Saloon	1 R,	built 1903	(SR 7930)
Saloon	3785,	built 1905	(SR 7919)
Saloon	3786,	built 1905	(SR 7920)
First	225,	converted 1903	(SR 7254)
Saloon Brake	3493,	converted 1903	(SR 7915)

Nos. 3785–7 were sent into traffic in April 1905. As built, the only external access to saloons Nos. 3785/6 was by the end doors, but in 1910 an additional door each side, leading directly into the large saloon compartment, was fitted to No. 3786; No. 3785 was similarly modified in 1911. As may be seen on the diagram, this alteration did not spoil the symmetry of the coach.

No. 3787 may have been one of the Saloons used as a 'club car' by the Association of Regular Kent Coasters, formed in 1912 with the objects of suggesting improvements in train services and having the right to reserve compartments for the season-ticket holders who were their members. This facility was withdrawn at the outbreak of World War I, and all three Saloons were now kept in readiness for working 'Imperial Specials' from Victoria or Charing Cross to Folkestone or Dover. These trains conveyed couriers and other important personages. Nos. 3785/7 were kept at Rotherhithe Road carriage depot for the Charing Cross services, and No. 3786 was at Victoria carriage depot. By 1917 the allocation was: 3785 at Victoria, 3786 at Ashford Works, 3787 at Charing Cross.

All three Saloons were taken into Southern Railway stock in 1923 and received new numbers 7919–7921.

No. 3785, renumbered 7919 at Eastleigh in December 1925, lost its Westinghouse brake gear in August 1930. In March 1937, the SR Board decided to authorise conversion of this vehicle into an Invalid Saloon to replace two ex-LSWR Invalid Saloons Nos. 7903/4 (the first of these was sold to the Longmoor Military Railway in 1938, the second was withdrawn in 1940). The interior of No. 7919 was extensively altered, only the lavatory and 'cabin' compartment at one end remaining the same. A bed, armchairs and a collapsible table were placed in the main saloon, the lavatory was shifted so that it adjoined this saloon, and a luggage compartment with double doors each side was installed at the opposite end of the coach. Access to the saloon also was by a set of external double doors on each bodyside. In BR days the Saloon was much in use for pilgrims travelling to Lourdes and when it was withdrawn in August 1959 it was replaced by four converted SR coaches, as this traffic had increased considerably over the years.

No. 3786 was renumbered 7920 at Eastleigh in October 1925, along with five other Royal Train vehicles. On 19th May, 1937, the ex-SE&C Royal Train worked from Victoria to Cosham in connection with the Fleet Review at Spithead: formation was recorded by Frank Box as 7914, 7930, 7920, 7254, 7915 and a corridor luggage van (2292). Departure from Victoria was at 3.45 pm and the booked arrival at Cosham was 2 hours later. The return on 21st May was from Portsmouth (South Jetty) at 2.50 pm, the journey again being allowed 2 hours. (*Southern Railway Magazine*, Vol. 20, p.85). No. 7920 ceased being used in the Royal Train in 1939 and was presumably stored during the War. In 1948 it was transferred to the service vehicles list as 1062 S and used for some while as a temporary office at Wimbledon station.

No. 3787 became SR No. 7921 in January 1927, later being altered to unclassed Saloon and seating capacity reduced from 24 to 19. Its withdrawal date is unknown, possibly 1942, but its body was sent to Southampton Docks, where it was observed in May 1947.

PICNIC SALOONS (SECOND CLASS)

Nos. 140–147 (SR Nos. 7922–7929)

Body length: 50 ft 1 in. Bogie centres: 33 ft 6 in.
Height, rail to roof: 11 ft 9 in. Compartments: 2.
Seats: 48. Lavatories: 2 (one to each saloon compartment).

These Picnic Saloons were built by the SEC in 1905, Nos. 140–3 emerging from Ashford in June and Nos. 144–7 in October. They had teak body framing with mahogany panels and mouldings, and the windows were bedded on felt. Each saloon compartment was equipped with four inward-facing lounge seats, each accommodating six persons, and there were four narrow tables placed along the centre-line of the coach. Access was by two doors each side, and each saloon included a droplight at each corner. Underframes consisted of angle soles with oak headstocks and channel iron bolster cross bars, all other parts being of oak. Each coach was lit by eight Duplex lamps and two single lamps, all controlled by a main switch at the end.

Heaters were added later: Nos. 144–7 in 1906 on the storage system, and No. 141 in 1911 and Nos. 140/2/3 in 1913 on the non-storage system. All eight were fitted with two additional heaters each in 1922.

In the summer service of 1922, six of the Picnic Saloons had regular workings on Kent Coast trains: 6.40 am Ramsgate Harbour to Cannon Street, 7.20 am Margate West to Cannon Street (two), 7.40 am Ramsgate Harbour to Cannon Street, 8.05 am (not Saturdays) Margate West to Cannon Street and 8.45 am Ramsgate to Victoria. These returned on the 3.20 pm Victoria to Ramsgate, 5.05 pm Holborn to Ramsgate, 5.10 pm Holborn to Margate, 6.12 pm Cannon Street to Ramsgate (two) and 7.00 pm Victoria to Ramsgate. All these were 'not Saturdays' except the 7.00 pm. There was a Saloon formed in the Saturday 1.15 pm Cannon Street to Ramsgate Harbour, but how the other saloons were 'balanced' on Saturdays is not clear.

The Southern Railway reclassed these Saloons as third, although seating capacity remained at 48. New numbers given were 7922–7929 between 1924 and 1929. In 1926 No. 7925 was running in 4-set 685 and SEC No. 145 was in 7-set 699, both of which ran on Ramsgate–Cannon Street business train services.

It is believed that in Southern days the Saloons were used in special school trains run at the start and finish of school terms, and in consequence were not often to be seen in traffic. During the War they were used in connection with Air Raid Precautions and firefighting, and withdrawn about 1943. Most ended as grounded bodies, noted in the late 1940s: 7922 at Wembley Hill, 7924 at Baynards, 7925 at East Croydon, 7928 at Orpington and 7929 at Chislet Colliery.

Dates of renumbering by the Southern are as follows:

SEC	*SR*	*Re-No.*	*SEC*	*SR*	*Re-No.*
140	7922	10/25	144	7926	10/28
141	7923	11/24	145	7927	6/28
142	7924	4/29	146	7928	12/28
143	7925	2/24	147	7929	12/25

THE 1905 BOAT TRAINS

In December 1904 a contract was made between the Metropolitan Amalgamated Railway Carriage & Wagon Co. of Saltley and the SE&CR for the former to build two boat trains and spare carriages to these trains. Six different types of coach were designed (a total of 22 vehicles) and the total cost was £39,968.

Train No. 1, for the Folkestone service, was intended to be made up of two Firsts (Plan AA), one Composite with saloon (Plan B), two Composites (Plan CC), two Tri-Composites (Plan EE) and two Third Brakes (Plan FF). Train No. 2, for the Dover service, was to have five Firsts (Plan AA), one Composite (Plan B), one Composite (Plan CC) and two Second Brakes (Plan D). Spare stock for these trains were two to Plan AA and two to Plan CC.

Details of the six types of coach are as follows:

FIRST LAVATORY. Plan AA. Nos. 3788–3796 (SR 7361–4, 7740–4)
Body length: 51 ft 1 in. Bogie centres: 34 ft 6 in.
Compartments: 5 plus coupé. Seats: 29.
Lavatories: 4, with access from 4 compartments.
Nos. 3788–90 delivered 6/05, 3791–3 7/05, 3794–6 8/05. £1,900 each.

COMPOSITE LAVATORY. Plan B. Nos. 3797/98 (SR Nos. 5354/55)
Body length: 51 ft 1 in. Bogie centres: 34 ft 6 in.
Compartments: 1 1st saloon, 4 2nd class. Seats: 11 1st, 28 2nd.
Lavatories: 5 (1 to 1st class, 4 to 2nd class).
No. 3797 delivered 7/05 and No. 3798 delivered 8/05. £1,915 each.

COMPOSITE LAVATORY. Plan CC. Nos. 3799–3803 (SR Nos. 5286–90)
Body length: 50 ft 1 in. Bogie centres: 33 ft 6 in.
Compartments: 3 1st, 3 2nd. Seats: 15 1st, 24 2nd class.
Lavatories: 3 (to 1st class).
Nos. 3799–3801 delivered 7/05, 3802/3 8/05. £1,898 each.

TRI-COMPOSITE LAV. Plan EE. Nos. 3804/05 (SR Nos. 5393/94)
Body length: 51 ft 1 in. Bogie centres: 34 ft 6 in.
Compartments: 2 1st, 2 2nd, 2 3rd. Seats: 10 1st, 14 2nd, 18 3rd.
Lavatories: 5 (2 to 1st class, 2 to 2nd, 1 to 3rd).
Both coaches delivered 7/05. £1,864 each.

SECOND BRAKE LAV. Plan D. Nos. 3806/07 (SR Nos. 3318/19)
Body length: 50 ft 1 in. Bogie centres: 33 ft 6 in.
Compartments: 2, plus guard and luggage. Seats: 14.
Lavatories: 2.
Both coaches delivered 8/05. £1,461 each.

THIRD BRAKE LAV. Plan FF. Nos. 3808/09 (SR Nos. 3292/93)
Body length: 50 ft 1 in. Bogie centres: 33 ft 6 in.
Compartments: 3, plus guard and luggage. Seats: 26.
Lavatories: 2 (access from 2 compartments).
Both coaches delivered 7/05. £1,449 each.

All 22 coaches had the standard body width of 8 ft 0¾ in. and height from rail level to top of roof of 11 ft 9 in., roof observatories on the brake coaches being 12 ft 9 in. high. Bogie wheelbase was 8 ft. Body construction used the then normal methods, and underframes were of oak apart from the soles, bolsters and end longitudinals, which were steel. Steam heating equipment, on the storage system, was fitted from the outset. In short, these boat train carriages represented the very best and most up-to-date practice of the period.

The Composite coaches that included a first-class saloon were particularly beautiful; the saloon had one entry door each side, two inward-facing settees plus three normal transverse seats as well as lavatory access. It was the perfect accommodation for a party of well-to-do gentlemen setting out for the Continent. Externally the coaches were recognisable by the two large windows each side, which identified the position of the saloon. Later, the settees were replaced by six individual armchairs, reducing the seating capacity from 11 to 9.

It is recorded that the coaches were sent into traffic in the following order: 31.7.1905 – 3789/90, 3797, 3800/01, 3804/05, 3808/09; 4.8.1905 – 3788, 3799; 22.8.1905 – 3791–96, 3798, 3802/03; 3806/07.

The initial formationof No. 2 Boat Train was 3789 First, 3797 Composite, 3800 Composite, 3804/05 Tri-Composites, and 3808/09 Third Brakes. Nos. 3788/92/99 were 'spare', but the other coaches were not recorded as having set numbers, although presumably they, or most of them, were formed into the Dover boat train. The admission of third-class passengers to boat trains was a new departure for the SE&C, and even then they still could not travel in the sacred Dover service but only to Folkestone. With the easing of the curvature of the lines in Folkestone Harbour station, long bogie stock was now permitted to run on the Harbour branch.

These new boat trains did not maintain their original formations for very long. No. 2 train (which worked the 2.20 pm Charing Cross to Folkestone Harbour and 9.05 pm return) included Firsts 3789/90, Composites 3797, 3801/02 and Tri-Composite 3805 in 1907, 1908 and 1909. No. 3 train, whose formation was not recorded in the carriage working notices, was scheduled to work the 11.00 am Victoria to Dover Pier and 5.20 pm return services. These included a 2-coach portion from and to Holborn Viaduct, attached or detached at Herne Hill, comprising a Lavatory First and Brake Second. By 1910 First No. 3793 and Brake Second No. 3807 were in Boat Train No. 3A, along with newer coaches, and later that year the formation of the 11.00 am Victoria to Dover included Firsts 3794/5 and Composites 3799 and 3803. Boat Train No. 3A in summer 1910 worked the 9.00 am Charing Cross to Dover Pier and 3.20 pm return services.

During 1908 Third Brakes 3808/09 were allocated to the Deal – GWR through train, one or the other forming part of the through portion.

In 1913 five of the Firsts, Nos. 3789/90/92/93/96, were converted to First Brakes by replacing one end compartment by a guard's compartment; double doors each side were fitted, but there was no raised observatory – instead, there were two small windows fitted in the end for the guard's use. The First Brakes seated 23 passengers. The SE&C seemed always to be short of brake coaches and often preferred to convert existing coaches rather than build new ones. These five were altered in pursuance of a scheme to make up the boat trains into five 5-coach sets.

During 1917–19 first No. 3788 was formed in boat train set No. 5, run in connection with Continental mails, but by 1920 this and all the other 1905-built coaches were 'spare boat' stock, not formed in any numbered sets. During 1918 Third Brake No. 3808 really hit bottom, for it was used as a temporary goods brake on London-area local goods trains, for which it was fitted with side lamp-irons.

All 22 coaches became SR property, and in September 1923 the second-class compartments were downgraded to third class, with a slight increase in capacity, as shown on the diagrams. The coaches gravitated to semi-fast trains and by the 1930s most had been formed into 'long sets' – usually eight or nine coaches – for summer Saturday holiday services between Victoria and Ramsgate. The following list shows Southern numbers, dates of renumbering, known set numbers and withdrawal dates.

COMPOSITES

SEC	*SR*	*Re-No.*	*Set*	*Wdn*	*SEC*	*SR*	*Re-No.*	*Set*	*Wdn*
3799	5286	1/27	666	4/51	3802	5289	7/24	526	/42
3800	5287	10/23	687	12/44	3803	5290	7/24	899	12/49
3801	5288	3/24	688	9/44					

COMPOSITES (continued)

SEC	*SR*	*Re-No.*	*Set*	*Wdn*	*SEC*	*SR*	*Re-No.*	*Set*	*Wdn*
3797	5354	7/24	693,913	1/52	3798	5355	9/26	666	4/51
SEC	*SR*	*Re-No.*	*Set*	*Wdn*	*SEC*	*SR*	*Re-No.*	*Set*	*Wdn*
3804	5393	11/28	919	2/42	3805	5394	11/26	526	/42

THIRD BRAKES

SEC	*SR*	*Re-No.*	*Set*	*Wdn*	*SEC*	*SR*	*Re-No.*	*Set*	*Wdn*
3808	3292	10/26	680,914	c11/42	3809	3293	10/28	687	4/45
SEC	*SR*	*Re-No.*	*Set*	*Wdn*	*SEC*	*SR*	*Re-No.*	*Set*	*Wdn*
3806	3318	10/23	896	4/51	3807	3319	1/24	903	8/45

FIRSTS

SEC	*SR*	*Re-No.*	*Set*	*Wdn*	*SEC*	*SR*	*Re-No.*	*Set*	*Wdn*
3788	7361	5/24	690?	c/41	3794	7363	6/26		11/41
3791	7362	1/24	899,L	3/52	3795	7364	2/25	910	/44

FIRST BRAKES

SEC	*SR*	*Re-No.*	*Set*	*Wdn*	*SEC*	*SR*	*Re-No.*	*Set*	*Wdn*
3789	7740	11/24	667	2/42	3793	7743	9/27	347	7/39
3790	7741	8/24	341	5/41	3796	7744	7/28	346	8/52
3792	7742	1/28	341,344	1/47					

Set 341 was a 10-coach 1st-class race set formed entirely of ex-SEC stock by 1931 and allocated to the London West District of the Southern. When not in use it was berthed at Barnes, Brentford or Strawberry Hill. It was disbanded about the middle of 1939. No. 7744 was a replacement of No. 7735 in Set 346 from about 1942 onwards; this set was berthed at Tattenham Corner during 1948 but from 1950 started working between Margate and Canterbury West on miners' train duties.

First No. 7361 was damaged in a mishap at Brockenhurst on 12th March, 1941, and subsequently cut up.

Five of the 1905-built coaches were converted to service vehicles after their withdrawal from capital stock, viz:

3293 to Mess & Tool van 235 S, 4/45. Norwood Junction.
3319 to Mess & Tool van 243 S, 8/45. Motive Power Dept. Wdn 1956.
5287 to Mess & Tool van 222 S, 12/44. Loco. Running Dept, Plymouth.
5393 to Stores Van 1705 S, 2/42. Stores Dept, Eastleigh.
7363 to Stores Van 1700 S, 11/41. Stores Dept, Eastleigh.

Some of the bodies were grounded as temporary accommodation and No. 5289 was noted at Exeter Central 10/46, 3292 at Tonbridge 5/46, 7740 at Orpington and 7741 at Angerstein Wharf 7/47.

THIRD BRAKES

Nos. 830–844, 856–860 (SR Nos. 3272–3291)

Body length: 50 ft 1 in. Bogie centres: 33 ft 6 in.
Compartments: 5, plus guard and luggage. Seats: 50.

The first batch of 15 of these Third Brakes was built by the SE&CR in December 1905 (Nos. 830–4), January 1906 (Nos. 835–9) and March 1906

(Nos. 840–4). The second batch, consisting of just five coaches, was constructed by the Metropolitan Amalgamated Railway Carriage & Wagon Co. at its Hadley Works, Wellington, and delivered to the SE&C in October 1906. Incidentally, the Hadley Works was in use for carriage construction only between 1905 and 1908; it had been a tramcar-building factory between 1900 and 1904, owned by G.F. Milnes & Co. (who had built two of the South Eastern's Hythe & Sandgate horse trams).

Roof observatories on these 20 coaches were to a modified design. Instead of the rounded top hitherto standard, there was now a flattened top to each 'birdcage', reducing the overall height from 12 ft 9 in. to 12 ft 6½ in., and this now became standard for all further construction. Such coaches could clear the loading gauge of the Metropolitan Railway.

Body construction used normal methods. The luggage compartment, 16 ft long, had one set of double doors on each bodyside giving access, and communicated with the adjoining guard's compartment by means of a sliding door which could be padlocked on the luggage compartment side. There were two electric lamps controlled by a switch in the luggage compartment. The guard's compartment included a dog box, coupling box, valve locker and letter rack and was lit by a single lamp controlled by a switch. The passenger compartments were lit by five Duplex lamps, each of eight candle-power, controlled by a main switch at the body end.

Nos. 856–60 were noted as being built to Drawings Nos. 2494 (body) and 2495A (underframe). Headstocks, soles, end longitudinals and bolsters were steel; cross bars and centre longitudinals were oak. This batch had steam heaters on the storage system when new, but the 15 Ashford-built coaches did not. The careful observer could distinguish the two batches by noting the position of the lozenge-shaped panel used for chalking on destinations on the bodyside. In the Metro batch it was placed midway between the guard's door and the luggage doors but in the Ashford batch it was located nearer to the guard's door.

For accountancy purposes the two batches differed also: Nos. 830–44 were built as renewals out of revenue, but Nos. 856–60 needed capital and cost £1,570 each.

A 5-compartment Third Brake was specified as part of the formation of the five-bogie 11.00 am Charing Cross to Dover and 2.25 pm return during 1908. Also included were a Tri-Composite Lavatory, Third No. 3464, Second No. 2323, a First and, from Cannon Street, a Lavatory Third Brake. In 1909 the 50-seat Third Brakes began to be formed into numbered sets. There was one each in 4-sets 19 and 20, and in 3-sets 23 and 24, 70, 71 and 72, 4-set 60 and 5-set 66.

Sets 23 and 24 worked two-day cyclic diagrams, which took in the 10.40 am Deal to Charing Cross, 10.35 pm (not Saturdays) Charing Cross to Tonbridge, 8.48 am (not Mondays) Tonbridge to Cannon Street and 3.18 pm Charing Cross to Deal via Minster. On Saturdays a set worked the 2.55 pm Charing Cross to Hastings and returned next Monday on the 7.05 am Hastings to Charing Cross.

From July 1909, Set 70 was allocated to the 10.40 am Holborn to Ramsgate Harbour and 2.35 pm return services. Train No. 66 worked the 5.45 am

Victoria to Dover and 12.10 pm return, whilst No. 60 was found on the 7.45 am Margate Sands to Charing Cross and 4.30 pm return if all was well.

In 1910 further 50-set Third Brakes were formed into numbered set trains: one in 3-set 82, No. 833 in 3-set 57 and one in No. 66A. Set 66 was altered to become a 3-set, and No. 71 was specially noted in the carriage working notice as including Third Brake No. 843 – which it retained for many years.

Most of the Third Brakes were ultimately formed into 3-sets along with Tri-Composite Brakes Nos. 148–162 and various Tri-Composites. Steam heating on the non-storage system was added to Nos. 841/4 in 1909, 832/4/6/40 in 1910, 837/8/43 in 1911, 830/1/3/5/42 in 1912 and 839 in 1913. During 1914 No. 857 ran as part of the Victoria portion of the Deal to North through service.

There were 14 Type 'B' 3-coach sets and their original numbers were 23, 24, 25, 57, 59, 61, 66, 67, 70, 71, 82, 83, 125 and 142. In 1915 most of these were renumbered to group them consecutively, the new numbers being 58 to 71: 57 became 58; 59, 61, 66, 67, 70 and 71 kept their old numbers; 24 became 69, 25 became 63 and 83 became 65. Each set included one of the 50-seat Third Brakes. The other six coaches were accounted for thus: three in Sets 128, 129 and 130, formed in 1917; one in 4-set 39, formed in 1919; one in 5-set 32 (1922) and one – No. 844 – loose.

In 1922 Set 32 worked the 9.05 am Bexhill to Cannon Street and 6.16 pm return. Set 39 worked on Mondays from Hastings to Cannon Street at 6.55 am, Tuesdays to Fridays from Tonbridge to Cannon Street at 8.04 am, and on Saturdays from Tunbridge Wells to Cannon Street at 7.49 am. The set returned on the 6.10 pm (not Saturdays) from Charing Cross to Sevenoaks Tubs Hill and empty to Tonbridge; on Saturdays it worked the 1.20 pm Cannon Street to Tonbridge and 5.55 pm thence to Hastings, being berthed there for Monday morning.

The Southern renumbered the 20 Third Brakes consecutively (Nos. 3272–91), and the 14 Type 'B' sets 58–71 became SR set Nos. 515–528; Set 130 became SR 566, but the other SE&C sets were disbanded and the Third Brakes placed in new SR sets.

No. 834 (SE&C set 32) became SR 3276 in Set 686.
No. 840 (SE&C set 128) became SR 3282 in Set 696.
No. 844 became SR 3286 and was placed in Set 687.
No. 857 (SE&C set 129) became SR 3288 in Set 685.
No. 858 (SE&C set 39) became SR 3289, believed to have been in Set 662.

Although the Southern usually repainted all the coaches in a set at the same time, it sometimes happened that set trains ran in mixed liveries. Such a set was 8-bogie No. 699, which R.W. Kidner observed on 20th May, 1929. Six of the coaches were in Southern green, but two – Third Brake No. 840 and Third No. 1399 – were still in SE&C brown, although they were marked on the solebars with the SR set number. No. 840 received its SR number in October 1929, and by 1931 was formed in Set 696 as shown above.

3-set 528 was disbanded early, its Third Brake (No. 3285) going to Set 640 by 1931. No. 3277 (Set 523) was withdrawn in June 1932 – probably as a result of accident damage – and was replaced in the set by No. 3289. Details of renumbering, set number allocations and withdrawal dates now follow:

SEC	*SR*	*Re-No.*	*Set*	*Wdn*	*SEC*	*SR*	*Re-No.*	*Set*	*Wdn*
830	3272	6/27	526	11/42	840	3282	10/29	696,896	1/58
831	3273	12/26	516	8/48	841	3283	9/26	517	10/43
832	3274	7/27	524	10/43	842	3284	12/27	525,921?	8/52
833	3275	3/29	515	4/48	843	3285	4/26	640	3/43
834	3276	8/29	686	12/51	844	3286	10/28	687	9/44
835	3277	3/28	523	6/32	856	3287	12/26	518	5/44
836	3278	6/27	520	12/46	857	3288	2/24	685,899	10/49
837	3279	11/28	566,903	1/58	858	3289	6/26	662,523	3/43
838	3280	3/27	519	1/53	859	3290	11/27	521	/47
839	3281	5/27	527	/47	860	3291	4/26	522,L,900	6/55

No. 3279 was transferred from Set 903 to Set 519 after the withdrawal in 1953 of No. 3280; in 1956, 9-set 519 was renumbered 900 and withdrawn in 1958. No. 3291, after the disbanding of Set 522 in 1951, became a loose coach allocated to the Kent & East Sussex line until that line's closure to passenger traffic in January 1954. It then ran in 9-set 900 until June 1955.

Eight Third Brakes were altered to service vehicles after withdrawal from capital stock, all becoming Mess and Tool Vans:

3272 to 1760 S, 11/42. Breakdown Van, Reading.
3274 to 1872 S, 10/43. Withdrawn 11/58.
3281 to 381 S, 1947. Motive Power Dept.
3283 to 1873 S, 10/43. Withdrawn 7/60.
3285 to 1821 S, 3/43. Breakdown Van, Brighton.
3287 to 1962 S, 5/44. Mobile living quarters, Woking.
3289 to 1820 S, 3/43. Breakdown Van, Brighton.
3290 to 378 S, 1947. Motive Power Dept.

THIRD BRAKE LAVATORY

Nos. 845–855, 963–972 (SR Nos. 3294–3314)

Body length: 50 ft 1 in. Bogie centres: 33 ft 6 in.
Compartments: 4, plus guard and luggage. Seats: 36.
Lavatories: 2 (access from 2 compartments).

The first batch was built by the Metropolitan Amalgamated RC&W Co. at its Hadley Works in 1906 and the second batch – 10 carriages – was Ashford-built during 1908. Dimensionally similar, the two groups differed chiefly in that the 1906 ones had roof observatories with round tops 12 ft 9 in. above rail level and the 1908 series featured the new flat-topped roof lookout only 12 ft 6½ in. above rail level. The Metro carriages were received and the Ashford carriages were completed on the following dates:

Nos.	*Received*	*Nos.*	*Built*
845	7/1906	963–67	7/1908
846–49	8/1906	968–72	11/1908
850–55	9/1906		

Nos. 845–55 were constructed to Drawing Nos. 2512 (body) and 2495A (underframe). Bodies and underframes used the same methods of con-

struction as Third Brakes Nos. 830–44. The later batch had underframes of steel: bulb angle steel soles, channel steel headstocks, channel steel bolsters, cross bars and longitudinals. Buffers were fitted with malleable iron guides and sleeves.

None of the 21 carriages included steam heating, with the sole exception of No. 854 which was fitted with storage system heaters when new. This increased the cost of the coach by £50, the other 10 Metro-built coaches costing £1,581 each. Between 1910 and 1914 the 20 unheated coaches received non-storage heaters.

In 1909 the 36-seat Third Brakes began to be formed into sets, which were allocated to specific daily workings: one each in Sets 18, 19, 20, 21, 22, 61, 68, 73 and 75, and two each in Sets 25, 26 and 62.

5-sets 25 and 26 each worked a two-day diagram as follows: 8.25 am Charing Cross to Dover Town, 12.50 pm return to Cannon Street, 6.55 pm Charing Cross to Dover Town. Next day – 5.25 am Dover Town to Charing Cross, 12.07 pm return, 5.00 pm Dover Town to Charing Cross. 6-set 62 also worked between Dover and Charing Cross from July 1909. 4-sets 21 and 22 were two other sets that each worked two-day diagrams, but this time on the Chatham Section: 9.50 am Victoria to Dover Harbour, 1.27 pm Dover Harbour to Victoria and 7.45 pm return. Next day – 8.20 am Dover Harbour to Victoria, 1.30 pm return, and 6.00 pm Dover Harbour to Victoria.

By 1911 at least some of the Third Brakes were being used in boat trains. During that year and 1912, Nos. 852 and 968/9 were altered to slip coaches and given the necessary detaching gear, with electric hooters for giving warning. These slip coaches could easily be identified by the small window that was cut into the brake end – a feature retained long after the slip apparatus fell out of use.

Steam heaters were fitted to Nos. 852, 972 in 1910; 846/7/9/50/5, 963/8/9 in 1911; 848/53, 966/7 in 1912; 845, 965/70/1 in 1913 and 851, 964 in 1914. This improvement cost £32 10s. per coach.

By 1914 the sets quoted above had been disbanded, and very few 36-seat Third Brakes remained attached to sets, though there was one in 3-set 55 (No. 851). Early in 1915, Nos. 848 and 971 were equipped with Westinghouse air brakes and formed into an un-numbered set with Tri-Composite No. 667 and ex-LC&D Composite No. 2719 for working through services between Ashford and Brighton.

Other sets known to have included a 36-seat Third Brake were No. 246 (formed 1916) and Nos. 257, 258 and 261 (formed 1917). No. 246 worked between Maidstone East and Holborn; Nos. 257/8 alternated between Tonbridge/Cannon Street and Chilworth/Cannon Street services; and No. 261 worked between Tonbridge and Cannon Street also.

Four carriages were used as temporary goods brakes for pilot services in the London area, although not all at the same time: No. 855 was so-used during 1916/7, No. 966 during 1917, and Nos. 847/9 during 1918. All reverted to passenger train use.

Six Third Brakes are known to have been operating in sets during 1922. 6-set 53 (Reading line) had No. 963 and 4-set 55 had No. 851. This train worked between Tonbridge and Cannon Street via Redhill. 3-set 246 included No. 970, working between Maidstone East or Swanley and London. 5-sets 257/8, with Nos. 964 and 971 respectively, worked between Dorking or Ash and Cannon Street. Finally, 5-set 261 (Third Brake No. 967) worked services in the Tonbridge/Redhill/Reigate area to and from London.

Although most of these sets seem to have been disbanded by the SR before the coaches came to be repainted green and given SR numbers, one at least was kept intact, all five coaches being sent to Ashford Works together. SE&C set 258 became SR set 688, with the formation:

Third Bke	3307	(SE&C 965)	Renumbered 12.10.23
Third	870	(SE&C 2910)	" "
First	7245	(SE&C 2632)	" "
Composite	5246	(SE&C 227)	" "
Third Bke	3313	(SE&C 971)	" "

Both the Third and the First were ex-LC&D vehicles; No. 7245 was soon replaced by Composite No. 5305 (built in 1889). Set 688 was involved in a collision at Cannon Street on 13th May, 1925, when working the 5.24 pm to Ash via Redhill.

SE&C Nos. 845–55 were given Southern numbers 3294–3304, and 963–72 became 3305–3314. Most of them were put in the later 9-coach excursion sets (numbered between 896 and 921) and no attempt was made to group them together; the sets really were a hopeless jumble of coaches, each train having different proportions of first class, third class, and lavatory accommodation.

Here is a list of the 21 Lavatory Third Brakes with dates that Southern numbers were applied, known set numbers, and withdrawal dates.

SEC	*SR*	*Re-No.*	*Set*	*Wdn*	*SEC*	*SR*	*Re-No.*	*Set*	*Wdn*
845	3294	7/27	910	6/44	963	3305	4/24	691,921	/48?
846	3295	8/26	898	4/51	964	3306	5/24	662,912	3/51
847	3296	9/26	913	10/44	965	3307	10/23	688	6/42
848	3297	8/26		8/35	966	3308	2/28	900	6/51
849	3298	1/26	899	9/49	967	3309	12/26	918	9/56
850	3299	3/24	689,669	7/52	968	3310	12/23	918	7/52
851	3300	8/27	691,672	9/51	969	3311	12/25	912	3/51
852	3301	1/29	907	12/43	970	3312	6/26	640,921?	10/52
853	3302	7/26	920	6/57	971	3313	10/23	688	6/42
854	3303	11/27	919	c12/41	972	3314	5/29	899,97	5/50
855	3304	1/28	919	c12/41					

In addition, No. 3300 was later in Set 921 then Set 897; and Nos. 3305/14 were both in 4-set 97 during 1942 and 1943. No. 3298 was withdrawn after collision damage at Hawkhurst on 17th September, 1949.

Those sets surviving into the early 1950s continued working summer Saturday Ramsgate services, but every year saw the withdrawal of one or two more and their replacement with corridor stock, no doubt to the satisfaction of holidaymakers who had perhaps been forced to sit in a compartment without lavatory access for the 79½-mile journey.

Only two of this type became service vehicles. No. 3294 was converted to a Breakdown Van No. 1970 S for the Locomotive Running Department in June 1944 and condemned in April 1957; No. 3301 was altered to a Mess &

Tool Van No. 1961 S for the Engineers' Department, used as mobile living quarters at Purley, and condemned in October 1962.

THIRD LAVATORY

Nos. 861–879 (SR Nos. 937–955)

Body length: 48 ft. Bogie centres: 33 ft.
Compartments: 7. Seats: 62.
Lavatories: 4 (access from 4 compartments).

The Gloucester Railway Carriage & Wagon Co. built these 19 coaches for the SE&CR in 1906, and they were delivered in the following order:

868–72	7/06	861/62	8/06
873–79	8/06	863–67	9/06

Each was sent into traffic about a month or two after having been received from the builders.

Constructed to Drawing No. 2498, the carriages had teak body framing with mahogany panels; soles, headstocks and bolsters were steel, with other parts of the underframe being oak. Compartments were only 5 ft 7½ in. across, the then standard dimension for third class. The centre compartment and both end compartments were without lavatory access. Nos. 862–867 were built new with storage heaters and cost £1,888 each, but the other 13, without heaters, cost only £1,826 each. (One register states that No. 861 also was built new with storage heaters, but a document entitled 'Carriage Stock Built by SER & SECR from 12th December, 1899' contradicts this with a note '861 Not Steam Heating'.)

At a cost of £32 10s. each, non-storage heaters were fitted to the remaining coaches between 1909 and 1916: Nos. 869 in 1909, 870/7 in 1911, 868/71/4 in 1912, 872/5/9 in 1913, 878 in 1914, 876 in 1915 and 873 in 1916.

No. 874 was recorded in one register as being fitted in May 1909 with a Maximus brake, but what this was exactly is not clear; anyway, it was not perpetuated, no other bogie carriage being so-distinguished.

Few of these Thirds were attached to numbered sets. From May 1909, No. 869 was placed in 4-coach Train No. 16, which regularly worked the 7.55 am Ramsgate to Charing Cross and 5.10 pm Holborn to Ramsgate (slipped at Faversham). In 1916 Train 16 was renumbered 31, and still included No. 869, although by 1917 it had no workings and was disbanded about 1919. No. 866 was formed into 4-coach Train No. 10, the Granville Express stock (renumbered Set 24 in 1915), this also becoming spare during World War I, and disbanded in 1918. After this, none of the 19 Thirds was attached to a set train.

The Southern renumbered the complete series as 937–955 between 1923 and 1929. Their use in Southern days was probably as strengthening vehicles or as part of 'scratch' un-numbered sets; during electrification of suburban services during the 1920s the steam rolling stock position on the Eastern Section seems to have been particularly chaotic. In later years almost all the Thirds were marshalled into 9-coach sets numbered between 903 and 921, tending to stay put until withdrawal. Here is a list of Southern renumbering dates, known set numbers and withdrawal dates:

SEC	*SR*	*Re-No.*	*Set*	*Wdn*	*SEC*	*SR*	*Re-No.*	*Set*	*Wdn*
861	937	12/27	903	5/45	871	947	1/29	910	5/44
862	938	4/27	909	9/44	872	948	7/27		6/42
863	939	2/27	921,917	3/57	873	949	10/26	909	9/44
864	940	10/24	921,917	3/57	874	950	12/28	913	4/47
865	941	9/26		3/37	875	951	7/26	909	7/44
866	942	12/27	910	5/44	876	952	9/24		4/38
867	943	2/27	909	10/44	877	953	11/23	657,919	5/42
868	944	1/26	913	12/51	878	954	6/24	919	12/41
869	945	9/27	905	1/48	879	955	4/28	921,917	3/57
870	946	6/26	921	?47					

Upon withdrawal the underframes of Nos. 941 and 952 were re-used on Post Office Vans Nos. 4914 and 4913 respectively. The body of No. 943 was sent to New Cross Gate; that of No. 953 to Hither Green; and that of No. 954 to Dunton Green.No. 948 became a Stores Van, No. 1733 S, based at Eastleigh. By 1957 the three surviving coaches in capital stock – all formed in 9-set 917 – must have been well overdue for withdrawal; even if physically in good condition, their accommodation was far below the standards then prevailing.

TRI-COMPOSITE LAVATORY

Nos. 667–681 (SR Nos. 5271–5285)

Body length: 50 ft 1 in. Bogie centres: 33 ft 6 in.
Compartments: 2 1st, 2 2nd, 2 3rd. Seats: 10 1st, 14 2nd, 16 3rd.
Lavatories: 6 (2 1st, 2 2nd, 2 3rd).

These Tri-Composites were the first to appear with lavatory accommodation to *all* compartments; the design was repeated in later batches having the same layout, although dimensions differed from batch to batch. The compartments were arranged '2 Lavs 2 1 Lavs 1 3 Lavs 3'.

Nos. 667–76 were built at Ashford and completed in May 1906, the remaining five emerging in July of that year. None was steam heated. Body framing was teak with mahogany panels and mouldings, and the quarter lights were bedded on felt, with mahogany mouldings. The underframes were constructed with angle soles, oak headstocks and channel iron bolsters and crossbars, all other parts being oak. Electric lighting was controlled by a main switch at the end and fittings comprised six Duplex lamps in the compartments and six single lamps in the lavatories. The 8 ft wheelbase bogies had the usual 3 ft 6 in.-diameter wheels.

From July 1906 three Tri-Composites were formed in the Granville Express train, which ran at 10.00 am from Ramsgate Harbour to Victoria and returned at 3.25 pm, scheduled journey times being only slightly more than two hours. The Victoria portion comprised a Brake Van, a Third, a Composite, the three Tri-Composites and an extra Third if required. The City portion comprised a Composite, a Third and a Brake Van, detached at Herne Hill on the up journey and reunited there on the down trip. Although no set number was given initially, the formation was described in the Carriage

Workings as a 'fixed train' which was to be kept intact and, just in case there was any uncertainty, there was an additional instruction: 'The Down Train must always be returned intact.'

The 'Granville' was formed of steam-heated stock during the 1906/7 winter, so it is thought that three Tri-Composites, built new with storage heaters, replaced the three unheated coaches believed to have been used initially.

No. 674 was formed into a 3-set, with Third Brake No. 830 and Tri-Composite Brake No. 153, certainly by 1912 as all three coaches were equipped with steam heating at the same time, emerging from Ashford in April 1912. The original set number was 24, but this became 69 in 1915. No. 676, formed with Nos. 856 and 149 into 3-set 61, was given heaters in January 1912; and No. 681 (with Nos. 841 and 150) was placed in a 3-set that later received the number 60. The 15 Tri-Composites received heating on the following dates:

681, 1909; 675, 1910; 671/2/3, 1911; 669/74/6/80, 1912; 670/7/8/9, 1913; 667/8, 1914.

No. 667 was equipped in 1915 with Westinghouse air brakes in addition to the automatic vacuum brakes with which it had been fitted since new; it was formed into the train, already mentioned in an earlier section, that worked the 8.27 am Ashford to Brighton and 1.55 pm return services, locomotives being changed at Hastings. Late in 1915 3-set No. 245 was formed for working between Chatham/Otford and Victoria; it included Tri-Composite No. 677. In 1918 the set worked between Maidstone East and Holborn; in 1919 between Sevenoaks and Holborn. Set 245 was renumbered 639 by the Southern Railway, probably around 1924.

The SR renumbered the series of 15 Tri-Composites as 5271–5285, and in September 1923 the second-class compartments became third class, seating 16 instead of 14 (total capacity 10 first, 32 third). The three vehicles in Type 'B' 3-sets 60, 61 and 69 remained in those sets, which were given SR numbers 517, 518 and 526. Set 526 was noted in June 1927 working the Southern-instigated Gillingham to Brighton (via Maidstone and Tunbridge Wells) through service.

No. 5281 was running in 6-set 696 by 1931 and No. 5272 in 7-set 686 by 1935. Other set numbers shown below refer to the position in the late 1930s and into the 1940s.

SEC	*SR*	*Re-No.*	*Set*	*Wdn*	*SEC*	*SR*	*Re-No.*	*Set*	*Wdn*
667	5271	10/23		/42	675	5279	12/24	912	3/51
668	5272	8/29	686	12/48	676	5280	12/26	518	12/43
669	5273	2/28	913	7/46	677	5281	1/28	696	6/51
670	5274	9/26		/42	678	5282	2/28	919	2/42
671	5275	12/27		2/42	679	5283	7/26	919	2/42
672	5276	6/25	912	3/51	680	5284	2/27	909	8/44
673	5277	8/26	909	8/44	681	5285	9/26	517	/43
674	5278	6/27	526	/42					

Nos. 5277/84 were condemned following damage by enemy action in 1944, it is believed at New Cross Gate. Six coaches were sent to various places as grounded bodies for temporary accommodation during and after

World War II: No. 5271 to Reading, 5273 Exeter Central, 5274 Exmouth Junction, 5275 Three Bridges locomotive depot, 5278 Stewarts Lane and 5283 West Croydon. Four became service vehicles:

5273 underframe to DS 3111 Match Wagon, 1948.
5278 underframe to 1826SM, Match Wagon to Grafton travelling crane.
5280 to Stores Van 1955 S in 4/1944, for storage of ARP clothing.
5282 to Stores Van 1706 S, 2/1942. At Eastleigh.

Last survivor was No. 5281 in 9-set 696, being withdrawn in mid-1951, although the set itself continued in use for some more years.

TRI-COMPOSITE LAVATORY

Nos. 880–888 (SR Nos. 5356–5364)

Body length: 51 ft 1 in. Bogie centres: 34 ft 6 in.
Compartments: 2 1st, 2 2nd, 2 3rd. Seats: 10 1st, 14 2nd, 16 3rd.
Lavatories: 6 (2 1st, 2 2nd, 2 3rd class).

The second batch of Tri-Composites was built by the Metropolitan Amalgamated RC&W Co. at its Britannia Works, Saltley (the former works of Brown, Marshalls & Co., taken over in 1902) and delivered to the SE&C in 1906. Although having the same layout as Nos. 667–81, these nine carriages were a foot longer over body, allowing the first- and second-class compartments to be a little wider, although the thirds were still a cramped 5 ft 7½ in. Delivery dates at Ashford were August (Nos. 880–4/6/7) and September 1906 (Nos. 885/8).

The bodies – to Drawing No. 2449A – were of normal timber construction. The underframes (Drawing No. 2495) had steel headstocks, soles, end longitudinals and bolsters, with oak cross bars and centre longitudinals. All nine coaches (which were built on Capital account) were equipped from the outset with steam heating on the storage system. Original cost of each vehicle was £2,067; prices were rising!

By February 1907 there was sufficient steam-heated stock to allow nine services in each direction to be formed entirely of such stock. One of these trains was the Granville Express, which included three of the Tri-Composites in its formation; from May 1907 it was numbered as Train No. 10. Formation of this train leaving Victoria was: Brake Van, Third, Composite, 3 Tri-Composites and Third (certain days only). At Herne Hill the City portion was attached to the rear: Tri-Composite (certain days), Composite, Third and Brake Van.

In late 1908 or early 1909 No. 888 was formed into a 3-set with Third Brake No. 2295 and Tri-Composite Brake No. 160 for London–Hastings–Ashford services; the train received the set number 59 in 1910. In October 1910 the Tri-Compo Brake was replaced by another, No. 162, and later (possibly 1911 or 1912) the Third Brake was replaced by 5-compartment Third Brake No. 831.

Another train service steam-heated by February 1907 was the Deal Express (Train No. 11), working the 8.32 am Deal to Victoria and 5.00 pm return. The formation of Train No. 11 is not shown in the carriage working notices, but in February 1911 its quoted formation included Tri-Composites Nos. 884, 885 and 886, Composite No. 894 and Third Brake (5-compartment) No. 857. By October 1914 Nos. 885/6 were in an un-numbered 3-vehicle portion (with Brake Van No. 104) based at Folkestone Junction. No. 887 in 1914 worked in the 10.25 am Deal to Victoria. Train No. 11, the Deal Express stock, was renumbered 25 in 1915 but disbanded a year later as in wartime there was no place for fast-running passenger trains; freight services were of greater importance.

Nos. 880–8 were given SR numbers 5356–5364 between 1926 and 1928, and the second class became third in the same way as Nos. 667–81 described in the previous section. Set 59 was renumbered 516 and kept the same formation until *c.*1938, when it was augmented to eight coaches – five plus the original three. Set 516 was withdrawn in 1948, and its original Composite No. 5364 (SEC 888) was transferred to 9-set 666 until its withdrawal in September 1951.

Summary of SR Composites Nos. 5356–64:

SEC	*SR*	*Re-No.*	*Set*	*Wdn*	*SEC*	*SR*	*Re-No.*	*Set*	*Wdn*
880	5356	11/26	526	/42	885	5361	12/25	919	1/42
881	5357	2/28	913	1/52	886	5362	11/26	695	2/51
882	5358	11/28		12/43	887	5363	1/27		1/42
883	5359	3/27		12/40	888	5364	12/26	516,666	9/51
884	5360	1/28	687	8/44					

No. 5356 was not the original Composite in Set 526 but was one of five vehicles added to the former 3-set to make it up to eight, there being a need for 'long' sets on the Victoria–Ramsgate main line; a need much reduced in wartime, for the whole set was withdrawn in 1942.

Set 695's history is fairly involved, as with most things to do with the SE&C. Formed by the SE&C as a 6-set,No. 87, for Dorking services, it was reduced to three coaches after 1924 and became SR set No. 695. All three vehicles were renumbered in July 1926: Composite Brake No. 1081 to Third Brake 3360, First No. 3508 to 7343, and Tri-Composite Brake No. 152 to Composite Brake No. 6611. By 1935 3-set 695 had its First replaced by Composite No. 5362, and later, during the 1940s, it was recorded as a 9-coach set, No. 5362 remaining in it until withdrawal early in 1951.

None of these Composites, after withdrawal, became a service vehicle but three bodies were noted as grounded off wheels at different locations: No. 5356 at East Croydon, No. 5361 at Gomshall in June 1948, and No. 5363 at Christchurch.

COMPOSITE LAVATORY

Nos. 889–891 (SR Nos. 5351–5353)

Body length: 51 ft 1 in. Bogie centres: 34 ft 6 in.
Compartments: 1 1st saloon, 4 2nd class.
Seats: 10 first, 28 second class.
Lavatories: 5 (1 to 1st class, 4 to second class).

These three coaches, which were very similar to Nos. 3797/8 of 1905, were built for the SE&C by Cravens Ltd of Darnall, Sheffield. They were received by the SE&C in October (Nos. 889/90) and November 1906 (No. 891). Built to Drawings Nos. 2204A and 2238A (body) and 2495 (underframe), these coaches differed from the 1905 pair in the saloon layout; two transverse seats were next to the lavatory compartment and external doors were nearer this end of the saloon. As before, two inward-facing settees, each seating four passengers, made up the rest of the accommodation in each saloon; this was probably not such a good layout as that found in Nos. 3797/8, in each of which, with a full-width transverse seat at the opposite end to the lavatory, the capacity was one passenger more. In 1912 the settees were replaced by six individual armchairs, reducing the total capacity of each saloon to eight, and a portable table replaced the fixed table.

Body framing was teak with Honduras mahogany panels. Underframes had steel headstocks, soles, end longitudinals and bolsters; cross bars and centre longitudinals were American oak. All three vehicles were steam-heated by Laycock's storage system from the start, and each cost £2,164 on Capital account.

The three Composites do not appear to have been attached to sets during the SE&C era, and no workings can be traced. On coming to the SR they gained new numbers 5351–5353 and the second class seating was altered to third class, seating 32 passengers. No. 5353 was put in 9-coach set No. 910, which was withdrawn complete in May 1944; No. 5352 was in 8-set 518 between *c.*1938 and 1943.

The body of No. 5351 was sent to Maidstone West and that of No. 5353 was observed at Southampton Docks in May 1947.

Summary

SEC	*SR*	*Re-No.*	*Set*	*Wdn*
889	5351	7/24		/42
890	5352	11/25	518	/43
891	5353	3/24	910	/44

COMPOSITE LAVATORY

Nos. 892–898 (SR Nos. 5291–5297)

Body length: 50 ft 1 in. Bogie centres: 33 ft 6 in.
Compartments: 3 1st, 3 2nd. Seats: 16 1st, 22 2nd class.
Lavatories: 4 (2 1st, 2 2nd).

Ordered from Cravens at the same time as Nos. 889–91 – March 1906 – these seven Composites were delivered between September and December 1906: Nos. 892/3 in September, 894/5 in October, 895 in November and 897/8 in December. They were built to Drawing Nos. 2492 (body) and 2495 (underframe), and both body and underframe construction were the same as those on Nos. 889–91. Compartments were arranged '1 1 Lavs 1 2 Lavs 2 2', so that neither of the two endmost compartments had lavatory access. From the start, all seven carriages were steam heated on the storage system.

From October 1907 No. 896 was booked to work, with a 6-wheel Brake Van, in the 2-coach Dover portion of the 2.20 pm Charing Cross to Folkestone boat train. No. 894 was part of Train 11 – the Deal Express stock –

in 1911, but by 1914 was scheduled to be formed in the 10.25 am Deal to Victoria and 2.50 pm return services, which included through carriages to and from Bradford and Manchester.

None of the seven was recorded in any set train during the 1920–2 period and when the SR inherited them it altered the second-class seating to third (with an increase from 22 to 26 seats) and renumbered the series as 5291–5297 between 1924 and 1929.

Whether any appeared in sets during the late 1920s is unknown but, most probably, they worked in semi-fast services, possibly even as 'back-up' stock for relief boat trains. By the late 1930s or early 1940s almost all were in sets, as summarised in the list below:

SEC	*SR*	*Re-No.*	*Set*	*Wdn*	*SEC*	*SR*	*Re-No.*	*Set*	*Wdn*
892	5291	9/27	917	1/53	896	5295	1/28	917	1/53
893	5292	1/29	674	5/42	897	5296	6/24	674	5/42
894	5293	8/26	640	/42	898	5297	9/26		12/42
895	5294	12/24	519,900	1/58					

Set 519 was one of the long-lasting 3-sets that had been made up to 8 coaches by 1941; No. 5294 was in that set at least from 1941 until 1956, when Set 519 was renumbered 900, running thus until withdrawal. No. 5297 was converted to Stores Van No. 1956 S in April 1944 for the storage of ARP clothing. After the War it was withdrawn in February 1946, having outlived its usefulness.

FIRST CLASS LAVATORY

Nos. 899–901 (SR Nos. 7358–7360)

Body length: 50 ft 1 in. Bogie centres: 33 ft 6 in.
Compartments: 1 saloon, 4 ordinary.
Seats: saloon 8, ordinary compartments 21.
Lavatories: 4, including 1 to saloon.

A new type of carriage was this bogie First incorporating a small saloon compartment, and ultimately there were three distinct groups, each of which was generally similar but dimensionally different. Nos. 899–901, the earliest batch, were ordered from Cravens at the same time as Composites Nos. 889–898, and on completion at the Darnall Works were delivered to the SE&C in October (No. 899) and November 1906 (Nos. 900/1).

The bodies (Drawing No. 2493) were constructed of timber. Each saloon, which was only 11 ft 8 in. long, had two transverse seats next to the lavatory, and two inward-facing settees each seating three passengers. In 1912 the settees were replaced by five armchairs in each saloon, a portable table being installed in place of the narrow, centrally-located fixed table. These changes reduced the seating capacity of the saloon to seven.

The underframes, to Drawing No. 2495, were the same in every respect as those on Nos. 889–898. Steam heating on the storage system was supplied from the outset.

Each coach cost £2,164, for which capital was required.

Unfortunately, no record of the use of these three Firsts can be found, as they do not seem to have been attached to set trains; but it is safe to assume that, from time to time, they formed part of the composition of the SE&C's best trains.

Nos. 899–901 were renumbered 7358–7360 by the SR. Two of them were placed in sets: No. 7358 was in 6-set 662 by 1931, and No. 7360 was in 5-set 693 by 1931, remaining in it until at least 1944. By 1935 both sets were given an extra coach each. Both Firsts were transferred to 9-coach sets in the 1940s. 7-set 662 in 1936 was booked to work the 7.24 am Reading to London Bridge and 12.43 pm (Saturdays) or 5.25 pm (Mondays to Fridays) return services. By this time these were the only remaining through trains between London and the Reading line; the provision of three full Firsts in Set 662 suggests that the services were still very popular with first-class season-ticket holders – though few of them would have used these trains west of Dorking. 6-set 693 was allocated to the ex-LC&D section and worked between London and Maidstone East until the electrification to that town in July 1939.

Summary of Firsts:

SEC	*SR*	*Re-No.*	*Set*	*Wdn*
899	7358	1/27	662,905	1/48
900	7359	1/27	347	4/42
901	7360	7/24	693,921	10/52

CORRIDOR COMPOSITE BRAKES

Nos. 902–916 (SR Nos. 6622–6636)

These 15 beautifully-designed carriages were built at Ashford in 1907 and, because they were intended to be used in through train services between the SE&C and the Northern lines, were fully equipped with side corridors and external end gangways – or, to use SE&C terminology, 'vestibules'.

There were three distinct varieties within the series. The first seven were Bi-Composites with first- and third-class accommodation only and were intended for through service to the Midland Railway, which had long ago abolished second-class. A group of four was constructed with first, second and third class accommodation for through service to the London & North Western Railway, and a final batch of four, also Tri-Composites but with an extra second-class compartment squeezed in, was intended for through service to the Great Western Railway.

Nos. 902–908, built May 1907. (SR Nos. 6630–6636)
Body length: 50 ft 1 in. Bogie centres: 33 ft 6 in.
Compartments: 2 1st, 4 3rd, guard. Seats: 6 1st, 24 3rd.
Lavatories: 2.

Nos. 913–916, built July 1907. (SR Nos. 6622–6625)
Body length: 50 ft 1 in. Bogie centres: 33 ft 6 in.
Compartments: 2 1st, 1 2nd, 2 3rd, guard. Seats: 8 1st, 6 2nd, 12 3rd.
Lavatories: 2.

Nos. 909–912, built Sept. 1907. (SR Nos. 6626–6629)
Body length: 50 ft 1 in. Bogie centres: 33 ft 6 in.
Compartments: 2 1st, 2 2nd, 2 3rd, guard. Seats: 6 1st, 12 2nd, 12 3rd.
Lavatories: 2.

As all the coaches were the standard SE&C width of 8 ft 0¾ in., the side corridor severely restricted the seating capacity of the compartments; firsts sat only 2-a-side, seconds and thirds only 3-a-side. Hinged doors gave access from the corridor into the compartments. To the passenger it must have seemed that the coach was all doors: external doors, internal doors, doors separating the first-class corridor from the third-class, gangway doors; Nos. 913–6 each had 25 doors per coach, and the other two types had no fewer than 27 each!

All 15 vehicles employed the same methods of construction. Body framing was teak with mahogany panels and mouldings. Roof observatories for the guard had the new style of flattened top, the overall height being 12 ft 6½ in. The guard's compartment was fitted with a letter rack, a balance seat, hand brake wheel and brake release valve, and there were external double doors each side. The underframes were built entirely of steel, with bulb angle steel soles, channel steel bolster bars, cross bars and longitudinals. The corridor brakes were the first SE&C coaches with all-steel underframes.

Another 'first' was that these corridor coaches were the first to be built new with steam heating apparatus on the *non*-storage system, and a plate indicating 'Steam Heating Non-Storage' was fixed to the left-hand corner of the sole bars. In addition, they were the first SE&C carriages to be fitted with a new pattern long draw-hook and short coupling, which would henceforth be standard; to indicate carriages so fitted, the draw bar plates were painted white.

Despite the through corridor, the designer still considered it essential that separate first- and third-class lavatories should be provided. A curious distinction was made in their respective frosted-glass windows: in the first-class lavatory it was a droplight, but in the other it was a fixed window with a ventilator above it.

Ray Tustin, writing about these corridor coaches in the *Model Railway News* Vol.27, p.8, described the livery as 'reddish maroon with gold transfers'. Vehicle numbers on the compartment side were placed between the two first-class compartments, and between the end third-class compartment and the guard's compartment. 'S.E.&C.R.' appeared on the centre-line underneath the windows, and 'GUARD'S COMPT.' on the van doors. The underframe was black and the roof was white.

All 15 carriages were built out of revenue as 'renewals', and for accountancy purposes Nos. 902–5 were Chatham Section stock, though in practice this designation was meaningless. With some justification the SE&C was sufficiently proud of its corridor coaches to send one example, No. 915, to the Franco-British Exhibition in 1908, where considerable publicity was attracted to them.

Presumably the coaches entered service on their intended workings. From July 1907 there was an SE&C through carriage from Deal and Dover to Manchester Central via Ludgate Hill and the Midland Railway. The south-bound carriage was attached at Herne Hill to a through carriage from Manchester London Road (LNW). Some were used purely on SE&C services, despite their intended use: for example, from May 1908, No. 902 was booked to run in the 2.20 pm Charing Cross to Folkestone, and this working continued through the following winter. Then in July 1909 Nos. 909–12 were allocated thus: one in Train No. 11 (the Deal Express) and three as Bexhill through coaches. The 10.15 am Deal to Manchester included a SE&C through coach to and from Willesden only, and a GW coach ceased to work in the train.

From July 1910 Nos. 909–916 were booked to be kept in the following train services:

One in Train 11 (8.32 am Deal to Victoria and 5.00 pm return).
One in 10.30 am Victoria to Bexhill.
Three as Charing Cross and Bexhill through carriages.
Two in Charing Cross to Deal through workings.
One spare at Deal.

That accounted for all the Tri-Composite Brakes, but as two were actually in use on through trains to and from the L&NWR it is felt that the reference 'Two in Charing Cross to Deal through workings' must be incorrect. The LNW carriage workings for July to September 1910 show an SE&C Brake Tri-Composite in the 10.15 am Deal to Manchester London Road; it was scheduled to leave Willesden at 2.20 pm formed with LNW stock from Eastbourne and an LSW Brake Tri-Composite from Bournemouth. The SE&C carriage was attached at Crewe to the 2.40 pm Euston to Manchester. It returned next day on the 10.10 am Manchester to Deal, formed with the LSW Brake Tri-Composite for Bournemouth. At Crewe they were attached to the 7.40 am Holyhead to Euston service and detached at Willesden, the SE&C coach running to Herne Hill via the West London line.

The 10.15 am from Deal also conveyed a through carriage for Manchester Central, detached at Herne Hill and worked via Ludgate Hill, Kentish Town and the Midland Railway. The return service left Manchester at 10.30 am; the through carriage, on arriving at Herne Hill, was joined to the coach from the LNW and continued on to Tonbridge, Ashford, Folkestone, Dover and Deal.

From October 1910 Bi-Composite Brake No. 908 was booked to work with a Slip Brake Composite between Charing Cross and Dover Town, detached from the 4.25 pm down and returning on the 7.25 pm up. In April 1911 Nos. 904/6 had their third-class compartments upgraded to second class 'for GW services'.

The through service between Deal and Birkenhead via Redhill, Reading, Leamington and Wolverhampton ran from 1903 until October 1916, being reinstated in 1922. The booked formation in summer 1914 of the 10.38 am leaving Deal was: GW Composite and SE&C Tri-Composite Brake for Leamington; SE&C Third Brake and Tri-Composite Brake (GW Composite Brake alternate days) for Wolverhampton; GW Brake Composite for Birkenhead; van and 3-set for Charing Cross. From 1st August, 1914 one train comprised mainly SE&C stock and the other mainly GW, but the Leamington portion always included a GW Composite and an SE&C Brake Composite regardless of which company's stock formed the remainder of the train. An SE&C Brake Composite now worked through to Birkenhead on alternate days.

From May 1915 the through portion was reduced in length: only a GW Brake Composite for Birkenhead and a Tri-Composite Brake (SE&C or GW alternate days) and SE&C Third Brake for Wolverhampton were now included in the 10.38 am from Deal, along with stock for Charing Cross. From 19th December, 1915, the line was blocked between Dover and Folkestone by a huge landslip, and the through GW train was arranged to start at Dover Harbour at 10.05 am and run via Minster to Ashford, the return service operating the same way. All coaches were labelled 'Wolverhampton, Birmingham, Leamington, Oxford, Deal and Dover.' This was a temporary arrangement, for in April 1916 the train was arranged to start and finish its journey at Folkestone Junction, Dover and Deal being left unserved. Incidentally, to conform to GW practice, SE&C stock working in this service had to be provided with side lamp brackets in addition to the usual ones.

Meanwhile, on the 10.25 am Deal to Manchester service, the Victoria portion from August 1914 included Composite Brake No. 908, Tri-Composite Brake No. 912, Composite No. 894 and Third Brake No. 857, returning on the 2.50 pm Victoria to Deal. In the Midland through portion an SE&C Composite Brake worked between Deal and King's Cross and in the LNW through portion an SE&C Third Brake worked between Deal and Willesden; other stock was provided by the respective 'foreign' companies in both directions. All were withdrawn in March 1915.

In 1921, with the restoration of Continental travel, several boat trains were newly formed and all 15 brake coaches were formed in them, along with Pullman cars, to which they were through gangwayed. All third-class seating was upgraded to second, so that Nos. 902–912 now seated 6 1st, 24 2nd, and Nos. 913–916 seated 8 1st, 18 2nd; all compartments now had electric bell communication with the Pullman car attendant, and moreover could be fitted with portable tables which, when not in use, were kept in the guard's compartment.

Boat sets and workings, from June 1922, were:

1 (including 915 and 916): 10.50 am Victoria to Dover Marine and 5.45 pm return.
3 (including 902 and 914): 9.15 am Victoria to Folkestone Harbour, 2.10 pm Dover Marine to Victoria.
4 (including 907 and 908): 8.55 am Victoria to Dover Marine and 2.40 pm return.
5 (including 905 and 903): 2.00 pm Victoria to Dover Marine and 9.00 pm Folkestone Harbour to Victoria.
6 (including 912 and 909): If required, 9.05 am or 1.50 pm Victoria to Dover Marine and 6.40 pm return.
7 (including 910 and 911): 8.15 am Dover Marine to Victoria and 8.00 pm return.
8 (including 904 and 906): 8.30 am Victoria to Folkestone Harbour and 8.30 pm return.

Pullman cars and any other corridor stock were marshalled between pairs of corridor brakes, and non-gangwayed coaches, even though part of the set, were put at the London end of the train.

With the advent of new boat train stock, the 1907-built carriages were taken off these workings and in 1924 the second-class seating was down-graded to third, capacity being unchanged. Southern numbers began to be applied as from April 1924: Nos. 913–6 became 6622–25, Nos. 909–12

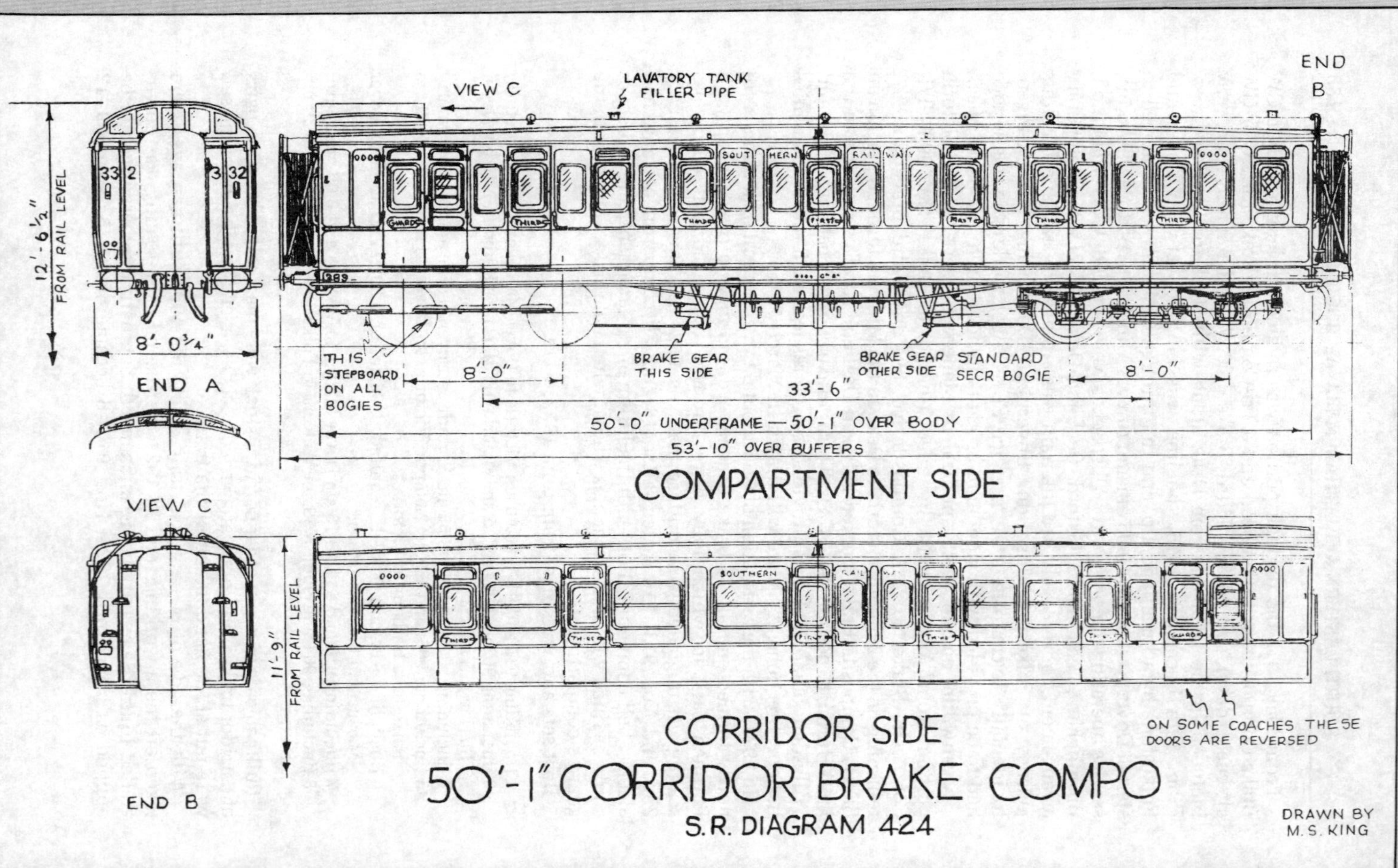

END B
VIEW C
LAVATORY TANK FILLER PIPE
12'-6½" FROM RAIL LEVEL
8'-0¾"
END A
THIS STEPBOARD ON ALL BOGIES
8'-0"
BRAKE GEAR THIS SIDE
BRAKE GEAR OTHER SIDE
STANDARD SECR BOGIE
8'-0"
33'-6"
50'-0" UNDERFRAME — 50'-1" OVER BODY
53'-10" OVER BUFFERS
COMPARTMENT SIDE
VIEW C
11'-9" FROM RAIL LEVEL
ON SOME COACHES THESE DOORS ARE REVERSED
CORRIDOR SIDE
END B
50'-1" CORRIDOR BRAKE COMPO
S.R. DIAGRAM 424
DRAWN BY M.S. KING

became 6626–29 and Nos. 904/6/2/3/5/7/8 (in that order) were renumbered 6630–36. Some were then restored to Dover–Birkenhead through train services, either working in pairs or with a Corridor Third marshalled between two of them. They remained on these services throughout the 1920s.

3-coach corridor sets 400 and 430 were formed, probably in 1925, with two Composite Brakes and an ex-LSW 1894-built 'Eagle' First in each. All six coaches received their SR numbers at Eastleigh in June 1925. The sets worked Charing Cross–Hastings services until the arrival of modern corridor stock on that line. R.W. Kidner recorded ex-SE&C Corridor Third No. 964 as an extra coach in Set 430, but it may have been part of the set as it, too, had been repainted at Eastleigh in June 1925. Another corridor set formed about 1925 was No. 389; this comprised Composite Brakes 6622/27 and Third No. 966, all repainted at Ashford in June 1925. Set 389 ran on the Central Section, working in 1928 the 8.05 am Hastings to London Bridge and 4.05 pm return services.

	Set 400	**Set 430**
Cor.Cpo Bke	6623	6629
Cor. First	7207?	7206
Cor.Cpo Bke	6636	6632

By 1931 the corridor Firsts had been replaced by ex-SEC Corridor Thirds and the 3-sets were now working Ashford–Brighton services.

After Sets 400 and 430 were disbanded three of the Corridor Brakes were formed into special-traffic sets 331 and 332, each with two Composite Brakes and seven ex-LSW Saloons (formerly dining cars). Set 331 included Brakes 6623/34 and Set 332 had Brakes 6632/36. 10-coach sets 336 and 337 were formed by 1931, each composed of two SE&C Corridor Brakes and eight ex-LSW non-corridor coaches. They were berthed at Eastleigh or Walton for summer traffic on the ex-LSW main line: Set 336 had Nos. 6625/26 and Set 337 had Nos. 6624/33.

In 1939 six of the Corridor Brakes were modified at Eastleigh for use in three casualty evacuation trains, each of which included an SR-built Saloon and nine SR Corridor Luggage Vans for carrying stretchers. Train No. 32 had Brakes 6628/30, Train No. 33 had Nos. 6626/35, and Train No. 34 had Nos. 6633/29. Clearly Sets 336/7 had been disbanded by then, coaches 6626 and 6633 going into the casualty evacuation trains, which were themselves disbanded about 1945.

Two 9-coach sets, Nos. 334/5, were formed about 1940 for the Western Section, using Corridor Brakes and ex-SE&C and ex-LSW non-corridor coaches. The sets were berthed at Barnes during 1941; Set 334 was at Hampton Court during 1945 and, reduced to eight coaches, at Hook during 1947 before being transferred to the Eastern Section. 9-set 335 was at Strawberry Hill by 1947 for a Saturday working, the 12.39 pm Waterloo to Basingstoke. The set was transferred to the Eastern Section during 1948. By then Set 334 had Composite Brakes Nos. 6624/5 and Set 335 had Nos. 6630/3.

By summer 1947 quite a few Corridor Brakes had been withdrawn and only Nos. 6624/5/8/9/30/2/3/4/6 remained in traffic. Three 2-coach sets had been formed about 1946 for Ashford–Rye–Hastings services, each formed of an SE&C Corridor Brake and an SR Corridor Third:

	Set 331	**Set 332**	**Set 333**
Cor.Bke Cpo	6634	6632	6636
Cor Third	989	988	985

Set 333 was withdrawn in 1951, 331 in 1953, and Set 332 lasted until 1958. 8-set 334 retained its SE&C Brakes 6624/5 until late 1952, the set being berthed at Lenham or Birchington. In May 1949 No. 6624 was noted marshalled 'the wrong way round', although Ray Tustin thought that this arrangement might not have been accidental but was done to bring the guard's compartment on to the platform of stations with short platforms.

The longest-lasting set composed entirely of SE&C corridor coaches was No. 389. Its original Composite Brakes, Nos. 6622/7, were withdrawn in 1947 and replaced by Nos. 6628/9, which remained in the set until its withdrawal in 1959. (The other coaches were six Corridor Thirds of 1921, which will be described in a later section.) Nos. 6628/9/32 were repainted by BR in its crimson lake and cream livery, which did not suit them very much, especially as the dividing line between the two colours blundered its way unimaginatively through the middle of the waist panels instead of following the raised mouldings. The Corridor Thirds in Set 389 appear never to have been painted in matching style. Set 389, berthed at Maze Hill during the 1950s, was always used for the summer Saturday 2.25 pm Charing Cross to Hastings and 7.10 pm return.

Summary of Corridor Composite Brakes

SEC	*SR*	*Re-No.*	*Set*	*Wdn*	*SEC*	*SR*	*Re-No.*	*Set*	*Wdn*
913	6622	6/25	389	/47	904	6630	10/25	335	11/51
914	6623	6/25	400,331	8/45	906	6631	11/25		8/35
915	6624	6/25	337,334	12/52	902	6632	6/25	430,332	6/58
916	6625	6/25	336,334	12/52	903	6633	4/24	337,335,917	3/57
909	6626	4/24	336	11/44	905	6634	4/24	331	10/53
910	6627	6/25	389	/47	907	6635	12/25		11/44
911	6628	4/24	389	2/59	908	6636	6/25	400,332,333	3/51
912	6629	6/25	430,389	2/59					

Nos. 6622/7 on withdrawal in 1947 were transferred to the service vehicle list as Breakdown Tool Vans Nos. 344 S and 345 S; No. 6624 became DS 3211 in 1953 and No. 6625 was renumbered DS 3193. These two were also Breakdown Tool Vans, and by 1960 were stationed at Stewarts Lane. The last two to be withdrawn, Nos. 6628/9, became 'Internal User' vehicles 081061 and 081062 for a few years at Folkestone. Now 52 years old, they were a tribute to the superb quality of construction that was normal for SE&C carriages.

THE 1907/8 BOAT TRAINS

At a meeting of the Locomotive, Carriage and Wagon Committee in December 1906 the decision was made to order two new boat trains from

Metropolitan Amalgamated Railway Carriage & Wagon Co. The contract, for nine Composites, eight Firsts and six Second Brakes, was drawn in April 1907. All the stock was delivered that same summer. A third, spare, boat train was later ordered from the same manufacturers, this one comprising five Composites, three Firsts and two Second Brakes, which were completed and delivered to the SEC in summer 1908. The 23 coaches of the first batch were built at Metropolitan's main works at Saltley, Birmingham, but the 10 later ones were the product of the Lancaster works, shortly before its closure in September 1908.

The coaches were of the following types:

COMPOSITE LAVATORY Nos. 930–938, 953–957 (SR 5311–5324)
Body length: 50 ft 1 in. Bogie centres: 33 ft 6 in.
Compartments: 3 1st, 3 2nd. Seats: 15 1st, 19 2nd class.
Lavatories: 4 (3 to 1st class, 1 to 2nd).
Lighting: 6 duplex and six single lamps.
Nos. 930–5 delivered 6/07, 936–8 delivered 7/07, 953–7 6/08.
Original cost: £2,445 each.

FIRST LAVATORY (with saloon) Nos. 939–946, 958–960 (SR 7347–7357)
Body length: 50 ft 1 in. Bogie centres: 33 ft 6 in.
Compartments: 1 saloon, 3 ordinary. Seats: 27.
Lavatories: 4 (one to each compartment).
Lighting: 6 duplex and four single lamps.
Nos. 939–46 delivered 7/07, Nos. 958–60 delivered 6/08.
Original cost: £2,520 each.

SECOND BRAKE LAVATORY Nos. 947, 948 (SR Nos. 3316, 3317)
Body length: 50 ft 1 in. Bogie centres: 33 ft 6 in.
Compartments: 5, plus guard. Seats: 35.
Lavatories: 5 (one to each compartment)
Lighting: 5 duplex, 6 single lamps.
Nos. 947/8 delivered 7/07.
Original cost: £2,303 each.

SECOND BRAKE (with saloon) Nos. 949, 950, 961, 962 (SR 3581/2/5/6)
Body length: 50 ft 1 in. Bogie centres: 33 ft 6 in.
Compartments: 1 saloon, 1 ordinary, plus luggage and guard.
Seats: 22. Lavatories: 2.
Nos. 949/50 delivered 7/07, Nos. 961/2 delivered 6/08.
Original cost: £2,001 each.

SECOND BRAKE LAVATORY Nos. 951, 952 (SR Nos. 3320, 3321)
Body length: 50 ft 1 in. Bogie centres: 33 ft 6 in.
Compartments: 2, plus luggage and guard. Seats: 14.
Lavatories: 2. Lighting: 2 duplex, 6 single lamps.
Nos. 951/2 delivered 7/07.
Original cost: £1,859 each.

Features common to all were a height from rail to roof of 11 ft 9 in., a height to top of roof observatories on the three brake coaches of 12 ft 6½ in., a bogie wheelbase of 8 ft, all-steel underframes, low-pressure steam heating on the non-storage system, compensating buffers with auxiliary buffers on the headstocks, and the new style of short coupling with long drawbar hook.

Nos. 951/2 each had a luggage compartment of truly gargantuan dimensions holding 4 tons and fitted with two sets of double doors (with louvre ventilators) on each bodyside. Luggage compartments on the saloon brakes were a little smaller, holding 3 tons and with one set of double doors each side. In contrast Nos. 947/8 had only a very cramped combined guard's and luggage compartment.

In the Firsts, each saloon was 19 ft 9 in. long and seated 12 passengers on a mixture of transverse fixed seats, movable armchairs and an inward-facing settee. The saloon in the Second Brakes (an innovation) seated 15 passengers: eight in two settees and seven on transverse fixed seats. In the Bi-Composites, the second-class passengers had the useful facility of a corridor which enabled all passengers to have access to the lavatory. As for the unfortunate third-class passengers, they were not admitted to any of the three boat trains.

The stock was sent into traffic as follows: Nos. 939/40 – 29.7.07; Nos. 930–3/5/6, 941–4, 949–52 – 31.7.07; Nos. 937/8, 945/6, 947/8 – 1.8.07; No. 934 – 2.8.07; Nos. 953–62 – 20.6.08. However, they were not kept together for very long but were mixed in with the 1905 stock. By 1908 Boat Train No. 2, for example, was formed mainly of 1905 stock but also included First No. 939 of 1907. In 1909 Boat Train No. 6A included First No. 944 and Composites Nos. 934/5 in its formation.

On 5th March, 1909, a boat train was involved in an accident at Tonbridge. The 9.05 am Cannon Street to Dover Harbour service, which included Second Brake 952, several mail vans, Composites 931/4, First 944 and Second Brake 951, was passing through Tonbridge station when it was hit by the 8.30 am Charing Cross to Dover Town via Redhill service, which had passed the home signal at danger. Both trains were running late. Although it was quite a spectacular smash, no carriages were damaged sufficiently to be beyond repair, and all later returned to service. Two of the vans at the front of the 8.30 am were not so fortunate.

By August 1910, Second Brakes Nos. 951 and 952 were allocated to the 10.38 am Deal to Reading service, one or the other being in the booked formation. Also in 1910, Boat Train No. 3A was shown as being formed largely of 1908-built stock, plus two new Pullman cars: 2nd Brake 961, Composites 953/4, Parlour Car *Corunna*, Buffet Car *Florence*, Firsts 3793, 960, 959, Composite 955 and Second Brake 3807. This train set worked the 9.00 am Charing Cross to Dover Pier and 3.20 pm return. The 11.00 am from Victoria to Dover Pier included Composite 957 and First 940, plus Pullmans *Savona* and *Valencia* and four 1905-built boat train carriages; the portion from Holborn to Dover, attached at Herne Hill, included Composite 956.

During 1915 and 1916 First No. 939 was recorded as being part of 4-set 24, berthed at Ramsgate Harbour. From 1916 to 1919 Boat Train No. 5 was in regular use and included Composites Nos. 937/8 and Firsts Nos. 946 and 3788, plus Pullman cars. During World War I, certain Firsts, because they incorporated saloons, were reserved for special traffic along with the entire-First Saloons Nos. 3785–7 described in a previous section. No. 943 was kept at Victoria during 1915 but was at Rotherhithe Road during 1917; No. 940 was kept at Folkestone Junction during that year. Saloon Brake No. 949 was one of the 'temporary goods brakes' in use during 1917.

No. 956 was equipped with water heaters in the lavatories in 1921, and No. 933 was similarly-fitted in 1922. By then only Nos. 940/1/5 were in regular boat train sets (941 in Set 3, 940/5 in Set 5) but Nos. 930–8/42/3/6/9/50/3–62 were designated 'spare boat' stock and could be drawn upon to make up 'scratch' boat trains when necessary.

The SR, when it came to renumber the saloon Second Brakes, showed the same indecision that it did with many other ex-SE&C second-class carriages. Initially, Nos. 949/50 were to be renumbered 4152/3 in the Second Brake series, and Nos. 961/2 were to be 4154/5. But in 1924 Nos. 949/50/61 were transferred to the *Third* Brakes list, Nos. 949/50 receiving their new numbers 3581/2 in 1928. No. 961, however, was transferred back *again* to the Second Brakes list as No. 4154, receiving this number in October 1926. No. 962, which had remained as a Second Brake, was duly renumbered 4155 in February 1927. Second class facilities were still required for boat trains because of through bookings to the Continent, and Nos. 4154/5 remained as back-up boat train stock until April 1934, when they were finally renumbered as Third Brakes 3585/6.

The other four Second Brakes, Nos. 947/8/51/2, became Third Brakes 3316/7 and 3320/1 without any hesitation, seating capacity being slightly increased in consequence.

The Composites were retained as first/second until 1924, when the second-class seating was altered to 20 third-class seats. These coaches received new numbers 5311–5324. The Firsts became Nos. 7347–57.

Below is listed the renumbering scheme, dates of renumbering, known SR set numbers, and withdrawal dates. (L = Loose coach.)

SEC	*SR*	*Re-No.*	*Set*	*Wdn*	*SEC*	*SR*	*Re-No.*	*Set*	*Wdn*
947	3316	8/24	686	12/51	953	5320	11/28	688	7/52
948	3317	9/28	662	11/39	954	5321	5/24		/44
951	3320	6/26	680	10/48	955	5322	5/24	912	3/51
952	3321	10/28	900,519,900	1/58	956	5323	9/26	335	11/51
949	3581	6/28	917,901?	1/53	957	5324	1/26	519,900	1/58
950	3582	11/28	901	1/53	939	7347	6/24	898,L	5/56
961	4154	10/26		see note	940	7348	6/28	906	8/55
962	4155	2/27		see note	941	7349	4/27	921	2/45
930	5311	10/27	516	/42	942	7350	11/27	303,920	5/55
931	5312	2/28	517	/43	943	7351	12/25	891,662	7/44
932	5313	9/26		1/40	944	7352	10/23	685,305	4/44
933	5314	5/28	906,896	5/56	945	7353	5/28	917,L	5/50
934	5315	3/27		6/40	946	7354	4/24	896	4/51
935	5316	8/28	900	12/56	958	7355	12/27	918	9/42
936	5317	1/28		8/40	959	7356	8/24		c/42
937	5318	8/24	688,?	11/52	960	7357	2/24	686,920,903	12/57
938	5319	1/29	403	4/53					

Note: Second Brakes 4154/5 were renumbered as Third Brakes 3585/6 and both were formed in Set 906; No. 3585 was withdrawn in August 1955 and No. 3586 was then transferred to Set 335 until its withdrawal in January 1957.

First No. 7351 was 6-set 891 by 1931 (the other five coaches being ex-LB&SC) and then in 7-set 662 by 1935; it was withdrawn following enemy action in 1944. Another casualty of war was First No. 7355, which was damaged and withdrawn at Lancing in September 1942.

Sets 662, 680, 685, 686 and 688 were all formed in the 1920s by the SR and each included at least one example from the list of 33 former boat train vehicles. As the years went by the sets were lengthened and re-formed, and the numbers shown in the above table show the position in the middle-to-late 1940s. The sets numbered in the 900s were formed in 1931/2 for special traffic and summer Saturday Kent coast services. They often appeared on hop-pickers' specials, especially in later years: for example, 9-set 906 was used for such a purpose on 19th September, 1948, when it ran from London to the Kent & East Sussex line (which had become part of British Railways in January 1948).

Composite No. 5319, along with other ex-SE&C vehicles, ran in 6-set 403 from about 1946 on the Western Section. Set 403 was originally an LSW corridor set but with the addition of these coaches it was now only 'part-corridor'. During summer 1947 it stood spare at Eastleigh, moving to Broadstone for the winter. Subsequently it worked in the Eastleigh district each summer and stood at Hook or Winchfield at other times. Upon withdrawal, No. 5319 was converted to Camping Coach CC 30 and was stationed at Amberley. Camping coaches provided cheap holiday accommodation for families during the 1950s and early 1960s and were the responsibility of the station at which they were berthed. The only condition imposed upon campers was that they had to use the railway at the start and finish of their holidays. In July 1966 CC 30 was withdrawn and transferred to the Western Region of BR as a departmental service vehicle, DW 150382.

Two coaches ultimately became service vehicles in the Southern Region list. First No. 7353 was renumbered DS 3160 in 1950 and was used at Lancing Carriage Works for moving materials about. It was marked 'C.&W. Engineers Dept. Lancing Works only (Trimming Shop)'. Third Brake Saloon No. 3582 became Staff Van DS 27 in 1954 and on withdrawal was purchased for preservation and kept at the South Eastern Steam Centre during the 1970s. This site, the former locomotive depot at Ashford, held several open days and the coach could be ridden in by visitors when it was hauled and propelled within shed limits by a steam locomotive. As the interior had been stripped in 1954 the visitor could have had no idea what an attractive coach it once was; the long lines of inward-facing bench seats with which the vehicle was now fitted gave a rather poor impression. When the South Eastern Steam Centre was closed much of the rolling stock was rescued and transferred to other locations, but unfortunately DS 27 does not seem to have been one of the items saved.

COMPOSITE LAVATORY

Nos. 981–1000 (SR Nos. 5325–5344)

Body length: 50 ft 1 in. Bogie centres: 33 ft 6 in.
Compartments: 3 1st, 3 2nd. Seats: 15 1st, 19 2nd class.
Lavatories: 4 (3 to 1st class, 1 to 2nd).

These coaches, to the same design as Nos. 930–8 and 953–7 described in the previous section, were built as renewals by the SE&C at Ashford and completed on the following dates:

981–85	11/1907	991–95	3/1908
986–90	12/1907	996–1000	6/1908

The buffers had malleable cast iron sleeves and there were auxiliary side springs of indiarubber. Initially only Nos. 985–90 were fitted with steam heating apparatus when new; each first-class compartment had a 5 ft heater, two of the second-class had a 3 ft 9 in. heater and the remaining second-class a 4 ft 6 in. heater (all six being of the non-storage type). The other 14 coaches received heating as follows: 996/7, 1909; 981/2/91/3, 1910; 983/92/4/5, 998–1000, 1911; and 984, 1912.

Three of the Composites were formed into new set trains for the 1909 summer train service. Train No. 67 comprised Composite 983, a Third and a Brake Van, and worked the 7.30 am Victoria to Dover Harbour and 3.45 pm return. Train No. 68 had a Third Brake, Composite No. 994, a non-lavatory Composite (3 1sts, 3 2nds) and a Brake Van, for the 9.05 am Dover Harbour to Victoria and 4.20 pm return. Train No. 69, formed with Composite No. 993, a Third and a Brake Van, was a 'City Portion' working the 9.45 am Holborn to Dover Harbour and 7.20 pm return.

No. 994 (Train 68) was involved in dynamo experiments during 1910 and 1911. On 26th August, 1910, it was fitted with Stone's 'CZ' trial dynamo, and apparently the agreement was that Stone's representative would keep a check on it and see to any repairs necessary. On 15th February, 1911, the lighting failed and the coach was 'stopped' at Grosvenor Road carriage depot (Victoria) for examination by the representative. He found that some of the contacts on the dynamo had burnt out. Some parts were renewed and No. 994 returned to traffic on the 4.20 pm down on 16th February, 1911. An inspection by Stone's representative at Ashford in April 1911 found everything in good order, but on 4th September, 1911, the light failed while the carriage was working the 3.15 pm Charing Cross to Deal, and the coach was 'stopped' next day. The fittings had been tampered with – by whom the report did not say.

Some other Composites were specified in short portions detached from or attached to the main train: in June 1910 No. 984 (with a Tri-Composite and Brake Van) was the Dover Town portion of the 3.18 pm Charing Cross to Deal; by October 1910 it had been replaced by No. 993. The portion returned from Dover at 7.25 pm. No. 1000 was similarly formed with a Tri-Composite and Brake Van and worked the 11.00 am Charing Cross to Sandwich and 4.40 pm return from October 1910.

During 1914 and 1915 No. 992 was recorded as being in Train 16, having replaced one of the Slip Brake Composites originally formed in. Also in 1914/5, No. 995 worked with Third Brake No. 3497 as a 2-coach portion berthed at Reigate.

By 1921, Nos. 981/5–90/6/7/9 were designated 'spare boat' stock and No. 995 was in Boat Train Set 7. No. 982 was part of 5-set 257 (which was berthed at Reigate or Ash for Cannon Street services) and No. 992 was in 4-set 55, which worked between Tonbridge and Cannon Street via Redhill. Set 55 later became SR set No. 672.

On becoming Southern Railway property Nos. 981/5–90/6/7/9 were initially retained as first/second Composites for boat train working until 1924, when the second class became third, seating 20 in each coach. Only Nos. 5331/4 appeared in Southern livery with the class label 'SECOND' on the doors. The remaining Composites were reclassified as first/third from 1923. All 20 were renumbered 5325–5344 between January 1924 and April 1929.

Three Composites were running in sets during the 1930s: No. 5326 in 6-set 687, No. 5336 in 4-set 672, and No. 5338 in 6-set 685. Others were added to sets during the late 1930s and the 1940s. In 1941 Set 685 was running on the Central Section, working the 7.00 am Brighton to London Bridge, 5.20 pm London Bridge to Tunbridge Wells West and 7.37 pm thence to Brighton.

Summary of Composites Nos. 981–1000

SEC	*SR*	*Re-No.*	*Set*	*Wdn*	*SEC*	*SR*	*Re-No.*	*Set*	*Wdn*
981	5325	12/28	917	11/52	991	5335	2/26	898	4/51
982	5326	10/28	687	8/40	992	5336	8/27	672,919	/43
983	5327	10/28	640,917	3/57	993	5337	4/27	901	12/49
984	5328	1/28	688	7/52	994	5338	1/24	685,666	4/51
985	5329	11/25	921	7/52	995	5339	1/24	520	12/46
986	5330	8/24	896,696?	11/55	996	5340	4/29	403	4/55
987	5331	2/24	918	7/52	997	5341	10/28	517	/43
988	5332	8/24	903,920	4/51	998	5342	11/26	640,?	8/52
989	5333	10/27	520	12/46	999	5343	12/24	688	7/52
990	5334	4/24	410	3/56	1000	5344	1/24	335	11/51

Sets 403 and 410 shown in the table were originally 3-coach ex-LSW corridor sets, but from about 1946 ran as 6-sets with ex-SE&C non-corridor coaches added and they worked certain Western Section extra train services or were kept for special traffic.

Set 403 included Composites 5319, 5340, 5347, 5349 and two ex-LSW Corridor Brake Thirds. Set 410 had only one ex-SE&C vehicle – No. 5334 – the remaining five coaches all being ex-LSW. For the summer 1947 services Set 410 was berthed at Basingstoke for semi-fast Waterloo services. Set 403, at this time, was berthed at Eastleigh but during each winter, when fewer trains were needed to operate the service, it usually sojourned at Hook.

TRI-COMPOSITE LAVATORY

Nos. 917–929 (SR Nos. 5380–5392)

Body length: 51 ft 1 in. Bogie centres: 34 ft 6 in.
Compartments: 2 1st, 2 2nd, 2 3rd. Seats: 10 1st, 14 2nd, 16 3rd.
Lavatories: 6 (2 1st, 2 2nd, 2 3rd class).

Ordered from Metropolitan Amalgamated RC&W Co. at the same time as the 1907 boat trains, these 13 Tri-Composites were all delivered in August 1907. Paid for out of revenue as renewals, each cost £2,388. They were almost identical to the Tri-Composites of 1906 (Nos. 880–888) but the second class compartments were 2 in. wider, the extra 4 in. being gained at the expense of the lavatories, which were slightly narrower. The coaches, which were built to Drawing No. 2449B, had all-steel underframes and compensating buffers with auxiliary buffers on the headstocks and the new standard couplings and drawhooks but were not at first steam heated. They were electrically lit with six duplex lamps in the compartments and six single lamps in the lavatories.

Steam heating was fitted in November 1907 to Nos. 917–20 and January 1908 to Nos. 921/2. The remainder were fitted in 1909 (929), 1910 (924), 1911 (923/7), 1912 (926/8) and 1914 (925).

From May 1909, Boat Train No. 6A included one of these coaches, No. 920, in the formation, which was booked as two Second Brakes, Firsts Nos. 3500 and 944, Composites Nos. 934 and 935, Tri-Composites Nos. 920 and two extra Composites if required. Services worked were the 9.05 am Cannon Street to Dover Pier and 3.25 pm return.

Five of this series of Tri-Composites were formed into 3-coach sets which later were classed as Type 'B', each including a 5-compartment Third Brake, a Tri-Composite and a Brake Tri-Composite. Set 66 was formed in October 1910, and all three of its coaches received steam heating in December 1912: Nos. 835, 928 and 151. The set that later became No. 68 was also in Ashford Works for steam heaters to be fitted in 1912: coaches 842, 926 and 158 emerged in September of that year.

Nos. 919 and 921 were formed with Third Brake No. 3496 into an unnumbered 3-set in October 1909 to work the 2.45 pm Hastings to Victoria and 6.00 pm return services. From May 1910 the workings were altered to 12.30 pm Hastings to Ashford, 2.18 pm Ashford to Victoria, and 6.00 pm thence to Hastings. By about 1912 No. 919 was the centre coach of Type 'B' set 67.

In the last year of the SE&C's existence Nos. 919/24/26/28/29 were running in Type 'B' 3-sets and the other eight coaches were loose. The SR renumbered all 13 to 5380–5392 between 1924 and 1929 and the second-class compartments were re-classed as third, total seating capacity of the four third-class compartments in each coach now being 32. The 3-sets remained intact and were renumbered 515, 520 and 523–5 in 1923. There seems no doubt that sets received Southern set numbers while the coaches remained in SE&C livery; Set 515, for example, retained SE&C livery until early 1929.

Of the other Composites, No. 5390 went to 5-set 334 in the 1930s, No. 5383 to 9-set 687 *c*.1940, No. 5384 to 8-set 897, No. 5388 to 9-set 900 and No. 5380 to 8-set 920, probably when they were first formed. No. 5381 was recorded running in a Western Section 2-set, No. 127, between about 1941 and 1945, before going to 9-set 335 and remaining there until withdrawal in 1951.

Sets 334 and 335 were both allocated to the London West district until 1947 but both were 'sent home' in late 1947/early 1948. In 1947 Set 334 had been berthed at Hook and Set 335 at Strawberry Hill (for the Saturday 12.39 pm Waterloo to Basingstoke).

Summary of Tri-Composites Nos. 917–929

SEC	*SR*	*Re-No.*	*Set*	*Wdn*	*SEC*	*SR*	*Re-No.*	*Set*	*Wdn*
917	5380	11/26	920	6/57	924	5387	6/27	520	8/40
918	5381	6/24	127,335	11/51	925	5388	1/24	900	12/56
919	5382	7/27	524	9/43	926	5389	12/27	525,896	1/58
920	5383	8/26	687,688,?	10/54	927	5390	8/26	334	1/58
921	5384	10/28	897	9/51	928	5391	3/28	523	/43
922	5385	4/27	897	9/51	929	5392	3/29	515	4/48
923	5386	10/27		3/45					

After withdrawal three coach bodies were grounded at different locations: No. 5382 at Newhaven (noted 6/47), 5386 at Farley Green MoS depot (5/48) and 5391 at Eastleigh (8/46).

TRI-COMPOSITE LAVATORY

Nos. 800–814 (SR Nos. 5365–5379)

Body length: 51 ft 1 in. Bogie centres: 34 ft 6 in.
Compartments: 2 1st, 2 2nd, 2 3rd. Seats: 10 1st, 14 2nd, 16 3rd.
Lavatories: 6 (2 1st, 2 2nd, 2 3rd class).

Built at Ashford in April (800–4), May (805–9) and July 1909 (810–4) as 'renewals', this final batch of Tri-Composites differed from the earlier 51 ft Tri-Composites only in compartment dimensions. First- and second-class compartments were slightly narrower to allow the long-suffering third-class passengers an extra 2 in. of leg-room in their two compartments, which were 5 ft 9½ in. across.

Buffers were fitted with malleable iron guides and sleeves, and incorporated auxiliary side springs. The steel underframes had bulb angle soles, channel steel headstocks and channel steel bolster crossbars. Initially only Nos. 810 and 811 had steam heating, though No. 813 received it only two months after leaving Ashford Works. Others were fitted as follows: 803–6/12, 1910; 800/2/8, 1911; 801, 1913; 814, 1914; 809, 1918; and 807, 1919.

Five of these 1909-built Tri-Composites were later marshalled in Type 'B' 3-coach sets, of which there were 14, originally with random numbers but in 1914/5 collected together and numbered 58–71. No. 800 was in Set 71 (with Third Brake No. 843 and Composite Brake No. 160, all three of which were given heaters in May 1911); No. 801 was in Set 70, with Nos. 839 and 154 (all being heated from February 1913). No. 805 was in Set 83, which later became Set 65.

3-set 246 was formed late in 1915 with a Composite, Tri-Composite and Third Brake for working in the Maidstone East/Swanley/Sevenoaks area; the Tri-Composite is known to have been No. 811 in 1920–2. At about this time, Nos. 808/12 were formed in Boat Train No. 3 and Nos. 810/13 were in Boat Train No. 4. No. 814 was designated 'Spare Boat'. These five were retained as Tri-Composites by the SR until 1924, when the second class was altered to third with a total seating capacity of 32; the other 10 became first/third Composites in 1923.

All 15 of the former Tri-Composites received their Southern numbers, which were applied as the coaches went into Works for overhaul between 1924 and 1929. The new numbers were 5365–5379. The five 3-coach sets that included one of this series of Composites, SE&C set numbers 62, 64, 65, 70 and 71, received the SR set numbers 519, 521, 522, 527 and 528. For some unknown reason Set 528 was disbanded before any of its coaches were painted in SR livery. In 1926 Third Brake No. 843 became SR 3285 and went to Set 640; Composite No. 800 became SR 5365 in 1927, running in 4-set 538 from about 1924 to about 1932; and Composite Brake No. 160 became SR 6619 in 1927, remaining as part of Set 528 but in a non-standard formation that comprised Third No. 1111 and another Composite Brake, No. 6638. No. 5365 eventually found its way into 3-set 516 when that set was augmented to eight coaches about 1938.

Most of the series seem to have been loose stock during the 1920s and 1930s. By 1941 No. 5373 had been formed with ex-LSW Third Brake No.

62 ft Corridor Brake Composite No. 6642, built as SE&C Corridor Brake First No. 2508 in 1921. Matchboarded lower panels, Maunsell bogies, L-section truss rods, Spencer's patent buffers at brake end and retractable buffers at opposite end. Faversham, 20th May, 1950. *D. Cullum*

Compartment side of Corridor Brake Composite No. 6642 at Blackheath on 23rd June, 1957, formed in corridor set No. 917. The three right-hand compartments were first-class and the other two were second-class. Pullman gangway and retractable buffers at inner end. *J.H. Aston*

40 ft 6 in. First No. 7239, built by the SER as No. 1954 in 1880. 'American' bogies, gas lighting, close-coupling, 'smoking' labels on the windows of three compartments. No. 7239 was withdrawn in 1928. *Author's Collection*

44 ft First No. 7298 at Templecombe, 23rd July, 1937. The coach was built by Metropolitan RCW in 1900 as a Composite, but was altered to a First by the SR in 1923. *H.C. Casserley*

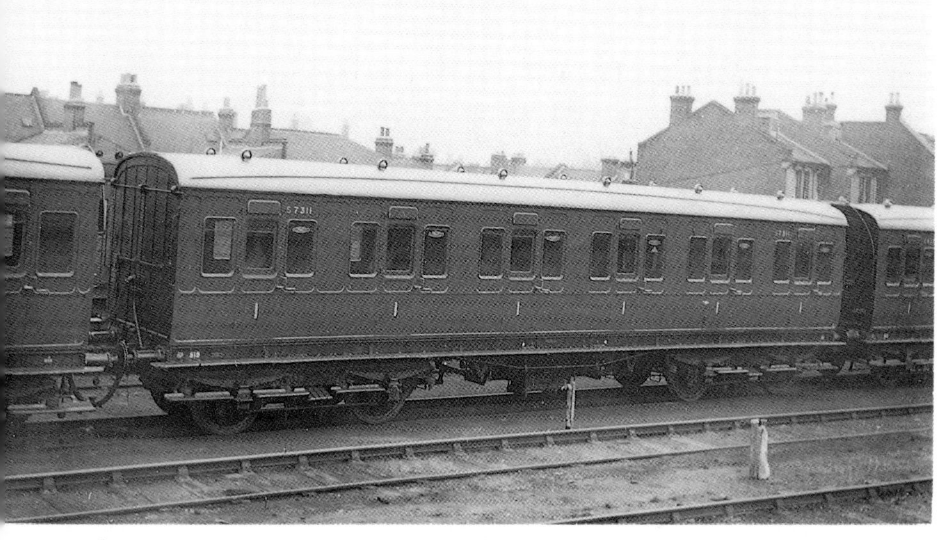

45 ft First No. 7311 in Set 519 at Maze Hill, 22nd March, 1951. As No. 188, this coach was constructed at Ashford in 1903, and was withdrawn as late as 1956.
D. Cullum

46 ft Lavatory First No. 7345 in Set 302 at Tonbridge, 29th May, 1950. This was the only ex-SE&C coach in the set. No. 7345 was built as No. 3510 by the Midland Railway-Carriage & Wagon Co. in 1904. Four of the five compartments had lavatory access.
D. Cullum

50 ft Lavatory First with saloon No. 7347, as painted by BR in lined red livery. It was built by Metropolitan Amalgamated in 1907 as SE&C No. 939 for a boat train. It is shown here at Eardley on 23rd July, 1956, two months after withdrawal from service. *H.C. Casserley*

SEC No. 3791 was built by Metropolitan Amalgamated for the 1905 boat train and is shown here as SR No. 7362 in Set 899 at Tattenham Corner on 13th April, 1948. Four of the compartments had lavatory access. Body length was 51 ft. *D. Cullum*

Five of the 1905-built 51 ft Lavatory Firsts were converted in 1913 to first brakes, the end compartment being replaced by a small luggage and guard's compartment, seen here at the right-hand end of No. 7744 (formerly 3796) in Set 346 at Tattenham Corner on 21st March, 1949. *D. Cullum*

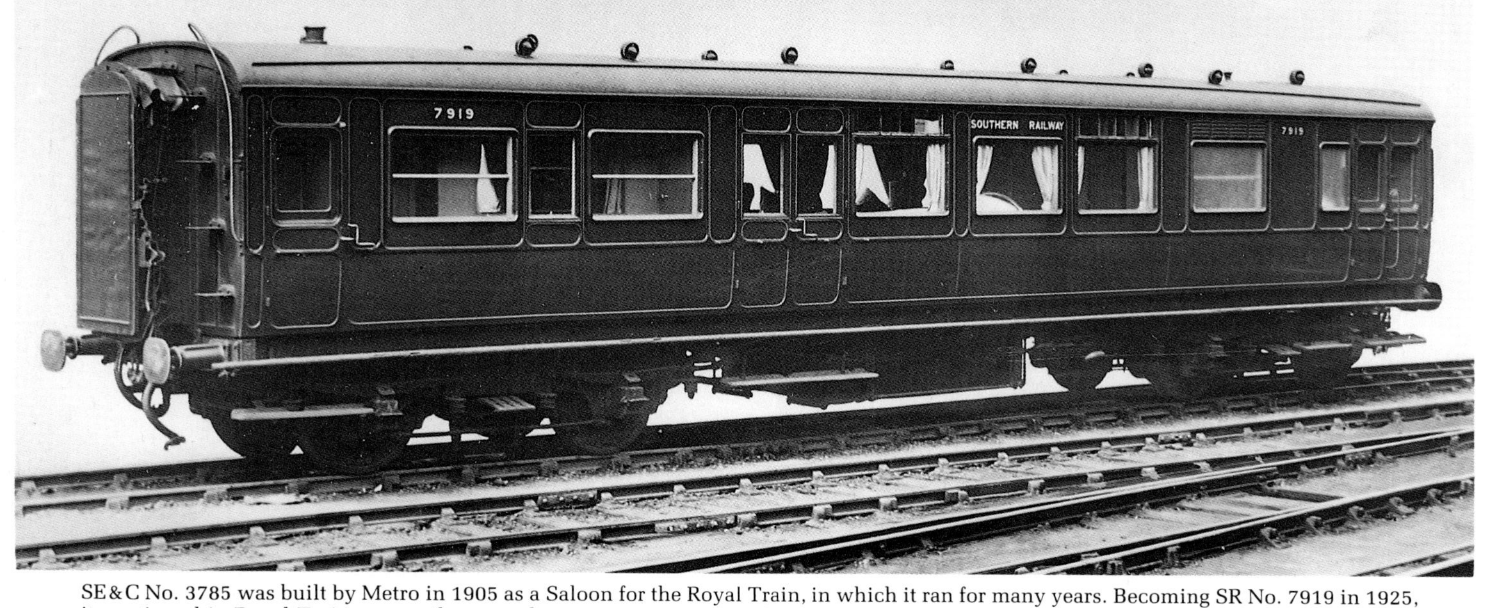

SE&C No. 3785 was built by Metro in 1905 as a Saloon for the Royal Train, in which it ran for many years. Becoming SR No. 7919 in 1925, it continued in Royal Train use until 1937, when it was reconstructed as an invalid saloon, in which form it is shown here on 3rd May, 1939. It was withdrawn in 1959. *SR (A2423)*

Kent & East Sussex Railway No. 60, in brown and cream livery, without lining, at Tenterden Town station, 4th October, 1975. This 54 ft coach, one of the few of this type not rebuilt for Isle of Wight service, was built in 1910 as SE&C No. 1106, became SR No. 3388 and was sold to the Longmoor Military Railway in 1943.
Author's Collection

Ex-SE&C coach body at Tenterden Town station, in use as staff accommodation. It was a 44 ft composite, built by Cravens in 1901 as SE&C No. 3448, and became SR No. 5240. The body was grounded at Ashford in 1942, but was later moved to Tenterden.
Author's Collection

Interior of first-class saloon of 60 ft Lavatory Composite No. 5450. Note the floral-patterned upholstery, window blinds which could be held in four different positions by means of notches on the window frames, and four droplight which could be held in position by a leather strap, the holes in which engaged with a 'button' on the door. *H.C. Casserley*

Interior of first-class saloon of 60 ft Lavatory Composite No. 5493. On the right is one of the four, inward-facing, moveable armchairs that were a feature of these comfortable saloon compartments. *H.C. Casserley*

Interior of saloon of Third Brake No. 3582, formerly a Second Brake. Even the second-class saloons were quite luxurious, although the inward-facing settee has a very low back. The floor is carpeted, and an advertisement for the Night Ferry sleeper service, then quite heavily promoted, may be seen to the right of the lavatory door.
D. Cullum

Typical third-class compartment interior: no armrests, walls planked in tongue-and-groove deal boards, and string-mesh luggage racks. The coach is K&ESR No. 61, formerly SE&C Composite Brake No. 1100 and SR Third Brake No. 3368. Tenterden, 4th October, 1975. *Author's Collection*

What happened when some ex-SER close-coupled coaches were deliberately wrecked on the Basingstoke & Alton Light Railway for a film made in 1928. On the left is a First and the other coach is a former Second. *Author's Collection*

Standard plate as fixed to solebars of SE&C-built coaches; this example is on Composite Brake No. 1061 on the Bluebell Railway. *Author's Collection*

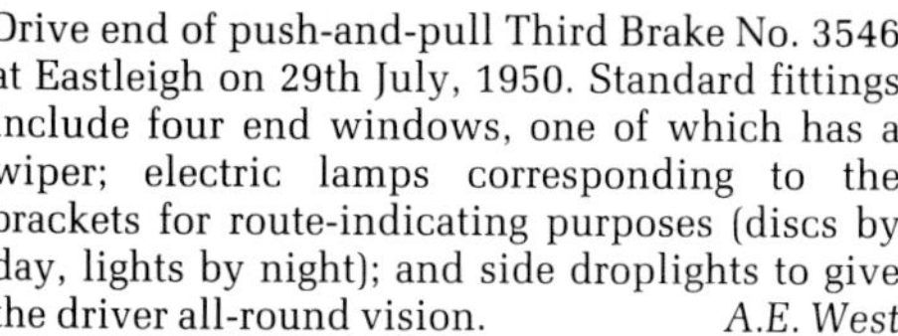
Drive end of push-and-pull Third Brake No. 3546 at Eastleigh on 29th July, 1950. Standard fittings include four end windows, one of which has a wiper; electric lamps corresponding to the brackets for route-indicating purposes (discs by day, lights by night); and side droplights to give the driver all-round vision. *A.E. West*

Inner end of push-and-pull set 662 (Compo No. 5503) at Eastleigh, 29th July, 1950. addition to the vacuum brake pipe above headstock, and the steam-heating pipe nex the coupling hook, there are three hoses use connection with the auto-train gear: the regul control pipe (blue), the main storage pipe (gre and the back pressure pipe (yellow). *A.E. W*

Spencer's patent buffer on SE&C 54 ft Composite Brake No. 1106 (K&ESR No. 60). Such buffers were fitted as standard from about 1907 onwards. *Author's Collection*

50 ft bogie guard's van No. 655, one of two built at Ashford in 1905, is the first vehicle behind class 'B1' 4–4–0 No. A450 on a down parcels train at Gravesend Central on 10th September, 1929. The centrally-placed roof observatory is clearly visible. *R.W. Kidner*

Ex-LC&D bogie guard's van in use in the Isle of Wight. It was built by the Midland Railway-Carriage & Wagon Co. in 1898 as No. 1191, becoming SE&C No. 569 and SR No. 649. Transferred to the Island in 1932 it was renumbered yet again and became 1011, later being encased in steel sheets. Ryde St Johns Road, 26th June, 1950. *D. Cullum*

SE&C Post Office Sorting Van No. 691, built in 1904. It was 50 ft over body, gangwayed at one end only and ran on Fox's bogies. There was no net apparatus. This van became SR No. 4951 in 1927 and was withdrawn in 1958. *Author's Collection*

A three-van 'set' of mail vans, photographed when new in 1904. No. 691 is extreme left; centre is No. 693 and right is No. 692. Both the last two were fitted with net apparatus and were gangwayed at each end. All three vans were gas-lit, and the tanks carrying the gas supply may be seen on the underframes. Nos. 692/3 became SR Nos. 4952/3. *SR (A4222)*

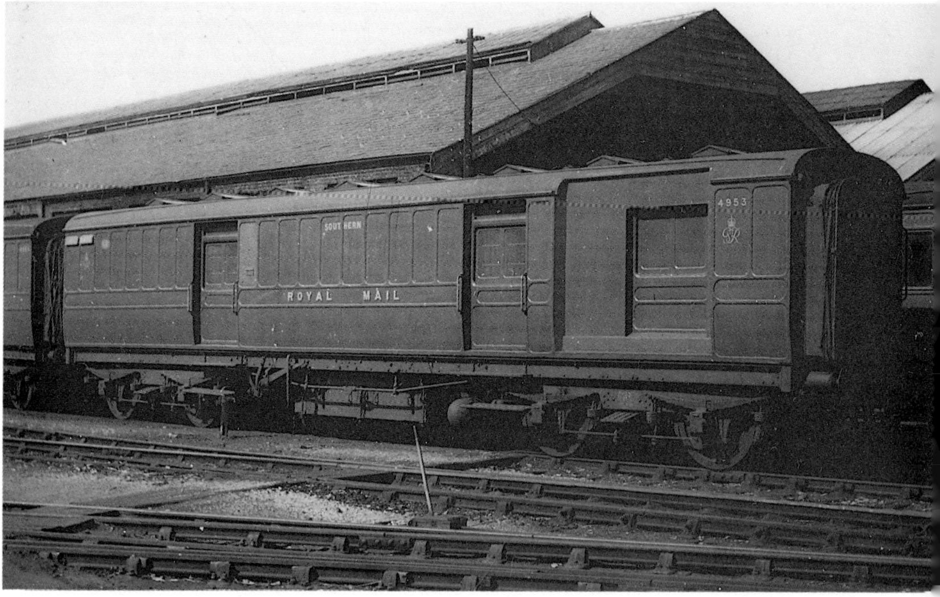

50 ft Post Office Van No. 4953 at Rotherhithe Road, 26th April, 1947. The gas lighting has now been replaced by electricity (note the battery boxes slung from the underframe). The handbrake lever to the left of the truss-rod is a later addition.

D. Cullum

One of two SER 44 ft Composites that included a luggage compartment at one end, SER No. 85, built in 1896. This became SR No. 5256, but was transferred to the service vehicles list as No. 901S in 1936. It is here shown at Stewarts Lane (Battersea) on 22nd May, 1948. *D. Cullum*

This Mess and Tool Van, DS 1537, was converted in 1940 from Post Office Van No. 4948, which was built by the SER in 1896. In 1942 the 44 ft body was placed on the underframe of SE&C First No. 7298. This van had a double roof and seven roof-lights of unusual shape. *Lens of Sutton*

DS 1838 was a Mess and Tool Van converted from Third No. 867 in 1943. This was built as a Composite by the Gloucester RCW Co. in 1899, had a body length of 44 ft and became SR No. 5195, when in 1936 it was altered to all-third. The corridor connection (*left*) was a later addition and the vehicle bears the paint date 2/55. *Lens of Sutton*

60 ft 10-compartment coach in use as part of the Lancing workmen's train, with individually-numbered compartments. It was built as a third in 1922, with Birmingham RCW Co. underframe and Ashford body, and became SR No. 1089. As DS 70053 it was placed in the Lancing Works train in 1959. *Lens of Sutton*

This vehicle was originally a Post Office Stowage Van, SR No. 4956, and was built at Ashford in 1907 as SE&C No. 112 (body length 50 ft). About 1958, after it was withdrawn, it was transferred to the 'internal user' list and renumbered 080539. Such vehicles did not normally travel on running lines. *Lens of Sutton*

3052 in Western Section 2-set 128, in which it remained for several years, until its withdrawal in 1953. Most of the others were attached to sets during the 1940s.

Summary of Tri-Composites Nos. 800–814

SEC	*SR*	*Re-No.*	*Set*	*Wdn*	*SEC*	*SR*	*Re-No.*	*Set*	*Wdn*
800	5365	9/27	538,516,900	12/56	808	5373	11/25	128	9/53
801	5366	5/27	527	9/46	809	5374	8/26	680	3/45
802	5367	3/27	519,896	11/55	810	5375	12/25	680,686?	12/51
803	5368	7/24	917	1/53	811	5376	2/26	640,?	6/56
804	5369	6/26	918	9/56	812	5377	9/28	680,686?	12/51
805	5370	4/26	522,897	1/58	813	5378	10/29	680,686?	12/51
806	5371	11/27	521	9/46	814	5379	3/25	334,636	12/56
807	5372	6/26	686	7/52					

SLIP BRAKE COMPOSITE LAVATORY

Nos. 976–980 (SR Nos. 6637–6641)

Body length: 50 ft 1 in. Bogie centres: 33 ft 6 in.
Compartments: 2 1st, 2 2nd, plus luggage and guard.
Seats: 10 1st, 13 2nd class. Lavatories: 3 (2 1st, 1 2nd class).

Built by the SE&C in January 1909 out of revenue as 'renewals', these five 'detaching' carriages had timber bodies and steel underframes. The innermost second-class compartment had access to a lavatory, situated at the very end of the coach, by means of a short corridor which also connected with the other second-class compartment. Access from the corridor to the 'cabin' compartment was by means of a sliding door with a sliding sash; this was a great improvement on hinged doors that swung out into the corridor and Nos. 976–80 were the first SE&C coaches to feature a sliding door between corridor and compartment.

The luggage compartment held 3 tons and access was by means of double doors each side, fitted with fixed door lights. It communicated with the guard's compartment by a sliding door which could be padlocked on the luggage compartment side. Fittings in the guard's compartment included a coupling box, locker, letter rack, balance seat, handbrake and an electric hooter (intended for giving warning whilst the slip portion was gliding silently into the station). In addition to the normal roof observatory, which was 12 ft 6½ in. above rail level, there was a small centrally-placed window in the end, so that the 'slip' guard could see where he was going whilst operating the detaching apparatus, applying the handbrake, and sounding the hooter if necessary.

Buffers were fitted with malleable iron guides and sleeves, working with auxiliary side springs of indiarubber. Bodyside quarterlights were bedded on felt, with 1½ in. teak mouldings. As with earlier stock, droplights were fitted to the first-class lavatories but fixed lights to the second-class ones – a very curious distinction.

From May 1909 Nos. 978 and 979, together with Lavatory Third No. 869 and Composite No. 2375, were formed as Train No. 16, which worked as part of the 7.55 am Ramsgate Harbour to Charing Cross and the slip portion of the 5.10 pm Holborn Viaduct to Ramsgate, which was detached at

Faversham. However, this set could not have maintained its correct formation at all during the summer of 1909, for each of the four coaches was sent to Ashford Works individually for the fitting of steam heating: No. 2375 in May, No. 978 in June, No. 979 in July and No. 869 in August. In each case the missing coach would have been replaced temporarily by one of 'corresponding description'.

Other slip portions from 1910 were the 4.25 pm Charing Cross for Dover Town, returning at 7.25 pm, and the 4.55 pm Charing Cross for Westerham, detached at Dunton Green off a Tonbridge train. This 2-coach portion, formed of a Slip Brake Composite and Tri-Composite, was numbered as Train 88 in July 1910 and worked up as part of the 8.37 am Westerham to Cannon Street.

Nos. 976/8–80 were steam heated in 1909 and No. 977 in 1910. By1914 No. 979 had been replaced in 4-set 16 by an ordinary Composite, No. 992, leaving only No. 978. The set was renumbered 31 in 1915, but in any case 'slipping' was discontinued during World War I. By 1914, 4-set 81, used on London–Tadworth services until it was disbanded in 1918, included a Slip Brake. In 1915 No. 978 was transferred from Set 31 to Set 24, being replaced by No. 977; the formation of Set 24 was recorded as: Slip Brake Composite No. 978, First No. 939, Composite No. 2374 and Third Lavatory No. 866. This, the Granville Express set, was originally numbered 10 and became spare in 1917. Sets 24 and 31 were disbanded in 1919, by which time No. 980 had been marshalled in 5-set 29 in replacement of a 6-wheeled Slip Brake Composite. Set 29 had long been the regular train on an Ashford to Holborn morning service, slipped at Herne Hill, but in June 1920 it was transferred to a Maidstone East–London service.

From 16th June, 1919, slip coach workings were restored and in summer 1922 four Brake Composites were regularly diagrammed, although none now formed part of a set train. The workings were:

6.48 am Ashford to Cannon Street and in 1.25 pm Charing Cross to Deal, detached at Ashford.

8.20 am Ashford to Holborn Viaduct, slipped at Herne Hill, and (not Saturdays) 2.13 pm Holborn to Swanley Junction, where it was attached to the 2.50 pm Victoria to Ashford. On Saturdays the coach worked throughout on the 2.50 pm Victoria to Ashford.

6.32 am Gillingham to Holborn Viaduct and 5.32 pm (not Saturdays) Victoria–Faversham, slipped at Swanley Junction, thence 6.15 pm to Gillingham.

9.47 am Gravesend West Street to Victoria (Tuesdays to Fridays) and 5.45 pm (not Saturdays) return, slipped at Swanley Junction.

'Slipping' was not favoured by the Southern Railway and the Herne Hill and Swanley Junction slips were discontinued in 1924; and a Faversham slip (from the 5.10 pm Holborn to Margate service) lasted until 1926, this being the last on any of the former LC&D lines. However, the coaches themselves continued in use for many more years, still retaining their distinctive window at the brake end.

Nos. 976–80 were given SR numbers 6637–6641 and eventually all were formed into sets. No. 6638 was first placed in 3-set 528, with Third No. 1111 and Brake Composite No. 6619; later No. 6619 was formed with No. 6641 and two Thirds as 4-set 668. Upon withdrawal of this set in about 1940 No. 6641 was transferred to 4-set 666; it is believed this set was later amalgamated with 4-set 667 to make an 8-coach set numbered 666 by 1944.

Summary of Slip Brake Composites

SEC	*SR*	*Re-No.*	*Set*	*Wdn*	*SEC*	*SR*	*Re-No.*	*Set*	*Wdn*
976	6637	5/28	920	6/57	979	6640	5/28	902,913	12/51
977	6638	7/27	902,688,917	3/57	980	6641	11/26	668,666	9/51
978	6639	10/29	669	4/51					

In 1935 9-set 902 was berthed at Stewarts Lane and booked to work the summer Saturday 10.10 am Victoria to Ramsgate and 2.50 pm return. By 1941 it was a 7-set based at Tunbridge Wells West for the 7.47 am to London Bridge and returning on the 5.50 pm from Victoria. By 1947 it was reduced to six coaches and, berthed at Eardley sidings (Streatham), had no regular workings; the set was withdrawn in 1948, although most of its coaches were transferred to other sets.

9-coach set 920, which included Composite Brake No. 6637, was one of the longer-lasting sets made up of ex-SE&C non-corridor stock. The coach seems to have attracted the attention of photographers, probably because that little window in the end alerted them to the fact that the coach was a one-time 'slip'.

During 1945 Set 920 (reduced to eight coaches) had been allocated to the Southern District at Weymouth for a regular Saturday working: the 2.02 pm Dorchester to Bournemouth and 10.30 pm return. Set 920 was back in the London East District by 1947, during which summer it worked the 9.50 am Victoria to Ramsgate and 2.38 pm return, both on Saturdays only. At other times it stood at Nunhead. Workings of Set 920 (9-coach since September 1949) on summer Saturdays in 1954 were: 9.32 am Gravesend Central to Margate and 4.23 pm Margate to Victoria. During summer 1956 it had no booked workings and stood spare at Maze Hill until its withdrawal in June 1957.

THE 1909 BOAT TRAIN

In May 1909 ten further boat train carriages were ordered from Metropolitan Amalgamated RC&W Co., these being six Composites, two Firsts, one Second Brake and one Third Brake, all of which were similar in appearance to the boat train carriages of 1907/8 but whose compartments differed dimensionally. The complete train, constructed at Saltley Works, Birmingham, was delivered in September 1909 and sent into traffic on 21st September, 1909, two weeks later. Capital was required to pay for it.

COMPOSITE LAVATORY Nos. 815–820 (SR Nos. 5345–5350)
Body length: 51 ft 1 in. Bogie centres: 35 ft.
Compartments: 3 1st, 3 2nd. Seats: 15 1st, 19 2nd class.
Lavatories: 4 (3 1st, 1 2nd).

FIRST LAVATORY (with saloon) Nos. 821, 822 (SR Nos. 7365, 7366)
Body length: 51 ft 1 in. Bogie centres: 35 ft.
Compartments: 1 saloon, 3 ordinary. Seats: 27.
Lavatories: 4 (one to each compartment).

SECOND BRAKE (with saloon) No. 823 (SR No. 3580)
Body length: 50 ft 1 in. Bogie centres: 34 ft.
Compartments: 1 saloon, 1 ordinary, plus luggage and guard.
Seats: 22. Lavatories: 2.

THIRD BRAKE LAVATORY No. 824 (SR No. 3315)
Body length: 50 ft 1 in. Bogie centres: 34 ft.
Compartments: 4. Seats: 36. Lavatories: 2 (to 2 compartments).

Composites Nos. 815–20 had the same compartment layout as Nos. 930–8, 953–7 and 981–1000 but as the body was one foot longer the compartments were more spacious. Firsts Nos. 821/2 also had a similar layout to Nos. 939–46 and 958–60 and the saloon, 19 ft 9 in. long, was the same length but the longer body allowed for more generous dimensions in the other compartments. Second Brake No. 823 was virtually indistinguishable from Nos. 949/50/61/62; the end compartment was an inch wider and the luggage compartment an inch shorter. Third Brake No. 824 had the same layout as Nos. 845–55 and 963–72 but the compartments were 2 in. wider and the luggage compartment correspondingly reduced from 17 ft 10½ in. to 17 ft 3 in. Another small difference was that the bogies of all these 1909-built carriages were spaced 6 in. further apart than on previous batches.

In each of the Composites was a short internal corridor giving access between the second-class compartments and the lavatory. As in the Slip Brake Composites described in the previous section, sliding doors, with frameless glass sashes fitted with Laycock's balancing arrangement, gave access from this corridor into the two 'cabin' compartments instead of the inconvenient hinged doors used on the earlier stock.

The whole train was steam-heated. Until March 1909 only stock intended for boat trains had heaters from the outset, but after that date all new carriages had them, and as older main-line carriages went through Ashford Works they too were fitted.

The 1909 boat train was the last one to be built in the Wainwright era, as well as being the last to appear with South Eastern-type mouldings, standard since the 1880s.

In 1913 a decision was made to place a notice in both English and French on the lavatory doors of all boat train carriages to indicate where the doors led to, following the General Manager's complaint that 'There is nothing whatever to show that the doors lead to a lavatory.' Other bi-lingual notices in boat train stock were ALARM SIGNAL/*SIGNALE D'ALARME*, with the usual warning of a £5 penalty; and DO NOT LEAN OUT OF THE WINDOW/ *NE PAS SE PENCHER AU DEHORS*, which was on an enamelled iron tablet, white with black letters, 8½ in. by 1½ in. The General Manager, Francis Dent, had suggested that the equivalent notices in German should also appear, but this was not done.

By 1913 the boat train carriages had been arranged to run as nine sets. Although the formations are unknown, the set numbers, service to which each train was allocated and the date that each train was last painted at Ashford Works have been recorded. This was the position in January 1913:

Train	*Service*	*Painted*
1	2.20 pm Charing Cross–Folkestone	9.1912
2	10.00 am Charing Cross–Folkestone	10.1912
3	10.57 am Victoria–Dover	12.1912
3A	Spare Boat (Dover)	7.1912
4	'Day Flushing'	5.1912
5	'Night Flushing'	4.1911
6	9.00 am Charing Cross–Dover Mail	9.1912
Spare	11.00 am Victoria–Dover	10.1911
52	9.00 pm Charing Cross–Dover Mail	2.1912

In 1913 these were reshuffled further when five of the 1905-built Firsts were converted into First Brakes and formed into five 5-coach boat sets lettered A, B, C, D and E. Each was formed:

Second Brake Saloon, two Composites (930 type), First with saloon, and First Brake (3789 type). There were also four 2-coach strengthening sets, formed: Second Brake (951 or 3806 type) and First Saloon. Sets A to E were given the numbers 7 to 11 in 1915/16, later classed 'XE' but disbanded about 1921.

By 1921 Nos. 815–8/20/1/3 were 'spare boat' carriages, No. 819 was part of Set 6 and No. 822 in Set 7 (removed by June 1922); No. 815 went to Set 3 in June 1922. No. 824 was in 5-set 256, which worked between Tonbridge and Cannon Street or Dorking and Cannon Street. First No. 822 received water heaters in its lavatories in 1922. Composite No. 818 was involved in a mishap at Milton Range Halt on 21st August, 1922, but was later returned to traffic.

As boat train stock, the Composites and the Second Brake kept their second-class accommodation until 1924, when it was downgraded to third class; seating capacity of the Saloon Brake was then increased to 26 and the 19 second-class seats in each Composite were increased to 20. No coach appeared in SR livery as a first/second Composite; No. 818 was the first to receive its Southern number, and this was not done until January 1925.

Third Brake No. 824 became SR 3315 and No. 823, originally allocated the number 4151 in the SR Second Brake series, actually became SR Third Brake No. 3580 in January 1925. Composites Nos. 815–20 became SR 5345–50 and Firsts Nos. 821/2 were renumbered 7365/6.

The coaches were distributed around various sets used on semi-fast and excursion trains during the late 1930s and early 1940s, as shown in the table below:

SEC	*SR*	*Re-No.*	*Set*	*Wdn*	*SEC*	*SR*	*Re-No.*	*Set*	*Wdn*
824	3315	10/28	909,98,905	1/48	818	5348	1/25	674,687,688	8/52
823	3580	1/25	680,640,918	8/56	819	5349	2/28	688,403	
815	5345	4/28	335	7/50	820	5350	3/26	918	10/49
816	5346	7/27	518	/43	821	7365	3/25		4/44
817	5347	2/29	403		822	7366	4/27	901	1/53

4-set 98 was used on Clapham Junction–Kensington Addison Road services between about 1943 and 1947. It was formed of three Thirds and a Brake Third, the latter recorded as being No. 3315. 6-set 403 was the Western Section part-corridor set mentioned in previous sections. Nos. 5347 and

5349, included in this set from about 1946, were downgraded to third class in June 1955 and renumbered 953 and 954 (numbers once carried by ex-SEC 48 ft Thirds); they remained in Set 403 until both were withdrawn in February 1957.

Only one of the 10 former boat train carriages became a service vehicle after withdrawal: this was First No. 7365, which in April 1944 was converted to a Stores Van No. 1958 S for the engineer's department. Finally, Composite No. 5346 was noted off wheels as a grounded body at Southampton Docks during the late 1940s.

THIRD LAVATORY

Nos. 1085–1089 (SR Nos. 956–960)

Body length: 50 ft 1 in. Bogie centres: 34 ft.
Compartments: 7. Seats: 62.
Lavatories: 4 (access from 4 compartments).

The final batch of coaches displaying the 'Ashford' style of bodyside mouldings in vogue since the 1880s, Nos. 1085–89 were built by the SE&C in November 1909. They had the same layout as Lavatory Thirds Nos. 861–79 of 1906, but as the body was 2 ft longer it was possible to make all the compartments 6 ft across instead of only 5 ft 7½ in. Built as 'renewals' for boat train services, Nos. 1085–89 employed the same methods of construction as the 1909 Brake Composites described in a previous section: steel underframes, wooden bodies, quarter lights bedded on felt with 1½ in. mouldings. All the Thirds had steam heating. The central and two outermost compartments were without lavatory access.

It is not known in which, if any, sets the Thirds were placed but between 1920 and 1924 all were noted as 'spare boat' stock. No. 1085 received water heating in the lavatories in 1922 – quite an amenity for third class passengers. On coming to the SR all five were renumbered 956–960 and eventually all found themselves in the 'special traffic' 9-coach sets, as summarised below:

SEC	*SR*	*Re-No.*	*Set*	*Wdn*	*SEC*	*SR*	*Re-No.*	*Set*	*Wdn*
1085	956	6/26	680,898	4/51	1088	959	?	898	4/51
1086	957	12/23	906,920?	6/57	1089	960	by 6/24	896	2/49
1087	958	?	901	1/53					

No. 958 was in 9-set 901 from about 1931 until 1953. On withdrawal in 1953, No. 958 was converted to a Camping Coach, No. CC 26, and continued in use as such until its final withdrawal in February 1961.

THREE-COACH SETS TYPE 'A' (50 ft STOCK)

By March 1909 there was sufficient lavatory-fitted bogie stock to work all the best train services on the South Eastern & Chatham but a great many other services had to keep going with old stock, including some of the really ancient four-wheeled carriages. The superintendent of the line, W. Thomson, therefore suggested that 'set trains' of non-lavatory bogie stock be built in order to allow the better six-wheeled stock to be modified for close-coupled trains on London suburban workings and the more decrepit carriages to be withdrawn.

He stated: 'I would point out that the Victoria–New Brompton, and the Charing Cross–New Brompton and Maidstone West services are the worst-equipped on the whole system and these should, unquestionably, be taken first in hand.' (New Brompton was renamed 'Gillingham' in October 1912.)

In fact, there was a change in policy: hitherto, the SE&C had provided lavatory-fitted stock only for fast trains, but these new sets, 32 coaches for which were ordered from Metropolitan Amalgamated RC&W Co., included a small number of lavatories even though the trains were designed for use on outer-suburban services. Ultimately, fourteen 3-coach sets were made up.

Metro constructed all the coaches for the first 10 sets plus two coaches for the eleventh. Ashford constructed one coach to go with the two built by Metro, plus a further three sets. Each of these comprised a Lavatory Composite, a Lavatory Brake Composite and a Brake Composite without lavatories. All were built at the end of 1909. The following year Ashford built three 4-coach sets, of which three vehicles were the same as those in the 1909 sets and the fourth was a Composite without lavatories.

These coaches were the first to display a new style of bodyside moulding in which the top panels were rounded in SE style but the waist panels were square-cornered after the fashion of the LC&D. This 'compromise' panelling, a sort of acknowledgement of LC&D practice, became standard until 1915. Quarterlights also were changed in shape: the top quarters were rounded in each corner but the lower part of the window was square-cornered, again as a reminder of the LC&D. This style was known as 'Ashford Gothic'.

Details of the vehicle types now follow:

COMPOSITE LAVATORY Nos. 1021–1034, 1067–1070 (SR Nos. 5415–5432)
Body length: 54 ft 1 in. Bogie centres: 38 ft.
Compartments: 4 1st, 3 2nd. Seats: 23 1st class, 23 2nd class.
Lavatories: 2 (1 1st, 1 2nd class).
Nos. 1021–30 by Metro 10/1909; No. 1031 by SE&C 11/1909; Nos. 1032–4 by SE&C 12/1909; Nos. 1067–70 by SE&C 6/1910.

COMPOSITE BRAKE LAVATORY Nos. 1035–1048, 1071–1074 (SR Nos. 3340–3357)
Body length: 50 ft 1 in. Bogie centres: 34 ft.
Compartments: 1 2nd, 5 3rd, guard. Seats: 8 2nd class, 48 3rd class.
Lavatories: 1 (serving 1 3rd class compartment)
Nos. 1035–45 by Metro 10/1909; Nos. 1046–8 by SE&C 12/1909; Nos. 1071–4 by SE&C 6/1910.

COMPOSITE BRAKE Nos. 1049–1062, 1075–1078 (SR Nos. 3322–3339)
Body length: 50 ft 1 in. Bogie centres: 34 ft.
Compartments: 1 2nd, 5 3rd class, guard. Seats: 8 2nd, 50 3rd.
Lavatories: none.
Nos. 1049–59 by Metro 11/1909: Nos. 1060–2 by SE&C 12/1909; Nos. 1075–8 by SE&C 6/1910.

COMPOSITE Nos. 1063–1066 (SR Nos. 5298–5301)
Body length: 50 ft 1 in. Bogie centres: 34 ft.
Compartments: 4 1st, 3 2nd class. Seats: 24 1st, 24 2nd class.
Lavatories: none.
Built by SE&CR 6/1910.

There were also six Lavatory Brake Composites, which had a different layout from Nos. 1035–48/71–4 and were formed into sets with older stock.

COMPOSITE BRAKE LAVATORY Nos. 1079–1084 (SR Nos. 3358–3363)
Body length: 50 ft 1 in. Bogie centres: 34 ft.
Compartments: 2 2nd, 4 3rd class, guard. Seats: 15 2nd, 38 3rd.
Lavatories: 2 (1 2nd, 1 3rd class).
Nos. 1079–80 by SE&C 4/1910; Nos. 1081–4 by Metro 4/1910.

All the coaches had 8 ft bogies, compensating buffers with malleable iron guides and sleeves, and steel underframes with bulb angle soles, channel headstocks, channel bolsters, crossbars and longitudinals. Wheels were 3 ft 6 in. in diameter. Body framing was teak with mahogany panels and mouldings, the quarter lights being bedded on felt with 1½ in. teak mouldings. Height from rail to roof was 11 ft 9 in., and guard's compartments were fitted with a roof observatory whose extreme height was 12 ft 6½ in. Interior fittings included a hand brake, shelf, valve and coupling lockers and a dogbox. All coaches had steam heating apparatus (non-storage system).

Metro delivered the 11 Lavatory Brake Composites first, on 18th October, 1909, then the following day the 10 Composites arrived. Finally, on 1st November, 1909, came the 11 non-lavatory Brake Composites from Saltley. Consequently when the sets were assembled by Ashford the coaches were not in numerical order. The 11 sets, one of which included an Ashford-built Composite (No. 1031), were numbered 90 to 100 and sent into traffic as follows: 16th November, 1909 – 94/97–100; 17th November, 1909 – 91/95/96; 22nd November, 1909 – 90/92/93. These were followed by the three Ashford-built sets, numbered 101 to 103.

Mostly the sets went into service on the trains for which they had been intended; London–Dartford–New Brompton–Maidstone West. But there were some main-line duties too, and from March 1910 new 3-sets were booked for such trains as the 7.45 am Dover Harbour to Cannon Street, 3.30 pm Victoria to Dover, 7.30 am Victoria to Dover Harbour and 12.00 noon return, 2.30 pm Dover Town to Charing Cross and 9.45 pm return. All these were 'cyclic diagrams', for only one set finished up at night at the place from which it had started in the morning; the exception was Set 103.

From March 1910 Set 103 was specially booked to work a daily out-and-home diagram on the Reading line, taking in the 7.12 am and 3.15 pm Reading to Charing Cross services and the 10.50 am and 7.16 pm Charing Cross to Reading trains. Composite No. 1032 in Set 103 had been fitted with Vickers Sons & Maxim electric lighting to give it a trial for comparison with Stone's lighting on Composite Brake No. 1046. An instruction was given that the set must not be separated, and in the event of failures the whole set had to be withdrawn. From 27th March, 1911, Set 103 worked the 5.20 am Cannon Street to Westerham, 8.37 am return, 3.08 pm Charing Cross to Reading and 7.53 pm return. Time was spent at Rotherhithe Road in the middle of the day and at night so that the dynamo cells could be examined and, if necessary, attended to. On 18th February, 1911, the lights failed on No. 1032 at North Camp while the train was on the 3.08 pm Charing Cross to Reading; and the set was returned to Rotherhithe Road for inspection. Within the next couple of days the dynamo was examined by VS&M's representative, who found that the cells were exhausted. After recharging, the set was ready for traffic again on 24th February.

By January 1911, when Set 103 had completed a year's working, the Vickers-equipped coach had been stopped on six occasions because of exhausted cells, whilst the Stone trial coach had not suffered any failure at all. Again, in May 1911, the Stone's dynamo was inspected and found to be 'in thoroughly good condition'. It was reckoned that the Vickers dynamo was not up to the job of recharging the cells while the carriage was working a stopping train, also that the demands of night-time working were too severe for it. The equipment itself was not faulty. The report to H.S. Wainwright on the working of Train No. 103 concluded that the Vickers equipment on No. 1032 'will not adequately meet the conditions on this line.'

The 4-coach sets of June 1910 were numbered 104 to 107 and went into service on four diagrams which took each set in turn to and from London and Edenbridge, Tonbridge, Tunbridge Wells, Maidstone West, Tonbridge, Westerham, Bromley North, Dorking, Bromley North, Edenbridge, Oxted and Rotherhithe Road for maintenance every four days or so. Each set in turn was berthed overnight at Rotherhithe Road, Tonbridge, Dorking and Rotherhithe Road. Specimen services worked were the 9.12 am Edenbridge to Cannon Street, 4.55 pm Charing Cross to Tonbridge, 9.44 am Westerham to Cannon Street, 11.40 pm Charing Cross to Dorking, 7.28 am Dorking to Charing Cross, 8.23 pm Charing Cross to Oxted and 9.52 pm Oxted to Cannon Street.

Loose Brake Composites Nos. 1079–84 were not formed immediately into sets so far as can be judged. No. 1081 may have been in 6-set 87 (London–Dorking) by 1914. Early in 1917 three 3-sets, Nos. 128–130, were formed with Brake Composites Nos. 1084, 1082 and 1083, Composites Nos. 1063/4/5, and Third Brakes Nos. 840, 857 and 837 of 1905. The sets were classed Type 'D'.

The 4-coach sets, Nos. 104–7, were renumbered 124, 125, 126 and 127 in 1915. Early in 1917 Nos. 124–6 were reduced to 3-coach by removing the 50 ft Composites, Nos. 1063–5 (which were transferred to Sets 128–30 as noted above), and only Set 127 remained as 4-coach, classed Type 'ZD', for Reigate–Cannon Street services. In 1920 Set 127 was moved across to Sevenoaks, from which base its daily workings included the 8.44 am Westerham to Cannon Street and 5.05 pm (not Saturdays) Cannon Street to Sevenoaks or 4.55 pm (Saturdays) Charing Cross to Sevenoaks.

3-set 79 was formed in 1915 for Gillingham–London services: it included two Composite Brakes Nos. 1079 and 1080 and Composite No. 690 of 1899. Based at Faversham during 1920, it was strengthened to six coaches for summer 1922 and, based at Ore, it worked the 7.35 am Hastings to Cannon Street and 5.04 pm return services.

On being inherited by the Southern Railway, 3-sets 90–103, which had run in their original formations since 1909, were renumbered 529 to 542 in the same order. 3-sets 124–126 became SR Nos. 563–565, and 4-set 127 was given the SR number 674. 6-set 79 became 6-set 693 and part of 6-set 87 became SR 3-set No. 695. 5-set 685 was formed with the brake coaches of SEC 3-set 129 and other odd coaches in February 1924; Set 128 was increased to 7 or 8 coaches and renumbered 699; and only Set 130 of the Type 'D' 3-sets kept its identity as SR No. 566. These odd sets were repainted in SR livery as follows:

SE&C Set 130		*Re-No.*	**SR Set 566**	
Third Bke	837	11/28	Third Bke	3279
Compo	1065	?	Compo	5300
Compo Bke	1083	11/28	Third Bke	3362
SE&C Set 127		*Re-No.*	**SR Set 674**	
Compo Bke	1078	1/25	Third Bke	3339
Compo Lav	1070	1/25	Compo Lav	5432
Compo	1066	1/25	Compo	5301
Compo Bke	1074	1/25	Third Bke	3357
		Re-No.	**SR Set 685**	
Third Bke	857	2/24	Third Bke	3288
Picnic Sal	143	2/24	Picnic Sal	7925
First	2386	2/24	First	7279
First Lav	944	10/23	First Lav	7352
Compo Bke	1082	2/24	Third Bke	3361
SE&C Set 79		*Re-No.*	**SR Set 693**	
Compo Bke	1079	7/24	Third Bke	3358
Second	2326	8/24	Third	936
Compo Lav	889	7/24	Compo Lav	5351
First Lav	901	7/24	First Lav	7360
Compo Lav	3797	7/24	Compo Lav	5354
Compo Bke	1080	7/24	Third Bke	3359
SE&C Set 87		*Re-No.*	**SR Set 695**	
Compo Bke	1081	7/26	Third Bke	3360
First	3508	7/26	First	7343
Compo Bke	152	7/26	Compo Bke	6611

Other coaches: SE&C No. 1084 (Set 699) was renumbered 3363 in January 1928 and Composites 1063/4 became SR Nos. 5298/9 in April 1928 and an unknown date. Most of the sets detailed above were later altered:

Set 566: renumbered 903 in 1948, with Thirds 970, 1064, 1056 and Composite 5332. 3362 to Set 896 in 1951, wdn 1/58.

Set 674: reduced to 3-set early 1930s, 5301 to Set 600. 3339/57 to Set 688 *c.*1943; 3339 wdn 7/52, 3357 to DS 1810 in 1949. 5432 to Set 687 *c.*1943, Set 688 *c.*1946; to DS 1898 in 1949.

Set 685: reduced to 3-set by 1930 with 3288, 7352 and 3361. Third 1097 and Compos 5228, 5338 added by 1935. 7352 replaced by 7297, by 1941. Set disbanded *c.*1943. 3361 to Set 666, wdn 9/51.

Set 693: 5351 replaced by 5224. Set wdn *c.*1945. 3358 to Set 921, wdn 1947; 3359 to Set 921, then Set 900 in 1951, wdn 12/56.

Set 695: 7343 replaced by Compo 5362, by 1935. 9-set by 1941. All wdn 2/51.

In 1931 4-set 674 was used for the 8.38 am Westerham to Cannon Street; 6-set 693 worked the 9.15 am Hastings to Charing Cross and 5.15 pm return; while 3-set 695 was booked for the 7.24 am Aldershot to London Bridge and the front portion of the 6.08 pm (not Saturdays) or 2.26 pm (Saturdays) London Bridge to Reading.

The Type 'A' 3-sets, Nos. 529–542, were repainted in Southern livery, with second-class marked down to third, and continued to run uneventfully on Eastern Section local services and a good many fast trains too.

On 27th June, 1937, the 8.17 pm Margate to Victoria via Canterbury West, Ashford and Maidstone East was arranged to call at Swanley Junction in order to pick up passengers off the late-running 10.00 pm train from Gillingham to Swanley who had missed their normal connection. The driver of the up Margate must have forgotten his out-of-course stop for his train went through signals and, entering the short up siding at speed, collided with a stationary wagon and two coaches in it. Four passengers were killed and 11 injured. The train was formed of 3-set 535 leading and an SR-built 4-set, No. 182. The front end of the first coach, No. 3341, was thrown on top of the locomotive tender, the guard's compartment was wrecked and the rear four compartments telescoped by the penetration of the second coach, No. 5418, in which the leading four compartments were destroyed. The third coach, No. 3324, was derailed but Set 182 was undamaged.

The result was that Set 535 was withdrawn; No. 5418 was rebuilt as a Driving Brake Composite (renumbered 6409), being paired with Third Brake No. 3324 in push-and-pull set No. 659 in April 1938. No. 6409 now had two first-class and four third-class compartments, seating 14 and 38 respectively, and at the drive-end four windows overlooking the track were put in. The Third Brake's body was unmodified, even retaining its roof observatory. No. 3324 was the sole push-and-pull vehicle to have a 'birdcage' and, as it turned out, the very last such vehicle to run on British Railways in passenger service! At first Set 659 was allocated to Yeovil for workings on the branch from Yeovil Junction, but in 1949 was transferred back to the Eastern Section for general push-and-pull workings. Latterly Set 659 became a very familiar sight on Tunbridge Wells West–Oxted services until at last it was withdrawn late in 1961.

Set 542 was another that was withdrawn following accident damage, which in this case was the result of a collision at Victoria on 17th July, 1946. Third Brake No. 3351 was sent to Eastleigh and its body was grounded there. The other 15 sets were withdrawn as follows:

Set No.	*Wdn*	
529	9/48	
530	6/51	
531	/51	3325 to Set 913?, then to Set 335 in 1952 and Set 346 in 1956, wdn 11/57; 3346 to Set 519, then to Set 335 in 1953, wdn 1/57; 5420 to Set 696, then 896, wdn 1/58.
532	3/42	3331/48 to breakdown vans 1730 S and 1731 S. 5422 body grounded at Dartford.
533	/52	3330/40 to Set 897; 5417 to Set 897, wdn 1/58. 3330/40 wdn 2/53, to DS 25/6.
534	11/47	

536	/51	3322 to Set 688, wdn 3/56; 3344 to Set 688, wdn 3/56; 5415 to Set 688, then 896, wdn 1/58.
537	1/52	3323 to DS 3207; 3349 to DS 3206.
538	10/44	
539	/53	3326/42, 5419 to Set 901. Wdn 12/56, 3/55, 12/56.
540	/49	3333/53 to Set 903, wdn 12/57, 1/58. 5427 wdn 3/49.
541	2/52	3334/52 to DS 3208, DS 3209.
563	12/52	3336/54 to DS 3212, DS 21. 5429 to Set 335, wdn 1/57.
564	4/51	
565	1/52	3338/56 to DS 3205, DS 3204.

Third Brake No. 3363 in the 1930s went to 9-set 901, remaining therein until 1952, after which it was withdrawn and became a service vehicle, DS 22, in June 1954. 7-set 903, which from 1951 included the two Third Brakes formerly in 3-set 540 as well as Composite No. 5300 from 3-set 566, was allocated to Tunbridge Wells West to work the 7.06 am to London Bridge and 5.20 pm return services until 1956, when it worked the 7.42 am East Grinstead to London Bridge and 4.20 pm return services until final withdrawal. No. 3333 was noted as being one of the first coaches to be painted in BR's red livery, in 1949.

Of the Composites Nos. 5298–5301, No. 5298 was altered in 1941 to work in push-and-pull set 715, of which the driving brake coach was an ex-London Brighton & South Coast Railway vehicle. This was withdrawn in March 1961. No. 5299 was placed in Set 600 which, with two other coaches, was made up to six coaches until its withdrawal in 1941. No. 5300, originally in Set 566, was transferred in 1948 to 7-set 903 as noted above and was withdrawn in December 1957. Finally, No. 5301, which had been in 4-set 674 then 6-set 600, was altered in 1942 for push-and-pull working and placed in Set 661. Two of the first-class compartments in No. 5301 were downgraded to third and the remaining firsts were altered to seat 4-a-side instead of 3-a-side; the makeup was now '3 3 3 1 1 3 3' and the seating capacity 16 first, 50 third. In this form it ran in Set 661 until its withdrawal in October 1961.

Many of the Third Brakes were converted to Mess and Tool Vans for breakdown trains, but No. 3363 (DS 22) became a gauging van fitted with springy 'bristles' on the roof to test the load gauge of various lineside structures, bridges and tunnels. This coach was withdrawn in 1978 and sold in August of that year to the Kent & East Sussex Railway. Nos. 1730 S and 1731 S, converted in 1942, were Breakdown Vans at Fratton and Guildford respectively. No. 3357 became a Mess and Tool Van No. DS 1810 at Norwood Junction and was scrapped at Newhaven in August 1960, as was DS 21 (formerly No. 3354). DS 3208 was more fortunate, for in February 1962 it was purchased by the Bluebell Railway, where, after some basic restoration, it entered service in June 1965. Lighting and heating had been stripped during its days as a service vehicle, but steam pipes were fitted in 1969. The coach was painted in plain maroon livery, with its old SE&C number 1061 displayed, and for many years it was worked very hard before being withdrawn, worn-out, for thorough overhaul – which had not yet occurred by 1991.

THREE-COACH SETS TYPE 'A' (54 ft STOCK)

Towards the end of 1910, the SE&C completed the construction of six 3-coach sets, Nos. 111–116, and these were followed in 1911 by further sets in two batches of seven, Nos. 117–123 and 126–132. All 20 sets were 'renewals' and were built to the same body style as the 1909 Type 'A' sets but differed in that the bodies were 54 ft in length, whilst the earlier sets had 50 ft brake coaches and a 54 ft centre coach. The 54 ft sets were designed from the outset to be indivisible in normal service, for only the centre coach was equipped with a dynamo for the electric lighting, supplying current for all three vehicles. If there was any sort of failure the whole set had to be withdrawn from traffic complete. Details of the coaches are shown below:

COMPOSITE LAVATORY. Nos. 1090–95, 1108–14, 1129–35 (SR Nos. 5395–5414)
Body length: 54 ft 1 in. Bogie centres: 38 ft.
Compartments: 4 1st, 3 2nd class. Seats: 22 1st, 24 2nd class.
Lavatories: 2 (serving 2 1st class).
Nos. 1090–5 built 12/1910; Nos. 1108–14, 6/1911; Nos. 1129–35 12/1911.
Built to Plan 3184A. Fitted with 'D' electric light dynamo (one dynamo and accumulator for the 3-coach train).

COMPO BRAKE LAVATORY. Nos. 1096–1101, 1115–21, 1136–42 (SR Nos. 3364–3383)
Body length: 54 ft 1 in. Bogie centres: 38 ft.
Compartments: 1 2nd, 5 3rd class. Seats: 7 2nd, 48 3rd class.
Lavatories: 2 (serving 1 2nd, 1 3rd class compartment).
Nos. 1096–1101 built 12/1910; Nos. 1115–21, 6/1911; 1136–42, 12/1911.
Built to Plan 3185A. Electric lighting, no dynamo. Nos. 1096–8/1115 with dynamo.

COMPOSITE BRAKE. Nos. 1102–07, 1122–28, 1143–49 (SR Nos. 3384–3403)
Body length: 54 ft 1 in. Bogie centres: 38 ft.
Compartments: 1 2nd, 6 3rd. class. Seats: 8 2nd, 60 third class.
Lavatories: none.
Nos. 1102–07 built 12/1910; Nos. 1122–28, 6/1911; Nos. 1143–49, 12/1911.
Built to Plan 3186A. Electric lighting, no dynamo. Nos. 1102–4/22 with dynamo.

Quarter-lights on these coaches were the 'Ashford Gothic' style, but after completion of these 60 vehicles a reversion was made to the 'all-four-corners-rounded' windows, although square-cornered waist mouldings were perpetuated until 1915.

Still experimenting with types of dynamo, the SE&C selected No. 1115 in Train 117 to be fitted with Vickers' trial equipment and its running was closely observed during 1911. On 21st August of that year there was a total failure of the lighting. It was apparent that Vickers dynamos were not up to the job and that Stone's equipment was greatly preferred by the SE&C.

The 20 sets worked all sorts of semi-fast and local trains, being used indiscriminately with the earlier and later-built 3-sets and never being allocated to any 'fixed' workings. Late in 1915, Sets 126–32 were re-numbered 104–110 as part of a 'tidying-up' exercise to allow all the Type 'A' sets to be numbered consecutively from 90 to 123. To enable this to happen, old Sets 104–110, which were a miscellaneous bunch, had to be renumbered also: 4-sets 104–7 to 124–7, 4-set 108 to 261, 10-set 109 to 260 and 5-set 110 to 256.

On coming to the Southern, Sets 104–123 were renumbered 543–562 in the same order, and between 1924 and 1928, as the sets went in for overhaul at Ashford (Set 561 at Lancing), their allocated SR coach numbers were applied. Lavatory Composite Brakes became Third Brakes (56 seats) Nos. 3364–83; non-lavatory Composite Brakes also became Third Brakes (70 seats) Nos. 3384–3403; and the 1st/2nd Composites were altered to first/thirds, seating 22 and 30 of each respective class and renumbered 5395–5414.

During 1927, L.G. Pegrum, one of the very few people to be recording details of ex-SE&C carriages at that time, noted against Sets 545/6 and 555/6 that they were used on boat trains.

Otherwise, the sets trundled uneventfully round the Eastern and Central Sections of the SR until, in October 1943, the first one was withdrawn. Set 552 (coaches 3388, 5398 and 3368) was sold to the Longmoor Military Railway, where the coaches were renumbered 13582–4. About 1955, the centre vehicle (No. 13584) was damaged and withdrawn, but the other two carried on, being used for regular passenger service until the closure of the LMR in October 1969, by which time they bore the numbers ARMY 5311/12. Sometimes they displayed roofboards lettered 'Liss–Longmoor Downs–Bordon'. The two lavatory compartments of No. 5311 had been sealed out of use, but the fittings were still there. Both coaches were purchased by the Kent & East Sussex Railway in September 1970 and, after some repair work (during the course of which the lavatories were opened up, photographed and re-sealed), they were repainted in brown and cream livery. The 7-compartment brake was given the KES number 60 and its companion became No. 61. Both coaches saw some use in passenger traffic from 1974 onwards, but were later withdrawn as both needed extensive overhauls.

Third Brake No. 3395 in Set 561 was withdrawn in 1942 and the remaining two coaches transferred to 8-set 640; and another withdrawal came in 1944 when Third Brake No. 3386 in Set 555 was damaged by enemy action and the other two coaches in the set were transferred to 9-set 913. All three coaches of Set 551 (Nos. 3389, 5397 and 3367) were transferred to 8-set 903 by about 1945. Set 546 was withdrawn completely in 1946, its Third Brakes Nos. 3380 and 3400 becoming Mess and Tool Vans Nos. 365S and 366S for the Redhill breakdown train.

Thus, the position in 1947 was that eight 54 ft coaches had been withdrawn, leaving 52 which, over the next two years, were converted at Lancing to be made suitable for further service in the Isle of Wight.

Much of the carriage stock there was overdue for replacement, but the problem was what to replace it with. In 1945 the Chief Civil Engineer had turned down certain Western Section 8 ft 6 in. stock as well as three types of Eastern Section 3-coach sets. Even withdrawn vehicles from electric trailer sets had been considered for re-conversion to steam stock for Island service but, finally, the decision was made to use the 54 ft SE&C stock, subject to the removal of roof observatories owing to a restricted loading gauge.

The Brake Thirds were given enlarged luggage compartments (with an

SR DIAG. No. 40.

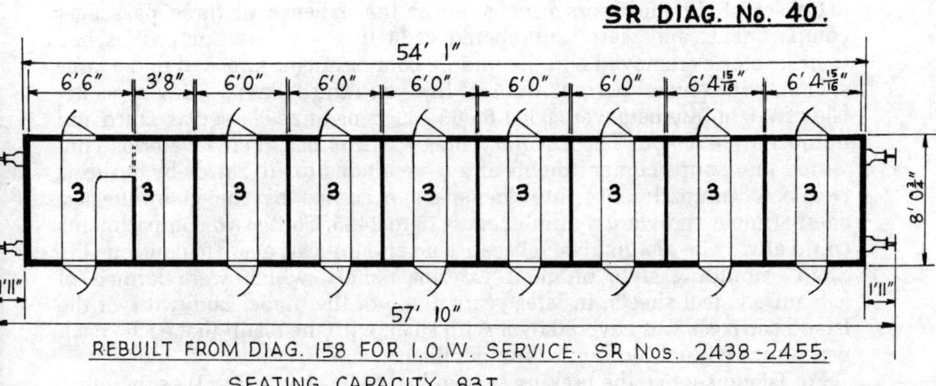

REBUILT FROM DIAG. 158 FOR I.O.W. SERVICE. SR Nos. 2438-2455.

SEATING CAPACITY 83T.

SR DIAG. No. 171.

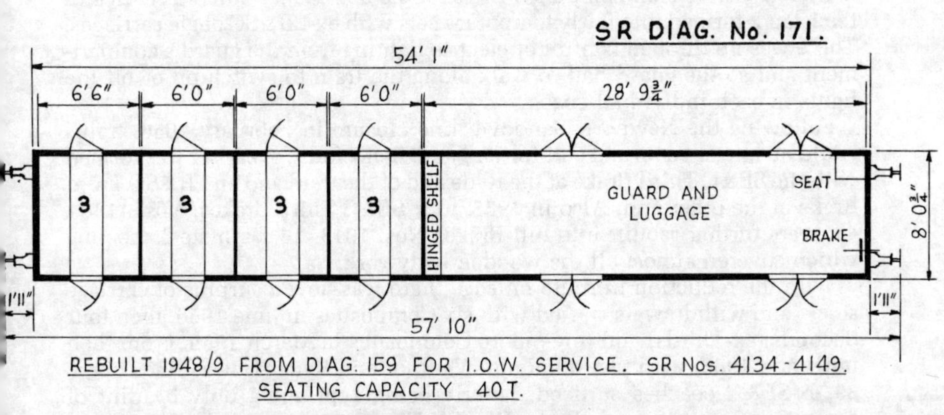

REBUILT 1948/9 FROM DIAG. 159 FOR I.O.W. SERVICE. SR Nos. 4134-4149.

SEATING CAPACITY 40T.

SR DIAG. Nos. 41, 376, 377 and 378.

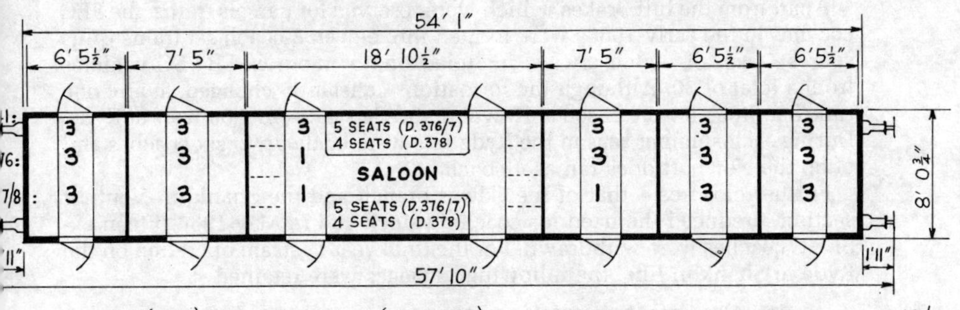

	SR (IOW) Nos. 2456-58	(DIAG. 41).	SEATING CAPACITY 70T.	1948/9
REBUILT FROM	No. 6365	(DIAG. 376).	,, ,, 18 F 50 T.	1947
DIAG. 313	Nos. 6364/68	(DIAG. 377).	,, ,, 26 F 40 T.	1947
FOR I.O.W. SERVICE	Nos. 6369-80	(DIAG. 378).	,, ,, 24 F 40 T.	1948/9

extra set of double doors each side) at the expense of three passenger compartments and were renumbered 4134 to 4149. The Composites had their lavatories removed and the middle compartments knocked into a large saloon, with several permutations of first- and third-class seating capacity; Isle of Wight numbers were 6364/65/68–80, plus three classed as Third and numbered 2456–58. The Lavatory Brake Thirds had their lavatories converted into coupé compartments and were altered to all-Thirds by building two new compartments into the space occupied by the guard/luggage compartment and were renumbered 2438 to 2455. These two compartments could always be distinguished because no attempt was made to continue the SE&C moulding style on their exterior panels, which were formed of galvanised steel sheets. In later years much of the timber bodywork of the Island carriages was covered over with steel, with the result that each coach was an individual, no two being identical.

For Island service the braking system had to be changed to Westinghouse air, and at the brake-ends two windows were fitted for the guard to observe the track. Conversion completed in 1949, the 52 coaches entered service in the Island, formed into fairly temporary sets with ex-LB&SC bogie carriages. There was no through control of electric lighting from the guard's compartment and so the guard had to walk along the train to switch on or off the lights in each individual coach.

Following the Newport–Sandown line closure in February 1956, trains could no longer be turned end-for-end and, henceforth, every set was formed with the SE&C Third Brake at the Ryde end of the train and an LB&SC Third Brake at the other end. Also in 1956, four SE&C Third Brakes, Nos. 4138–41, were further rebuilt into full Brakes Nos. 1013–16, with steel sheeting which covered almost all the wooden bodywork.

With the reduction in route mileage there was now a surplus of carriage stock, and withdrawals started with six Composites in June 1956, then four Seconds (ex-Thirds) and three more Composites in March 1959. From then until mid-1966, with just the Ryde–Ventnor and Ryde–Cowes lines open, 39 ex-SE&C coaches sufficed, latterly being kept going only by dint of careful maintenance by Ryde Works. These 39 comprised 15 83-seat Seconds, two 70-set Seconds (2456/8), 12 Brake Seconds, six Composites seating 24 first- and 40 second-class passengers, and four full Brakes (1013–6).

Apart from the full Brakes, which were reserved for parcels trains, the SEC coaches in the early 1960s were formed into eleven 3-coach set trains (plus spares), each of which always included one or more ex-LB&SC vehicles from a total of 30. Although the formations constantly changed, at any one time Sets 485–8 were based at Newport and Sets 490–4/7/500 were at Ryde. During each summer season the Ryde sets were made up to six coaches and often the Newport ones ran as 4-coach.

Further closures – that of the Cowes branch and the Shanklin–Ventnor section – reduced the need for coaching stock and in May 1966 fifteen ex-SE&C coaches were withdrawn. For the final year of steam operation on the Ryde to Shanklin line, the following carriages were retained:

11 83-set Seconds Nos. 2438/40/42/47/49–55.
7 40-seat Second Brakes Nos. 4135–37/42/43/45/49.
2 Composites (24 1st, 40 2nd) Nos. 6375/76.
4 Brake Vans Nos. 1013–16. Total 24.

All these were withdrawn at the end of 1966, but three were rescued by the Wight Locomotive Society, these being Brake Seconds Nos. 4145 and 4149 (formerly 3390 and 3402) and Composite No. 6375 (formerly 5412); and all three may be seen in SR malachite green livery at Haven Street, Isle of Wight.

Summary of 54 ft Coaches used in Isle of Wight

Original SR No.	*IOW No.*	*To IOW*	*Wdn*	*Original SR No.*	*IOW No.*	*To IOW*	*Wdn*
3365	2438	/48	12/66	3396	4139	48	*
3372	2439	/48	5/66	3398	4140	/48	*
3373	2440	/48	10/66	3399	4141	/48	*
3374	2441	/48	3/59	3403	4142	/48	10/66
3376	2442	/48	10/66	3391	4143	/48	12/66
3377	2443	/48	3/59	3389	4144	/49	5/66
3378	2444	/48	5/66	3390	4145	/49	1/67
3379	2445	/48	5/66	3387	4146	/49	5/66
3366	2446	/48	5/66	3401	4147	/49	5/66
3375	2447	/48	c12/66	3397	4148	/49	5/66
3364	2448	/48	3/59	3402	4149	/49	1/67
3371	2449	/48	10/66	5403	6364	/47	3/59
3367	2450	/49	10/66	5404	6365	/47	3/59
3382	2451	/49	12/66	5410	6368	/47	3/59
3370	2452	/49	c12/66	5395	6369	/48	6/56
3381	2453	/48	c12/66	5399	6370	/48	5/66
3369	2454	/49	12/66	5405	6371	/48	6/56
3383	2455	/49	10/66	5407	6372	/48	6/56
5402	2456	/48	5/66	5409	6373	/48	5/66
5397	2457	/49	3/59	5401	6374	/49	6/56
5413	2458	/49	5/66	5412	6375	/49	1/67
3384	4134	/48	5/66	5400	6376	/49	12/66
3385	4135	/48	10/66	5414	6377	/49	5/66
3392	4136	/48	10/66	5396	6378	/49	6/56
3393	4137	/48	1/67	5408	6379	/49	6/56
3394	4138	/48	*	5406	6380	/49	5/66

*Nos. 4138–41 rebuilt as brake vans 1013–16, 1956; withdrawn 1966.

Note: Nos. 2438–55 were 83-seat Thirds, Nos. 2456–58 were 70-seat Thirds with same layout as Composites, Nos. 4134–49 were Third Brakes and Nos. 6364/65/68–80 were Composites.

1013	reconstructed	10/1956;	withdrawn	12/66
1014	"	9/1956;	"	12/66
1015	"	12/1956;	"	12/66
1016	"	4/1957;	"	12/66

THREE-COACH SETS TYPE 'C' (60 ft STOCK)

'Longer still and longer' might well have been the motto of Ashford Works for, after the construction of series of 50 ft and 54 ft carriage sets a very bold decision was made to introduce sets composed of coaches with bodies each 60 ft in length. No other railway in the south of England at that time had carriages of so great a length; the London & South Western's maximum was 56 ft and the 'Brighton's' was only 54 ft. The SE&C's Type 'C' 3-coach sets, of which 62 were constructed between 1912 and 1915, and a further 10 to a modified design between 1915 and 1921, were the final flowering of the H.S. Wainwright seed for, during the course of construction, ill-health forced the resignation in November 1913 of the respected locomotive, carriage and wagon superintendent. For 31 years there had been a Wainwright in charge of carriage design at Ashford; their successor was R.E.L. Maunsell, from Inchicore.

Of the 62 Wainwright sets built, some by contractors and the remainder by Ashford, all had identical 8-compartment Third Brakes and 7-compartment Lavatory Composite Brakes, all guard's compartments being equipped with the standard roof observatory. The centre coach of each set was a Composite Lavatory with first-class saloon with two wide (fixed) windows each side, but after 30 of these had been built the design was slightly modified, presumably to improve ventilation: the later vehicles had *one* wide and *two* narrow windows (one of which was a droplight) each side.

COMPOSITE LAVATORY (with saloon)
Nos. 1150–6/75–8, 1203–10/53–6/80–6 (SR Nos. 5433–5462)
Body length: 60 ft 1 in. Bogie centres: 43 ft 6 in.
Compartments: 1 saloon 1st, 3 ordinary 1st, 3 2nd class.
Seats: 26 1st, 24 2nd class. Lavatories: 2 (to 1st class).
Electric lighting, with dynamo. Saloon with two wide windows each side.

COMPOSITE LAVATORY (with saloon)
Nos. 1211–22/57–62, 1301–7/20–2/31–3 (SR Nos. 5463–5493)
As above, but saloon had one wide and two narrow windows each side.

COMPOSITE BRAKE LAVATORY
Nos. 1157–63/71–4, 1223–52, 1287–1300/23–9 (SR Nos. 3476–3537)
Body length: 60 ft 1 in. Bogie centres: 43 ft 6 in.
Compartments: 2 2nd, 5 3rd class, guard. Seats: 13 2nd, 40 3rd class.
Lavatories: 2 (1 o 2nd class, 1 to three 3rd class compartments).
Electric lighting, without dynamo.

THIRD BRAKE
Nos. 1164–70/79–1202/63–79, 1308–18/35–7 (SR Nos. 3404–3465)
Body length: 60 ft 1 in. Bogie centres: 43 ft 6 in.
Compartments: 8, guard. Seats: 80. Lavatories: none.
Electric lighting, without dynamo.

Dates of construction now follow. The undermentioned were built at Ashford Works:

1150–70	6/1912	1297–1300, 1304–6/11–14	2/1914
1278/9/85/6/92/3	2/1913	1307/15–8/20–2/3–6	7/1914
1276/7/83/4/90/1	3/1913	1327/31/35	11/1914
1273–5/80–2/87–9	4/1913	1328/32/36	3/1915
1294–6, 1301–3/8–10	10/1913	1329/33/37	6/1915

Seventy-two coaches (formed in 24 sets) were built by Metropolitan Amalgamated Railway Carriage & Wagon Co., which in 1912 changed its name to Metropolitan Carriage Wagon & Finance Co.:

1171–82	6/1912	1191–4, 1211–4, 1231–4	10/1913
1183–6/1203–6/23–6	12/1912	1195–8, 1215–8, 1235–8	11/1913
1187/8/1207/8/27/8	2/1913	1199–1202, 1219–22, 1239–42	12/1913
1189/90, 1209/10/29/30	3/1913		

And 30 coaches (10 sets) were built by Cravens Ltd of Darnall, Sheffield, as under:

1243/4/53/4/63/4	6/1913	1248/58/68	9/1913
1245/6/55/6/65/6	7/1913	1249/50/59/60/69/70	10/1913
1247/57/67	8/1913	1251/2/61/2/71/2	11/1913

Many visitors have commented on the excellence of the Trio-'C' sets. They were beautiful riding vehicles, better indeed than much of the contemporary corridor stock operating on the northern lines. First-class seating was very comfortable and the armchairs in the saloon compartments were positively luxurious; interiors were well insulated from the noise of the wheels travelling over rail-joints, although as was to be expected the third-class seating was nothing like as comfortable, being narrow and minimally padded. The heating could be regulated by the passenger, if he had sufficient strength to operate the huge brass handle situated above the seat-back.

The sets were originally numbered 135–138 and from 143 onwards in order of construction until Set 193 came out in February 1914. After that things became a little confusing, partly because of a belated desire to fill the missing numbers 139 to 142 in order to have a consecutive sequence for the Type 'C' sets. The July 1914 construction comprised Type 'C' Sets 195, 196, 197 and 142; the original Set 142 had been a Type 'B' 3-set, which was renumbered within the range 58 to 71. Next came Sets 194, 139 and 140 between November 1914 and June 1915; to accommodate the last two the original Sets 139 and 140 needed renumbering and 4-set 139 duly became 52 (Caterham and Tadworth branches) and 5-set 140 became 257 (Tonbridge–Cannon Street) late in 1915.

A note should be made about Composite No. 1319 (SR No. 5494), which was formed in Set 193, built at Ashford in February 1914. It was a plain-panelled vehicle, without the usual mouldings, although the interior layout was the same as that of its predecessors and the brake coaches with which it ran were panelled in the usual way. Clearly it was a prototype coach, for it was not until October 1915 that the first complete 3-coach set built in plain style emerged from Ashford. The brake coaches, moreover, had no roof observatories. The feature that typified SE&C carriage design more than anything else had at last been abolished as far as new construction was concerned.

Back in July 1913, even before Wainwright was gone, it had been suggested in internal correspondence that the observatories should be abolished on the 3-coach sets, although it was not thought necessary to raise the height of the roof. Edwin Cox, superintendent of the line, saw no reason why the observatories should be perpetuated any longer. In August 1913 he wrote to the General Manager, Francis Dent:

'We have considered this question, and are of the opinion that the time has arrived when the roof observatories of Guard's compartments, in the new Coaching Stock, can be dispensed with, the brake compartment being re-arranged accordingly. In all cases there should be end "lookouts" to the Guard's compartment as in the recently converted Boat Train Units.' (A reference to the five Firsts of 1905 that were altered in 1913 to Brake Firsts without roof observatories.)

Thus, plans were prepared for further Trio 'C' sets with re-arranged brake compartment, two windows in the end overlooking the track, and with all the bodysides devoid of moulding. Externally they were austere vehicles; internally the layout of seating and compartments was identical to the earlier 'C' sets. Only 10 sets were built, all at Ashford, between 1915 and 1921; essential war work prevented Ashford from constructing rolling stock at the pre-War rate of rapidity.

COMPOSITE LAVATORY (with saloon)
Nos. 1334/45–7/9/57/8/63–5 (SR Nos. 5495–5504)
Details as for Nos. 1211 etc.

COMPOSITE BRAKE LAVATORY
Nos. 1330/42–4/50/61/2/69–71 (SR Nos. 3538–3547)
Details as for Nos. 1157 etc.

THIRD BRAKE
Nos. 1338–41/8/59/60/6–8 (SR Nos. 3466–3475)
Details as for Nos. 1164 etc.

Dates sent out from Ashford were:

1330/34/38	10/1915	1341/44/47	12/1916	1358/60/62	2/1920
1339/42/45	7/1916	1348–50	10/1917	1366/7/63/4/9/70	3/1921
1340/43/46	9/1916	1357/59/61	1/1920	1365/68/71	5/1921

Set numbers were 141 and 198 to 206, allocated in order of construction. To make way for Set 141, the old set of that number (5-coach, allotted to a Tonbridge–London service) had to be renumbered 258 late in 1915. There was now a consecutive run of set numbers for all 72 Type 'C' sets – 135 to 206.

Sets 198 to 200 were built originally without heaters, although they were through-piped. Nos. 199 and 200 received steam heating complete in May 1920 and No. 198 did so in June 1921. Sets 201–6 had 'L'-section truss-rods to support the underframes.

No individual Type 'C' set was ever allotted to a specific train service, nor was any train booked for working by a Type 'C' as opposed to any other of the 3-coach sets. All 'mucked-in', and all types were just as likely to turn up on fast trains to Dover or Ramsgate as they were on slow trains to Addiscombe Road, Bromley North, Caterham or Dartford. The sets went round and round from working to working, with brief rest periods for maintenance every few days at depots such as Rotherhithe Road or Victoria. The 3-coach sets, of four different types, were coded by the SE&C 'Trio' and also had telegraphic codes for identification, as under:

Type 'A'	code XA	Sets 90 to 126	*Total:* 37
Type 'B'	code XB	Sets 58 to 71	*Total:* 14
Type 'C'	code XC	Sets 135 to 206	*Total:* 72
Type 'D'	code XD	Sets 128 to 130	*Total:* 3

All these 126 sets were indivisible in traffic and in the event of any failure the whole set had to be 'stopped'. Consequently there needed to be quite a number of spare sets standing about to allow for mishaps, normal maintenance and cleaning. In 1919, for example, there was always one set for cleaning at Dover, Hastings and Margate West, as well as one spare set at Ashford, Folkestone Junction, Reading and Tonbridge, and two spares at both Rotherhithe Road and Victoria: 11 sets. The summer 1922 train services required 108 Trio sets working in traffic on weekdays, leaving 18 spare.

The SE&C was clearly as keen as ever on retaining second-class accommodation on its system, quite apart from its use on boat trains (because of through bookings to the Continent), for the very last Trio 'C' sets had second-class built in. Since the abolition of second-class on the L&SWR from 22nd July, 1918, the SE&C was the only important railway in Great Britain to keep it for Continental, main-line *and* suburban traffic. The LB&SCR and Great Eastern still kept it for Continental traffic, and the Great Northern and GE kept it for suburban services. The Southern Railway officially abolished it in September 1923, but the actual accommodation remained unaltered for some while; as second-class coaches went through Works for repainting in new livery the seating was altered by removing arm-rests, if any, and the 'SECOND' labelling changed to 'THIRD'. It is not thought that Trio sets, as long as they remained in SE&C livery, had their large figures '2' on the doors changed to '3'.

SE&C sets 135 to 206 were given the SR set numbers 567 to 638 in exactly the same order as the SE&C numbers, and were repainted at Ashford or Lancing between 1923 and 1929. At some stage, Third Brake No. 3464 (SE&C 1336) had been involved in an accident and as a result its roof observatory was removed and replaced by end windows; it was the only rebuild of its type and the set it was in (SR 571) was always an oddity because the coach at the other end still had its 'birdcage'. R.W. Kidner noted it in 1928.

L.G. Pegrum noted in 1927 that Sets 608, 609, 611–13, 619 and 620, most of which were still in SE&C livery, were used in boat trains. Otherwise, the Southern used the sets on local and semi-fast trains on both the Eastern and Central sections and gave them the code 'R' (for 'Rover') in the carriage working notices. Presumably they were called Rover sets because they 'roved' all over the system, with free interchange between the Central and Eastern Sections, no set ever being allocated permanently to any particular depot. They were, indeed, called 'interchangeable sets' in the working books.

On 20th August, 1927, the 10.51 am Charing Cross–Margate via Maidstone East line train was derailed at Bearsted, the locomotive and seven coaches leaving the rails; the train included in its makeup Set 621 (still in SE&C livery), Third No. 918 and Composite No. 5369 as well as sundry vans and ex-LSW and ex-LBSC vehicles. No serious damage was done.

In March 1931 the Southern Railway Board approved a proposal to modify the electric lighting on 83 Eastern Section 3-sets. Because the train sets were now used on slower services than they were originally designed for, the single dynamo per set was unable to supply sufficient current and so an additional dynamo with extra battery capacity was fitted to each set train. To keep expenditure to a minimum, in characteristic SR style, the dynamos employed were second-hand. The work was completed by March 1933.

About 1933 or 1934 Set 600 was made up to six coaches by the addition of Composites Nos. 5299 (ex-'loose' stock) and 5301 (ex-Set 674) and First No.

7278; it was then used on a morning Hastings to Charing Cross via Cannon Street service, until about 1940. Its booked workings in May 1941 were the 5.35 am Margate to Rochester (daily) and 7.38 pm Saturdays excepted, 5.30 pm Saturdays and Sundays return services. The set was withdrawn at the end of 1941, Nos. 5299 and 7278 being condemned. The other four coaches lasted rather longer, for in mid-1942 they were converted into two push-and-pull sets. No. 3505 had the brake compartment altered, being fitted with driving controls, the roof observatory was removed and four windows in the end and one each side were provided for the driver; the handbrake column was moved from the wall to the floor and the lavatories were stripped, their windows being panelled over. No. 5473 also had the lavatories stripped and panelled over, two first-class compartments nearest the end were downgraded to third and the remaining two first-class compartments (including the saloon) had their seating altered from 3-a-side to 4-a-side, total seating capacity of the composite being 20 1st, 50 3rd. Nos. 3505 and 5473 were numbered as push-and-pull Set 660 from September 1942. Third Brake No. 3433, also from Set 600, was similarly altered for push-and-pull and fitted with driving controls, being paired with Composite No. 5301 from the same set to become push-and-pull Set 661 in September 1942; two first-class compartments in the Composite required downgrading to third, but the seating in the Third Brake was unaltered and in this case there were no lavatories to be eliminated. Seating capacity of No. 5301 was now 16 1st, 50 3rd.

Sets 660 and 661 were normally allocated to the Crowhurst–Bexhill West branch; despite the journey time being a mere 10 minutes, two sets were always needed to work the service because of the desirability of connecting at Crowhurst with all main-line trains, which usually ran at awkward times. Later, during 1960 and 1961, Sets 660/1 became a very familiar sight to passengers travelling between Tunbridge Wells West and Oxted, but they were compared unfavourably with modern corridor stock in use on the through London trains. Set 660 was withdrawn in November 1961 and Set 661 in October 1961.

Plain-panelled 3-set 630 was deleted in 1941 and Composite No. 5496 withdrawn, presumably because of accident or enemy action damage. Third Brake No. 3467 was fitted up for push-and-pull working, initially as a 'loose' driving trailer. The brake compartment was altered in the same manner as those of Nos. 3433 and 3505, with four windows overlooking the track and two side windows, but there was no roof observatory to remove. At the same time No. 3539, from Set 630, was similarly converted, but here the two former second-class compartments were upgraded to a rather sub-standard first class and the lavatories stripped, leaving the short internal corridors to lead nowhere. As the coach was now a Brake Composite it needed renumbering, and took the number 6410 (originally that of an ex-LSW coach) running as a loose trailer between June 1941 and May 1947. Seating capacity was now 13 1st, 40 3rd class.

In May 1947 No. 3467 was paired with an ex-LB & SC Trailer Composite to replace the original Third Brake in Set 714, and then worked various Eastern Section push-and-pull services until withdrawal came in August 1961. Also in May 1947, No. 6410 was paired with ex-LSW Third No. 608 to form a new push-and-pull set, No. 37, for Central Section services; this Third on being withdrawn in July 1954 was replaced by an ex-LB&SC Third, No. 2193. They were an ill-matched pair: one coach with mouldings, the other without; one coach with plain arc roof, the other with a semi-elliptical one. Despite this, Set 37 ran until December 1960, after which it was sent to Newhaven for scrapping.

The next sets selected for conversion to push-and-pull working were Nos. 637 and 638 (plain-panelled), which were deleted from the 3-set lists in September 1950 and June 1952 respectively. The body and interior alterations were done as on earlier ones: lavatories stripped, first-class reduced to two compartments per set, four windows built at the drive-end. In 1950 coaches 3546 and 5503 became 2-set 662, which was sent to the Western Section as 'relief set' to other push-and-pull sets and based at Eastleigh, working, when required, services in the Bournemouth area. In late 1961 it was transferred to the Tunbridge Wells area for Oxted line push-and-pull services, and when withdrawal came in May 1962 it was the last push-and-pull set formed of ex-SE&C stock still in existence.

Two coaches of Set 638, Nos. 5504 and 3547, were converted in 1952 to trailers for push-and-pull Set 663, for use on the Eastern and Central Sections. It was withdrawn in May 1961. No. 3474, the Brake Third left over from the conversion of Set 637, replaced Lavatory Third Brake No. 3053 (ex-L&SW) in push-and-pull Set 31 on the Western Section in 1951, being withdrawn in March 1961; No. 3475, spare from the conversion of Set 638, was used to replace the ex-LB&SC Third Brake in Set 715 in 1952; this set had already had its original Composite replaced by an SE&C one, No. 5298, back in 1941. Withdrawal of Set 715 was effected in March 1961.

The final push-and-pull set created from former SE&C stock was No. 656, a replacement of the original push-and-pull Set 656, which was withdrawn in October 1956. The 'new' one was made up from Second Brake (former Third Brake) No. 3542 and Composite No. 5499 – from 3-set 633, deleted in October 1956 and its other Second Brake (3470) withdrawn – and sent into traffic in time for the 1957 summer services. Set 656 was Eastern- or Central-based until its withdrawal in January 1962, latterly appearing regularly on Tunbridge Wells–Oxted services.

In 1951 Set 572 was deleted and its coaches transferred to 8-set 898. No. 3465 was withdrawn in September 1958; Nos. 5493 and 3537 went in January 1958.

The only other permanent alteration to a Trio 'C' set was made in 1955 to No. 636, which was strengthened to 6 coaches by the addition of Thirds Nos. 1090 and 1101 and Composite No. 5379 and given a regular summer service to work: the 9.09 am Tonbridge to Hastings and 4.50 pm return. In December 1956 No. 5379 was withdrawn and replaced by a Second, No. 968. Further strengthened to 7 coaches in March 1958 (with SR-built Corridor Composite No. 6287) Set 636 was withdrawn in July 1959, just after the start of that year's summer services. This was the last set in traffic to consist of all three original coaches of a Trio 'C', plus the extra coaches.

No permanent change was ever made to any other of the 60 ft sets, of which the first to be withdrawn was No. 584 in January 1954. Over the next few years withdrawal continued steadily, as BR-built stock arrived to take over the working of services formerly the preserve of the Trios, until in October 1958 the last one, No. 620, was condemned. Only the augmented set, No. 636, now remained, as mentioned above, and after this was eliminated only the few push-and-pull sets survived for a few more years.

The dates of withdrawal of the Trio 'C' sets were:

Set	*Wdn*	*Set*	*Wdn*	*Set*	*Wdn*	*Set*	*Wdn*
567	2/56	578	3/56	589	10/57	601	8/57
568	12/56	579	4/57	590	1/58	602	2/58
569	2/56	580	1/58	591	11/55	603	11/57
570	11/54	581	5/54	592	10/58	604	2/56
571	/56	582	7/57	593	11/55	605	3/58
572	/51	583	2/58	594	6/54	606	4/56
573	11/57	584	1/54	595	7/58	607	2/57
574	11/57	585	1/57	596	1/58	608	12/56
575	11/57	586	5/57	597	5/57	609	11/57
576	3/57	587	1/56	598	6/57	610	3/56
577	11/57	588	9/56	599	3/58	611	1/58

Set	*Wdn*	*Set*	*Wdn*
612	10/55	623	5/58
613	10/54	624	7/57
614	4/57	625	6/58
615	6/55	626	5/57
616	12/55	627	6/54
617	4/57	628	6/57
618	1/57	629	6/58
619	9/56	631	1/57
620	10/58	632	12/57
621	4/57	634	8/58
622	3/56	635	5/58

Set 567 scrapped at Newhaven, 3/56
Set 604 scrapped at Newhaven, 3/56
Set 571 was renumbered 600 in December 1956 and withdrawn in June 1958.

Many of the Second Brakes were found suitable for conversion, after their withdrawal from passenger service, into departmental coaches, often as breakdown train vehicles, whilst some others became 'internal user' at various fixed locations. Below are listed all the known conversions.

3407 to Sleeping and Mess Coach DS 99, 1956.
3410 to Instruction Coach DS 33, 1/56. Carriage & Wagon examiners. Renumbered 083180, *c.*1977. Clapham Junction. Sold to Bluebell Railway, August 1982.
3424 to Breakdown Van DS 129, 3/56. Tonbridge in 1960.
3434 to DS 134, *c.*1958. Ashford.
3443 to DS 98, 1956. Norwood Junction.
3446 to Breakdown Van (staff) DS 124, 10/55. Gillingham.
3448 to Breakdown Van DS 126, 3/56. Bricklayers Arms; Ashford in 1960. Wdn and sent to Queenborough, 5/65.
3452 to Internal User 080640, *c.*1957. Chichester.
3455 to DS 133, *c.*1958. Ashford. Wdn and sent to Bynea, 1/66.
3457 to Mess & Tool Van DS 180, 5/58. Faversham. Wdn 1960 and scrapped at Newhaven, August 1960.
3460 to Internal User 080637, *c.*1957. Chichester.
3466 to Internal User 080681, 1958.

3472 to Internal User 080691, 4/58. Salisbury. Condemned 6/61.
3473 to DS 70080, 4/60. Lancing Works Train. Wdn 8/64.
3477 to DS 116, mobile workshop and messroom, *c*.1958. Brighton.
3479 to Sleeping & Mess Coach DS 100, 1957.
3484 to Internal User 080621, *c*.1957. Lancing Works.
3492 to Internal User 080638, *c*.1957. St Mary Cray.
3496 to DS 128, 3/56. Breakdown Van. Tonbridge in 1960.
3511 to DS 136, 2/58. Mobile Laboratory.
3515 to DS 130, 1956. Breakdown Van, Staff & Tool. Ashford in 1960.
3518 to DS 125, 10/55. Breakdown Van, Tool. Gillingham.
3520 to DS 127, 3/56. Breakdown Van, Ashford in 1960.
3527 to DS 132, 1956. Civil Defence Training School.
3543 to DS 70019, 2/59. Wdn 2/65.
3544 to Internal User 080692, 4/58. Salisbury.
5492 to Internal User 080909, 5/58. Gillingham.

CORRIDOR THIRDS

Nos. 1351–1356 (SR Nos. 962–967)

Body length: 54 ft 1 in. Body width: 8 ft 4 in.
Height from rail to top of roof: 12 ft 3 in. Bogie centres: 38 ft.
Compartments: 8. Seats: 48. Lavatories: 1.

This batch of six coaches, built at Ashford and dated October 1920, indicated a complete change of direction in SE&C carriage design. The old days of Wainwright were truly gone for ever, and the 'new and improved' SE&C was making every effort to demonstrate what a fine railway it really was.

The coaches, which were steel-clad, were the first to exceed the standard width of 8 ft since the Vestibuled Cars of 1897 and, moreover, were 6 in. higher than other stock, the roof having a high arched profile. Each of the compartments seated six passengers, access from the corridor being by sliding door. There were only four external doors on the corridor side: one at each end and two in the centre, but on the compartment side of the coach a door gave access to every compartment. At one end of the coach was a lavatory, but at the other end, where one would have expected to find another lavatory, there was only a small alcove where portable tables were stored. These tables could be fitted up in the compartments if required.

Wide windows were provided in the corridors, and the bodysides had a much more pronounced curve at the waist than did the older wooden-panelled stock. Bogies, of 8 ft wheelbase, were Fox's patent pressed steel type, but No. 1352 (later SR 963) was equipped with Maunsell's new type of bogie. British Standard Gangways were fitted at each end of the coaches.

The Corridor Thirds were designed to work with the 1907 Corridor Brake Composites and with Pullman cars in boat trains; a useful facility was that every compartment had electric bell communication to the Pullman car attendant. Nos. 1351 to 1354 were formed, one each and in numerical order, in boat train sets 4, 5, 6 and 7; and Nos. 1355 and 1356 were 'spare boat' stock.

During the 1924/5 period the Corridor Thirds were taken off boat train services and sent to Works for repainting in SR livery. Nos. 1353/6 were

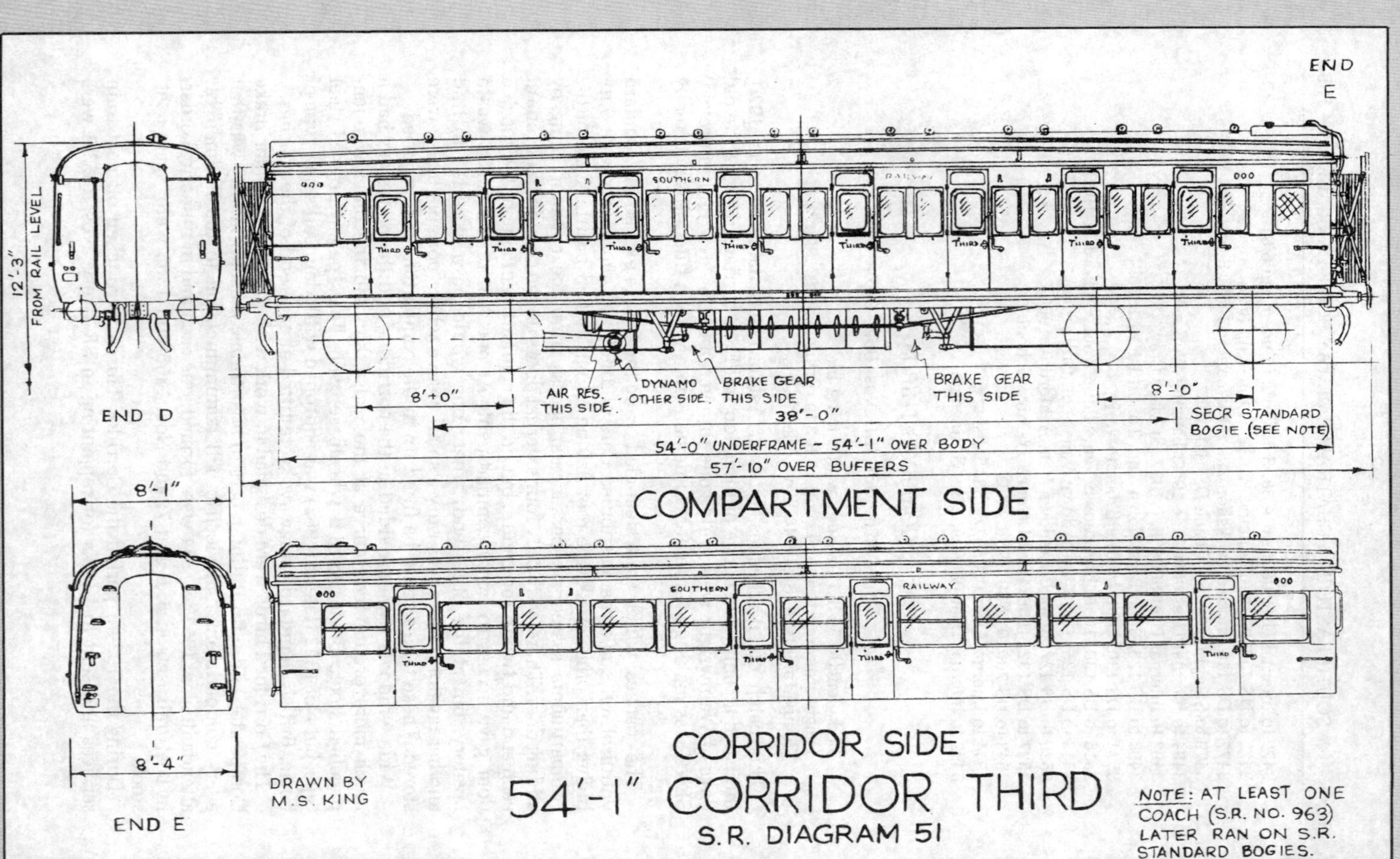
END E
12'-3" FROM RAIL LEVEL
END D
8'+0"
AIR RES. THIS SIDE
DYNAMO OTHER SIDE
BRAKE GEAR THIS SIDE
38'-0"
BRAKE GEAR THIS SIDE
8'-0"
SECR STANDARD BOGIE (SEE NOTE)
54'-0" UNDERFRAME - 54'-1" OVER BODY
57'-10" OVER BUFFERS
COMPARTMENT SIDE
8'-1"
8'-4"
END E
CORRIDOR SIDE
DRAWN BY M.S KING
54'-1" CORRIDOR THIRD
S.R. DIAGRAM 51
NOTE: AT LEAST ONE COACH (S.R. NO. 963) LATER RAN ON S.R. STANDARD BOGIES.

done at Eastleigh and the other four at Ashford. The new numbers were 962 to 967; of these, No. 966 was formed in 3-set 389 from June 1925 and worked on the former LB&SC, between Hastings and London Bridge via Lewes and East Croydon. No. 963 was observed in Set 400 and No. 964 was in Set 430 during 1928 (both on London–Tunbridge Wells–Bexhill through services) but may not have been part of the sets as the observer, R.W. Kidner, noted them as 'extra coaches'. Some of the Corridor Thirds worked with Corridor Brake Composites on Dover–Birkenhead services during the 1920s, until replaced by new SR-built stock.

However, during the early 1930s all six Corridor Thirds were collected together and formed, with Corridor Brake Composites Nos. 6622/7, into one 8-coach set, No. 389, which remained unchanged until mid-1947. Set 389 worked on the Ramsgate via Chatham main line during the 1930s, but after the War its regular summer Saturday outings were on the Hastings line. When not in use it normally slumbered at Maze Hill.

Nos. 963/6 were withdrawn in October 1955 and replaced by two 1921-built Corridor Thirds, Nos. 1010/11; a 1923-built Corridor First, No. 7374, had already been added to the formation in 1954. The set was withdrawn in February 1959 and the remaining four Corridor Thirds (now Seconds) were condemned; by this time Set 389 was the last remaining to be formed entirely of ex-SE&C corridor stock. Nos. 962/4/5/7 were scrapped at Newhaven in June 1959.

Summary of Corridor Thirds

SEC	*SR*	*Re-No.*	*Set*	*Wdn*	*SEC*	*SR*	*Re-No.*	*Set*	*Wdn*
1351	962	1/25	389	2/59	1354	965	1/25	389	2/59
1352	963	4/24	389	10/55	1355	966	6/25	389	10/55
1353	964	6/25	389	2/59	1356	967	6/25	389	2/59

10-COMPARTMENT THIRDS

Nos. 1372–1437 (SR Nos. 1054–1112, 968–974)

Body length: 60 ft 1 in. Body width: 8 ft 0¾ in.
Height from rail to top of roof: 11 ft 9 in. Bogie centres: 43 ft 6 in.
Compartments: 10. Seats: 100.

During the early 1920s, when the SE&C was evolving its electrification plans, a decision was made to construct a large number of high-capacity third-class coaches that could be incorporated in the future electric trains although, for the moment, they would run as steam-hauled carriages. In all, 66 of these very austere and somewhat uncomfortable carriages were built between 1921 and 1923.

The first 20 (Nos. 1372–91) were delivered in August 1921; bodies were by Birmingham Railway Carriage & Wagon Co. and underframes by Gloucester Railway Carriage & Wagon Co. The next 10 were built complete by Birmingham and No. 1392 was delivered in August, Nos. 1393–7 in October, and 1398–1401 in November 1921. All 30 of these displayed the same body style as that of the last 10 Trio sets. They were followed by 20 with SE&C-built bodies and underframes by Birmingham RC&W: Nos. 1402–6 in April, 1407–11 in August, 1412–16 in November and 1417–21 in

December 1922. Of these, Nos. 1402–11 were matchboarded with mahogany slats arranged vertically along the lower part of the body. Nos. 1412–21 looked very different as they were steel-panelled, the windows having almost square corners, and had ‘tin’ door ventilators, officially referred to as ‘Special MM Ventilation’. Nos. 1422–37, entirely Ashford-built, were also in this style: Nos. 1422–9 were dated December 1922, 1430/1 April 1923, and 1432–7 June 1923.

The bodies had almost straight sides, whilst the compartments, although only slightly narrower than those of the Trios, were far from luxurious, having rather narrow bench seating. Despite their intended use on suburban services, the Thirds in fact found themselves working in fast trains. During the summer of 1922, many Victoria to Ramsgate trains included two 100-seat Thirds in their formation, and a few of the Folkestone, Hastings and Bexhill services included one. The traffic people must have been delighted with the new Thirds, for with two of these in each of the busy holiday trains they soon cleared away the crowds.

All the Thirds entered service in dark brown livery, unlined and lettered in gold, blocked with white; roofs were white and underframes black. During the first half of 1923, No. 1383 was repainted dark blue, similar to Somerset & Dorset Joint Railway livery, picked out with white lines around the quarter lights (noted in *The Railway Magazine*, July 1923). Possibly it ran in this style until November 1928, when it gained its SR number and, presumably, green livery.

When the 1923 renumbering scheme was drawn up Nos. 1372–1430 were allotted the numbers 9058–9116 in the electric trailer Thirds list, following on from the 46 ft Thirds. Nos. 1431–7, on the other hand, were scheduled to remain as steam-hauled coaches and were allotted the numbers 968–974, which all eventually were carried. Shortly afterwards the Southern revised its plans for electric stock and the 10-compartment Thirds had no place in the scheme of things. Instead, No. 1372–1430 were allotted a spare batch of ‘steam’ numbers, 1054–1112, and between 1927 and 1929 were so renumbered. Two of them shared the distinction of being the very last ex-SE&C carriages to be renumbered, these being Nos. 1399 (SR 1081) and 1414 (SR 1096), which were repainted at Ashford and both formally dated 23rd December, 1929.

Most of them were placed in sets used on semi-fast and excursion trains. In 1929 R.W. Kidner recorded 7-set 640 as including No. 1055 and 6-set 662 as including No. 1057. On 20th May, 1929, he observed No. 1399 – still in SE&C livery – in 8-set 699. No. 1059 was noted as having been formed – presumably for only a short time – in Trio Set 526; by April 1931 the Third was seen running in a mixed un-numbered set. The set number 526 was removed at Blackheath on 8th April, 1931.

4-set 667, which included two Thirds, was formed by about 1931. Something of a curiosity, its makeup was: Third Brake No. 3259, Thirds Nos. 974 and 1094, and Brake First No. 7740. On 31st August, 1931, it worked as a portion of the 11.00 am Charing Cross to Dover. Set 667 was a ‘general service and relief train’ berthed at Blackheath (later Maze Hill), always working with the similarly-formed 4-set 666 as a semi-permanent 8-coach train. After 1941 Set 666 became 8-coach and Set 667 was deleted.

Another 4-set with two Thirds was No. 668, which comprised two Brake Composites (Nos. 6619 and 6641) and Thirds 1068 and 1111. No. 6619 was later replaced by a 50-seat Third Brake. Berthed at Margate during 1934/5, this was another set that worked in tandem, its faithful companion being 4-set 669. Set 668 was withdrawn about 1940, its Thirds being transferred to Set 669, now augmented to 9 coaches.

By 1940 all 66 Thirds were formed in sets of varying descriptions, three of them being push-and-pull sets. In March 1937 the Southern had decided to form three such sets using three ex-LSW 50 ft composites lengthened to 57 ft or 58 ft on underframes left over from fire damage, together with three ex-SE&C 10-compartment Thirds. Sets 656, 657 and 658, formed of converted Composite Brakes Nos. 6406–8 and Thirds Nos. 1057, 1077 and 1088 in November and December 1937, were intended for use on Eastern Section push-and-pull services, such as Gravesend Central–Allhallows-on-Sea.

Set 656 was withdrawn in October 1956, its Third being transferred to loose stock; Set 657 was withdrawn complete in August 1961, having worked latterly on Tunbridge Wells–Oxted services; and Set 658 was withdrawn in July 1958.

About 1944, two Thirds were converted to push-and-pull but for use only as strengthening vehicles to make up the normal 2-coach train to 3 coaches at busy times: these were No. 1093 (ex-set 760), allocated to the Swanage branch; and No. 1098, allocated to the Lymington branch. They replaced Thirds Nos. 877 and 883 in these duties,and lasted many years, not being withdrawn until November 1961 (1093) and December 1962 (1098). No. 1098 was purchased by the Bluebell Railway, upon which it arrived on 2nd May, 1963.

10-compartment Thirds began appearing on the West London Extension line, between Clapham Junction and Kensington Addison Road, from about 1942. Two 4-sets, Nos. 97 and 98, were formed, each with a Brake Third and three Thirds; by 1944 the sets were three coaches plus one Third as required. The formations were as follows:

Set 97		**Set 98**	
Third	1106	Third	1087
Bke 3rd	3314	Bke 3rd	3315
Third	1071	Third	1107
Third	974 if reqd	Third	1094 if reqd

No. 974 was specially allocated to Clapham Junction–Kensington services until about 1956. Set 97 was in use until 1949/50 but Set 98 was withdrawn late in 1946.

During the 1950s, as the special traffic sets formed largely of ex-SE&C stock were withdrawn, there seemed to be a reluctance to withdraw the ten-compartment Thirds along with them. It is not as if the Thirds were particularly beautiful and worth keeping, but much more to do with the fact that they were useful from the point of view of capacity. If not transferred to surviving sets, the Thirds were added to the 'loose vehicles' list, which reached its maximum extent of 27 vehicles in 1957.

In 1958, eleven Thirds (now Seconds) were sent to the Western District where they were formed with Southern-built Corridor Brake Composites as

2-coach sets Nos. 100–110; the Seconds remained in these sets for about a year, when they were replaced by Southern Open Seconds. Also during the early part of 1958, 12 further Seconds were given the necessary fittings (at Lancing) to enable them to work as push-and-pull trailers: of these, nine were loose, mostly working in Brighton–Horsham–Guildford services, and three were formed into sets as replacements for withdrawn coaches. No. 1066 went to Set 1 in July 1958; No. 1074 to Set 652 in September 1957; and No. 1103 to Set 6 in May 1958.

Push-and-pull Sets 1 and 6 were Western Section stock. Set 6 was withdrawn in March 1959 after being damaged at Bournemouth Central. Set 1 lasted a couple of years longer; indeed, towards the end of 1961 it was transferred to the London Central District where it joined the miscellaneous collection of push-and-pull sets working between Tunbridge Wells and Oxted. Set 1 was always worth looking out for, but its stay was short; withdrawal came in July 1962. Set 652, which was always allocated to the Eastern or Central Sections (its Brake Composite was of L&SW origin, reconstructed in February 1935), latterly worked on the Oxted push-and-pull services until its withdrawal in August 1962.

Of the Seconds not converted for push-and-pull, Nos. 969/72, 1058–61/4/5/9/70/2/6/82/3/5/6/96/7 and 1102/6/9/10 were loose coaches in 1958 divided between the Southern District and the London Central/London East Districts. In May 1959 a replacement 5-coach set for working Clapham Junction–Kensington services was created, using four 10-compartment Seconds (Nos. 1059, 1069, 1109 and 1076) and a Southern-built Corridor Brake Second, the set being numbered 156. It was withdrawn late in 1961.

During 1960 ten 'loose' seconds were regularly diagrammed to work in Oxted line trains. Of these, two were attached to the 6.34 am East Grinstead to London Bridge and 8.01 am London Bridge to Tunbridge Wells West, and one worked in the 5.26 pm East Grinstead to Victoria and 6.48 pm return. There were two in the 7.00 am Forest Row to London Bridge, returning in the 5.37 pm London Bridge to East Grinstead. Two worked in the 8.26 am Tunbridge Wells West to London Bridge and 6.31 pm London Bridge to Forest Row. Three more were attached singly to certain Tunbridge Wells–Victoria services. They provided much-needed extra capacity to overcrowded trains, which by then were almost entirely formed of corridor stock; this, although more comfortable than the non-corridor vehicles, was somewhat deficient in seating capacity. Thus, the discerning passenger had the choice of standing in a corridor with lavatory access, or sitting in a moderately cramped compartment without! From about August or September 1961 the 100-seat Seconds began to be replaced by SR 64-seat Corridor Seconds and, by the end of the year, most of the remaining SE&C coaches were gone. The only 'loose' Seconds to survive into 1962 were Nos. 972 and 1058.

After withdrawal, several were sent to the carriage 'dump' on the Ardingly branch, and on 20th December, 1961, the Southern Carriage and Wagon Society noted Nos. 969/71, 1057/61/4/9/70/82/97 there. Another resting place for withdrawn stock was Gatwick, and No. 1055 was recorded there about the same time.

Nos. 971 and 1070 were purchased by the Bluebell Railway – which was still physically connected to the Ardingly branch then – and they arrived at Horsted Keynes on 24th February, 1963. However, No. 1070 did not stay long, because it had broken windows, and was later exchanged for a similar coach. No. 1069 was reserved, but this too was found to be in poor condition, and the choice fell upon No. 1098, which arrived on the private railway on 2nd May, 1963. Both Nos. 971 and 1098 are steel-clad, and the chance to save an example of one of the earlier mahogany-panelled seconds was lost. The Bluebell has found the 100-seat coaches to be as useful as did their previous owners, and they have hardly ever been out of traffic for more than a short time. At first No. 971 was painted plain blue without any lettering, and No. 1098 remained in British Railways green for some years. In June 1970 No. 1098 was restored to SR malachite green and two years later No. 971 appeared similarly adorned; since then both have always been repainted malachite at every overhaul.

The last survivors on BR were eight that had been transferred to the service vehicles list for working in the Lancing Workmen's train in 1959/60, replacing old LSW 48 ft coaches. This newly-constituted train did not last long, for Lancing Carriage Works was closed in 1965.

No.	*Re-No.*	*Wdn*	*No.*	*Re-No.*	*Wdn*
970	DS 70054	7/64	1089	DS 70053	7/64
1063	DS 70065	3/65	1102	DS 70069	7/63
1067	DS 70052	2/64	1105	DS 70066	7/64
1087	DS 70064	11/63	1112	DS 70067	1/64

The long tradition of having each compartment individually numbered externally was maintained with these conversions. The train, which was not advertised to ordinary passengers, ran between Brighton and Lancing once each working day, and was berthed at Holland Road, near Brighton, overnight and at weekends. Even before the closure of the carriage works patronage of the train had declined, not necessarily because of a reaction against the presence of 100-seat coaches.

Summary of 10-Compartment Thirds

SEC	*SR*	*Re-No.*	*Sets*	*Wdn*
1431	968	1/28	900 636, 11/56	7/59
1432	969	6/28	900 L, 11/56	9/61
1433	970	4/29	903 110, 3/58	To DS 70054, 11/59
1434	971	7/29	896 L, /58 P & P, 4/58	9/61
1435	972	7/29	698, 640, 918, /52, 340 10/56, L /58	7/62
1436	973	8/29	896 L /58 P & P, 4/58	2/62
1437	974	9/29	667 to /42, 97 /42, L /50	12/59
1372	1054	2/27	902 /39, 688 /49, 346 /58	6/59
1373	1055	2/27	640 /29, 902 /39, 688 /49, L 5/59	11/61
1374	1056	4/29	903 L 3/58 P & P 2/58	7/61
1375	1057	11/26	662 /31, 656 11/37, L 10/56	9/61
1376	1058	7/27	918, 696 /50, L 12/56	7/62
1377	1059	5/27	900, L 11/56, 109 3/58, 156 5/59	12/61
1378	1060	2/27	905 /41, 335 /48, L 11/56, 346 11/58	7/59

1379	1061	7/27	902, 669 L /54	9/61
1380	1062	3/29	669 L /54	11/54
1381	1063	9/27	902 /39, 335, L 11/56, 104 3/58	To DS 70065, 2/60
1382	1064	3/29	903 108 3/58, L /58	8/61
1383	1065	11/28	666 335 /52, L 11/56	8/58
1384	1066	3/29	896 P & P 7/58 Set 1	6/62
1385	1067	12/27	906 /41, L /56, 107 3/58	To DS 70052, 9/59
1386	1068	7/27	668, 669, L /55, 346 /58	6/59
1387	1069	7/28	906, L /56, 156 5/59	8/61
1388	1070	2/27	905 /41, 335 /48, L 11/56	9/61
1389	1071	1/29	899, 97 /42, L /52, 346, L 11/58	2/59
1390	1072	6/28	906 /41, L /56, 346 11/58	6/59
1391	1073	2/27	898 /41, L P & P 3/58	12/61
1392	1074	1/27	905 /41, 335 /48, L 11/56, 652 1/58	8/62
1393	1075	3/29	918, ?, L /57, 46 11/58	3/59
1394	1076	12/27	901 /37, L 11/56, 156 5/59	12/61
1395	1077	4/28	657 12/37	8/61
1396	1078	1/28	901 /37, L 11/56, 46 11/58	3/59
1397	1079	3/29	900, 696 /56, L 12/56, 46 11/58	3/59
1398	1080	3/29	897, 103 3/58	7/59
1399	1081	12/29	903 /41, L /50, 519 /51, 900 12/56, L P & P 2/58	10/61
1400	1082	3/28	906 /41, L /56	8/61
1401	1083	9/27	901, /37, L 11/56	11/58
1402	1084	10/27	640, 669, L /55	6/57
1403	1085	12/27	917 /41, L 12/56	11/58
1404	1086	1/29	666 /50, 917 /52,L 12/56	2/59
1405	1087	3/29	899, 97 /42, 98 /44, 918 /47, L 9/56	To DS 70064, 2/60
1406	1088	10/27	658 12/37	6/58
1407	1089	9/29	897 /41, 101 3/58	To DS 70053, 11/59
1408	1090	9/29	898 /41, 636 /55	7/59
1409	1091	8/29	680 /31, 640 /49, 688, L 5/59	8/59
1410	1092	7/29	898 /41, L P & P 3/58	7/61
1411	1093	6/29	760 /35, L P & P /44	11/61
1412	1094	7/29	667 to /42, 98 /44, 897 /47	11/58
1413	1095	9/29	897 /47, 100 3/58	9/59
1414	1096	12/29	920 /41, L /57	6/59
1415	1097	3/29	685 /35, 666, 688, L /52	8/61
1416	1098	6/29	918, L P & P /44	12/62
1417	1099	12/29	686 /35, 688, L 5/59	4/61
1418	1100	6/29	898 /41, L P & P 3/58	7/61
1419	1101	9/29	669 /41, 636 /55	7/59
1420	1102	8/29	920 /41, L /57, 106 2/59	To DS 70069, 2/60
1421	1103	9/29	896 /41, P & P 5/58 Set 6	Damaged B-mouth Ctl, 3/59
1422	1104	6/28	900, 898 L P & P 3/58	7/61
1423	1105	9/29	897 /41, 102 3/58	To DS 70066, 2/60
1424	1106	1/29	899, 97 /42, L /52	10/61
1425	1107	11/29	899, 97 /42, 98 /44, 918 /47, L 9/56, 106 3/58	10/58
1426	1108	3/29	905 ? Enemy Action	12/40
1427	1109	1/28	901 /37, L 11/56, 156 5/59	12/61
1428	1110	9/28	680 /31, 640 /49, 696, L 12/56	Damaged Gillingham 15/9/60

1429	1111	7/27	528, 668, 669 /41, L /55, P & P 4/58	5/61
1430	1112	9/28	917 /41, 901 /53, L 11/56, 105 3/58	To DS 70067, 2/60

Dates against set numbers are approximate and indicate only that a coach was running at that time in the set quoted. 'L' stands for loose vehicle. SR Nos. 1084–93 were matchboarded with mahogany slats.

THE 1921 BOAT TRAIN

Although the eight carriages comprising this magnificent corridor boat train were not completed until August 1921, planning for a new type of train had begun as far back as 1913.

During that year, plans were being drawn for a new boat train of traditional design, with normal roof profile, roof observatories, ordinary door lights and luggage racks only 9 in. wide. But the General Manager, Francis Dent, was far from satisfied. In June 1913, after having suggested the addition of notices in the train in English, French and German, he went on to say:

> Then there is the question of racks, which are still of the old diminutive size. It is impossible to reduce the hand baggage and it is a common occurrence for the seats, floor and entrance to the lavatories to be blocked with hand baggage for the simple reason that the racks are not large enough. The racks could easily be made twice the size and the loading of the trains would be facilitated.

And so the drawings were altered to show luggage racks with a width of 13 in. instead of 9 in.

In July 1913 Dent wrote to the superintendent of the line, Edwin Cox, suggesting that if the roof observatories were discontinued the roof height could be raised by 6 in. Cox agreed:

> We recommend that, in the case of the Boat Trains, the roofs of the vehicles should be raised, throughout, to the extent of 6 in. in centre, so as to afford more accommodation for hand luggage on the larger racks that are being introduced.
>
> We do not recommend that the roofs of the carriages in the other services shall be raised, but consider that the Guard's observatories in future new Block Sets should be dispensed with.

So the drawings were altered to show roofs to the new height and without observatories, and doors with frameless sash lights after the Great Northern Railway pattern.

In fact this boat train was never built, but the ideas and improvements connected with it were incorporated in the 1921 stock, the construction of which was recommended to the Board on 10th July, 1919, at an estimated cost of £32,000. Four types of carriage were designed and built, all at Ashford Works, and sent out in August 1921.

CORRIDOR SECOND CLASS Nos. 2501–2503 (SR Nos. 4159–4161)
Body length: 62 ft. Body width: 8 ft 0¾ in.
Height, rail to top of roof: 12 ft 2 in. Bogie centres: 44 ft.
Compartments: 7. Seats: 42. Lavatories: 2.
Pullman gangways both ends.

CORRIDOR SECOND BRAKE No. 2504 (SR No. 4156)
Body length: 62 ft. Body width: 8 ft 0¾ in.
Height, rail to top of roof: 12 ft 2 in. Bogie centres: 44 ft.
Compartments: 6, plus guard. Seats: 36. Lavatories: 1.
Pullman gangway at inner end only.

CORRIDOR FIRST CLASS Nos. 2505–2507 (SR Nos. 7367–7369)
Body length: 62 ft. Body width: 8 ft 0¾ in.
Height, rail to top of roof: 12 ft 2 in. Bogie centres: 44 ft.
Compartments: 6. Seats: 24. Lavatories: 2.
Pullman gangways both ends.

CORRIDOR FIRST BRAKE No. 2508 (SR No. 7745, later 6642)
Body length: 62 ft. Body width: 8 ft 0¾ in.
Height, rail to top of roof: 12 ft 2 in. Bogie centres: 44 ft.
Compartments: 4, plus 1 saloon, and guard.
Seats: 16, plus 4 in saloon. Lavatories: 1.
Pullman gangway at inner end only.

These handsome vehicles, so different from any previous SE&C carriage stock, were designed by R.E.L. Maunsell and his chief draughtsman L. Lynes. They were the first to have Pullman gangways (for working with new Pullman cars), the first to have so great a body length as 62 ft, and (apart from saloons and the railmotors) the first to have entry doors – which opened inwards – at separate vestibules instead of leading directly into each compartment. The lower panels of the body were matchboarded with vertical slats, and centrally-placed upon each body was a plywood disc on which was the Managing Committee's coat of arms. Livery was 'standard brown', gold-lined, with white roofs and black underframes.

Underframes were rolled-steel, with non-adjustable 'L'-section trusses. Bogies, of 8 ft wheelbase, were a type that became standard for the Southern Railway, and had laminated side bearing springs and helical bolster springs.

First-class compartments were upholstered in green corded cloth, and the interiors finished in walnut with sycamore panels; corridors had the lower panels of slatted walnut and sycamore panels above and between the windows. Second-class compartments were trimmed in red, black and orange velvet, and interiors were mahogany, as were the corridor panels (slatted).

All compartments were fitted with portable tables which, when not in use, were kept in a cupboard at the end of the coach; and all compartments had electric bell communication with the Pullman car attendant. Vickers' single-battery electric lighting was fitted, with through control from the guard's compartments; in addition there were individual lamps over each seat in the first-class compartments, separately controlled by switches immediately below the lamps.

Nos. 2503–08 were formed in Boat Train No. 2, with two Pullman cars in the centre, working the 11.00 am Victoria to Dover Marine and the 5.55 pm return services. No. 2502 remained spare, and No. 2501 was placed in Boat Train No. 5. By summer 1922 No. 2502 was in Train No. 2 and No. 2506 relegated to 'spare'.

Two further corridor boat trains, each of eight coaches, were built at Ashford during 1923; in these a half-compartment replaced one of the lavatories in the all-firsts and all-seconds. Further examples of boat train stock – known as 'Continentals' – were introduced by the Southern Railway, with the body width increased to 8 ft 6½ in. All were gangwayed within the set, with retractable buffers; at the outer ends, where there were no gangways, Spencer's patent buffers were fitted. The post-Grouping 'Continentals'

SECR DIAG. No. S.3066/2. **SR DIAG. No. 233, later 55.**

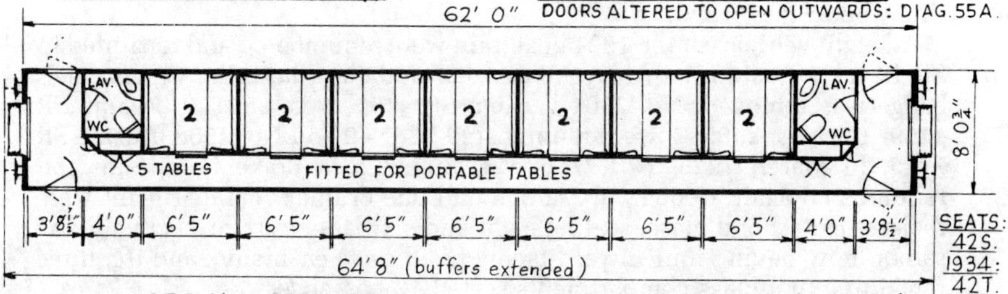

62′ 0″
DOORS ALTERED TO OPEN OUTWARDS: DIAG. 55A.
LAV.
WC
2
2
2
2
2
2
2
LAV.
WC
8′ 0¾″
5 TABLES
FITTED FOR PORTABLE TABLES
3′8½″
4′0″
6′5″
6′5″
6′5″
6′5″
6′5″
6′5″
6′5″
4′0″
3′8½″
64′8″ (buffers extended)
SEATS:
42S.
1934:
42T.

SEC Nos. 2501-2503. SR Nos. 4159-4161 (1010-1012).

SECR DIAG. No. S.3066/1. **SR DIAG. No. 245, later 169.**

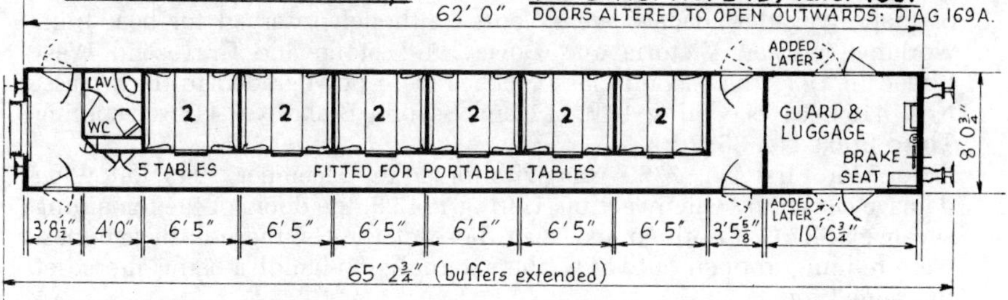

62′ 0″
DOORS ALTERED TO OPEN OUTWARDS: DIAG 169A.
ADDED LATER
LAV.
WC
2
2
2
2
2
2
GUARD & LUGGAGE
BRAKE
SEAT
8′ 0¾″
5 TABLES
FITTED FOR PORTABLE TABLES
ADDED LATER
3′8½″
4′0″
6′5″
6′5″
6′5″
6′5″
6′5″
6′5″
3′5⅝″
10′6¾″
65′ 2¾″ (buffers extended)

SEC No. 2504. SR No. 4156 (3587).

SEATS: 36S. 1934: 36T.

SECR DIAG. No. S.3053/3. **SR DIAG. No. 494.**

62′ 0″
DOORS ALTERED TO OPEN OUTWARDS: DIAG. 494A.
LAV.
WC
1
1
1
1
1
1
LAV.
WC
8′ 0¾″
5 TABLES
FITTED FOR PORTABLE TABLES
3′8½″
4′0″
7′6″
7′6″
7′6″
7′6″
7′6″
7′6″
4′0″
3′8½″
SEATS:
24F.
64′8″ (buffers extended)

SEC Nos. 2505-2507. SR Nos. 7367-7369.

SECR DIAG. No. S.3053/1. **SR DIAG. No. 550, later 427.**

62′ 0″
DOORS ALTERED TO OPEN OUTWARDS: DIAG. 427A.
ADDED LATER
LAV.
WC
1
1
1
1
(2)
SALOON
GUARD AND LUGGAGE
BRAKE
SEAT
8′ 0¾″
4 TABLES
FITTED FOR PORTABLE TABLES
ADDED LATER
3′8½″
4′0″
7′6″
7′6″
7′6″
7′6″
3′5½″
7′6″
11′6½″
65′ 2¾″ (buffers extended)

SEC No. 2508. SR No. 7745 (6642).

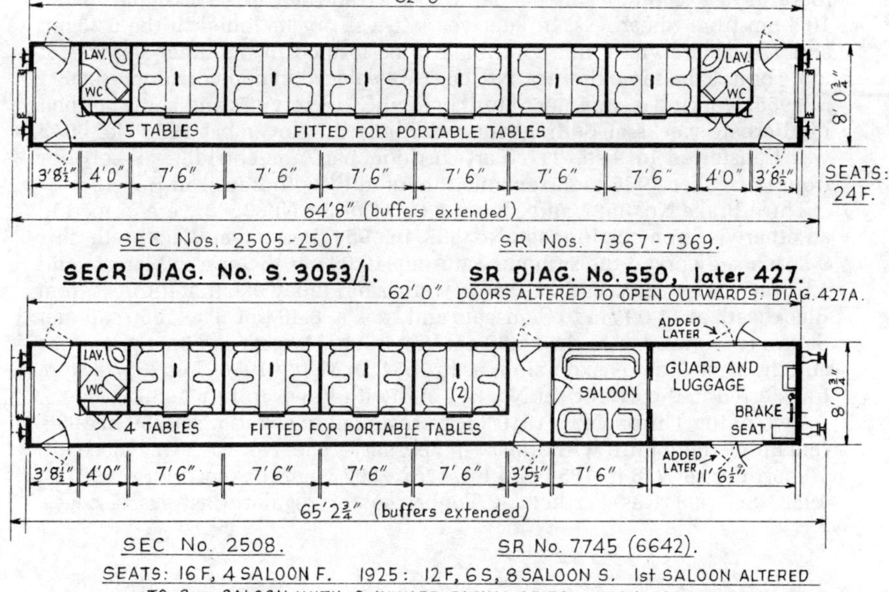

SEATS: 16F, 4 SALOON F. 1925: 12F, 6S, 8 SALOON S. 1st SALOON ALTERED TO 2ND SALOON WITH 8 INWARD-FACING SEATS. 1934: 12F, 6T, 8 SALOON T.

are dealt with in greater detail in *Maunsell's SR Steam Carriage Stock* (Oakwood Press, 1990).

All eight vehicles of the 1921 boat train were renumbered and repainted in SR livery at Ashford in November 1923 and the Managing Committee's badge was removed: No. 2504 became SR 4156, Nos. 2501–3 became SR 4159–61, Nos. 2505–7 were renumbered 7367–9 and No. 2508 became SR 7745. In March 1925, No. 7745 was altered to a Brake Composite and renumbered again to 6642; its saloon and one ordinary compartment were reclassified second class, seating eight and six passengers respectively, the saloon now having four inward-facing fixed seats each side, and the three remaining first-class compartments seated 12 passengers.

During the 1927–1928 period some of the Continental stock ran in numbered sets 510, 511 and 512, but no further details are known. For most of their lives the coaches were 'loose', although reserved for boat train working between Victoria and Dover, Folkestone and Gravesend West Street. In 1934 the second class coaches were downgraded to third class, Nos. 4159–61 becoming 1010–12 and Second Brake No. 4156 becoming Third Brake No. 3587.

Corridor First No. 7369 was withdrawn in December 1940 following damage caused by enemy action. During 1947/8, the doors of the remaining seven ex-SE&C 'Continentals', also those of the Southern-built vehicles, were re-hung to open outwards, the external grab-handles being altered at the same time.

Between 1947 and about 1954 Composite Brake No. 6642 was berthed at Faversham for working as a single coach every weekday on the 4.40 am Faversham to Sheerness. During summer 1947 it also worked, with other stock, the 6.35 am Sheerness to Sittingbourne and 7.10 am return; the 8.00 am Sheerness to Sittingbourne and 8.27 am thence to Faversham (Saturdays excepted) and on Saturdays it returned to Faversham on the 10.8 pm from Sheerness. In later years it was not included in the 6.35 am and 7.10 am services, but continued to be formed in the other services at more or less the same timings. No. 6642 was placed in non-corridor 8-set 901 in 1955, working in summer Saturday Kent Coast services and being berthed in alternate weeks at Bellingham or Walmer. In November 1956 No. 6642 was transferred to 9-set 917 (part-corridor, part non-corridor; all-corridor from December 1956) and remained there until withdrawal in July 1959.

Third Brake No. 3587 and SR-built Third Brake No. 3588 were formed in an otherwise non-corridor set, No. 897, in 1953. Berthed at Blackheath, this 9-coach set worked the summer Saturday 10.06 am Victoria to Margate and 4.52 pm return services in 1954, as well as a Sunday excursion direct from Blackheath at 11.09 am to Ramsgate and back at 8.48 pm. The 1956 summer Saturday working were the 11.30 am Victoria to Margate and 3.34 pm return and the same Sunday excursions as in 1954. In March 1958 Nos. 3587/8 were transferred to 9-corridor set No. 211 and withdrawn in July 1959.

Two of the Thirds, Nos. 1010/11, were added to corridor set 389 in 1955, remaining there until withdrawal in February 1959; No. 1012 was placed in 10-corridor set 938 in 1954 and First No. 7367 went to 9-corridor set 937 in 1958. Set 938 was berthed at Tonbridge for regular Hastings services, including the 7.54 am Wadhurst to Charing Cross and 4.20 pm Charing Cross to Hastings.

The SE&C-built 'Continentals' were rendered extinct in 1959, although a handful of the SR-built version survived until 1961.

Summary of 1921-built 'Continental' Stock

SEC	*SR*	*Re-No.*	*Third*	*Re-No.*	*Set*	*Wdn*
2501	4159	11/23	1010	/34	389	2/59
2502	4160	11/23	1011	/34	389	2/59
2503	4161	11/23	1012	/34	938	7/59
2504	4156	11/23	3587	6/34	897,211	7/59
2505	7367	11/23	–	–	937	1/59
2506	7368	11/23	–	–	–	1/58
2507	7369	11/23	–	–	–	12/40
2508	7745	11/23	6642	3/25	669,901,917	7/59

SECR DIAG. No. S.2773/2. SR DIAG. No. 51.

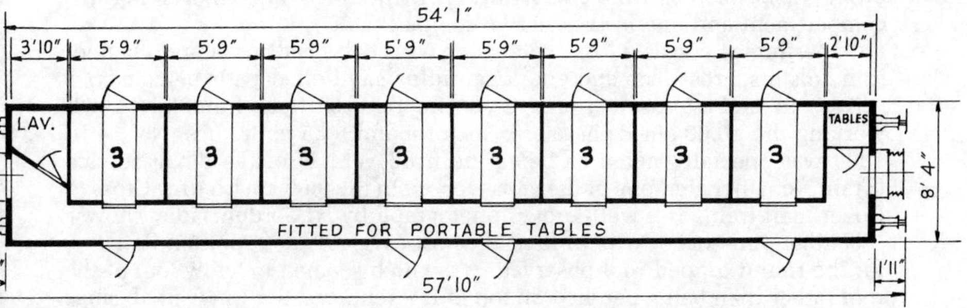

SECR Nos. 1351-1356. SR Nos. 962-967.

SEATING CAPACITY 48 T.

SECR DIAG. No. S.2811/4. SR DIAG. No. 52.

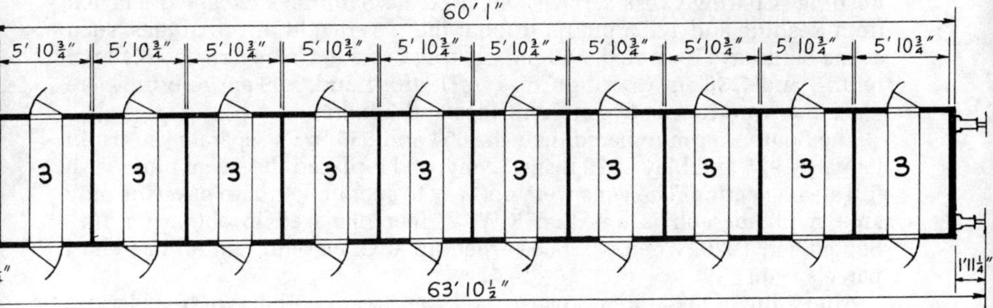

SECR Nos. 1372-1437. SR Nos. 1054-1112, 968-974.

SEATING CAPACITY 100 T.

Chapter Five

Non-Passenger-Carrying Stock

SE&CR Bogie Brake Vans

Although the SE&C built quantities of 6-wheeled brake vans for use in passenger trains, there were only two bogie vans; even the Chatham had managed to have six built! SE&C Nos. 14 and 15 (numbered in a separate van list) were completed by Ashford in November 1905 as 'renewals' of Chatham Section stock.

The vans were 50 ft 1 in. by 8 ft 0¾ in. over body, and height from rail level to the top of the centrally-placed guard's observatory was 12 ft 8½ in. 8 ft wheelbase bogies at 33 ft 6 in. centres were provided. Body framing was teak with mahogany panels and mouldings, and the elliptical roof comprised iron carlines and ash segments. The guard's compartment was in the centre with one door on each side; the two luggage compartments (each holding up to 4 tons) had two pairs of doors each side for each compartment, and communication with the guard's compartment was by sliding door. The luggage doors were fitted with fixed lights, and the guard's doors had normal droplights. The vans were electrically lit with three lamps in each luggage compartment and one in the guard's compartment.

Underframes consisted of angle soles with oak headstocks and channel iron bolsters, cross bars and end longitudinals, all other parts being oak.

Nos. 14 and 15 were in the Granville Express train from July 1908, working the 10.00 am Ramsgate to Victoria and 3.25 pm return. No. 14 in 1909 was specially noted as being the front vehicle of the down service (Train No. 10). Later, one of the vans worked in the 9.00 am Charing Cross to Dover mail train, as a well-known photograph by H. Gordon Tidey shows.

Neither van was ever permitted to work over the Metropolitan Railway, for the round-topped roof observatory – which seemed to 'grow' out of the roof rather than being perched on top of it – rendered the vans out of gauge for that line. The vans could work over any part of the SE&C except the Canterbury & Whitstable line, which boasted a tunnel of ridiculously small bore.

In the summer of 1922, Nos. 14 and 15 worked cyclic diagrams of which the six ex-LC&D bogie vans were a part. Most of the workings took in Reading–Charing Cross services, such as the Saturdays Excepted 9.08 am from Reading and 12.55 pm return; but there were odd 'fill-in' duties, such as the Saturdays Excepted 5.50 pm Charing Cross to Orpington and 6.48 pm return, and 7.38 am Charing Cross to Dartford and 9.09 am return. There were also workings between Tonbridge and London.

The Southern renumbered the vans 654 and 655 in its separate van list in January 1925 and May 1929 respectively, and replaced the steam pipes with full steam heating. The vans were not easy to spot in Southern days; the only known photograph is one that R.W. Kidner managed to obtain on 10th September, 1929, when No. 655 turned up at Gravesend Central in a short parcels train.

After a life of just under 30 years both vans were withdrawn from service in 1935: No. 654 in June and No. 655 in July.

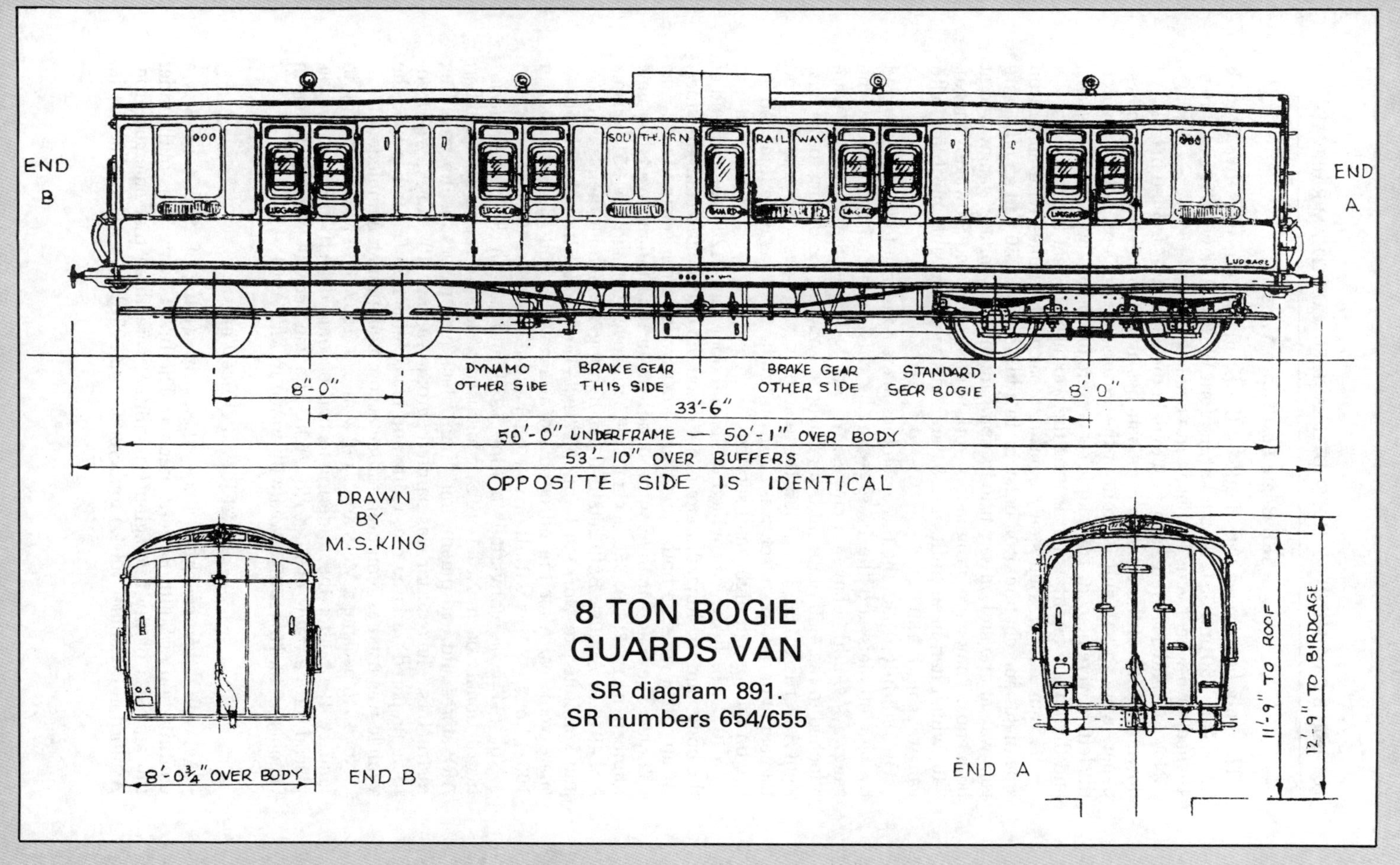
END B
END A
SOUTHERN RAILWAY
DYNAMO OTHER SIDE
BRAKE GEAR THIS SIDE
BRAKE GEAR OTHER SIDE
STANDARD SECR BOGIE
8'-0"
8'-0"
33'-6"
50'-0" UNDERFRAME — 50'-1" OVER BODY
53'-10" OVER BUFFERS
OPPOSITE SIDE IS IDENTICAL
DRAWN BY M.S.KING
8 TON BOGIE GUARDS VAN
SR diagram 891.
SR numbers 654/655
8'-0¾" OVER BODY
END B
END A
11'-9" TO ROOF
12'-9" TO BIRDCAGE

SER Bogie Post Office Vans

The only bogie mail vans built by the South Eastern were two Sorting Vans, Nos. 350 and 351, which left Ashford Works in May 1896. Until then, 4-wheel or 6-wheel vans had been in vogue.

Nos. 350 and 351 were each 44 ft over body, which was framed in teak. All down one side of the interior were benches at which the letters and newspapers were sorted, and in front of the sorters were pigeon holes in which the letters were placed. Telescopic seats were provided, the vans were gaslit, and there were facilities for heating the wax used to seal the mailbags.

The vans had pressed steel bogies and oak underframes with angle iron sole plates and channel iron bolsters. In addition, No. 350 had an off-centre gangway at one end only, while its companion was similarly gangwayed at both ends. They were designed to work with a 6-wheeled Stowage Van, No. 240, which had been built in 1881 and was most probably not fitted with gangways until 1896.

On 18th July, 1896, the three vehicles made a test run to Dover, attended by SER officials and the Press, with the chief object of seeing how the gangways would behave on curves. All was well, and the three vans were attached to the 4.50 pm train from Dover to London. According to the *East Kent Advertiser*, 25th July, 1896, the telescopic gangways were 4 ft wide and the length of the 3-van 'set' was close on 126 ft. The vans were intended for use on the foreign night mail service.

In 1911 No. 351 was provided with a 3 ft door about 12 ft from the end of the body, and the hinged doors panelled on the outside to match the sides. At an unknown date both vans were downgraded from sorting to stowage vehicles. They came to the Southern Railway in 1923 and received their new numbers in 1927: No. 350 became 4947 in November and No. 351 became No. 4948 in August. Both retained gas lighting throughout their existence, and continued to work on Cannon Street–Dover mail trains, probably as spare vehicles. After the introduction of a new SR-built Stowage Van in 1937, No. 4947 was withdrawn in 1939 and its sister in 1940.

No. 4947 was converted in June 1939 into an Air Raid Precautions instructional coach, No. 1449 S, composed of lecture room, gas chamber, ARP stores and equipment, and living/sleeping quarters for the travelling instructors. The exterior was painted chrome yellow with 'A.R.P. We've got to be prepared' in large red, white and black letters. In December 1945 the vehicle was used as temporary office accommodation at Wimbledon.

No. 4948 became a Mess and Tool Van, No. 1537 S, in May 1940 and, in January 1942, after the underframe had become defective, the body was placed on the frame of First No. 7298. The van became a mess kitchen in October 1943. No. 1537 S was withdrawn in May 1961.

SE&CR Post Office Vans

As with other coaching stock, the body styling of mail vans was a continuation of South Eastern practice. The first Sorting Vans built under the auspices of the Managing Committee were three that emerged from Ashford in December 1904, numbered 691 to 693. They measured 50 ft 1 in.

by 8 ft 0¾ in. over body, and the height from rail level to the top of the roof lights was 12 ft 3¾ in. Bogies, of 8 ft wheelbase with wheels of 3 ft 6 in. diameter, were set at 33 ft 6 in. centres.

The body framing was teak with mahogany facia and panels. Carrying capacity was about 5 tons. No. 691 had a gangway at one end only, and did not include net apparatus. Nos. 692/3, on the other hand, did have net apparatus, and were gangwayed at both ends. Each van had a 2 ft 3 in. door and No. 691 had two sliding doors with 3 ft 9 in. openings. The other two vans had, in addition to the two sliding doors, a 4 ft opening which 'at present' was fixed. The vans were gas-lit, at a time when electric lighting was normal; but presumably the Post Office still preferred gas lighting. No. 691 had 13 single burners and Nos. 692/3 had 14; each of the three in addition had 6 double burners (lamps) and two burners for wax heating.

Underframes comprised angle soles, wood headstocks, channel iron bolster cross bars and iron end longitudinals, the remainder being oak. When new the vans would have been used on the Dover mail services, as bogie mail vans were not permitted to run to Folkestone Harbour at that time.

The next two Sorting Vans to be built were Nos. 130 and 131, which Ashford completed in December 1906 as 'renewals'. General dimensions were the same as those of Nos. 691–3, and again the vans were gas-lit.

Body framing was teak with mahogany panels and mouldings. No. 130 was fitted with one 2 ft 3 in. door on one side and two sliding doors with 3 ft openings on the other side. No. 131 was fitted with two double doors on one side and two sliding doors with 3 ft openings on the other side. The gas lighting included 6 double burner lamps and two double burners for heating wax in each van; No. 130 also had 14 single lamps and No. 131 had only 12. The vans each had two end gangways, off-centre, with 6 ft 1 in. by 3 ft opening and sliding doors. On the bodyside, in large capital letters, were the words 'Royal Mail. *Malle Royale.*'

Underframes consisted of angle soles, wood headstocks, channel iron bolsters, iron cross bars and end longitudinals, other parts being of oak. Steam pipes were included, later altered to steam heating complete. Bogies were pressed steel, fitted with Timmis's bolster springs.

The two vans were built for the 'Day Continental' and 'Inland' mail train services, and the sorting tables and pigeon-holes were arranged to suit the requirements of the different services, No. 130 having a slightly different layout from its sister.

In April 1907 the SE&C completed five Stowage Vans to go with the Sorting Vans, and they were numbered 110–114 as 'renewals'. They were the only bogie mail stowage vans ever built by the SE&C, as well as being the last 8-wheel vans of any description. Body length was 50 ft 1 in.; height from rail to roof 11 ft 8½ in. and to the top of the deck lights – of which there were four – measured 12 ft 2 in. The body had two sliding doors each side, each with an opening of 4 ft, and there was a cross partition in the centre, with a doorway 6 ft 4 in. by 4 ft. Carrying capacity was 9 tons; electric lighting was provided by six lamps; and the vehicles were through piped for steam heating.

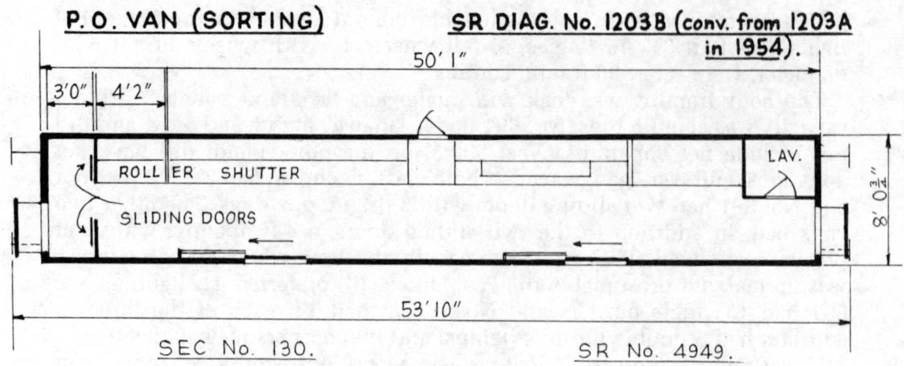
P. O. VAN (SORTING)
SR DIAG. No. 1203B (conv. from 1203A in 1954).
50' 1"
3'0"
4'2"
LAV.
ROLLER SHUTTER
SLIDING DOORS
8' 0¾"
53'10"
SEC No. 130.
SR No. 4949.

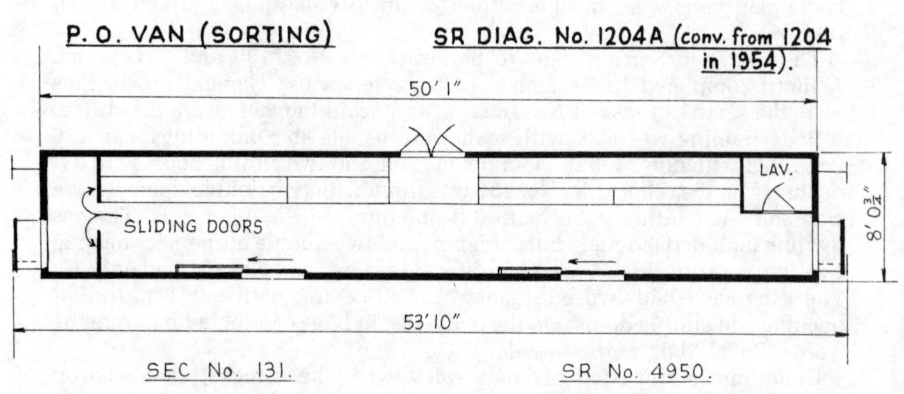
P. O. VAN (SORTING)
SR DIAG. No. 1204A (conv. from 1204 in 1954).
50' 1"
LAV.
SLIDING DOORS
8' 0¾"
53'10"
SEC No. 131.
SR No. 4950.

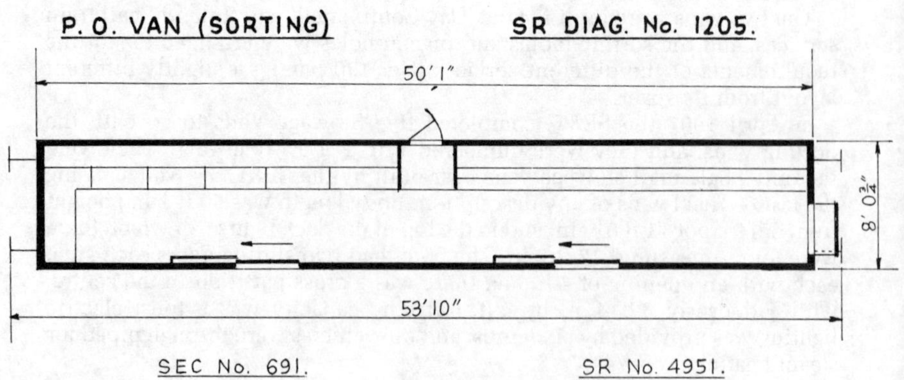
P. O. VAN (SORTING)
SR DIAG. No. 1205.
50' 1"
8' 0¾"
53'10"
SEC No. 691.
SR No. 4951.

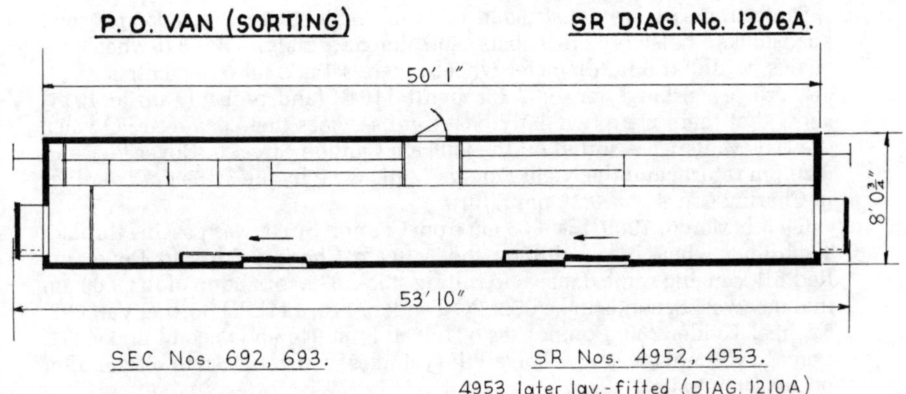
P. O. VAN (SORTING)
SR DIAG. No. 1206A.
50′ 1″
8′ 0¾″
53′ 10″
SEC Nos. 692, 693.
SR Nos. 4952, 4953.
4953 later lav.-fitted (DIAG. 1210A)

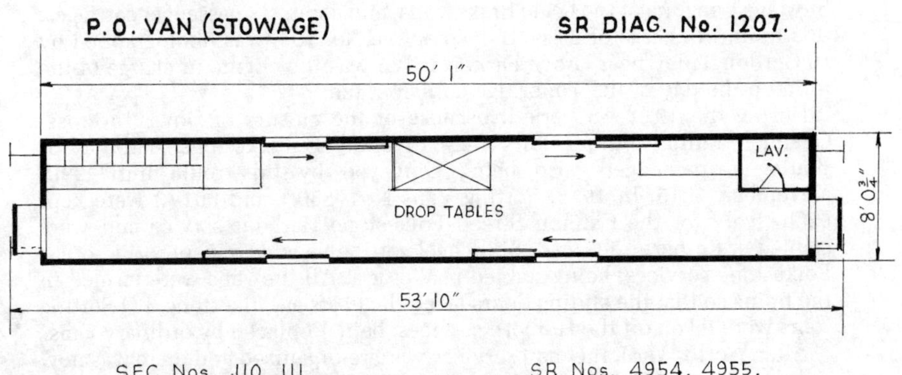
P. O. VAN (STOWAGE)
SR DIAG. No. 1207.
50′ 1″
LAV.
DROP TABLES
8′ 0¾″
53′ 10″
SEC Nos. 110, 111.
SR Nos. 4954, 4955.

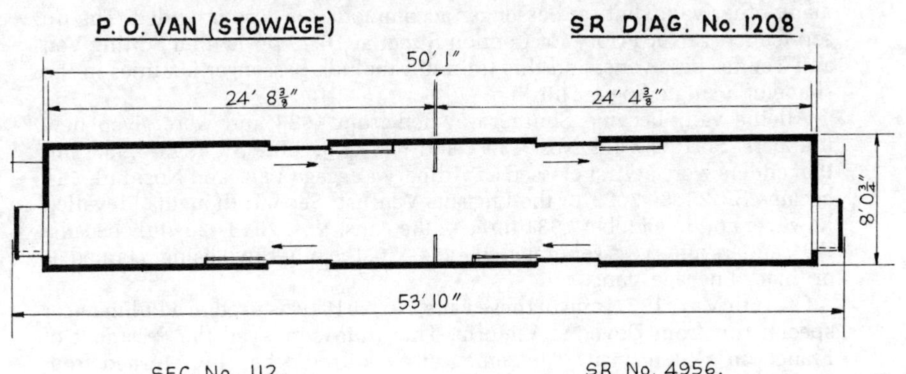
P. O. VAN (STOWAGE)
SR DIAG. No. 1208.
50′ 1″
24′ 8⅜″
24′ 4⅜″
8′ 0¾″
53′ 10″
SEC No. 112.
SR No. 4956.

Underframes were constructed of bulb angle steel soles, channel steel headstocks, bolsters, cross bars and longitudinals. The 8 ft-wheelbase bogies, with 3 ft 6 in. diameter wheels, were set at 33 ft 6 in. centres.

Carriage workings for 1907 through to 1910 (and probably up to 1914) show that there were two daily boat train services that conveyed PO vans: the Day Mails were sorted on the 9.05 am Cannon Street to Dover Pier and 3.20 pm return, and the Night Foreign Mails went by the 3.45 am Dover Pier to Charing Cross and 8.58 pm return.

On 5th March, 1909, the 9.05 am from Cannon Street was passing through Tonbridge when it was hit by the 8.30 am Charing Cross to Dover via Redhill, causing some damage to rolling stock. The formation of the 9.05 am that day was: Second Brake 952; PO Tenders 110, 111; PO Sorting Van 693; 6-wheel Tender 280; Composites 931, 934; First 944 and Second Brake 951. Damage was not too severe and all the vehicles were returned to service after necessary repairs.

At a later stage, the formation of the 9.00 am Continental Mail train comprised two bogie Stowage Vans, a bogie Sorting Van, the 6-wheel Stowage Van, one of the bogie Brake Vans, and about six passenger carriages; this train, in charge of class 'E' locomotive No. 165, was photographed by H. Gordon Tidey near Grove Park, No. 165 was the engine in charge of the train on the day of the Tonbridge collision, too.

During the 1914–18 period, because of the closure of Dover to cross-Channel traffic, all the mails were diverted to Folkestone Harbour for Boulogne, passengers also being conveyed by this route until 29th November, 1915. In 1915, Sorting Vans Nos. 350/1 and 691–3 were kept exclusively for the Cannon Street–Folkestone Harbour service and were stabled at Rotherhithe Road. Six-wheel sorting vans were kept to Victoria–Folkestone services, being stabled at Victoria. All the vans were formed in the trains so that the sliding doors faced the boats at Folkestone. PO Sorting Vans were taken off the Holborn services, being replaced by ordinary vans.

After World War I, the mail services were re-organised and there was now only one single night service in each direction, requiring the use of two Sorting Vans and two Tenders. The down service left Cannon Street at 11.48 pm for Dover Priory conveying one Sorting Van and one Tender, plus many other vans, but no passenger accommodation was provided. The up service left Dover Priory for Cannon Street at 10.40 pm with a Sorting Van and Tender plus vans, and this train did include passenger facilities in the shape of a single bogie Third.

All the vans became Southern-owned from 1923 and were given new numbers. Sorting Vans Nos. 130/1 and 691–3 became SR 4949–4953, but the tenders were at first classed as ordinary Luggage Vans and Nos. 110–114 became SR 2018–2022 in the Luggage Van list. Second thoughts prevailed however and in October 1931 three of the vans, Nos. 2018–20, duly became PO Tenders and were renumbered 4954–56, the other two being retained as ordinary Luggage Vans.

On 16th May, 1927, one of these vans, No. 2018, was used in a Pullman car special run from Dover to Victoria. This train conveyed the President of France on a State visit. The same van was used when he returned from London to Dover three days later.

At various unknown dates Nos. 4949/50/53/54/55 were lavatory-fitted, but the other three vans never received those facilities. Nos. 4951/2 became dual braked. Nos. 4949–53 all had their gas lighting replaced by electricity, and all the sorting vans were given steam heating complete.

Allocations of vans during 1937–39 were:

4949/50 (sorting), 4956 and SR-built 4957 (stowage): London Bridge–Dover.
4951 (sorting), 4954 (stowage): Holborn–Newhaven.
4952 (sorting): Spare to 4951 at Stewarts Lane.
4953 (sorting): Spare to 4949/50 at Rotherhithe Road.
4955 (stowage): Spare to 4954/56 at Stewarts Lane.

The Holborn–Newhaven service was worked as a van train between London and East Croydon, where it was attached in the down direction to the evening Victoria–Newhaven boat train. It returned on the early morning up boat train, being detached at East Croydon and worked as a separate van train back to Holborn.

All the mail services were suspended during World War II and the cars were stabled at Epsom Downs station. Some were used temporarily for ARP purposes. After the War the London Bridge–Dover postal services were reinstated but the Holborn–Newhaven workings remained in a state of suspension; the 1947 allocations of cars were exactly the same as those shown for 1937–39, except that No. 4951/4 had 'Workings Suspended' marked against them. In fact these two continued to be allocated theoretically to the Holborn–Newhaven service for several more years, but the workings never were restored. No. 4951 was withdrawn in May 1958 and No. 4954 was then allocated to the London Bridge–Dover service. Nos. 4949/56 were withdrawn in August 1958.

In 1951 No. 4952 was altered from a Sorting to a Stowage Van, and became the spare car to No. 4956.

The final allocations during 1959 and 1960, when five ex-SE&C mail vans remained in service, were: 4950/53/54: London Bridge–Dover. 4952/55: Spare. All were now well over 50 years old, and steam haulage was nearly at an end; gradually ex-Great Western Post Office vans, newly-fitted with electric heaters and intended for electric or diesel-electric haulage, were introduced on the Dover mail service and the five SE&C vans were withdrawn during 1960. During this whole period the timings had scarcely varied: 11.50 pm from London Bridge and 10.40 pm up from Dover, the latter service still conveying a single passenger carriage.

Summary of SEC Post Office Vans

SEC	*SR*	*Re-No.*	*Wdn*	*SEC*	*SR*	*Re-No.*		*Wdn*
130	4949	10/23	8/58	110	2018	9/26	To 4954 10/31	12/60
131	4950	1/27	6/60	111	2019	11/27	To 4955 10/31	3/60
691	4951	4/27	5/58	112	2020	7/27	To 4956 10/31	8/58
692	4952	11/28	12/60	113	2021	11/23	To 221 S, 1/45	
693	4953	9/27	12/60	114	2022	1/29	To 188 S, 11/44	

No. 2021 altered to Mess and Tool Van 221 S, Engineer's Painting Department, London East Division, in January 1945.

No. 2022 altered to Mess and Tool Van 188 S for the Chief Engineer, Bellingham. Withdrawn 1961.

No. 4951 to Internal User 081039, *c.*1959. 'Lancing Works Only.'

No. 4956 to Internal User 080539, *c.*1958.

Chapter Six

Steam Rail Motor Carriages

The South Eastern & Chatham Railway's experiments with steam railcars have been well dissected by previous writers, and in the present volume the eight vehicles are included only for the sake of completeness. The cars were never shown in SE&C Carriage Registers and clearly were not regarded as 'proper' carriages; they did in fact have their own separate number series, both the locomotive and the carriage portions of each railcar bearing the same number.

To start with, the SE&C ordered two cars from the Metropolitan Amalgamated Railway Carriage & Wagon Co. and two 0–4–0 tank locomotives from Kitson of Leeds. The locomotives (Kitson Nos. 4292/3) were received by the SE&C on 16th January and 2nd February, 1905, and were numbered 1 and 2. Compared with normal locomotives they were tiny, with wheels only 3 ft 7 in. in diameter and a wheelbase of 8 ft. Side tanks extended the whole length of the unit, and the boiler had a Belpaire firebox. The carriage portions were delivered on 24th February, 1905. Each of the bodies was 48 ft 4 in. in length and 8 ft 6 in. wide, with a recessed end where were located the guard's and luggage compartment, the width of this being only 7 ft 9 in. over mouldings. At this end was a bogie of 8 ft wheelbase, but at the locomotive end the carriage was supported by a large bearing below the firebox, the locomotive itself acting as a 'bogie'. Height of the car from rail to top of roof was 11 ft 9¾ in.

Total length over buffers of the combined unit was 64 ft 10½ in., and the total wheelbase was 51 ft 6 in. Layout of the car comprised an entrance vestibule (recessed); saloon 19 ft 10 in. long (four windows each side); smoking saloon 14 ft 11 in. long (three windows each side); entrance vestibule, guard/luggage and driver's compartment (all recessed). The ordinary doors opened inwards but the luggage doors opened outwards as normal. The general saloon compartment seated 32 passengers and the smoking compartment 24, all third-class; total capacity of the car was 56. The roof profile was deceptive; it appeared to be a plain arc but in fact was slightly elliptical although not all like the normal SE&C elliptical roof. On the roof there were 10 torpedo ventilators; there was also a ventilator above each of the side lights, which could not themselves be opened. Later, the third and sixth windows (viewed from the inner end of the cars) were altered to pairs of droplights to increase ventilation, and the number of roof ventilators was increased from ten to fourteen. The end driving compartment had one large window on the offside and two smaller windows, one of which was a droplight, on the nearside.

Both the locomotives and the coaches were painted lake, and the arms of the Managing Committee appeared twice on each bodyside. No. 1 was put to work on the Sheppey Light Railway, whilst No. 2 entered service on the Strood–Chatham Central branch, the cars being fitted with the appropriate destination boards. No. 1 was serviced at Sheerness and No. 2 at Strood.

In March 1905 William Thomson, superintendent of the line, reported to Vincent Hill, General Manager, that the working of No. 1 car on the Sheppey Light Railway (Queenborough to Leysdown) was entirely satisfactory, and he expected that when the summer season arrived a trailer or two could always be attached to carry the extra passengers. Harry Wainwright had informed him that the daily saving in coal consumption was about six shillings with railcars. On lines where higher speeds were permitted, the savings would be even greater. The car working the Chatham Central branch sometimes had to be replaced by an ordinary train on days when cheap tickets were issued, but this was later circumvented by transferring the issue of cheap tickets to the Chatham main line so that the whole branch service could be worked by the car. Thomson was greatly in favour of extending the use of steamcars on other short branches; his advice was taken and six more cars were ordered. His recommendation that they should have a first-class compartment and greater luggage space, however, was not heeded.

Six locomotives were ordered from Kitson and six carriage portions from the Metropolitan Amalgamated RC&W Co. The locomotives (Works Nos. 4376–81) differed from the original pair by having shorter side-tanks. Nos. 3 and 4 were delivered to the SE&C on 6th March, 1906; Nos. 5 and 6 on 22nd March; and Nos. 7 and 8 on 7th April, 1906. The carriage portions, which were built at the Oldbury Works of Metropolitan Amalgamated, were dimensionally the same as the original two but differed in detail. The bodyside windows were narrower, with a consequently larger panel between each; the third and sixth seating bays viewed from the inner end had pairs of droplights instead of a large fixed window; there were 14 roof ventilators; and at the driving end there were four equal-sized windows, of which the nearside and offside two were slideable. As photographic evidence is lacking there is some uncertainty about the window layout here, but the previous statement is believed to be correct.

The original allocations of the steamcars from 1906 to about 1907 were:

No. 3 at Tonbridge, for the Dunton Green–Westerham branch.
No. 4 at Bricklayers Arms, for the Elmers End–Hayes branch, also the Woodside–Selsdon Road joint line.
No. 5 at Strood, for the Hundred of Hoo line.
No. 6 at Sheerness, for the Sheppey Light Railway, replacing No. 1.
No. 7 at Tonbridge, for the Otford–Sevenoaks line.
No. 8 at Ashford, for the Lydd and New Romney branch.

Photographs show that Nos. 3, 4 and 8 did in fact work on the lines for which they were intended. No. 4 carried the destination board 'West Wickham & Hayes Branch', and No. 8 was boarded 'New Romney and Dungeness Branch'. However, the cars did not stay attached to individual lines for very long but moved around a great deal, being tried out on almost every branch line.

From photographs taken of the cars it is clear that Nos. 1 and 2 worked services between Hastings and Rye from about 1907, by which time the windows and ventilators had been altered to match those of the later six cars. No. 4 also worked between Hastings and Rye at some stage. No. 5 was at Dover Priory, probably for working the Hythe and Sandgate branch. No. 6 also worked that line, and No. 7 in 1910 worked services between Orpington and Bickley. No. 1 was on the Sandgate branch by 1910. Other steamcar-worked services included Crystal Palace–Beckenham Junction until December 1915 and the Elham Valley line during 1912 and 1913. From

December 1908 a steamcar was put to work on a local Dartford–Gravesend service of seven return trips each day, continuing until about January 1916.

The railcars soon went out of fashion. Although they could haul a tail-load they were not really powerful enough to do so, and the whole point of the cars, to reduce costs incurred by the engine 'running round' its train at terminal points, was lost if there was an extra coach. So withdrawal began in 1914, when No. 3 (at Hastings shed) was taken out of service in June. Next to go was No. 1 at Bricklayers Arms in March 1915, then Nos. 5 and 6 (Orpington and Dover respectively) in December 1915. Nos. 4 and 8, both of Slades Green, went in June 1918, leaving Nos. 2 and 7 to work the last remaining steamcar service, that between Hastings and Rye. These two were taken out of service in February 1920.

All the cars were stored after withdrawal, and even then they were moved around; there were three kept in the tunnel on the closed Greenwich Park branch, four stored at Sidley on the Bexhill West branch, and Nos. 5 and 6 were stabled at Crystal Palace High Level between 1922 and 1924.

Their new owners, the Southern Railway, who abhorred wasting anything that could be re-used, decided to take the carriage portions and convert them into ordinary coaches. Two 2-coach sets were made out of four of the cars, arranged with the brake-ends outermost, and to save expense the inner ends rested on a common bogie; in other words, the sets were articulated. Two further 2-coach sets were made out of the remaining four cars but, because they were intended for use in the Isle of Wight and there would have been difficulties in transporting articulated cars on the 'floating crane' across the Solent, they were not articulated. The locomotives were condemned in April 1924.

2-coach sets 513 and 514, each formed of a Brake Third and a Third (seats being placed in the former luggage compartment) were completed at Ashford in April 1924. Set 513 had No. 3560 and 975 (formerly Nos. 3 and 8); and Set 514 was formed of Nos. 3561 and 976 (formerly Nos. 1 and 2). Steel panelling covered the original wooden mouldings. The Brake Thirds retained their original seating capacity of 56, but the Thirds were increased to 65 each. Each of the Brake Thirds had two large windows in the brake-end, although No. 3561 was later modified and featured two small windows, with the set number displayed in between. The sets were the only articulated stock ever to run on the Southern, and they worked the Sheppey Light Railway (either singly or in pairs if traffic required) until its closure in December 1950. They were not equipped for push-and-pull working and the locomotive had to 'run round' at Queenborough and Leysdown, but there were only four return trips a day. The sets sported destination boards lettered 'Sheppey Light Railway'.

2-coach sets 481 and 482, intended for service in the Isle of Wight, were made up at Lancing in September and November 1924, each formed of a Brake Third and a Composite. They were fitted for push-and-pull working and had Westinghouse air brakes. Set 481 had Nos. 4110 and 6366 (formerly Nos. 5 and 4); whilst Set 482 was formed of Nos. 4109 and 6367 (formerly Nos. 6 and 7). They were given steel panelling, and also were gangwayed between the coaches, although not at the outer ends. The Brake Thirds retained their original seating (56) but in the Composites the 32-seat saloon remained third-class and the former smoking saloon was altered to first class with 10 seats. There were also five 1st-class seats in the former luggage compartments.

Sets 481/2 were duly dispatched across the Solent on 26th April, 1925, for Isle of Wight service, and worked on the Bembridge branch, though not 'push-and-pull'. They do not seem to have been very successful there for in May 1927 they were sent back to the Mainland. After that they went into a sort of 'limbo' until in April 1930, at Lancing, the coaches were renumbered into the main ex-SE&C number series – although the original Isle of Wight set numbers were retained. Coach numbers in Set 481 were now 3584 and 5580, and those of Set 482 were now 3583 and 5581. The sets, still push-and-pull fitted, were re-converted to vacuum braking in July 1930. They were sent to work the Gravesend West Street branch, and in this connection could be seen running on the Chatham main line between Farningham Road and Bromley South.

R.W. Kidner's earliest observation of Set 481 on the Swanley Junction–Gravesend West Street service was in January 1931, but it is probable that both the sets had been introduced on that service in summer 1930. They worked it until May 1934, occasionally appearing on Swanley Junction–Sevenoaks services as well (observed in January 1932). By June 1934 Sets 481 and 482 were transferred to Tonbridge to work the Dunton Green–Westerham branch, which they were to do with only an occasional break until 1959. The timetable was usually arranged so that one set was berthed at Westerham overnight while the other returned to Tonbridge.

In 1941 the first-class accommodation was formally downgraded to third, although the actual seating was retained and the Composites were not at first renumbered into the third-class series. This did not occur until 1951, when Nos. 5580/1 became Nos. 914/5. Seating capacity of the ex-Composites was 48 third-class.

Meanwhile, articulated sets 513/4, after the closure of the Sheppey Light Railway, were transferred in 1951 to Weymouth to work the Portland service until this succumbed to closure in March 1952. After this the sets were retained briefly for 'Special Traffic' – it has been said that Set 514 went to Exmouth – but later in 1952 were transferred to the London West District for working the Clapham Junction–Kensington Olympia unadvertised passenger service. This they did until 1957, often with a 10-compartment Third to provide additional capacity. Finally in 1957 Set 513 was sent to the Eastleigh district to work certain Totton to Fawley trains, and Set 514 went to Salisbury for working the Salisbury–Ismiston workers' train. Set 513 was withdrawn in October 1957, but Set 514 lasted until October 1959.

Sets 481/2 did not usually escape far from the Tonbridge–Dunton Green–Westerham rut. During 1947 the set returning to Tonbridge after the morning service on the Westerham branch did a 'fill-in' from Sevenoaks to Otford and back: a little-known steam passenger working over an electrified line. In 1959 Set 481 was sometimes seen on the Gravesend–Allhallows line (the Hundred of Hoo branch), but December 1959 saw the withdrawal of this set. Its companion had not much longer to live, for it was taken out of service in March 1960. By this time the sets wre distinct curiosities: they still retained their inward-opening doors, there were still bars across the saloon drop-

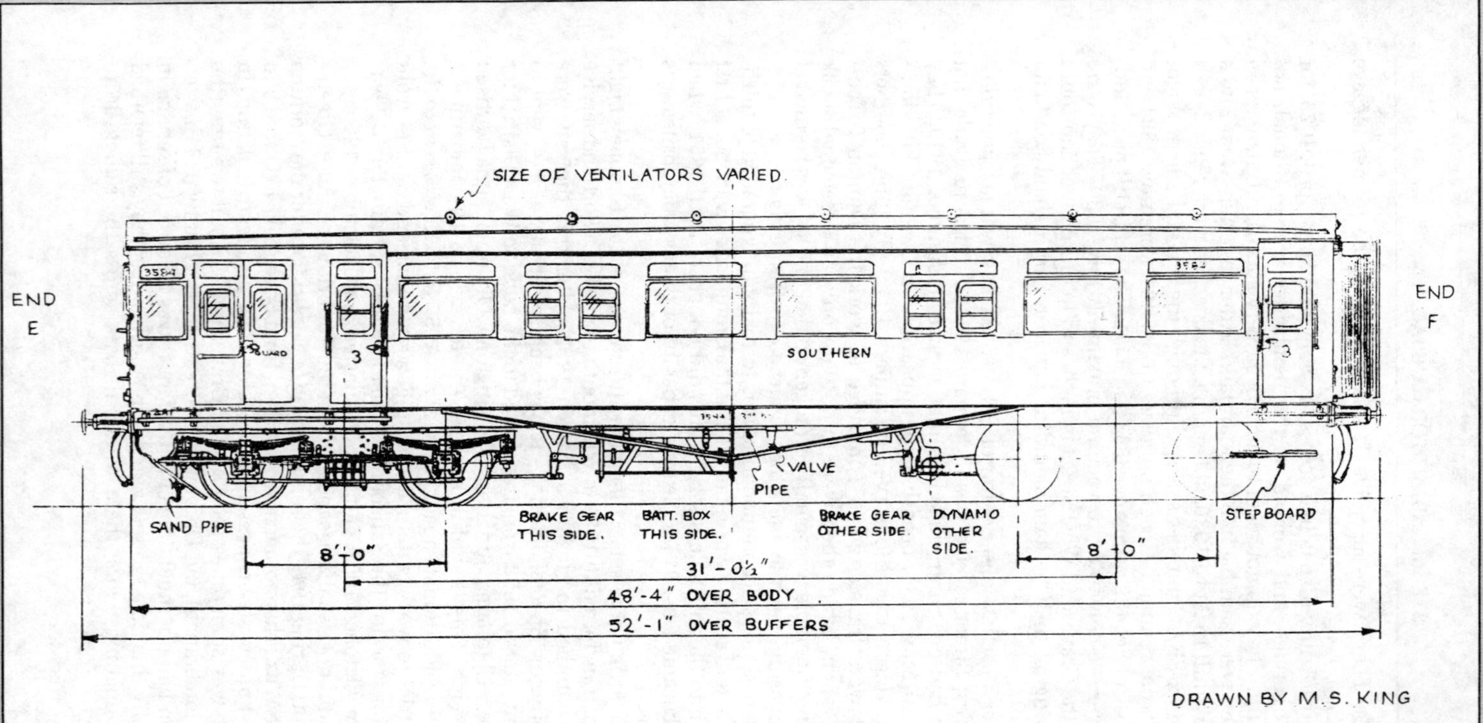

SIZE OF VENTILATORS VARIED.
END E
END F
3584
GUARD
3
SOUTHERN
3584
3
SAND PIPE
BRAKE GEAR THIS SIDE.
BATT. BOX THIS SIDE.
VALVE
PIPE
BRAKE GEAR OTHER SIDE
DYNAMO OTHER SIDE.
STEP BOARD
8'-0"
8'-0"
31'-0½"
48'-4" OVER BODY
52'-1" OVER BUFFERS
DRAWN BY M.S. KING

BRAKE THIRD

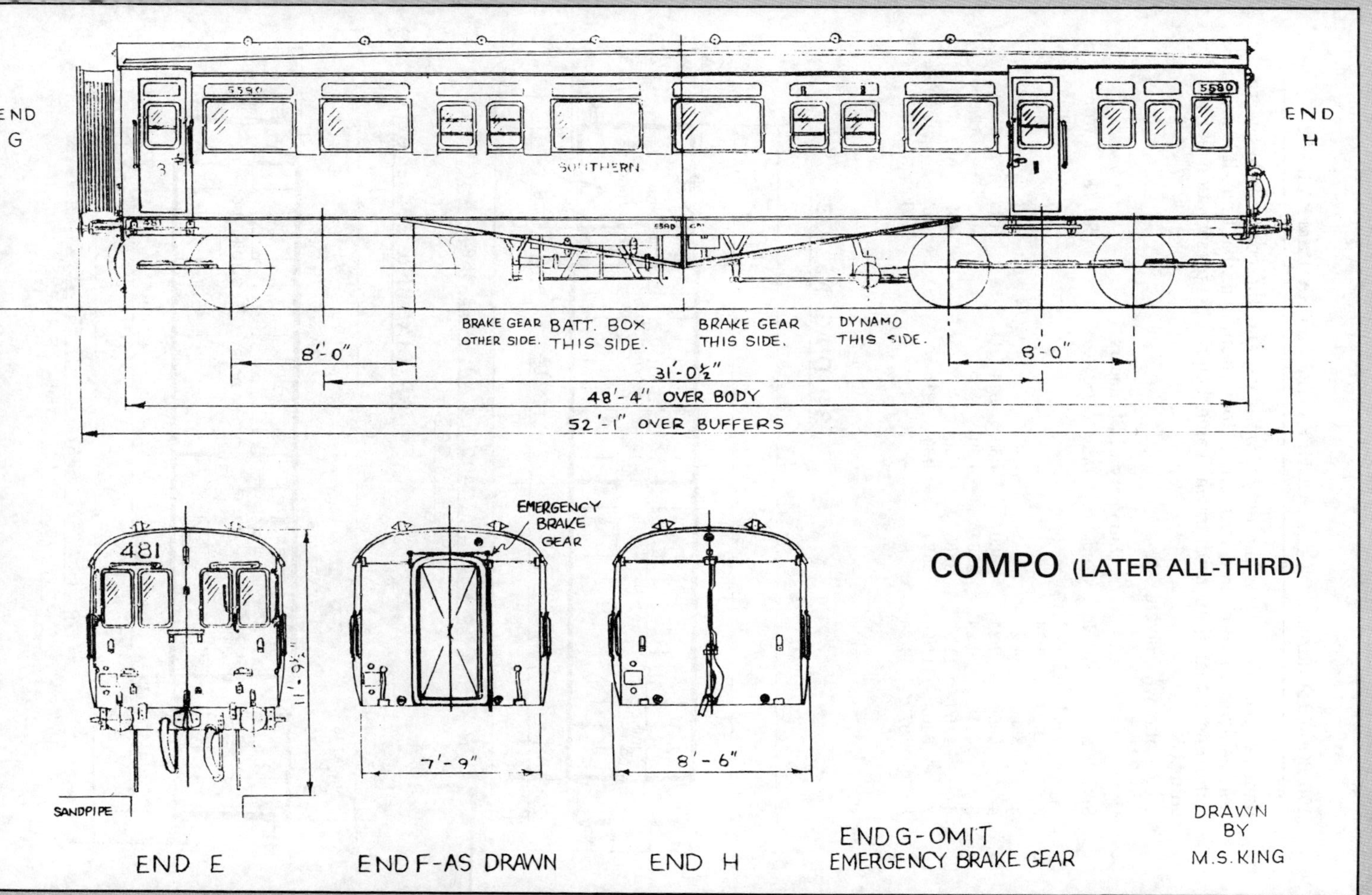
END G
END H
5590
5580
SOUTHERN
3
1
481
BRAKE GEAR OTHER SIDE.
BATT. BOX THIS SIDE.
BRAKE GEAR THIS SIDE.
DYNAMO THIS SIDE.
8'-0"
8'-0"
31'-0½"
48'-4" OVER BODY
52'-1" OVER BUFFERS
EMERGENCY BRAKE GEAR
481
11'-9½"
7'-9"
8'-6"
SANDPIPE
COMPO (LATER ALL-THIRD)
END E
END F-AS DRAWN
END H
END G-OMIT EMERGENCY BRAKE GEAR
DRAWN BY M.S.KING

lights, as well as across the door droplights, and the coach bodies were noticeably short compared with other stock running at that time. It is most unfortunate that their withdrawal came before the preservation era got going.

Not one was saved.

Summary of Steamcars

SEC	*SR*	*Re-No.*	*2nd No.*	*Date*	*3rd No.*	*Date*	*Set No.*	*Wdn*
1	3561	4/24	–	–	–	–	514	10/59
2	976	4/24	–	–	–	–	514	10/59
3	3560	4/24	–	–	–	–	513	10/57
4	6366	9/24	5580	4/30	914	/51	481	12/59
5	4110	9/24	3584	4/30	–	–	481	12/59
6	4109	11/24	3583	4/30	–	–	482	3/60
7	6367	11/24	5581	4/30	915	/51	482	3/60
8	975	4/24	–	–	–	–	513	10/57

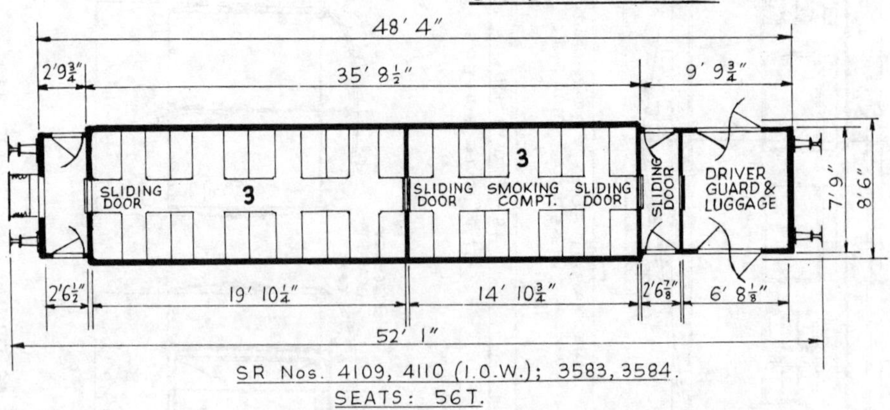

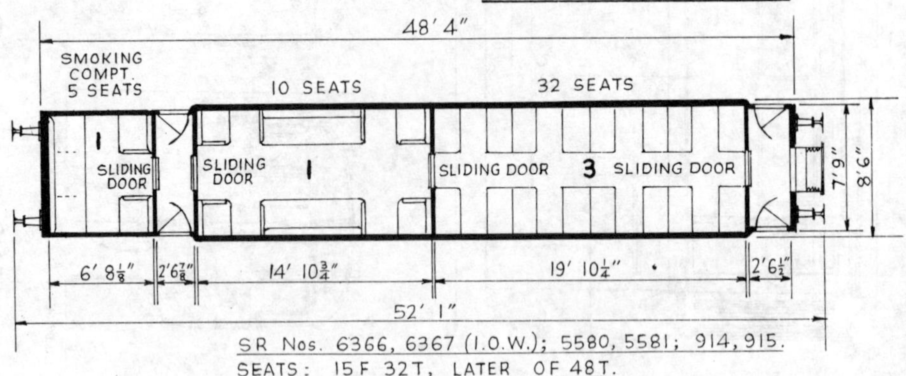

LIST OF TYPE 'A' THREE-COACH SETS

SEC Set	*Third Brake*	*Compo Lav.*	*Compo Bke Lav.*	*Reno'd*	*SR Set*	*Third Brake*	*Compo Lav.*	*Third Bke Lav*
90	1056	1027	1040	11/25	529	3329	5421	3345
91	1054	1029	1042	5/24	530	3327	5423	3347
92	1052	1026	1041	1/28	531	3325	5420	3346
93	1058	1028	1043	3/24	532	3331	5422	3348
94	1057	1023	1035	1/25	533	3330	5417	3340
95	1059	1031	1045	3/29	534	3332	5425	3350
96	1051	1024	1036	9/24	535	3324	5418	3341
97	1049	1021	1039	6/27	536	3322	5415	3344
98	1050	1030	1044	6/24	537	3323	5424	3349
99	1055	1022	1038	6/28	538	3328	5416	3343
100	1053	1025	1037	7/27	539	3326	5419	3342
101	1060	1033	1048	1/29	540	3333	5427	3353
102	1061	1034	1047	1/29	541	3334	5428	3352
103	1062	1032	1046	2/26	542	3335	5426	3351
124	1075	1067	1071	10/26	563	3336	5429	3354
125	1076	1068	1072	12/27	564	3337	5430	3355
126	1077	1069	1073	1/26	565	3338	5431	3356
104	1143	1129	1136	6/27	543	3397	5408	3377
105	1144	1130	1137	9/26	544	3398	5409	3378
106	1145	1131	1138	12/26	545	3399	5410	3379
107	1146	1132	1139	11/27	546	3400	5411	3380
108	1147	1133	1140	7/27	547	3401	5412	3381
109	1148	1134	1141	10/26	548	3402	5413	3382
110	1149	1135	1142	7/27	549	3403	5414	3383
111	1102	1094	1096	5/28	550	3384	5399	3364
112	1107	1092	1099	5/27	551	3389	5397	3367
113	1106	1093	1100	12/24	552	3388	5398	3368
114	1105	1095	1101	12/24	553	3387	5400	3369
115	1103	1090	1097	7/27	554	3385	5395	3365
116	1104	1091	1098	3/24	555	3386	5396	3366
117	1122	1108	1115	10/24	556	3390	5401	3370
118	1123	1109	1116	11/26	557	3391	5402	3371
119	1124	1110	1117	3/26	558	3392	5403	3372
120	1125	1111	1118	1/26	559	3393	5404	3373
121	1126	1112	1119	6/24	560	3394	5405	3374
122	1127	1113	1120	11/27	561	3395	5406	3375
123	1128	1114	1121	7/24	562	3396	5407	3376

TYPE 'D' THREE-COACH SETS

SEC Set	*Compo Bke Lav*	*Compo*	*Third Brake*	*SR Set*	*Third Bke Lav*	*Compo*	*Third Brake*
128	1084	1063	840	–	3363	5298	3282
129	1082	1064	857	–	3361	5299	3288
130	1083	1065	837	566	3362	5300	3279

LIST OF TYPE 'B' THREE-COACH SETS

SEC Set	*Third Brake*	*Tri-Compo*	*Tri-Cpo Bke*	*Reno'd*	*SR Set*	*Third Brake*	*Compo Lav.*	*Compo Brake*
58	833	929	155	3/29	515	3275	5392	6614
59	831	888	162	12/26	516	3273	5364	6621
60	841	681	150	9/26	517	3283	5285	6609
61	856	676	149	12/26	518	3287	5280	6608
62	838	802	157	3/27	519	3280	5367	6616
63	836	924	148	6/27	520	3278	5387	6607
64	859	806	159	11/27	521	3290	5371	6618
65	860	805	156	4/26	522	3291	5370	6615
66	835	928	151	3/28	523	3277	5391	6610
67	832	919	161	7/27	524	3274	5382	6620
68	842	926	158	12/27	525	3284	5389	6617
69	830	674	153	6/27	526	3272	5278	6612
70	839	801	154	5/27	527	3281	5366	6613
71	843	800	160					

Set 71 was split up and never became SR Set 528. Third Brake No. 843 went to Set 640 and was renumbered 3285 in April 1926; Composite No. 800 was added to 3-set 538 to make it up to four coaches from 1924, being renumbered 5365 in September 1927; and Compo Brake No. 160 remained as part of a re-formed Set 528, with 10-compartment Third No. 1429 and Compo Brake No. 977. These three were renumbered 6619, 1111 and 6638 respectively in July 1927.

Alterations to the other sets, and withdrawal dates, follow:

Set 515:	increased to 8-set *c*.1938.	Wdn 4/48
Set 516:	increased to 8-set *c*.1938.	Wdn 8/48
Set 517:	increased to 8-set *c*.1938.	Wdn /43
Set 518:	increased to 8-set *c*.1938.	Wdn 4/44
Set 519:	increased to 8-set *c*.1938. 3280 wdn 1/53, 5367 to Set 896? wdn 11/55, 6616 to Set 900, wdn 9/53.	
Set 520:	increased to 8-set *c*.1938.	Wdn 12/46
Set 521:		Wdn 9/46
Set 522:	wdn 1951. 3291 to Loose, then Set 900, wdn 6/55; 5370 to Set 897, wdn 1/58; 6615 to Set 669, wdn 12/53.	
Set 523:	3277 wdn 6/32, replaced by 3289 ex Set 920?	Wdn 2/43
Set 524:		Wdn 5/43
Set 525:	wdn 1951. 3284 to Set 921? wdn 8/52. 5389 to Set 896, wdn 1/58. 6617 to Set 896, wdn 12/54.	
Set 526:	increased to 8-set, *c*.1938.	Wdn 9/42
Set 527:		Wdn 9/46
Set 528:	renumbered 668. 6619 wdn 8/33, 6638 replaced by 6641, Third 1068 added. 6619 replaced by Third Brake.	

LIST OF TYPE 'C' THREE-COACH SETS

SEC Set	*Third Brake*	*Compo Lav.*	*Compo Bke Lav*	*Reno'd*	*SR Set*	*Third Brake*	*Compo Lav.*	*Third Bke Lav*
135	1179	1175	1171	3/27	567	3411	5440	3483
136	1180	1176	1172	7/27	568	3412	5441	3484
137	1181	1177	1173	6/28	569	3413	5442	3485
138	1182	1178	1174	11/27	570	3414	5443	3486
139	1336	1332	1328	12/24	571	3464	5492	3536
140	1337	1333	1329	9/26	572	3465	5493	3537
141	1338	1334	1330	10/26	573	3466	5495	3538
142	1318	1320	1323	11/25	574	3462	5488	3531
143	1164	1150	1157	2/28	575	3404	5433	3476
144	1165	1151	1158	11/27	576	3405	5434	3477
145	1166	1152	1159	9/27	577	3406	5435	3478
146	1167	1153	1160	2/24	578	3407	5436	3479
147	1168	1154	1161	12/27	579	3408	5437	3480
148	1169	1155	1162	5/24	580	3409	5438	3481
149	1170	1156	1163	6/28	581	3410	5439	3482
150	1183	1203	1223	9/28	582	3415	5444	3487
151	1184	1204	1224	1/29	583	3416	5445	3488
152	1185	1205	1225	7/28	584	3417	5446	3489
153	1186	1206	1226	7/28	585	3418	5447	3490
154	1187	1207	1227	7/28	586	3419	5448	3491
155	1188	1208	1228	11/27	587	3420	5449	3492
156	1189	1209	1229	11/23	588	3421	5450	3493
157	1190	1210	1230	6/28	589	3422	5451	3494
158	1191	1211	1231	12/27	590	3423	5463	3495
159	1192	1212	1232	2/28	591	3424	5464	3496
160	1193	1213	1233	6/29	592	3425	5465	3497
161	1194	1214	1234	7/28	593	3426	5466	3498
162	1195	1215	1235	9/23	594	3427	5467	3499
163	1196	1216	1236	7/28	595	3428	5468	3500
164	1197	1217	1237	11/23	596	3429	5469	3501
165	1198	1218	1238	10/23	597	3430	5470	3502
166	1199	1219	1239	10/23	598	3431	5471	3503
167	1200	1220	1240	12/23	599	3432	5472	3504
168	1201	1221	1241	12/23	600	3433	5473	3505
169	1202	1222	1242	2/24	601	3434	5474	3506
170	1263	1253	1243	3/28	602	3435	5459	3507
171	1264	1254	1244	7/27	603	3436	5460	3508
172	1265	1255	1246	7/28	604	3437	5461	3510
–	1266	1256	1245	6/28	605	3438	5462	3509
174	1267	1257	1247	4/26	606	3439	5475	3511
175	1268	1258	1248	3/29	607	3440	5476	3512
176	1269	1259	1249	6/28	608	3441	5477	3513
177	1270	1260	1250	8/28	609	3442	5478	3514
178	1271	1261	1251	10/28	610	3443	5479	3515
179	1272	1262	1252	1/24	611	3444	5480	3516
–	1273	1280	1287	7/28	612	3445	5452	3517

LIST OF TYPE 'C' THREE-COACH SETS – continued

SEC Set	*Third Brake*	*Compo Lav.*	*Compo Bke Lav*	*Reno'd*	*SR Set*	*Third Brake*	*Compo Lav.*	*Third Bke Lav*
181	1274	1281	1288	10/24	613	3446	5453	3518
182	1275	1282	1289	6/28	614	3447	5454	3519
183	1276	1283	1290	1/28	615	3448	5455	3520
–	1277	1284	1291	9/27	616	3449	5456	3521
185	1278	1285	1292	11/27	617	3450	5457	3522
–	1279	1286	1293	1/29	618	3451	5458	3523
187	1308	1301	1294	7/28	619	3452	5481	3524
188	1309	1302	1295	11/27	620	3453	5482	3525
189	1310	1303	1296	1/28	621	3454	5483	3526
190	1311	1304	1297	2/24	622	3455	5484	3527
191	1312	1305	1298	5/24	623	3456	5485	3528
192	1313	1306	1299	2/24	624	3457	5486	3529
193	1314	1319	1300	4/24	625	3458	5494	3530
194	1335	1331	1327	6/24	626	3463	5491	3535
195	1316	1321	1324	10/23	627	3460	5489	3532
196	1317	1322	1325	4/24	628	3461	5490	3533
197	1315	1307	1326	5/24	629	3459	5487	3534
198	1339	1345	1342	7/27	630	3467	5496	3539
199	1340	1346	1343	10/26	631	3468	5497	3540
200	1341	1347	1344	2/26	632	3469	5498	3541
201	1348	1349	1350	6/27	633	3470	5499	3542
202	1359	1357	1361	5/24	634	3471	5500	3543
203	1360	1358	1362	11/25	635	3472	5501	3544
204	1366	1363	1369	4/26	636	3473	5502	3545
205	1367	1364	1370	10/26	637	3474	5503	3546
206	1368	1365	1371	4/27	638	3475	5504	3547

SOUTHERN RAILWAY SETS OF EX-SE&CR COACHING STOCK

Formations quoted below are either as shown in SR carriage working notices or from observations noted by various people.

Vehicle No.	FORMATION.	Berth.
	Set 331 (1935-41)	
6623	Cor.Cpo.Bke.	
7821	Cor.Saloon*	
7822	Cor.Saloon*	
7823	Cor.Saloon*	
7824	Cor.Saloon*	EY
7825	Cor.Saloon*	
7826	Cor.Saloon*	
7827	Cor.Saloon*	
6634	Cor.Cpo.Bke	
	Set 332 (1935-41)	
6632	Cor.Cpo.Bke	
7828	Cor.Saloon*	
7829	Cor.Saloon*	
7830	Cor.Saloon*	
7831	Cor.Saloon*	EY
7832	Cor.Saloon*	
7834	Cor.Saloon*	
7838	Cor.Saloon*	
6636	Cor.Cpo.Bke	
	Set 334 (N.D.)	
6624	Cor.Cpo.Bke	
5379	Compo Lav.	
5390	Compo Lav.	
7336	First Lav.	
6633	Cor.Cpo.Bke	
	Set 335 (1936)	
--	Bke Cpo.Lav.	
--	2 Thirds	
--	3 First Lav.	CY
--	3 Thirds	
--	Bke Cpo.Lav.	
	Set 336 (1936)	
6625	Cor.Cpo.Bke	
--	3 Lav.Thirds	
--	2 Lav.Compos	BR
--	3 Lav.Thirds	
6626	Cor.Cpo.Bke	
	Set 337 (1936)	
6624	Cor.Cpo.Bke	
645	Lav. Third*	
643	Lav. Third*	
647	Lav. Third*	
5072	Lav. Compo*	TW
646	Lav. Third*	
644	Lav. Third*	
4605	Lav. Compo*	
4591	Lav. Compo*	
6633	Cor.Cpo.Bke	

Vehicle No.	FORMATION.	Berth.
	Set 341 (c.1931)	
7741	First Bke Lav	
7257	First	
7314	First	
7315	First	
7322	First	LW
7276	First	
7268	First	
7261	First	
7258	First	
7742	First Bke Lav	
	Set 344 (1938-41)	
7737	First Brake	
7308	First	
7262	First	
7323	First	
7319	First	LW
7335	First	
7344	First	
7305	First	
7742	First Bke Lav	
	Set 345 (1936)	
--	Cpo.Bke Lav.	
--	6 Thirds	CH
--	First Bke Lav	
	Set 346 (1936)	
7735	First Brake	
7280	First	
7301	First	
7302	First	
7266	First	LW
7273	First	
7284	First	
7321	First	
7312	First	
7739	First Brake	
	Set 347 (1936)	
7736	First Brake	
7255	First	
7261	First	
7314	First	
7295	First	LW
7325	First	
7259	First	
7342	First	
--	First	
7743	First Bke Lav	

Vehicle No.	FORMATION.	Berth.
	Set 389 (1935-41)	
6622	Cor.Cpo.Bke	
966	Cor.Third	
964	Cor.Third	
967	Cor.Third	
962	Cor.Third	
963	Cor.Third	
965	Cor.Third	
6627	Cor.Cpo.Bke	
	Set 481	
3584	Tlr 3rd Bke	
5580	Tlr Compo	WTM
	Set 482	
3583	Tlr 3rd Bke	
5581	Tlr Compo	WTM
	Set 490 (1931-38)	
4139	Third Bke*	
2423	Third	
2424	Third	
6394	Compo	IOW
6385	Compo *	
4140	Third Bke*	
	Set 491 (1931-38)	
4141	Third Bke*	
2422	Third	
2425	Third	
6386	Compo *	IOW
6395	Compo	
4107	Third Bke*	
	Set 492 (1931-39)	
4138	Third Bke*	
2421	Third	
2426	Third	
6396	Compo	IOW
6384	Compo *	
4106	Third Bke*	
	Set 493 (1931-33)	
4109	Third Bke	
2427	Third	
6397	Compo	IOW
2428	Third	
6398	Compo	
4110	Third Bke	

(1933 : 4110 repl. by 4117, 6398 repl. by 6359.)

* Coach not of ex-SE&C origin.

BERTHING STATION. CY - Chertsey. BR - Bracknell. CH - Christchurch. EY - Eardley. LW - London West. IOW - Isle of Wight. TW - Twickenham. WTM - Westerham.

	Set 640 (1944-46)	
3312	3rd Bke Lav.	
972	Third	
1084	Third	
5327	Compo Lav.	
5342	Compo Lav.	
5376	Compo Lav.	
5406	Compo Lav.	
3375	3rd Bke Lav.	
	Set 669 (1941-50)	
3299	3rd Bke Lav.	
1111	Third	
1062	Third	
1101	Third	
1068	Third	BGM
1061	Third	
5244	Compo	
5232	Compo	
6639	Compo Bke Lav	
	Set 680 (1941-44)	
3320	3rd Bke Lav.	
5378	Compo Lav.	
1091	Third	
5377	Compo Lav.	
5374	Compo Lav.	
5375	Compo Lav.	
956	Third Lav.	
1110	Third	
3580	3rd Bke Lav.	
	Set 688 (1946-48)	
3339	3rd Bke.	
5318	Compo Lav.	
5343	Compo Lav.	
5383	Compo Lav.	
5348	Compo Lav.	DL
5328	Compo Lav.	
5432	Compo Lav	
5320	Compo Lav.	
3357	3rd Bke Lav.	
	Set 695 (1941-48)	
3360	3rd Bke Lav.	
5252	Compo Lav.	
7329	First	
7326	First	
885	Third	EY
217	Third *	
5253	Compo Lav.	
5362	Compo Lav.	
6611	Compo Bke	

	Set 696 (1947-50)	
3266	Third Dke	
290	Third *	
361	Third *	
5241	Compo	
181	Third *	NB
7281	First	
5281	Compo Lav.	
3282	Third Bke	
	Set 896 (1941-48)	
3265	Third Bke	
1103	Third	
7354	First Lav.	
971	Third	EY
973	Third	
1066	Third	
5330	Compo Lav.	
960	Third Lav.	
3318	3rd Bke Lav.	
	Set 898 (1941-47)	
3269	Third Bke	
959	Third Lav.	
1100	Third	
1090	Third	
1092	Third	WU
7347	First Lav.	
5335	Compo Lav.	
1073	Third	
3295	3rd Bke Lav.	
	(1947: 7347 removed.)	
	Set 899 (1943-49)	
3288	Third Bke.	
5228	Compo	
873	Third	
5245	Compo Lav.	
5227	Compo	
847	Third	BH
5290	Compo Lav.	
7362	First Lav.	
3298	3rd Bke Lav.	
	Set 900 (1941-48)	
--	9 coach	MH
	Set 901 (1941-49)	
--	9 coach	CP
	Set 902 (1947-48)	
6638	Cpo Bke Lav.	
1055	Third	
1063	Third	
7291	First	EY
1054	Third	
6640	Cpo Bke Lav.	

	Set 903 (1947)	
3367	3rd Bke Lav.	
5397	Compo Lav.	
5332	Compo Lav.	
970	Third	BGM
1064	Third	
1056	Third	
1081	Third	
3389	Third Bke.	
	Set 905 (1941-45)	
3252	Third Bke	
878	Third	
945	Third Lav.	
1060	Third	
1070	Third	
1074	Third	
5239	Compo	
7358	First Lav.	
3267	Third Bke	
	Set 906 (1941-51)	
3585	3rd Bke Lav.	
7348	First Lav.	
1072	Third	
1082	Third	
1067	Third	BH
5314	Compo Lav.	
957	Third Lav.	
1069	Third	
3586	3rd Bke Lav.	
	Set 908 (1941-50)	
3258	Third Bke.	
922	Third	
5235	Compo	
924	Third	MK
923	Third	
3261	Third Bke	
	Set 912 (1947-48)	
3306	3rd Bke Lav.	
7332	First	
5279	Compo Lav.	
930	Third	
995	Third	MH
5276	Compo Lav.	
5322	Compo Lav.	
921	Third	
3311	3rd Bke Lav.	
	Set 913 (1947)	
--	9 coach	MH

BERTHING STATION. BGM - Bellingham. BH - Blackheath. CP - Crystal Palace. DL - Deal. EY - Eardley. MH - Maze Hill. MK - Margate (Miners' Train). NB - New Beckenham. WU - Wadhurst.

* Coach not of ex-SE&C origin.

	Set 917 (1947-50)	
3253	Third Bke.	
5368	Compo Lav.	
5325	Compo Lav.	
5295	Compo Lav.	
1085	Third	BI
5291	Compo Lav.	
1112	Third	
3581	3rd Bke Lav.	

	Set 918 (1947-49)	
3309	3rd Bke Lav.	
204	Third *	
284	Third *	
1087	Third	
1107	Third	MH
5369	Compo Lav.	
5331	Compo Lav.	
5350	Compo Lav.	
3310	3rd Bke Lav.	

	Set 920 (1941-48)	
3302	3rd Bke Lav.	
1096	Third	
5380	Compo Lav.	
1049	Third	ND
1102	Third	
1044	Third	
7357	First Lav.	
6637	Cpo. Bke Lav.	

	Set 921 (1947)	
3359	3rd Bke Lav.	
955	Third Lav.	
7360	First Lav.	
893	Third Lav.	
946	Third Lav.	HH
892	Third Lav.	
940	Third Lav.	
939	Third Lav.	
3358	3rd Bke Lav.	

Note :- Dates shown indicate only when the set was running in the given formation, not when the set was introduced or withdrawn.

SFTS AS RUNNING IN 1956, 1957 AND 1958

	Set 335 (1956)	
3586	2nd Bke Lav.	
1060	Second	
1070	Second	
1074	Second	BH
1063	Second	
1065	Second	
5429	Compo Lav.	
3346	2nd Bke Lav.	

	Set 346 (1957)	
1044	Second	
1054	Second	
3325	2nd Bke	MK
1071	Second	
1068	Second	

	Set 519 (1954-56)	
3279	2nd Bke	
231	Second *	
1081	Second	
5324	Compo Lav.	
5294	Compo Lav.	MH
5238	Compo Lav.	
217	Second *	
184	Second *	
3321	2nd Bke	

(Set renumbered 900, 12/56.)

	Set 636 (1957)	
3473	2nd Bke.	
1090	Second	
5502	Compo Lav.	MH
968	Second	
1101	Second	
3545	2nd Bke Lav.	

	Set 897 ?(1954-57)	
3587	Cor.Bke 2nd	
1095	Second	
1089	Second	
5370	Compo Lav.	
5417	Compo Lav.	BH
1094	Second	
1105	Second	
1080	Second	
3588	Cor.Bke 2nd	

	Set 900 (1955-56)	
3589	Cor.Bke 2nd	
969	Second	
1059	Second	
5365	Compo Lav.	
5316	Compo Lav.	BH
5388	Compo Lav.	
1079	Second	
968	Second	
3359	Cor.Bke 2nd	

	Set 901 (1955-56)	
3326	2nd Bke	
1076	Second	
1078	Second	
1083	Second	BS
1109	Second	
1112	Second	
5419	Compo Lav.	
6642	Cor.Bke Cpo.	

	Set 903 (1954-57)	
3333	2nd Bke	
5300	Compo.	
1056	Second	
1064	Second	EG
970	Second	
7357	First Lav.	
3353	2nd Bke Lav.	

	Set 917 (1954-56)	
6633	Cor.Bke Cpo.	
1086	Second	
329	Second Lav.*	
1085	Second	
940	Second Lav.	BH
939	Second Lav.	
955	Second Lav.	
5327	Compo Lav.	
6638	Lav. Bke Cpo.	

	Set 918 (1955-56)	
3580	2nd Bke Lav.	
204	Second Lav.*	
284	Second Lav.*	
5369	Compo Lav.	MH
972	Second	
1087	Second	
1107	Second	
3309	2nd Bke Lav.	

* Coach not of ex-SE&C origin.
BERTHING STATION. BI - Bexhill West. BH-Blackheath. BS-Bromley South. EG-East Grinstead. HH-Herne Hill. MH-Maze Hill. MK-Margate. ND - Nunhead.

No.	Vehicle	Berthing
	Set 495 (1932/34)	
4113	Third Bke	
2432	Third	
6399	Compo	IOW
4114	Third Bke	
	Set 496 (1933-47)	
4115	Third Bke	
2433	Third	
6360	Compo	IOW
4116	Third Bke	
	Set 497 (1933-39)	
4110	Third Bke	
2418	Third	
2419	Third	IOW
2420	Third	
6358	Compo	
	Set 498 (1934-40)	
4118	Third Bke*	
2434	Third	
2436	Third	
2437	Third	IOW
6388	Compo	
4121	Third Bke*	
	Set 499 (1934-47)	
4122	Third Bke*	
2435	Third	
6400	Compo	IOW
4123	Third Bke*	
	Set 513	
3560	Third Bke	
975	Third	SLR
	Set 514	
3561	Third Bke	
976	Third	SLR
	Sets 515 to 527, 529 to 599	
--	--	R
	Set 600 (1935-41)	
3433	Third Bke	
5299	Compo	
5301	Compo	
7278	First	
5473	Compo Lav.	
3505	3rd Bke Lav.	
	Sets 601 to 638	
--	--	R
	Set 640 (1935)	
--	9 bogies	BH

* Not ex-SE&C.

No.	Vehicle	Berthing
	Set 662 (1935)	
3306	3rd Bke Lav	
1057	Third	
7330	First	
7351	First Lav.	
7358	First Lav.	
1044	Third	
3317	3rd Bke Lav.	
	Set 666 (1935)	
--	4 bogies	MH
	Set 667 (1935)	
3259	Third Bke	
974	Third	
1094	Third	MH
7740	First Bke Lav	
	Set 668 (1933)	
6619	Compo Bke	
1068	Third	
1111	Third	MK
6641	Cpo Bke Lav	
	Set 669 (1935)	
--	4 bogies	MK
	Set 674 (1935)	
3339	3rd Bke	
5432	Compo.Lav.	R
3357	3rd Bke Lav.	
	Set 680 (1935)	
--	9 bogies	NB
	Set 685 (1935)	
3288	3rd Bke	
1097	Third	
5228	Compo	
7352	First Lav.	
5338	Compo Lav.	
3361	3rd Bke Lav.	
	(1939: 7352 repl. by 7297.)	
	Set 686 (1935)	
3276	3rd Bke.	
1099	Third	
5272	Compo Lav.	
7357	First Lav.	
5189	Compo	
920	Third	
3316	3rd Bke Lav.	
	Set 687 (1935)	
3286	3rd Bke.	
5326	Compo Lav	
7297	First	
7296	First	
5287	Compo.	
3293	3rd Bke Lav.	

No.	Vehicle	Berthing
	Set 688 (1935)	
3307	3rd Bke Lav.	
5288	Compo Lav.	
5246	Compo Lav.	
3313	3rd Bke Lav.	
	Set 689 (1931-5)	
3260	3rd Bke	
5191	Compo	
7325	First	
3299	3rd Bke Lav.	
	Set 691 (1931-35)	
3300	3rd Bke Lav.	
7271	First	
5254	Compo Lav.	
7255	First	
3305	3rd Bke Lav.	
	Set 693 (1935-41)	
3358	3rd Bke Lav.	
936	Third	
5354	Compo Lav.	
7360	First Lav.	
5224	Compo	
3359	3rd Bke Lav.	
	Set 695 (1935)	
3360	3rd Bke Lav.	
5362	Compo Lav.	R
6611	Compo Bke.	
	Set 696 (1935)	
3266	3rd Bke	
5281	Compo Lav.	
5230	Compo	
7279	First Lav.	
5241	Compo	
3282	3rd Bke	
	Set 705 (N.D.)	
619	6wh Bke Van	
5225	Compo	H
	Set 760 (1935)	
582	6wh Bke Van	
1093	Third	MA
5546	Compo	
	(1939 : Van repl. by Bke 1st 7735.)	
	Set 775 (1939)	
3912	3rd Bke *	
5239	Compo	R
878	Third	
	Set 797 (1939)	
3890	3rd Bke *	
5220	Compo	W
3989	3rd Bke *	

BERTHING STATION. BH-Blackheath. IOW-Isle of Wight. H-Hawkhurst Branch. MA-Maidstone West. MH-Maze Hill. MK-Margate. NB-New Beckenham. R-Rover 3-sets. SLR - Sheppey Light Railway. W-Western Section.

No.	Coach	Berthing
	Set 896 (1935)	
--	9 coach	DL
	Set 897 (1935)	
--	9 coach	BH
	Set 898 (1935)	
--	9 coach	SL
	Set 899 (1935)	
--	9 coach	SL
	Set 900 (1935-41)	
3308	3rd Bke Lav.	
969	Third	
1059	Third	
5388	Compo Lav.	
5316	Compo Lav.	HH
1104	Third	
968	Third	
1079	Third	
3321	3rd Bke Lav.	
	Set 901 (1935-41)	
3363	3rd Bke Lav.	
5337	Compo Lav.	
1078	Third	
1076	Third	
7366	First Lav.	BH
958	Third	
1083	Third	
1109	Third	
3582	3rd Bke Lav.	
	Set 902 (1935)	
--	9 coach	SL
	Set 903 (1935)	
--	9 coach	MH
	Set 905 (1935)	
--	9 coach	SL
	Set 906 (1935)	
--	9 coach	HH
	Set 907 (1935)	
--	9 coach	HH
	Set 908 (1935)	
--	9 coach	SL
	Set 909 (1935)	
--	9 coach	MH
	Set 910 (1935)	
--	9 coach	WAL
	Set 912 (1935)	
--	9 coach	GP
	Set 913 (1935)	
--	9 coach	RD
	Set 914 (1935)	
--	9 coach	BH
	Set 917 (1935)	
--	8 coach	MH
	Set 918 (1935)	
--	8 coach	BGM
	Set 919 (1935-41)	
3303	3rd Bke Lav.	
895	Third Lav.	
5336	Compo Lav.	
5361	Compo Lav.	
5282	Compo Lav.	HH
5283	Compo Lav.	
953	Third Lav.	
954	Third Lav.	
5393	Compo Lav.	
3304	3rd Bke Lav.	
	Set 920 (1935)	
--	8 coach	MH
	Set 921 (1935)	
--	10 coach	MK

SOME POST-WAR SET FORMATIONS

No.	Coach	Berthing
	Set 331 (1946-53)	
6634	Cor.Cpo.Bke	
989	Cor.Third *	AD
	Set 332 (1946-58)	
6632	Cor.Cpo.Bke.	
988	Cor. Third*	AD
	Set 333 (1946-50)	
6636	Cor.Cpo.Bke	
985	Cor. Third*	AD
	Set 334 (1946-50)	
6624	Cor.Cpo.Bke	
10	Third *	
175	Third *	
5390	Compo Lav.	
5379	Compo Lav.	SL
267	Third *	
16	Third *	
6625	Cor.Cpo Bke	
	Set 335 (1948-50)	
6630	Cor.Cpo.Bke	
1074	Third	
5345	Compo Lav.	
5381	Compo Lav.	
5344	Compo Lav.	EY
5323	Compo Lav.	
1070	Third	
1060	Third	
6633	Cor.Cpo.Bke	
	Set 346 (1946-49)	
3590	3rd Bke Lav	
900	Third	
901	Third	
902	Third	
903	Third	HH
904	Third	
905	Third	
906	Third	
7744	1st Bke Lav	
	Set 389 (1947-53)	
6628	Cor.Cpo.Bke	
965	Cor. Third	
963	Cor. Third	
962	Cor. Third	
967	Cor. Third	BH
964	Cor. Third	
966	Cor. Third	
6629	Cor.Cpo.Bke	
	Set 515 (1941-47)	
3275	Third Bke	
5233	Compo	
5392	Compo Lav.	
868	Third	MH
5221	Compo	
7257	First	
7322	First	
6614	Compo Bke	
	Set 516 (1944-47)	
3273	Third Bke	
5365	Compo Lav.	
5364	Compo Lav.	
886	Third	CP
888	Third	
871	Third	
5236	Compo	
6621	Compo Bke	
	Set 519 (1941-49)	
3280	Third Bke	
5324	Compo Lav.	
5238	Compo	
5367	Compo Lav.	WAL
184	Third *	
5294	Compo Lav.	
7311	First	
6616	Compo Bke	

* Coach not of ex-SEC origin.

BERTHING STATION. AD-Ashford. BGM-Bellingham. BH-Blackheath. DL-Deal. CP-Crystal Palace. GP-Grove Park. HH-Herne Hill. MH-Maze Hill. EY-Eardley. MK-Margate. RD-Rotherhithe Rd. SL-Stewarts Lane. WAL-Walmer.

WORKING OF 'LONG' SETS OF EX-SE&CR STOCK, VICTORIA–RAMSGATE LINE, SUMMER SATURDAYS, 1947

9-set 695	7.50 am Victoria–Ramsgate, 1.30 pm Margate–Victoria.
8-set 516	8.50 am Victoria–Ramsgate, 3.42 pm Margate–Victoria.
9-set 669	8.55 am Victoria–Margate, 11.43 am return; 2.54 pm Victoria–Margate, 5.30 pm return.
9-set 896	9.46 am Victoria–Margate, 2.15 pm return.
8-set 920	9.50 am Victoria–Ramsgate, 2.38 pm return.
9-set 901	10.26 am Victoria–Margate, 2.47 pm return.
9-set 921	10.46 am Victoria–Ramsgate, 3.35 pm return.
9-set 334	11.06 am Victoria–Ramsgate, 5.03 pm Margate–Victoria.
8-set 515	11.26 am Victoria–Ramsgate, 4.23 pm Margate–Gravesend Ctl.
9-set 905	11.30 am Victoria–Margate, 2.42 pm Herne Bay–Victoria.
9-set 346	11.35 am Victoria–Ramsgate, 8.20 pm return.
8-set 519	10.20 am Ramsgate–Victoria, 3.06 pm return.
9-set 897	9.30 am Margate–Victoria, 12.55 pm Victoria–Ramsgate, 5.30 pm Ramsgate–Victoria. To Margate on Sunday.
9-set 688	9.25 am Ramsgate–Victoria, 1.20 pm return.
9-set 680	10.40 am Ramsgate–Victoria, 2.26 pm Victoria–Margate.
8-set 666	11.13 am Broadstairs–Victoria, 2.46 pm Victoria–Ramsgate.
8-set 696	6.43 am Cannon Street–Ramsgate, 12.40 pm Ramsgate–Victoria.
8-set 903	9.46 am Bromley South–Ramsgate, 1.48 pm Dumpton Pk–Victoria.
9-set 913	9.41 am Gravesend Ctl–Margate, 4.20 pm Herne Bay–Victoria.
9-set 918	2.06 pm Gravesend Ctl–Ramsgate, 5.20 pm Margate–Victoria.
9-set 900	11.00 am Gravesend Ctl–Margate, 6.20 pm Herne Bay–Victoria.

Note: Empty stock workings in connection with the above are not shown. Only one set, No. 669, managed two return trips during the day.

WORKING OF 'LONG' SETS OF EX-SE&CR STOCK, CHARING CROSS–HASTINGS LINE, SUMMER SATURDAYS, 1947

9-set 640	10.34 am Charing Cross–Hastings, 1.55 pm return. 4.30 pm Charing Cross to Margate. To London Bridge on Sunday.
8 Cor. Set 389	2.25 pm Charing Cross–Hastings, 7.10 pm return.
9-set 912	2.40 pm Charing Cross–Hastings. Return Sunday on 8.10 pm Hastings to Charing Cross.

Index

INDEX TO SE&CR BOGIE COACHES UNDER SR NUMBERS

POST OFFICE VANS

SR Numbers	*Diagram Number*	*Page*	*SR Numbers*	*Diagram Number*	*Page*	*SR Numbers*	*Diagram Number*	*Page*
4947	1201	184	4950	1204	188	4954–4955	1207	189
4948	1202	184	4951	1205	188	4956	1208	189
4949	1203A	188	4952–4953	1206A	188			

FIRST BRAKES

7735–7739	548	110	7745	550	178
7740–7744	549	114			

SALOONS

7912–7913	613	53	7918	617	74	7922–7929	621	113
7914	614	61	7919	618	111	7930	622	75
7915	615	61	7920	619	111	7931	623	22
7916–7917	616	74	7921	620	111			

Note. In some cases the SR numbers shown were not actually applied.

PASSENGER GUARDS VANS

SR Numbers	*Diagram Number*	*Page*
648–653	889	48
654–655	891	182